ONE WE

Limits to Privatization

How to Avoid too Much of a Good Thing

A Report to the Club of Rome

Edited by
Ernst Ulrich von Weizsäcker
Oran R. Young
Matthias Finger

With
Marianne Beisheim

London • Sterling, VA

First published by Earthscan in the UK and USA in 2005

ISBN: 1-84407-177-4 hardback

Typesetting by MapSet Ltd, Gateshead, UK
Printed and bound in the UK by Cromwell Press Ltd
Cover design by Andrew Corbett

For a full list of publications please contact:

Earthscan
8–12 Camden High Street
London, NW1 0JH, UK
Tel: +44 (0)20 7387 8558 (main)
Fax: +44 (0)20 7387 8998
Email: earthinfo@earthscan.co.uk
Web: **www.earthscan.co.uk**

22883 Quicksilver Drive, Sterling, VA 20166-2012, USA

Earthscan publishes in association with the International Institute for Environment
and Development

A catalogue record for this book is available from the British Library

Library of Congress Cataloging-in-Publication Data

Limits to privatization : how to avoid too much of a good thing : a report to the
Club of Rome / edited by Ernst Ulrich von Weizsäcker, Oran R. Young, Matthias
Finger.
     p. cm.
  Includes bibliographical references and index.
  ISBN 1-84407-177-4 (hardback)
  1. Privatization. I. Weizsäcker, Ernst U. von (Ernst Ulrich), 1939- II. Young,
Oran R. III. Finger, Matthias.

HD3850.L56 2005
338.9'25--dc22

                                          2004025170

This book is printed on elemental chlorine free paper

Contents

PART I INTRODUCTION

PART II PRIVATIZATION IN MANY SECTORS: CASE STUDIES AND SNAPSHOTS

NATURAL RESOURCES AND RELATED INDUSTRIES

PART III PRIVATIZATION IN CONTEXT

PART IV GOVERNANCE OF PRIVATIZATION

PART V CONCLUSION

List of Figures

List of Boxes

Foreword by the President of the Club of Rome: Beware of Extremes

Beware of extremes! This is the first sentence in this new Report to the Club of Rome. Indeed, our world is suffering from going to the extremes. Our societies let extreme poverty persist in a world of affluence. Extreme inequalities trigger hatred and despair. Political and religious extremists seek salvation in violent and terrorist assaults. Unrestricted growth based on outdated technologies can lead to ecological disasters.

The Club of Rome stands for a balanced view of world affairs. We have looked at the limits to growth, the limits to certainty and the limits to governability in a globalized world. The new report now looks at the limits to privatization.

Twenty years of the neo-liberal revolution have yielded thousands of examples of privatization around the world. The privatization of telephone services was mostly seen as progress towards modernization, higher efficiency and lower prices. In the case of postal services, lower prices did not arrive – rather, to the contrary. The privatization of British Rail was experienced as a debacle and was recently reverted, in part. Privatized education systems in Chile, Kazakhstan and the US may have improved the quality at the top but eroded the quality at the bottom.

As the subtitle of the report says, privatization is a good thing. It is a good thing for certain purposes and under certain conditions. It is high time, after these 20 years of rather haphazard experience, to try and define the conditions under which privatization can produce benefits for the people. Likewise, we should become aware of conditions under which privatization is likely to worsen the situation and for whom.

Privatization is meant to enhance economic efficiency and has been conspicuously successful in this regard. Efficiency alone, however, does not lead to justice or equitable distribution. The latter is, instead, the task of the democratic state.

Democracy, on the other hand, can be dangerously weakened by the process of privatization. Democracy is meant to invite citizens, poor and rich alike, to participate in public affairs. But what happens if citizens see the most tangible *public* affairs vanish from the agenda of their municipalities and being transferred to private-sector companies? Citizens are not invited to take part in board or shareholder meetings of remote and anonymous foreign companies. Citizens may express their frustration by shrugging their shoulders on democracy.

One of the answers given in this report is that the state should fully remain in charge of defining and monitoring the quality of services. If citizens are not satisfied, they must have a right to complain, not only as individual customers, but also as active political animals.

The Club of Rome is grateful to receive this report, offering an experience-based assessment of privatization. The 'Lessons Learned from Privatization' in Part V (if not the entire report) should become obligatory reading for World Bank officials, for local and national politicians worldwide and for managers of companies now offering services to the public at large.

Prince El Hassan Bin Talal
President of the Club of Rome
Amman, Jordan, October 2004

Preface

Privatization is one of the defining features of our era. Starting on a small scale during the 1960s and 1970s, it has grown into a mighty force affecting all sectors of the world's societies. Today, there are thousands of privatization initiatives under way, ranging from wholesale liquidation of state enterprises in countries with economies in transition, to the establishment of privatized telecommunications and security services in a wide range of societies. Privatization is shifting the balance between the public domain and the private sector sharply towards the latter. The impacts of this dramatic shift are already being felt by all those living today; they will be felt by those who come after us for some time to come.

How should we respond to this social tidal wave? We are convinced that there is no substitute for a systematic evaluation of evidence from the real world in coming to terms with the privatization movement. We have looked at many cases of privatization occurring all over the world and in a wide range of issue areas.

Our examination of the experience with privatization has led us to conclude that there is both good privatization and bad privatization. We take seriously criteria of evaluation that include a concern for justice (who are the winners and who are the losers in specific cases of privatization?), as well as a concern for the protection of planetary life-support systems (is privatization implicated in the onset of disruptive global changes?). In the process, we seek to identify conditions that govern the consequences of privatization. Our goal is to make a contribution to balanced and constructive policy-making regarding privatization.

Concerns about the dramatic weakening of democracy were among the motives for a decision by the German Bundestag (parliament) to set up a new Study Commission on Globalization. That was just a few weeks before the Seattle World Trade Organization (WTO) Ministerial Conference in November 1999. Ernst von Weizsäcker, MP, was elected chairman of the commission, and subsequently he was invited to give lectures about globalization all around the world.

Some of these lectures and the ensuing discussions were instrumental in shaping the idea for a book on the limits to privatization and on the need to 'reinvent democracy' under the conditions of globalized markets. It was clear from the beginning that a single author could not possibly cover the entire field of new experiences with privatization, so diverse in different continents. Ernst von Weizsäcker invited Oran Young and, later, Matthias Finger to join him in an editorial team. Moreover, many contributors from around the world helped to fill the book with authentic experiences and analyses.

We are honoured and grateful to have had the Club of Rome accompany us in the process of making this book. And we are proud that it received the rare status of a Report to the Club of Rome.

Ernst Ulrich von Weizsäcker   **Oran R. Young**   **Matthias Finger**
Berlin and Stuttgart,   *Santa Barbara, CA,*   *Lausanne,*
Germany   *USA*   *Switzerland*

September 2004

Editors' Acknowledgements

Three people, in particular, were involved in the making of the book. The daily work was coordinated in an admirable manner by Marianne Beisheim in Berlin from 2002 onwards. Maria Gordon in Oran Young's Californian team did a great job in editing all case studies or 'snapshots' – and some other sections – and by asking pertinent questions greatly helped in bringing those contributions into a publishable form. Towards the end, the editors enjoyed the exquisite editorial assistance of Roger Levett from Bristol. We are extremely grateful to Marianne, Maria and Roger.

A loose team of young idealists in Berlin helped to maintain the good spirits over the two years of production; each one of them contributed at least one section to the book, among them Jochen Boekhoff, Ruth Brand, Andreas Obser, Jürgen Scheffran, Ralf Südhoff and, of course, Marianne Beisheim, Beate Klein and Martin Stürmer.

Several others supported the project at times, among them Bianca Barth, Ingo Bauer, Miriam Frömel, Herbert Girardet, Georg von Graevenitz, Tim Gürtler, Katharina Hay, Georg Kristian Kampfer, Mario Meinecke, Brian Power, Nele Schneidereit and John Züchner.

The illustrations were brought into an attractive and uniform shape by Hans Kretschmer, Wuppertal, in collaboration with Martin Stürmer.

We gratefully acknowledge the generous financial support given by the ZEIT Stiftung Ebelin und Gerd Bucerius in Hamburg and the Avina Foundation in Zurich. The Friedrich Ebert Foundation – namely, Jürgen Stetten – helped to arrange an authors' meeting in Berlin and organized a side event on Limits to Privatization during the World Social Forum in Mumbai, India, in January 2004.

The *Social Watch Report 2003* contained roughly 50 brief snapshots of privatization in different countries, edited by Roberto Bissio, Uruguay, who kindly agreed to our making ample use of his Report in our book.

The Club of Rome took an intense interest in the topic of the book and offered important time slots to it during its annual conferences in Ankara, 2002, Amman, 2003, and Helsinki, 2004. Several club members, including Ricardo Díez-Hochleitner (Spain), Leonor Briones (the Philippines), Eberhard von Koerber and Patrick Liedtke (both Switzerland), Manfred Max-Neef (Chile), Uwe Möller (secretary-general), Franz Josef Radermacher (Germany), Roseann Runte (USA), Mihaela Y. Smith (UK), Keith Suter

(Australia) and Raoul Weiler (Belgium), took the trouble of reviewing earlier stages of the book and offered very helpful comments. The editors are proud that the book received the unusual honour of being accepted as a new *Report to the Club of Rome*. We are particularly grateful to HRH Prince El Hassan Bin Talal, president of the Club of Rome, for a meaningful Foreword to our book.

Jonathan Sinclair Wilson of Earthscan took the risk of accepting the book at a stage when its quality was still inadequate, to put it mildly. We greatly appreciate Andrea Service's excellent copy-editing and the professional manner of Frances MacDermott and colleagues at Earthscan in producing the book.

PART I

Introduction

Limits to Privatization

Ernst Ulrich von Weizsäcker, Oran R. Young and Matthias Finger

Seeking a balance

Beware of extremes! What is needed is a proper balance: between freedom and order, between innovation and continuity, and – the topic of this book – between the private sector and the public domain.

Different actors will have their own preferences about the best balance between each pair of extremes. Poorer people may favour more order and a bigger public domain, while affluent people may want more freedom and more private ownership. Many believe private ownership promotes efficiency and wealth creation. Yet, even affluent countries committed to the productive value of private ownership seek a balance between the private sector and the public domain, regardless of the tone of the rhetoric they employ.

Striking a good balance between private and public is the theme of this book. Thus, we address one of the great issues of our times. Which services, including health, education and welfare systems, as well as law enforcement, infrastructure and finance, can be entrusted safely to the private sector? Are there good reasons to keep a sizeable proportion of a society's land and natural resources within the public domain? Under what circumstances is it better for the state to own and operate (some of) the means of production? Where functions are performed by private companies, what sorts of rules and regulations should govern them?

There are no simple answers to these questions. Yet, some important observations about recent developments are coming into focus. The thesis we develop in this book is that the recent and continuing swing towards privatization is in danger of becoming too much of a good thing. It may carry us beyond reasonable limits and produce undesirable consequences that outweigh the undeniable benefits of many forms of privatization.

In this book we describe and explore privatization in a range of sectors. Thousands of cases exist worldwide. Some have been successful by any reasonable standard, but others have failed. We have collected and selected, to the best of our ability, examples from around the world and from all relevant sectors.

What goes wrong attracts the attention of the media much more than what goes well. Never mind. It is widely assumed that privatization is a good thing; there is more need to understand its limitations and hazards than to confirm the assumptions underlying the trend.

At the time when our plans emerged to write this book, in 2001, we knew of no systematic worldwide study of privatization across all sectors. In the meantime, the World Bank has published a highly useful assessment of privatization of infrastructure in developing and Eastern European countries (Kessides, 2004). This policy research report is unusually candid about failures, although it maintains the Bank's general assertion that privatization enhances efficiency, enlarges access to essential services and helps solve many development problems.

Before assessing actual experience through a series of short case studies and snapshots, we need to flesh out what we mean when speaking of limits to privatization and suggest strategies for rectifying the growing imbalance that has emerged in this realm. The following sections of this introductory chapter set the stage for our investigation.

A word on definitions

Like most prominent policy concepts, 'privatization' has a cluster of overlapping meanings. In this book, we use the term in its widest sense to refer to all initiatives designed to increase the role of private enterprises in using society's resources and producing goods and services by reducing or restricting the roles that governments or public authorities play in such matters. This is often carried out by a transfer of property or property rights, partial or total, from public to private ownership. But it can also be done by arranging for governments to purchase goods and services from private suppliers or by turning over the use or financing of assets or delivery of services to private actors through licences, permits, franchises, leases or concession contracts, even when ownership remains legally in public hands. There are even cases such as 'build-operate-transfer' contracts, where the private sector creates an asset, operates it for a certain length of time, and then transfers it into public ownership. Where necessary, we use more technical definitions in accordance with the relevant literature.

Privatization is not the same as deregulation, which means the removal or attenuation of restrictions, including requirements and prohibitions, imposed by a public authority on the actions of public or private actors or, in essence, any reduction of state control over the activities of societal actors. Privatization often comes with deregulation, and especially the removal of exclusive rights and the opening-up of a service to competition. But either can occur without the other. A major theme running through the book is that the success or failure of privatization is often strongly influenced by the kind and degree of regulation accompanying it.

We draw a distinction, as well, between privatization/deregulation and liberalization, which means actions by governments to stimulate competition among companies in markets. Liberalization can take a variety of forms, ranging from anti-trust measures to the elimination of subsidies and the introduction of incentives to stimulate competition between private actors. Although they are separate phenomena, privatization/deregulation and liberalization often go together. In this book, we focus on privatization/ deregulation, referring to liberalization as it affects privatization.

Changing role of the state

Throughout much of the 19th and 20th centuries, governments assumed responsibility for an ever-expanding range of societal functions, in particular social and health functions. Later during the 19th century, but especially in the beginning of the 20th century, governments also played a crucial role in supplying *infrastructure*, such as highways, airports, port facilities, telecommunication and postal services, water supply and reservoirs, sewerage and irrigation systems, hospitals, schools, and, increasingly, in maintaining these facilities. Some infrastructure was actually built and initially owned by private entrepreneurs and later nationalized, notably many railways, power grids and telecommunication networks.

Nationalization was one of the central programmatic ideas of *communism* from the days of the Russian revolution onward. After World War II, communism spread further, and state-owned infrastructure *and industries* became the normal state of affairs throughout the communist bloc. But nationalization took place also in many Western countries, as well, notably in Europe and Latin America. Ideology (often socialist rather than communist) played a part. But nationalization was often motivated by pragmatic assessments that capital could be raised more readily and cheaply by the state, or services delivered in a more efficient, coordinated and effective way, if managed in the public interest as coherent and integrated systems rather than left to a patchwork of private companies who would inevitably put their individual commercial interests first. It is sobering to note how similar these arguments for nationalization – accessing investment, service responsiveness and efficiency – are to some of those advanced 30 to 40 years later to justify privatizing the same services.

States emerging from colonial rule during the 1960s and 1970s saw ownership and responsibility for essential infrastructure as the most natural task of the state. By the end of the 1970s most of the world's governments had assumed far-reaching responsibilities for their infrastructure and various means of production.

During recent decades, however, the tide has begun to flow in the opposite direction. Since the 1980s, preceded by economic theory generated in the 1960s but significantly pushed by globalization, technological developments, market expansion and the growth of private operators, a new trend has emerged of questioning the state's dominant role and of strengthening the private sector. This trend has manifested itself mainly in the privatization of an array of activities previously included in the public domain, together with deregulation in the form of opening previously protected industries to competition and of reducing restrictions on the activities of private enterprises.

During the 1960s, the spirit of privatization went against established cycles of change and took on an air of courageous endeavour. Economists such as Friedrich von Hayek, Milton Friedman and Ronald Coase paved the way.[1] They treated the then fashionable search for social equity as inefficient, partly dishonest and demoralizing for high achievers and thus, in the end, counterproductive to its own aims.

Neo-conservative politicians embraced their ideas as a basis for attacking affirmative action and other equity measures in the US, the UK and elsewhere. Socialist and equity concerns were seen as a form of romanticism or a cover-up for state cronyism, if not as a dangerous ideological support for the arch enemy, the Soviet Union.

In political battles to promote the emerging neo-liberal and neo-conservative paradigms, the most widely used term was 'economic efficiency'. The efficiency code was used successfully to delegitimate 'inefficient' state functions in an ever-growing array of sectors. The ideological adversary at the time was Keynesianism. Neo-conservatives said that Keynesian deficit spending was only leading to or deepening 'stagflation', the unpleasant combination of high inflation rates and high unemployment that was characteristic of the late 1970s (see, for example, Bruno and Sachs, 1985). A lean and efficient state, by contrast, would promote tax reductions, low inflation and better services – and that from the private sector. The enlarged private sector, not the state, would take care of economic growth and technological progress. In retrospect, nobody would seriously deny that the paradigm shift has been successful by its own standards of efficiency.

But can we afford to assume that these arguments will hold for all cases? Or are their limits to privatization in the sense of thresholds beyond which the costs of privatization outweigh the benefits?

Forms of privatization

In this book, we devote particular attention to four broad categories of privatization, ranking from 'weak' to 'strong' privatization:

1 putting state monopolies into competition with private or other public operators;
2 outsourcing, in which governments pay private actors to provide public goods and services;
3 private financing in exchange for delegated management arrangements, often with a view to transferring ownership to the state after a period of profitable use; and
4 transfers of publicly owned assets into private hands.

The first category includes cases in which governments alter the rules of the game to allow private enterprises to engage in specific activities. This might

Form	Brief description	Examples in this book
Conventional government agency	Administrative unit of government, establishment in the executive branch of the government	—
Performance-based organization	Government agencies, in which agency officials are rewarded on the basis of performance	—
Government corporation	Owned by the government, but intended to be entrepreneurial. It acts much like private corporations and is freed from many restrictions imposed on government agencies.	German rail; Telecom Uruguay; Skyguide
Service contract	A contract for the maintenance of a specific service by a private entity	Police services in Frankfurt, Germany
Management contract	The government pays a private operator to manage facilities, yet retains much of the operating risks	Railway Services, Portugal
Lease contract	A private operator pays a fee to the government for the right to manage the facility and takes some of the operating risks	Rostock Water
Build-operate-transfer (BOT) arrangement	A private entity builds, owns and operates a facility, then transfers ownership to the government at the end of a specified period	Thames Water; Telecommunication, Brazil
Concession	A private entity takes over the management of a facility or a state-owned enterprise for a given period during which it also assumes significant investment and operational risks	—
Partial privatization / divestiture	The government transfers part of the equity in the state-owned company to private entities (operators, institutional investors). The private stake may or may not imply private management of the facility.	Budapest Sewerage Works
Full privatization / divestiture	The government structures a public service as a state-owned company and transfers 100% of the equity in the state-owned company to private owners	MDK Pirdop Copper Refinery, Bulgaria; TPG Post

Figure 1
The public–private continuum. Different possible service
delivery models from fully public to fully private with some illustrations.

result in competition between private and public operators. In order to match private-sector efficiency, the public operator often takes efficiency as a measure of performance. Examples for this category include the granting of permission for private airlines to compete with national airlines, the authorization of private universities and hospitals and the deregulation of the electricity market.

The second category includes all those cases in which governments contract with private enterprises to supply specified goods and services previously provided by public agencies. Arrangements of this kind have a long history, going back, in the case of France, to the late 19th century. But recent decades

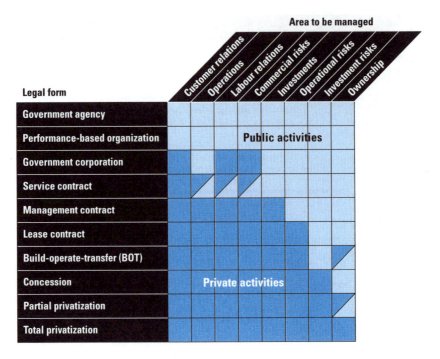

Figure 2
Schematic overview illustrating different mixes of public and private activities. Government
activites are light shaded, private activities dark.

have witnessed an explosion of new arrangements of this sort, dealing with
services ranging from education through healthcare, public transportation,
security systems and on to prisons.

The third category involves the financing of infrastructure but, increasingly,
also other projects (e.g. schools, hospitals and museums) by the private sector.
These include build-operate-transfer (BOT) arrangements, concessions and
lease contracts. The World Bank has been especially active in developing
sophisticated models where the private sector provides the money in exchange
for various forms of delegated management arrangements so that the
investments can be paid back. Originally only practised in developing
countries, this approach to financing public investments is increasingly
common in industrialized countries.

Perhaps the simplest and most familiar of these categories is the last one,
the transfer of publicly owned assets into private hands. Historically,
governments have often sold public land to private owners or granted more
limited use rights, such as the right to harvest standing timber on public lands.
More recently, we have witnessed a rising tide of sales of all or part of publicly
owned enterprises, such as national airlines, telecommunication companies,
petroleum companies and other energy companies.

In all cases, governments may impose more or less stringent regulations
restricting the actions of private enterprises. Land may be transferred with

easements, allowing public access for specified purposes (e.g. hiking, berry-picking). Government contracts with private corporations may or may not include requirements about service standards, access, prices, auditing, reporting and such like. Authorization to enter new markets may or may not include regulations dealing with occupational safety and health or with the treatment of pollutants.

Points of departure: Polar perspectives

Historically, arguments about privatization have often been polarized between extreme statist and extreme libertarian positions. The statist view, held by many socialists throughout the 20th century, is that it is desirable for the state to own property and to provide public services; moreover, state agencies can be trusted to act in the public interest without needing any external regulation or scrutiny. The libertarian view, exemplified by Milton Friedman, calls not only for transferring property rights from the public domain into private hands, but also for minimizing regulations and restrictions on the actions of owners of private property.

Statists assume that the public sector will automatically operate in the public interest because there is no profit motive to make it do anything else; libertarians believe that the mechanism of competition driven by profit-seeking will guarantee that private providers will respond to what users of services want – because those who fail to do so will be driven out of business by those who succeed. Thus, these two views, in one sense polar opposites, share the assumption that the right *ownership* of public assets is the key to good results.

Both contrast with the view that effective regulation is the key to ensuring that services act in the public interest. The problems experienced with unregulated or weakly regulated private ownership have led many to conclude that private ownership can bring benefits if, but only if, there is a strong framework of regulation to ensure that companies look after the needs of all their customers and support broader public policy goals, such as environmental protection and equal opportunities. 'Privatization – but with strong regulation' is perhaps the most popular position at the time of writing, and many of the examples in the book provide evidence supporting it.

However, arguments for regulation do not apply only to private ownership. Some now argue for public ownership, but with strong independent regulation to ensure that public services operate in the interests of their users, rather than of their staff, and to keep up the pressure to improve efficiency and effectiveness, which is otherwise absent from services that face neither competitors nor shareholders. Perhaps this kind of regulation could have prevented the complacency, inefficiency and unresponsiveness in many public services that made privatization seem attractive or even essential. Some of the examples in this book are of initiatives to make public service providers more accountable, responsive and self-critical in order to improve performance without resort to privatization.

The two axes of public versus private ownership and weak versus strong regulation thus imply four possible combinations (see Figure 3).

Level of regulation	Ownership	
	Public	**Private**
Minimal	*Most public services before 1980 (all in former Soviet states)*	*Most 'classic' privatizations through 1980s*
Strong	*Recent experiments as alternative to privatization*	*More recent privatizations*

Figure 3
Four possible combinations of ownership and regulation.

Of course, this is a simplification. As we have noted already, there are many different models of ownership, and even reducing them to a continuum from public to private is a simplification. Likewise, there are many more aspects of variation in regulation than just a line from 'strong' to 'weak'. Moreover, all four positions assume that governments are stable and capable of regulating and enforcing property rights. This assumption seems increasingly unrealistic in many societies for reasons having nothing to do directly with privatization.

Figure 3 should make one point clear. Privatization is not about doing away with regulation as some followers of Milton Friedman seem to believe. To the contrary, as Hernando de Soto (2000) argues, private ownership may require particularly reliable regulation to protect weak and small against the steamrolling powers of the rich.

Figure 3 should not be treated as more than a rough summary. Nevertheless, these first-order distinctions are helpful in drawing attention to the twin dangers of market failure and government failure. They may also help us to avoid confusing the ideal and the actual or, in other words, comparing ideal forms of privatization with the gritty realities of public supply or vice versa.

'Horses for courses'

Different forms of privatization fit different societal and cultural conditions. Forms of privatization that produce positive results under some conditions fail miserably under other circumstances. In some settings, privatization has even given rise to corrupt practices and a tendency to defraud the general public. More generally, there are *limits to privatization* in the sense of boundaries beyond which the negative consequences or costs of privatization outweigh any benefits.

Thus, the central concerns of this book are:

- What are the limits to privatization in the sense of boundaries beyond which the net results typically turn negative?
- What conditions determine the location of these limits in particular issue areas and in specific social/political systems?
- What systems of regulation are needed to avoid or minimize both market and government failures?

- How can the best balance be achieved in allocating social functions or tasks between the private sector and the public domain?

Generic pros and cons

The consequences of privatization, deregulation and liberalization are context specific. Identical structures or property rights or regulatory systems can, and often do, produce divergent results in different social settings. Many of those who promoted privatization in the wake of the collapse of the Soviet Union learned this lesson the hard way. For the victims, that lesson was even harder! It is always important, therefore, to evaluate the consequences of privatization or liberalization in context rather than judging specific situations on the basis of broad generalizations.

Even so, we can identify the major categories of arguments advanced by advocates of privatization and liberalization, as well as the core concerns of those who oppose these trends.

Proponents of privatization advance three broad types of arguments in one form or another:

- Privatization promotes efficiency and enhances social welfare by creating incentives to allocate resources to their highest and best use and by encouraging individual owners to invest in longer-term initiatives in the expectation that they will reap the resultant gains over time.
- Transferring property from the public domain to the private sector and reducing regulatory restrictions increases personal freedom, avoids the effects of rigid bureaucracies, and reduces corruption and cronyism in public places.
- A combination of private property and appropriate incentives and rules produces equitable results in the sense of rewarding those who work hard, take risks and exercise ingenuity. As such, it also leads to creativity and innovation.

For their part, opponents of privatization advance a parallel set of propositions:

- Privatization tends to weaken the state and its capacity to care for social equity. By weakening the state, privatization also erodes the significance of democratic participation at national and sub-national levels.
- Privatization subordinates broader public goods, including long-term ecological and cultural values, to commercial imperatives.
- The need of private providers to make a commercial return (in the form of profits, dividends, rents and/or interest) adds to the cost of providing public services.
- Commercially optimal decisions are often suboptimal for public goals; competition forces providers to ignore externalities.
- The private sector never really does take over risks in public service provision. Where costs exceed revenues, private operators respond by

demanding subsidies, raising charges, cutting necessary investment and maintenance, or walking away.

These considerations ought to be treated as a checklist of queries in terms of which to interrogate specific situations involving calls for privatization and liberalization, or their reversal. The results of such evaluative efforts will vary from one functional area to another, as well as from one social setting to another. But the use of such a checklist provides some assurance that the results will be based on a systematic assessment of the pros and cons of specific proposals.

The shape of things to come

We proceed by presenting a set of short case studies and even shorter snapshots designed to cover the spectrum from successful instances of privatization to outright failures evaluated in terms of a range of criteria.

Some cases simply examine the trend towards privatization, including its early motives, driving forces and consequences. These cases illustrate where the trend began – in what countries and in which functional sectors. Other cases show initial enthusiasm yielding to increasing frustration. Still others feature initial scepticism giving way to satisfaction on all sides.

In many cases – increasingly visible today – the costs of privatization and liberalization outweigh the benefits. Public protests, blatant corruption in the process of selling or transferring public assets, and clear breaches of the basic commitments are all visible signs of this failure.

Each of our case studies and snapshots seeks to answer at least *one* of the following questions:

- Has the *quality of services* improved or deteriorated as a result of privatization; have existing services disappeared or new services been created or added?
- Has privatization altered incentives in such a way as to improve *efficiency or cost effectiveness*?
- Has privatization led to increasing or decreasing *investments in infrastructure*?
- Has *competition* been increased through the process of privatization?
- Has the pursuit of efficiency led to *distributive consequences* that are manifestly unfair or inequitable?
- Has privatization/deregulation generated *collective action problems* in the sense of situations in which individual rationality leads to social outcomes that are undesirable for all? If so, have these problems been handled in a cooperative and fair manner?
- Has privatization/deregulation affected the supply of *public goods*, such as the fulfilment of basic human needs or the protection of the planet's life-support systems?
- Has privatization/deregulation affected rates of *(un)employment* or otherwise affected basic *social welfare*?

Box 1 An emerging controversy in the European Union: The Service Directive

Based on the Lisbon Strategy, the European Commission has made a proposal for a Service Directive, dated 13 January 2004. This draft directive is causing heated controversies in the European Union (EU), notably in the countries with high social standards. The reason is simple. The draft directive intends to liberalize remunerated services throughout the EU and gives clear preference to the country-of-origin principle over the country-of-delivery principle. This means that, for example, poor social standards of a country of origin (of the service supplier) automatically become legitimate and applicable in whichever country of delivery. Higher social standards in the recipient country will systematically be undercut. And public authorities that have so far been responsible for quality services will come under massive pressure to get the same job done cheaper, by subcontracting those services.

The whole draft directive is seen as highly biased and selective as regards the intentions of the Lisbon Strategy in that objectives of harmonization at a high social standard are completely neglected. Assuming that the European Commission, currently presided over by José Manuel Barroso, sticks to this biased interpretation of the Lisbon Strategy, it can be expected that liberalization and privatization will meet with fierce resistance in many EU countries.

- How was the *process of privatization* (bidding process, contracting, monitoring, etc.) organized? Has proper *regulation* been installed?
- In what ways has privatization/liberalization affected the role of *democratic controls and democratic participation*?
- Has privatization/liberalization undermined or augmented *cultural diversity*?
- Are *gender* effects visible or expected?
- Has privatization/liberalization encouraged *capacity-building* in such forms as training individuals and exposing small and medium-sized companies to the discipline of international markets?
- Has privatization/liberalization increased or decreased the effects of *corruption* in the public domain or in the private sector?
- How has *globalization* affected the results arising from privatization/liberalization within *individual societies*?
- Has the *local economy* been included into the process or have local firms profited from technological transfer and capacity-building?

Different case studies and snapshots illuminate different questions. We have presented them as readable narratives or vignettes, rather than attempting to force them into a standardized format. We have not been able to pursue all of the intriguing questions that they raise. Nevertheless, we believe that our efforts have produced some important insights regarding limits to privatization. Understanding and evaluating privatization as one of the mega trends of our time must be a 'work in progress'. We invite readers to arrive at their own assessments of experiences with privatization.

Box 2 Public goods

Public goods concern us all. The Earth's atmosphere and an educated public are public goods. So are security and the existence of a trustworthy legal system.

Economists have thought a lot about public goods. They have developed definitions and found ways of determining whether something deserves to be classified as a public good.

Mancur Olson (1965) was one of the pioneers in this endeavour. He spelled out the criterion of *non-excludability*: if a good is provided to any individual member of a group, no one else in the group can feasibly be excluded from consuming it, as well. Olson actually spoke about 'collective goods'; but the two terms are used interchangeably in the literature.

Other authors have added the criterion of *non-rivalness*. This means that the consumption of a good by one member of the group does not reduce the availability or value of that good to other members.

Some goods we would naively regard as public goods do not meet these two criteria. If water is a scarce resource (e.g. in a dry country), its consumption by some will have a negative effect on its availability to others. And as the emergence of markets in water makes clear, it is often possible to create exclusion mechanisms that regulate the supply of water.

Efforts to supply public goods give rise to the 'free-rider' problem. Free riders are those who enjoy a public good without contributing to its production, preservation or replenishment. If many members of the group choose this course, the public good will be undersupplied or not supplied at all. It is often assumed that the state should manage public goods in order to avoid this problem.

Political decisions can create exclusion mechanisms, shifting a good from the status of public good to private good in the process. The introduction of permits governing emissions of sulphur dioxide, for example, has turned certain aspects of the Earth's atmosphere into private goods.

Recently, a debate has arisen concerning the idea of 'global public goods'. Inge Kaul and Ronald Mendoza (2003, p95) say that global public goods are 'goods whose benefits extend to all countries, people and generations'. They distinguish among the global natural commons (e.g. the high seas), *global human-made commons* (e.g. radio and television broadcasts) and *global policy outcomes or conditions* (e.g. a peaceful world order) (Kaul and Mendoza, 2003, p100).

In order to advance future research, we suggest establishing an interactive website to support a worldwide search for knowledge on limits to privatization. We shall be happy to cooperate with others and would be delighted to see an improved second edition of this book published two or three years after this first one!

PART II

Privatization in Many Sectors: Case Studies and Snapshots

INITIAL REMARKS

Oran R. Young

In this critical section of the book, we consider a wide range of concrete situations in which societies have chosen combinations of privatization and deregulation during the recent past. Formally speaking, our examples do not constitute a representative sample of the thousands of experiments with privatization and deregulation that have made privatization one of the mega trends of our times. Nevertheless, we have cast our net widely and included a large number of cases covering a diversity of situations.

These cases range across numerous functional areas or sectors, including natural resources and extractive industries, a variety of other industries and many social services. They pertain to all of the world's regions, as well as to advanced industrial societies, countries with economies in transition and developing countries. We are confident that the examples we describe include the major types of privatization and that our findings are robust, despite the fact that our sample is not representative of the entire universe of cases of privatization.

Throughout our work on the limits to privatization, we have pursued a strategy of maximizing breadth rather than depth. Thus, we have chosen to sample a wide range of situations involving privatization and deregulation rather than to engage in an in-depth account of a small number of cases. Some of the contributions included go into the details; but others are extremely brief, often identifying a single point of interest rather than developing a real case study. We call these shorter pieces snapshots to differentiate them from actual case studies.

Our goal has been to identify the main issues associated with privatization as a mega trend rather than to dissect individual cases in sufficient detail to offer specific policy recommendations. We want to pinpoint the most important factors that determine the balance between the positive and the negative impacts of privatization. When we come to discuss strategies for rebalancing the private and the public in Parts III to V of our book, we will be seeking to formulate general conclusions rather than to redress the problems of privatization in individual cases.

Water

SOLVING WATER-SUPPLY PROBLEMS IN BOLIVIA: BEYOND COCHABAMBA

Ralf Südhoff

In the year 2000, a symbol for private water supply was born: Cochabamba. The privatization of the water system of Cochabamba, Bolivia, became a notorious failure. Bechtel Corporation pulled out after furious demonstrations against its plan to increase water prices. However, since then Cochabamba has become a symbol so powerful that it casts its shadow over positive examples of successful privatizations – even when these other examples are located just 250km from Cochabamba, such as Bolivia's capital, La Paz.

For many, another disaster seemed inevitable in La Paz. In 1997, South America's poorest country handed over its capital's water supply to the world's most powerful water corporation, Suez Lyonnaise des Eaux. The reform was due to a number of problems that had arisen simultaneously during the 1990s. Bolivia's urban population had doubled since the 1970s, chiefly due to migration from rural parts of the country. One of the fastest growing cities was El Alto, once a small suburb of La Paz. By the early 1990s it had grown to 350,000 inhabitants (2003 figures provide even a total between 600,000 and 700,000 of mostly impoverished people). Yet, infrastructure, including water supply, had failed to keep pace.

For this reason, the Bolivian government adopted a major water programme in 1990 with the aim of substantially improving the public water supply in its burgeoning cities. The World Bank provided financial support for the project – until 1997. At that point, the World Bank experts sounded the alarm. Improvements in water and sewerage services in the La Paz metropolitan region – and in Cochabamba – were making far slower progress than planned. SAMAPA (Servicio Autonomo Municipal de Agua Potable y Alcantarillado), the municipal water company, was two years behind the agreed schedule. A wastewater management project supported by German development agencies already faced an overall delay of 3.5 years. Seven years after the public water programme was launched, less than one household in three in El Alto had a sewerage connection, and even in more prosperous La Paz, sewage from one household in every three flowed untreated into the Rio Seco (and from there into Lake Titicaca). Almost half of the piped water seeped away through leaks or was not paid for. At the same time, the poorest rapidly growing districts still had not been connected to the potable water supply. Although coverage in the La Paz metropolitan region was relatively high from the very beginning (at around 85 per cent), the poorest inhabitants still had no access. As the population in El Alto kept growing at about 5 per cent per year, the number of people with no access increased and ever more people had to buy their water from dealers who often charged ten times the regular price.

Two reasons were cited for SAMAPA's problems. First, the company was said to be too linked to politics, with a supervisory board composed mainly of local and national politicians. Second, the company lacked the financial resources to invest in supplying the poor marginal areas and, indeed, had no incentive to do so (Komives and Brook Cowen, 1998).

Therefore, in July 1997, the World Bank made privatization of La Paz water distribution (but not the processing plants or reservoirs) a pre-condition of its loans' extensions. The tender process took place in April 1997 and the 30-year concession was awarded to the French–Bolivian–Argentine consortium AISA (Aguas del Illimani S.A.), of which the French company Suez owned 59 per cent of the shares. A detailed catalogue of measures was agreed, especially for the first five years. A nationally based regulation agency was to monitor the progress.

Five years later, substantial progress had been made both in equity terms of water access and in efficiency terms of water supply. Following investment by AISA totalling US$53 million, the number of water connections rose as planned from 154,000 to 225,000 in 2002 – an increase of 45 per cent. Most of the connections (45,000) have been supplied in the poor districts of El Alto. The number of households connected to the sewerage system in El Alto has increased from 30 per cent to 54 per cent (contractual target: 43 per cent). In La Paz, around 90 per cent of households are now connected to the sewerage system (contractual target: 77 per cent).

In a direct comparison, too, AISA's performance is well ahead of the public water company SAMAPA. During the first three years after privatization, AISA supplied around 60 per cent more new water connections and 180 per cent more sewerage connections than SAMAPA in its last three years of operation.

At the same time, water prices were frozen for the first five years. Shortly before the tender process took place, prices were increased and an 'increasing block tariff' was introduced in line with social needs. On average, the price of water increased by 38 per cent, but fell for approximately one third of customers. This balanced result occurred because, first, the block tariff is based on consumption, with a social pricing structure being introduced for the first 30 cubic metres; and, second, the old basic charge that corresponded to consumption of around 10 cubic metres per month was abolished. The new price was based solely on consumption and therefore led to cost savings for the poorest and most frugal customers as the average consumption in El Alto was just about 8 cubic metres per month. In 2001, the average monthly water bill thus amounted to the local currency equivalent of US$1.90, with average monthly income standing at around US$134 during this period. The charges imposed by Bolivia's only private operator became among the lowest in the country.

Alongside these improvements in the equity of water access, AISA was also able to achieve substantial improvements in the efficiency of water supply. Although AISA initially took SAMAPA's entire workforce of 640 people onto its payroll, it later gradually shed around one third of these jobs while substantially expanding the network and significantly increasing company turnover. With respect to overall employment goals – which had not been part of the contract – this resulted in around 220 job losses. At the same time, the company substantially improved efficiency – for example, by dismantling tiers of management, decentralizing its operations, and introducing new information technology (IT) systems. On average, AISA now employs two members of staff per 1000 connections, compared with a figure between five and nine for Bolivia's public water utilities. A more efficient and consistent invoicing procedure has slashed the outstanding debts owed to the company and reduced the share of 'non-revenue water' from 48 per cent to 40 per cent. Compared with the public utilities company, which rarely covered its costs despite the low level of investment, costs as a proportion of total revenue have fallen to around 75 per cent under AISA. Therefore, AISA has not needed subsidies and has paid a US$3 million annual licence fee to the government (Komives, 1999; Foster, 2001).

Thus, contrary to widespread concerns about trade-offs between efficiency and equity under privatization, AISA increased efficiency and converted a substantial part of these efficiency gains into equity gains – which had been a condition of the original tender.

This proved essential. Suppliers in other countries had tended to focus almost exclusively on water price. Contracts were typically awarded to the bidder offering the lowest tariffs. In La Paz, the regulatory agency fixed the price for five years and focused on investment. Thus, the contract was awarded to the supplier promising the highest investment in new connections. The tender's stated objective was to supply water to as many people as possible in the low income bracket, not to hold down water prices across the board.

Moreover, anti-poverty provisions and contractual obligations helped to ensure Suez's participation in a water policy focusing on the poor people in the region, whereby Suez's water business in La Paz was utilized for social objectives. The concession contract, among other stipulations, states that at least 50 per cent of new connections must be supplied in poor districts. Various penalties apply for failing to meet these targets. The block tariffs resulted in cross-subsidies in line with social needs. The contractual agreements were monitored by a fairly independent regulatory agency.

Nevertheless, after five years of privatization, the case of El Alto still has some way to go to become a model of best practice. For example, a risk typically associated with interventionist policies has become a reality in El

Alto, where excessively rigid conditions imposed by the state impinge upon flexibility. For instance, the regulatory agency stipulated that all new potable water connections had to be high-quality domestic connections. This excluded cheaper interim solutions, such as communal connections, or technically simpler options and made new connections unnecessarily expensive (specified maximum price: US$150; Arevalo-Correa, 2000). Other regulations granted too much flexibility to the investor. For example, AISA had exclusive rights as a supplier in the whole area from the very beginning. Following this rule, in some districts other sources such as standpipes had to be closed down even when AISA was not yet able to offer its service.

It took a couple of years for the regulatory agency to ease these provisions and to allow, for example, 'condominial water systems' with lower standards and alternative suppliers. This also illustrates a structural failure. Integrating the customers in the process could have avoided such shortcomings from the very beginning. However, with respect to 'participation programmes' and 'stakeholder processes', La Paz is surely no model for other cases (Crespo and Laurie, 2002).

At the same time, the agency acted without due care in setting some criteria for better supply. For example, the concession contract states that AISA must supply water connections to all households in districts with a specific minimum population density. However, these districts were not fixed. Assessment of progress, therefore, was difficult since 'population density' is something of a grey area in places with many illegal settlements and rapid population growth. According to AISA, the obligation was fulfilled in 2001, and onwards, as the company was no longer receiving requests for connections from such areas. Thus AISA could claim a supply rate of 100 per cent. However, such a claim, based on the weak criterion of density, is hard for a regulatory agency to verify.

These examples of shortcomings illustrate that regulation is a continuing process of checks and balances between the state and the operator. The La Paz case also demonstrates that the state need not be the loser in this game if it manages, in particular, to set up a strong regulator. This is shown, too, by the city's 2003 price negotiations with Suez.

The contract had stipulated that the levels of tariffs were to be renegotiated in 2002. However, the government delayed the renegotiation, which had quite a negative impact on AISA's revenue situation. After the company achieved profits of US$8.5 million in 1999, yields fell to US$5.7 million in 2001, not counting expenses, such as servicing investment loans. In 2003, experts feared that the company's financial situation could deteriorate significantly to the detriment of future investment. An independent study recommended an average price increase of 22 per cent, and AISA made suggestions about how this could be implemented without harming the poor. Even after this increase, water prices in La Paz and El Alto would still be among the lowest in the country. However, due in part to the events in Cochabamba, the political climate in Bolivia had become far less conducive to privatization, and water price increases were viewed as a highly sensitive political issue, especially in the wake of elections in 2002. Finally, both sides agreed, in 2003, on some financial incentives (such as higher prices for new connections) equivalent to a price increase of just over 10 per cent. Water tariffs themselves remained unchanged since the start of the privatization.

In conclusion, four lessons can be learned from the La Paz case so far:

1 Private water supply can meet both equity goals and efficiency goals if the incentives for the investor are set intelligently and from the very beginning, including the tender.
2 Even small details of regulations and contractual provisions influence the outcomes of private-sector participation. They must be considered and phrased far more carefully than has often been the case elsewhere, with predictably disastrous results.
3 If sufficient attention is paid to these details (if necessary, by taking external advice as in La Paz), even small states or cities can involve large private corporations in a water-supply programme designed to improve the situation of the poor.
4 If privatization is conducted this way, far better results can be achieved than by an inefficient public utilities company.

However, La Paz, just as much as Cochabamba, is not the symbol for water privatization. Nor is it the best model for water supply. Bolivia, in particular, demonstrates how important it is to think on a case-by-case basis. In Cochabamba, the state's initial failure was compounded by a poorly thought-out privatization programme; in Santa Cruz, Bolivia's third largest city, a public supplier is achieving good results because it is a highly transparent co-operative organization which has developed strong community links over the last 25 years; while in La Paz, an inefficient public company did not get the job done and was outperformed by the biggest multinational corporation of the world's highly contested water industry (Nickson, 1998; OED, 2002).

A 'WATERL'EAU' IN GRENOBLE, FRANCE[1]

Martin Stürmer

For the French, Grenoble is widely known as the 'Waterl'eau' of the privatization of water services. 'Waterl'eau' is a play on words that parallels Napoleon's first great defeat at the Battle of Waterloo with Grenoble's water service privatization. Corruption and overpricing led to a wide range of national commissions and legal processes that signify, in some sense, a defeat for the French method of privatization. The principal actors in this story include local politicians, a group of civic associations, as well as the local Ecology party and Suez,[2] the second largest water services company worldwide.

In general, French municipalities have always been responsible for water services themselves. Today, half of them accomplish this through a municipally owned enterprise formally separated from the city council (in French: *régie*).

Method	Contract (COGESE, 1989–1995)	Joint-venture (SEG, 1996–1999)
Entry fees	• Illegal recovery of entry fees which had to be paid to the city council by COGESE through charging users	• City council forego eliminated entry fees
Tariff formula	• Inflation indexing on wrong basis • Retroactive invoicing inflating bills	• Adjustment to consumption levels / price increases if consumption steady
Sub-contract-ing	• Privileged access to sub-contracting / discrimination against other bidders	• Water supply and sanitation subcontracted to SGEA (100% Suez) / decreasing remuneration of SEG versus increasing remuneration of SGEA • SGEA subcontract services to Suez (e.g. legal services, accounting, customer services, technical assistance, vehicles, IT, management of SGEA)
Creative account-ing	• Inflated costs of debt service • Transfer of receipts to Suez after 11 years of contract • City council to finance works without recovering costs	• City council share liability for damages caused by COGESE • City council assume €5.4 million of COGESE losses • City council forego dividends in favour of Suez
Legal powers	• Secrecy of documents	• Effective veto for Suez over decisions, despite minority shares

Figure 4
Techniques for overcharging used by Suez.
Source: adapted from Hall and Lobina (2001, p17).

The other half, representing about 80 per cent of the population, delegates service provision to private water companies.

Grenoble, a city in south-eastern France, had a population in 2003 of about 150,000.[3] For a century, the city council managed efficient water services, providing good quality water at low prices to consumers. Financially sound, despite its low prices, the service was profitable and regularly contributed to the municipal budget.

In 1983, however, Alain Carignon, then mayor of the city of Grenoble, initiated a new policy in favour of private-sector participation in all public services. He was a prominent member of the conservative Gaullist party and also became national deputy minister responsible for the environment. After his re-election in 1989, Carignon went ahead with the privatization of the city's water services. In spite of strong opposition from consumer and citizens associations, trade unions and the local Ecology party, the Grenoble City Council voted to award a 25-year long water supply and sanitation contract to COGESE (Compagnie de Gestion des Eaux du Sud-Est), a subsidiary of Suez.

The 'Waterl'eau' began in 1993. Under pressure from some civic associations and the local Ecology party, a number of corrupt public service concessions, including 'le système Carignon', were publicly exposed by legal investigators. The investigators concluded that the privatization had occurred

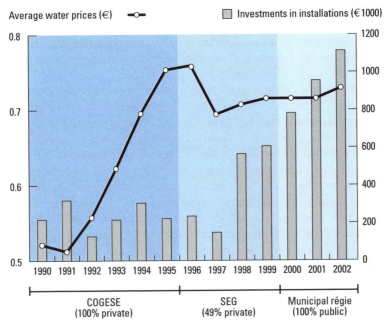

Average water prices (€) —o—   ☐ Investments in installations (€ 1000)

COGESE
(100% private)

SEG
(49% private)

Municipal régie
(100% public)

Figure 5
Prices and investments from fully private to fully public operation in Grenoble. Privatization has led to rising prices and lower investments. Following illegal pricing and corruption under privatization, the water service was finally re-municipalized in 2001. This welcome transition resulted in a stabilization of prices and an increase in investment.
Source: data from Raymond Avrillier, vice-president of the metropolitan region of Grenoble, 8 September 2003, based on reports by the Régie des eaux de Grenoble.

in exchange for kickbacks by Suez to fund Carignon's electoral campaign and other gifts to all major political parties, totalling approximately €3 million. Carignon and a chief executive of Suez were subsequently convicted of accepting and paying bribes. In 1996, they were sentenced to four years and one year in prison, respectively.[4]

The courts also ruled that the COGESE contract had damaged the municipality and consumers. The company had used a number of techniques, including fictitious accounting and manipulated indexation, in order to inflate prices (see Figure 4). The regional audit office estimated in 1995 that the total cost of these practices to the citizens of Grenoble, over the 25-year life of the COGESE contract, was approximately €180 million.[5]

In the wake of this scandal, council elections in 1995 saw the birth of a new local government, including the Socialist party and the Ecology party. While the Ecologists favoured termination of the contract and a re-municipalization of water services, the majority of the coalition was deterred by the prospect of having to pay high compensation to Suez.

Nevertheless, a solution had to be found, and in 1996 the Société des Eaux de Grenoble (SEG), was created. It was 51 per cent owned by the municipality and 49 per cent by Suez, allowing Suez to continue to maintain veto power over all major decisions. Immediately after its creation, SEG subcontracted water services for 15 years to the Société Grenobloise de l'Eau et de l'Assainissement (SGEA), a 100 per cent subsidiary of Suez (Avrillier, 1996, p17).

While the city council agreed to share liability for any damage caused by the former COGESE, the new joint venture allowed Suez to boost its profits once again. Corruption was stopped; but the city council suffered from a lack of sufficient knowledge needed to handle the contract with Suez. For example, the contract provided that the price of water would increase if consumption fell below 12.8 million cubic metres a year. This meant an immediate price increase in a city where consumption was already falling. Furthermore, the city council lost control over the formation of subsidiaries because the SGEA itself subcontracted several services at extremely high prices to other divisions of Suez (Figure 4 illustrates the other methods used to overcharge).

However, the local Green party and some citizen associations continued the legal fight. In 1996, the French Council of State deemed illegal the original decision to delegate the water service to COGESE. Furthermore, in 1998, the Grenoble Tribunal declared the city council's decisions concerning the new SEG/SGEA and some pricing methods void. In the end, all charges for the whole period of 1990–1998 had thus been invalidated.

After debating various options, the city council voted in 2000 to finally re-municipalize water supply under a *régie* (i.e. a municipally owned enterprise formally separated from the council). This form was chosen as the best option to ensure the transfer of all staff who had been employed by COGESE and the SEG/SGEA. A regional *régie* was created for water sanitation.

This re-municipalization has helped to re-establish a much a higher degree of transparency and has banished the culture of corruption and overcharging. As Figure 5 shows, water tariffs stabilized and at the same time the municipality could afford higher levels of investment in installations.

Grenoble is not an isolated case. Several national commissions have identified a wide range of corruption, kickbacks and overcharging in France in the context of delegated water services. For example, the Commission for Economics of the French Parliament states that these practices have enabled the growth of some French industrial groups that are now entering world markets (Tavernier, 2001, p10). Other reports by the National Audit Office and the High Commission on Public Service point out the significant difference in prices between private and municipal water services (Tavernier, 2001, pp22ff). Consequently, further examples of re-municipalization followed in France: Castre, Chatellerault, Neufchateau and others.

The privatization of water services saw no improvement in cost efficiency, and consumer prices went up for no apparent reason. Moreover, privatization took place in a highly corrupt environment and enabled further illegal practices by shrinking democratic control. The 'Waterl'eau' of Grenoble shows that even in France local governments lack sufficient knowledge to formulate regulations for the delegation of their water services to private companies.

Finally, it is worth noting that the resolution of the case of Grenoble and its successful re-municipalization were made possible by the effective French legal system and a ten-year effort by civil society. In addition, a return to a municipal service was legally possible and a working public model of provision was available. Such conditions do not exist in all countries where multinationals such as Suez act. It follows that this 'Waterl'eau' should not be considered a strictly French phenomenon.

MANILA: A SUCCESS STORY TURNED SOUR

Dörte Bernhardt

Until recently, the privatization of the water services of Manila, capital of the Philippines, seemed to be a success story. The World Bank, the International Monetary Fund (IMF) and government officials would refer to it favourably. Big water corporations, such as Vivendi/Veolia or Suez/Ondeo, used the example to convince more potential customers.

In December 2002, however, one of the two operators in Manila, Maynilad Water Services, was in deep financial distress and pulled out of its 25-year lease agreement. The regulatory commission had rejected an additional water rate increase to 27 pesos per cubic metre (approximately 49 US cents[6]). Maynilad Waters claimed that the city had not met its obligations and brought the dispute to the International Chamber of Commerce. The company then began to seek more than US$300 million in compensation from the government. However, this claim was legally rejected and Maynilad Water had to get on with the task of complying with its contract.

With 12 million residents, the metropolitan area of Manila is one of the biggest and fastest growing settlements in the world. During the mid 1990s, one third of the population had no access to the public water system. A public sewage system was almost non-existent. Water losses due to leakages from badly kept pipes and illegal withdrawal had been extremely high. Poor people especially had to rely on wells, public water stations and water vendors who often charged ten times the official tariffs. The local government officials were unable to stop the vicious circle of poor services, with subsequent insufficient revenues, that led to a lack of resources for investment. Even credits from international finance institutions such as the Asian Development Bank (ADB) did not improve the situation and only helped, finally, to leave the public Metropolitan Waterworks and Sewerage System (MWSS) with a debt of US$880 million (Esguerra, 2001, p1).

MWSS and, therefore, the Manila water situation in general, were considered un-reformable. However, in 1995, the Philippine Parliament (Congress) passed the Water Crises Act that gave President Fidel Ramos the authority to enter into contracts with private companies.[7] In 1992, after Ramos took office, he successfully resolved the Philippines' worst power crisis by partial privatization. Previously, nearly three years of power blackouts had hit Manila and its industrial areas, sometimes by as much as eight hours a day, with a tremendous effect on the economy. Now Ramos hoped to tackle the water crisis accordingly.

As a result of advice from the International Finance Corporation (IFC), the private sector lending arm of the World Bank, a privatization and international bidding process was started in Manila. This was hailed internationally as a significant improvement over previous similar deals – for example, by setting up a regulatory office and a dispute settlement mechanism. The service area was split into two, as in Paris and Jakarta. Foreign engagement was limited to 40 per cent. The lowest bidders won the contest. Manila Water Company Inc (MWCI) now serves the eastern part of town, with one third of the population. MWCI is co-owned by the US construction company Bechtel, the UK water company United Utilities and the Ayala Corporation. Maynilad Water Services International (MWSI) was granted the rights to operate and expand water and sewage service to the western part of town. MWSI is co-owned by the Benpres Holdings Corporation (59 per cent), which belongs to the Lopez family, and the French water company Suez (40 per cent). The Ayala and the Lopez family are among the richest and most influential families in the Philippines.

Manila Water had promised to run the concession by charging only a quarter (27 per cent) of existing rates (4 US cents compared to 16 US cents; Esguerra, 2001, p4). Maynilad Water offered to charge only 4.96 pesos, which is 57 per cent of the then current price. It planned to expand the infrastructure for the 7.5 million households covered by the concession. Other promises of Maynilad Water included '100% infrastructure coverage by 2007, US$7.5 billion new investments over 25 years. Unaccounted water would fall to 32% in 2007 and the city would save US$4 billion over 25 years' (Public Citizen, 2003). Water was predicted to be available within ten years for everybody in the city. The two bidders even took over all foreign debts of the MWSS. These very tempting offers by the two companies calmed down any protest against privatization, namely from trade unions or civil society.

Only a year into the contract, Maynilad Water asked for the first rate increase. In 2001, the price rose to 12 US cents, with subsequent hikes to 20 US cents, 21 US cents and 28 US cents (Public Citizen, 2003). This translates to an additional US$1.6 to US$2.7[8] on the monthly water bill for an ordinary Filipino family. 'Shortly before Maynilad Water took control, MWSS retired almost 2000 workers to lower costs and 6 months into the contract 750 workers were laid off' (Public Citizen, 2003). Because Maynilad Water was unable to contain costs and to realize the revenue potential of the asset assigned to it, its creditworthiness was at stake. The company 'tried to put the blame on the Asian financial crisis, which, while no doubt led to serious foreign exchange losses, had little to do with, for instance, water delivered to customers that is not billed due to metering mistakes, stealing, tampering, etc.' (Esguerra, 2001, p2). Maynilad Water argued further that climate change caused more severe El Nino events and that subsequent droughts decreased the water availability from the Angat reservoir by 40 per cent, resulting in loss of revenues (see Figure 6). Finally, the public partner, MWSS, was blamed for delaying the provision of water.

Maynilad continued to seek contract renegotiations, including continual rate increases, postponement of its obligations to meet investment and non-revenue water reduction targets. The contract provided three mechanisms to adjust prices, whether upwards or downwards: inflation, rate re-basing and extraordinary price adjustment (EPA). The revenues grow with the pace of inflation. Every five years, a review of tariffs ensures 'fair returns'. EPAs may be initiated once a year to capture the financial effects of certain unforeseeable events to the concessionaire:

> *Probably the most controversial contract renegotiation involved the pass through to consumers of foreign exchange losses. This ensured that Suez could continue to use its major foreign corporate suppliers and consultants (rather than local sources) while billing consumers to cover for the effects of peso devaluation* (Public Citizen, 2003).

Even critics admit that the water service contracts in Manila create a fair deal that allows all stakeholders – government, the companies and consumer – to reap benefits and, more importantly, to change the arrangements in an open and negotiated process should unforeseen or extraordinary events happen. There are sufficient guarantees for a fair return for efficiency-maximizing companies and adequate protection against risks that the companies may face (Esguerra, 2001, p5f). But in December 2002, when Maynilad Water tried to pull out of the contract, it was obvious that the success was theoretical and largely on paper. Maynilad Water and, to a lesser extent, Manila Water did not meet the obligations (e.g. water prices went up and water losses were still higher than promised). Dive bidding and a long-lasting corporate muddle, as well as government, public authorities, donors and lenders, who let it happen, turned the promising process in Manila into a failure. In 2004, Maynilad is compulsorily still in contract; but there is an ongoing bail-out process (Tubeza, 2004).

THAMES WATER UTILITIES LIMITED, UK[9]

Matthias Finger and Roger Levett

Thames Water was created as a company in 1989 as a result of its privatization by the Thatcher government. Originally, water services in the UK – as in most other countries of the world – had been run by local municipalities, publicly owned local water companies and a few private operators. They were essentially controlled through ownership and their prices were capped. In the UK, in 1974, water services were reorganized into ten regional water authorities, each covering a river basin area, and each responsible for water quality, water supply and sanitation in the area. Authorities were made accountable to national government as opposed to local government.

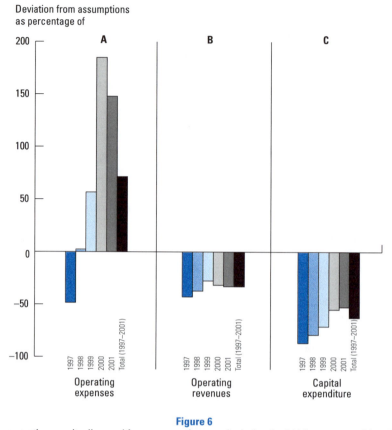

Figure 6
How operating results diverged from assumptions made during the bidding process. Maynilad underestimated expenses (A) and overestimated operating revenues (B). As a result, it cut capital expenditures (C).
Source: data from Esguerra (2001, pp8, 31ff); data for 2000 and 2001 from Esguerra (pers. comm. 2003).

Company start-up and scale

In 1989 the water authorities – including Thames Water Utilities Limited – were privatized, mainly with the aim of leveraging private funds for infrastructure upgrading and investment. Companies received a 25-year concession (i.e. a 25-year monopoly from the government), along with a write-off of all the utility company's debts, some start-up money and an exemption from taxes on profits. In 1989, Thames Water supplied water to 7 million customers in the London and Thames Valley, and treated wastewater of approximately 11 million customers. It had over 6000 employees and an annual turnover of approximately UK£870 million. When sold to the German transnational multi-service utility company RWE in 2002, Thames Water was the largest water and wastewater company in the UK.

Liberalization/privatization

Thames Water, along with the other nine UK water authorities, was floated approximately 20 per cent below market price. Pre-tax profits rose over 100 per cent in the next ten years (1990–1999), and water prices increased by approximately 30 to 40 per cent. Salaries of top managers were also raised significantly, something which was heavily criticized in the public arena.

Regulation

Privatization created a need for much greater regulation of the sector. Three regulatory authorities were set up: the Office of Water (OFWAT) to regulate prices, investment and profits; the Drinking Water Inspectorate to set, monitor and enforce purity standards in water delivered; and the National Rivers Authority to protect the aquatic environment by licensing water abstractions and wastewater discharge (which was subsequently subsumed into the Environment Agency, with broader powers for integrated management of river catchments).

Thames's operational context

London is one of the biggest concentrations of water demand and wastewater production in the world. It was a 19th-century pioneer in piped water and sewerage, so much of its infrastructure is now technically obsolete (for example, combined sewerage and rainwater pipes, which discharge untreated sewage into rivers when storm surges exceed treatment plant capacity), operating far above its original design capacity under quite unforeseen pressures (especially the literal pressure of traffic on below-road pipes) and crumbling with age. It is also extremely difficult and expensive to repair or replace because of the density of building, roads and other underground services that have grown up, often unplanned, around it.

Because of its large customer base and small catchment area with modest rainfall (south and east England are cloudy but, contrary to general belief, not very wet), Thames Water has less water available per resident than any other part of the UK. The company uses 55 per cent of available rainfall to supply its customers, twice as much as in any other UK water supply area and very high by developed world standards. Climate change is likely to increase demand and reduce supply, while planning policies have favoured housing growth without any reference to water availability. Most technically feasible and environmentally acceptable sources of water are already being exploited, some to excess. Most of the catchment area, with its high landscape, amenity and/or farming qualities, features high land values and wealthy residents ready to be militant in defence of their environment, so any new supply investment is expensive and politically difficult.

Performance after privatization

Assessment of Thames's performance after privatization should therefore consider not whether Thames has been less than perfect, but whether any alternative could have performed better given these somewhat daunting constraints.

Water quality and environmental impacts, already very high by world standards at privatization, have continued to improve incrementally since. Thames Water has occasionally been fined for environmental and public health violations. But these cases have been very rare considering the scale of the company's operations. According to data published by the regulators, standards are now generally higher than ever before. It seems likely that increasing public and political expectations would have led public-sector water utilities to improve standards over the same period, too. But, equally, there is no evidence that the privatized company has done any worse than it would have in the public sector.

Investment has widely been considered to have been insufficient after privatization, and the regulators are perceived as not capable of forcing water companies to invest sufficiently in order to guarantee security of supply (including the reduction of leakages) in the long run. But this is not necessarily an argument against privatization. Despite some successful big projects (notably a large new ring main around London), it is widely agreed that there had been a major investment shortfall for decades before privatization, especially in replacing older water distribution pipework in London.

This kind of investment greatly accelerated as a result of pressure from the incoming Labour government in 1997, notably the 'water summit' called by the Deputy Prime Minister John Prescott in response to mounting public and media concerns about water shortages, high leakage and costs. Arguably, the separation of regulators, companies and politicians made the issues more transparent and open to public scrutiny, and it was easier for Prescott to take on (unpopular) private companies than it would have been if they were in the public sector. Moreover, Thames Water managers complained that this political intervention showed that there was still not enough independence or separation. Specifically, they objected to Prescott responding to emotive and poorly informed public pressure by requiring OFWAT to set targets for leakage reduction, rather than for the overall aim of security of supply, which, they argued, could be achieved much more cost effectively by expanding supply.

However, this can be seen as an example of the success of the system: that it is still possible for the democratic political process to make privatized utilities do things for broader policy reasons, in this case avoiding the need for new environmentally damaging water supply investments, even if they are commercially suboptimal for the companies. The growing vulnerability of southern England to water shortages because of climate change may vividly confirm the wisdom of this decision. So, again, the conclusions for privatization are mixed and complex.

Employment in the sector fell approximately 20 per cent in the ten years following privatization, but had already fallen by about 40 per cent after the creation of the water authorities (1974–1989). Finally, the issue of *industry concentration* arises, where, ten years after privatization, five of the ten water companies, including Thames Water, had been taken over by transnational corporations, a process which is set to continue, if not to accelerate.

Thames Water's experience also raises some interesting points about the relationship between privatized utilities, public agencies and consumers. OFWAT requires water companies to encourage householders to change from un-metered supply, charged on the basis of property value (the norm in England), to metered supply. Thames Water believes this will help to cut consumption, in general, but not at times of shortage. The reason? When a water company puts out an appeal to reduce consumption during a drought, un-metered customers generally do their bit; but a lot of metered customers take the attitude of 'I'm paying for it; I'll keep buying as much as I want.' Turning water into a commodity bought by the litre makes it like any market commodity, and breaks any sense of social obligation to use an essential resource responsibly.

Raising the price of non-essential water use high enough in times of shortage might curb consumption as effectively as the sense of social responsibility does now – and arguably more fairly. Such smart real-time variable metering is technically feasible. But current regulatory rules require water companies not to discriminate between customers, and this means prices cannot vary too much between metered and un-metered customers.

During the late 1990s, Thames Water carried out research which showed that the majority of their customers would be happy to pay a bit more on their water bills in order to pay for environmental improvements. OFWAT vetoed this on the grounds that the consumer interest, which it represented, was in keeping prices down. If true, this suggests that the regulator is enforcing a narrower, more selfish and short-term notion of the consumer interest than consumers themselves wish (i.e. telling them that they cannot think as citizens when they are being consumers).

This is one example of a more general complaint that water companies are caught between the Drinking Water Inspectorate wanting to push purity ever upward regardless of diminishing returns or any sense of proportion over risk, the Environment Agency wanting to safeguard aquifers, again regardless of any broader consequences, and OFWAT always trying to push prices down, none of them with any remit to take account of the others' aims.

WATER PRIVATIZATION IN TANZANIA: MIXED RESULTS

Jürgen Scheffran

In order to improve the efficiency of water delivery in impoverished countries, the World Bank and the International Monetary Fund (IMF) push governments to enter public–private partnerships, often involving privatization. The record of such privatization seems to be mixed. Certainly, state-owned water supplies are often ineffective; but they have a built-in tendency to provide cheap or free water to the urban poor. Privatization, on the other hand, tends to exclude the poor from an affordable clean water supply (Bayliss, 2001).

Safe water supplies could save the lives of many children in Africa. This is one of the reasons why water privatization is a key issue in African countries. Proponents believe it brings efficiency, opponents that it hurts the poor. In the case of Tanzania, arguments exist for both positions.

Water privatization in Dar es Salaam

The water supply and sanitation infrastructure of Tanzania's largest city, Dar es Salaam, built in the 1970s, outdated and deteriorating rapidly by 2003, was causing estimated water losses of more than 30 per cent through leakage and illegal tapping. The Dar es Salaam Water and Sewerage Authority (DAWASA) has been described as suffering 'from poor billing and revenue collection and inadequate water sources, both in terms of quality and quantity' (Akande, 2002). In need of money, the Tanzanian government agreed, in the context of debt relief, to the IMF request to privatize the DAWASA as part of a process of privatizing over 300 state-owned enterprises.

However, the government had first to invest US$145 million to upgrade DAWASA, in order to sell off the company. To finance the cost of upgrading, the government needed credit. On 31 May 2002, the African Development Bank (ADB) announced an agreement with the Tanzanian government for a loan of approximately US$47 million, partially to finance the Dar es Salaam water supply and sanitation project. The remaining US$98 million was borrowed from the World Bank, the European Investment Bank and Agence Française de Développement. In May 2003, the World Bank agreed to borrow an additional US$61.50 million for the restructuring (Afrol, 2003).

According to the ADB, the project aims at improving the 'accessibility, quality, reliability and affordability' of the water services to the population, contributing 'to poverty reduction and improving the economic and social well-being of the people of Tanzania by providing them with a better access to clean water, thereby reducing the incidence of water-borne diseases among the vulnerable groups'. The handling of the problem, however, raised suspicions that the project's aim was not poverty reduction, but rather finding a buyer for DAWASA by significantly increasing its value through the government's investment in infrastructure and customer billing. As a result, the water service in Dar es Salaam may improve, but at considerable cost for customers and the city, increasing national debt rather than reducing it. The company expects high profits while the state of Tanzania carries the financial risk.

Kiliwater: A rural success story?

Kiliwater, the largest privatized water company in Tanzania, provided a different experience. It was established in 1995 with financial assistance and support from the Gesellschaft für Technische Zusammenarbeit (GTZ), a

German government-owned corporation for international cooperation. By 2003, Kiliwater was serving approximately 335,000 people (62,000 households), mostly farmers, in the eastern and north-eastern part of Mount Kilimanjaro.

About half of the distributed water is locally collected; the other half is transported to the Amboni Reservoir through the 14.6km-long East Kilimanjaro Trunk Main (EKTM-I), built between 1964 and 1969. The distribution network, about 700km in length, built between 1960 and 1978, was expanded in 1993 by about 100km with GTZ support. There are approximately 7300 water supply stations, 975 of them public and more than 2000 equipped with water meters. In the more densely populated areas, 400m became the maximum distance to a filling station.

Kiliwater tripled the number of water connections in households, partially repaired the rusted governmental pipe network which lost millions of litres of water every month, and installed hundreds of water meters. During a normal drought, about 20,300 cubic metres of water, or 61 litres per capita per day (l/cd), should have been available for the population in the service area. However, supply losses reached at least 35 per cent, making only 39 l/cd available (KfW, 2002). By 2003, there was an increasing need to repair and modernize the old EKTM-I, particularly the pipes of a diameter too small to transport the needed water. In addition, some parts of the region could not be reached by the EKTM-I.

Even though the project provider was able to continuously reduce its deficit, only 70 per cent of the operational costs could be covered from revenue. On the one hand, the provider could not supply sufficient water in regions with traditional water shortage and high willingness to pay; on the other hand, in 2000 of the 6500 connected households payment did not depend upon actual supply but was fixed. In this case, customers consuming a lot (notably by diverting drinking water for irrigation) paid only a little. The installation of water meters with lockable meter chambers could end this practice, but would surely meet with resistance. People do not easily accept obligations to pay for what they see as a public or common good provided free by nature. Moreover, poorer ones are unable to pay their water bills. But without a price tag, people (in any part of the world) have little inclination to conserve water as a scarce resource.

In order to reduce the conflict potential, Kiliwater implemented a policy of support for the participation of communities in decision-making, particularly selected water user groups who were most urgently in need of improved water services and favoured consumption metering. A system was introduced of water committees, where arbitrators from the villages at Kilimanjaro would decide in public meetings who should receive a particular amount of water for free and who should pay. By 2003, three experimental communities had been selected for testing this decentralization of responsibilities from the water company to the water users.

The 'privatization' of Kiliwater cannot be seen as an outright privatization because much of the funds for infrastructure came from foreign aid, which made it easier to include public goals in the company's mission, such as guaranteed access to drinking water at World Health Organization (WHO) quality standards, and improved service at least 20 hours a day throughout the year at very affordable prices.

The participatory approach taken at Kiliwater seems to have helped to increase a sense of common responsibility. It also helped to find solutions in ensuring water supply for the poor, a matter of central importance in African water privatization. As stated by David Smith, water expert of the United Nations Environment Programme (UNEP) (Sina, 2003), if poverty inclusion fails, then water privatization in Africa fails.

BUDAPEST SEWAGE WORKS: PARTIAL PRIVATIZATION OF A CENTRAL EUROPEAN UTILITY

Alexander Juras and Todd Schenk

The economies of Central and Eastern Europe took a shift towards a more liberal, less centrally planned paradigm during the early 1990s. This shift was accompanied by a wave of privatization. Industries and assets, most of which were previously state owned and run, were transferred to the private sector in the belief that private markets would be more competitive, bringing supply and demand closer to equilibrium, and thus more efficient. Privatization also coincided with a reduction of the role of government in the lives of the population, and thus became equated with freedom. Especially when multinational firms were involved, privatization was seen, too, as a way of attracting capital and raising funds for government debt repayment or social services.

In this climate, countries felt compelled to privatize not only manufacturing and non-essential services, but even sectors that were traditionally publicly owned in Western Europe and/or North America, such as education utilities and healthcare.[10] Municipal water and sewer works were no exception.

Budapest sewage works

Budapest's municipal sewer works (Fóvárosi Csatornázási Múvek Részvénytársaság, or FCSM) was partially privatized in November 1997 under a deal giving 25 per cent plus one share to a consortium composed of two multinational corporations (MNCs), Compagnie Générale des Eaux and Berliner Wasser Betriebe.[11] A special purpose corporation (SPC), with an added investment of €22.7 million by the European Bank for Reconstruction and Development (EBRD), was formed at the end of 1998 (EBRD, 1999). As of 2003, the majority stake of the company remained in the hands of the city of Budapest.[12]

The EBRD's reason for supporting this privatization was the belief that private firms experienced in managing utilities could improve the efficiency of operations and reduce operating costs (EBRD, 1999). While the municipality remained the majority owner, management control was handed to the private operators and their remuneration linked to efficiency gains made.

Partial privatization

An interesting trait of this privatization arrangement is that only a 25 per cent stake of the company was transferred to private hands, making it a 'partial privatization'. This afforded the municipality some control, potentially giving them power to protect the public interest. However, this may have been mitigated by the privatization agreement, which gives management rights to the private partners, thus limiting the authority of the municipality. The quote of Miklos Szalka in 'Sewerage prices' indicates the frustration that this limiting of authority created. The arrangements giving management rights to the foreign partners expire after 25 years.

Two disadvantages of partial privatization are that it reduces the income that the government makes from the sale and diminishes the willingness of the minority interests to make large capital investments in the operation. These are two of the key reasons for privatizing in the first place.

Sewerage prices

According to a Public Services International Research Unit study, sewerage prices in Budapest in 1998, a year after privatization, were 350 per cent more than in 1994, causing concern over affordability (Hall and Lobina, 1999, p8). The increased rates were justified as necessary by the newly privatized FCSM to fund much-needed investment. However, both the city council and citizens of Budapest were dismayed by the increase, believing it unjustified considering the lack of substantial physical improvements to the system. Miklos Szalka, vice-president of the municipal maintenance committee at the time, was quoted in the *Nepszabadsag* newspaper on 16 December 1998:

> *The sewerage company has proposed a 25–30 per cent price increase, and the main argument for this is the costs of development... Unfortunately, it is now clear that these powerful foreign companies do not want to make investments using their own capital – on the contrary, they take as much money as possible from the country, including their management fees* (Hall and Lobina, 1999, p7).

It should be noted that a Foundation for Customers in Budapest and for People with Outstanding Charges (HÁLÓZAT), created through a decision of the General Assembly of Budapest in 2001, served to mitigate the effects of higher rates on consumers unable to pay by providing assistance with outstanding charges. However, this is financed from public funds. From an environmental point of view, higher rates are not necessarily negative. More accurate pricing is an effective way of promoting efficiency, as consumers tend to be more conservative with their water usage when it is more expensive.

Interestingly, this has not been the case in Budapest. The amount of sewage collected remained approximately the same throughout this time (FCSM, 2003).

Quality of service

According to its annual report, the basic tasks of FCSM are 'to collect and treat sewage and rainwater generated in the area of Budapest and to discharge [this treated waste] into the receptor [the Danube]' (FCSM, 2003, p11). The quality of its collection and processing systems since privatization therefore becomes the best measure of improvement by the company.

The most important factor in terms of quality is the impact of the operation on the environment. According to the EBRD, an independent environmental 'due diligence' audit carried out in 1997, prior to the partial privatization, found several violations of Hungarian and European Union (EU) environmental standards. The Environmental Action Plan developed by FCSM as part of the privatization process mandated a 16-year timeline for bringing the operation into full compliance.

While 16 years may sound rather un-ambitious, the large scale of the sewage works, and therefore the work entailed, must be recognized. According to the ERBD, the work required was given a price tag of around €1 billion. The improvements, mandated as part of the privatization agreement, were designed to greatly increase the system's biological treatment capacity.

While Budapest's sewer network, and therefore capacity for biological treatment, provides broader coverage than other Hungarian municipalities, in 1998, 6 per cent of those supplied with municipal water were not connected to the wastewater system, representing a gap in collection (Somlyódy and Shanahan, 1998, p13). The length of the Budapest sewer network, however, increased substantially from 4413km in 1998, immediately following privatization, to 4799km in 2002 (see Figure 7).

Wastewater treatment by 2003, however, remained highly inadequate. In 2002, only 22 per cent of the sewage and rainwater collected was treated biologically, and a further 9 per cent was screened for nutrients. Despite major improvements to their North-Pest Biological Treatment Facility in 2002, the total biological treatment capacity of FCSM was still only 280,000 cubic metres per day by the end of the year, and significantly less than the daily average of sewage and rainwater collected in 2002, which was 660,000 cubic metres (FCSM, 2003, p12). Furthermore, it must be considered that the load on the system is much higher during rainy periods and lower in dry ones. As Figure 7 shows, little improvement was made in this area following privatization, and by 2003 the majority of wastewater was still released back into the environment with little or no processing.

An EBRD Operation Performance Evaluation Review (OPER), conducted in 2003, also seems to have reached the conclusion that service improvements have been minimal. The OPER summary states that 'the range and scope of services has not been markedly increased, at least from a consumer's perspective, since the wastewater coverage area remained basically the same "with" and "without" the project' (EBRD, 2003, p2). OPER rated environmental performance as only 'satisfactory' and attributed no environmental changes to the bank's investment.

Management

Both Vivendi and Berlinwasser, as the MNCs were renamed, have a great deal of experience in managing utilities. As mentioned previously, the primary reason given for instigating the partial privatization was to bring their expertise and efficiency and quality standards into what was seen as an inefficient and under-performing state enterprise.

While the management's concern for the physical state of the sewage system or for the utility's customers has been questioned, it has, at least on paper, made changes in management practices. For example, both ISO 9001 and ISO 14001 quality management standards were introduced in 2001 (FCSM, 2003, p3).

It is interesting to note that the only component rated as 'excellent' in the EBRD's OPER, which was introduced previously, was FCSM's corporate performance 'in view of dividend payments and current ratios over recent years' (EBRD, 2003, p2). This would indicate that the MNCs have turned FCSM into a healthier corporation; what is uncertain is whether on not this improvement is benefiting its customers both now and in the future.

Investment

Investment in improvements to Budapest's sewage works has come from various sources. The most significant project for the improvement of FCSM's infrastructure, since privatization, was signed in 1999 and is set to run until 2006. It was created with the aim of significantly improving the environmental performance of the operation by expanding the capacity of the North Budapest and South Pest Wastewater Treatment Plants, and to establish the North Buda Wastewater and Rainwater Pumping and Primary Collection System. Funding included grants from the Hungarian government (US$10 million), wastewater revenues from the city of Budapest (US$21.4 million), an EU Phare grant (US$18.6 million) and a World Bank loan (US$29.5 million) (World Bank, 1999).

The city of Budapest, the sewage works' largest shareholder, has invested a great deal. The FCSM's business report for 2002 states in its introduction that: 'These [2002] projects have been completed mostly by capital investment provided by the Municipality of Budapest' (FCSM, 2003, p3). In 2002, the municipality provided some 1160 million Hungarian forints (€4,640,000) for significant improvements to the North-Pest Wastewater Treatment Plant alone.

What is interesting is the relatively small investment provided by the two multinational corporations. Although these corporations exercise control in management, and are remunerated for this, their capital investments have been limited to their initial investments in the SPC. The addition of the EBRD to

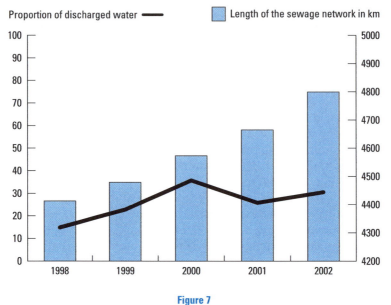

Figure 7
Length of Budapest sewage network and proportion of sewage treated. Despite increased length of the Budapest sewage network, sewage treatment percentages remained at a dismal 30 per cent.
Source: data from FCSM (2003).

the special purpose company in 1998 was seen by many as a way for the MNCs to reduce their investment costs even further, effectively refinancing their involvement at rates lower than the market would provide. In other words, the EBRD investment improved the financial situation of the MNCs rather than providing capital to FCSM.[13]

The capital investments made in FCSM since privatization have come either from the municipality, which previously fully owned the utility, or other sources that would also provide loans or grants to fully private enterprises, such as the Hungarian government, the EU and the World Bank. Given this, it would appear that an increase in investments or grants has not been due to privatization.

Conclusion

Few would argue that reforms were not needed throughout the utilities markets of Central and Eastern Europe. What is less certain is that privatization is a necessary impetus for this to happen.

While FCSM improved sewerage operations after privatization, adding to the sewage network and treatment capacity, it greatly increased the rates it charged consumers and paid a significant sum to the MNCs involved in the form of management fees. Furthermore, much of its improvements resulted from grants and loans from agencies and governments, not because the operation was privatized.

Other municipalities have chosen alternative paths. As a public waterworks company, Debrecen expanded its pipe network at less cost than projected by a previously proposed private partner (Hall and Lobina, 1999, p9). It was also found to be more responsive to local needs and interests. The lesson, overall, seems to be that privatization is not necessarily key to effective management and investment.

MANAGEMENT SUCCESS AT ROSTOCK, GERMANY[14]

Ernst Ulrich von Weizsäcker

Rostock was the major seaport of the former Democratic Republic of Germany (GDR), and historically a proud member of the Hanseatic League of North European trading cities. Around 200,000 inhabitants live in the city of Rostock, some 60,000 in its neighbourhood.

During GDR times, every conceivable public service was in state hands. Alas, services were also run down and technically un-modern, to put it mildly.

After German unification, the municipal authorities of greater Rostock decided to outsource the regional waterworks and leased it to Eurawasser, a joint venture of Thyssen Handels Union (holding 51 per cent, but chiefly as inactive shareholders) and Lyonnaise des Eaux, now Ondeo, Paris, holding 49 per cent. Eurawasser GmbH (Ltd), in turn, is split into a number of local companies, including Eurawasser Rostock, which control the local management of wastewater treatment and the distribution of water to customers.

Eurawasser Rostock invested the impressive sum of €225 million after 1993, mostly to comply with German and European standards, including the European Union (EU) Drinking Water Directive. Some €55 million went into upgrading water to drinking water standards and its distribution, another €170 million into a near-complete restoration and modernization of the wastewater collection and treatment system. Both systems – water supplies and wastewater treatment – are seen as top quality by world standards.

Eurawasser shouldered the risks of guaranteeing supply quantities and quality and the entire costs of capital and daily operation, with prices guaranteed for 25 years except for inflation adjustment. Furthermore, after 25 years, the leasing contract can be renewed; but the municipalities have the right to return to self-management after that period. The contract therefore also requires Eurawasser to maintain the value of the capital stock by building up reserves equivalent to capital depreciation.

During the leasing period, the local authorities of Rostock and its neighbours retain the right to control, monitor performance and instruct the private operator concerning measures resulting from legal changes. All company measures regarding prices, investments and other changes have to be licensed anew. A board consisting of equal numbers of private and public representatives oversees the compliance of the contract.

The Rostock water leasing is broadly acknowledged as a success story by the public and by the media. Even the PDS (Partei des Demokratischen Sozialismus), the successor to the Communist party, which is governing the respective *Land* (region) of Mecklenburg-Vorpommern in coalition with the SPD (Sozialdemokratische Partei Deutschlands), proudly boasts of the quality of the water management system in the largest and economically most dynamic city of the region.

This success is built on two pillars: the world class water management of the private operator, Ondeo, and the maintenance of a decisive position of the public authorities in ensuring the public good of high-quality drinking water. To be clear about terminology, the Rostock success story is not about private ownership but about the private management of the water and wastewater service.

Metals and Cement

PRIVATIZATION OF THE MINING SECTOR IN ZAMBIA: THE CASE OF ZAMBIA CONSOLIDATED COPPER MINES (ZCCM)

Brenda Mofya and Brighton Lubansa

Mining in Zambia dates back to 1899 when the first viable ore was discovered (Kangwa, S., 2001). However, organized mining activities began during the early 1900s in Zambia's Kabwe, Kansanshi, Bwana Mkubwa, Roan, Nkana, Mufulira, Nchanga, Konkola and Chibuluma mines in the Central and Copperbelt provinces. Although the country had substantial mineral wealth, copper and cobalt had the most economic potential. The mines, which were at first developed by settlers, eventually came under the control of two large mining groups, Anglo American Corporation (AAC) and Roan Selection Trust (RST).

In order to stabilize their labour force, mining companies established permanent settlements, providing housing and associated social and community services, including sponsoring street lighting, piped and treated water supply, electricity supply, sewage disposal, public health, education, markets, refuse collection and disposal, roads, storm water drain maintenance, fire-fighting services, social and sports clubs, hospitals and schools. In this way, social provision for a large number of workers began as a private affair.

Nationalization

At the time of independence in 1964, Zambia inherited a fairly prosperous economy with a well-established private sector. Expatriate business interests, multinational corporations and commercial farmers mainly dominated in this open market-oriented economy. The copper industry, which was the mainstay, remained under the control of AAC and RST until 1968/1969, when the government announced a programme of nationalization of privately owned companies through the Mulungushi/Matero reforms. The justification given was that since the economy of the country was largely in the hands of foreigners, nationalization was inevitable as the only way of providing an opportunity for indigenous Zambians to participate in the economy. President Kaunda is said to have been particularly concerned with what he called 'our friends who have kept only one foot in Zambia in order to take advantage of the economic boom, the other in South Africa, Europe, India or wherever they come from, ready to jump when they have made enough money, or when they think that the country no longer suits them'.

With effect from August 1969, the rights of ownership and or partial ownership of all mining activities reverted to the state, obliging former owners to offer 51 per cent of their shares to the government. On 1 January 1970, AAC and RST were renamed Nchanga Consolidated Copper Mines (NCCM) and Roan Consolidated Mines (RCM), respectively, and later amalgamated to form Zambia Consolidated Copper Mines (ZCCM) Ltd in 1982. The provision of housing and associated social services continued under ZCCM.

Like other cases of state-owned enterprises, ZCCM failed to perform for a variety of reasons, including the fluctuation of copper prices on the world market. Since mining exports accounted for over 80 per cent of Zambia's foreign exchange, the general economic performance of the country as a whole began deteriorating. This led to increasing external borrowing to finance economic activity and, in turn, to increasing foreign debt. In addition, overall government spending on social services decreased.

Restructuring/privatizing ZCCM

Kenneth Kaunda's government signed an agreement during the early 1980s with the International Monetary Fund (IMF) and the World Bank to reform the economy. However, it backed out of some aspects of the extremely harsh measures required under structural adjustment, attempting what one commentator called 'reform with a face' (Social Watch, 2003). Eventually, the poor performance of the economy resulted in government failure to facilitate economic growth and wider participation. It also gradually undermined the legitimacy of the leadership of Kenneth Kaunda's United National Independence Party (UNIP). A groundswell of support developed for the Movement for Multiparty Democracy (MMD). MMD's leader, former Mine Workers' Union leader Frederick Chiluba, won elections in 1991 on a platform of free-market reforms. The emphasis here was on the beneficial role of free markets, open economies and the privatization of inefficient public enterprises. Acting on this ideology, the MMD government passed the Privatization Act in 1992, establishing the Zambia Privatization Agency to plan, implement, manage and control the initiative.

The decision to sell ZCCM had several aims: the transfer of control and responsibility for its operations to private-sector mining companies as quickly as practicable; the mobilization of substantial amounts of committed new capital for ZCCM's operations; the realization of the value of ZCCM assets and retention of a significant minority interest in its principal operations; the transfer or nullification of ZCCM's liabilities, including its third-party debt; diversification of ownership of Copperbelt assets; an increase in Zambian participation; and accomplishment of privatization as quickly and transparently as would be consistent with good order, respect for the other objectives and the observation of ZCCM's existing contractual obligations.

A team was appointed in 1993, among other tasks, to scout for investors/buyers and negotiate the conditions of purchase. Following this appointment and a four-year long debate on the best mode of sale to employ, an agreement was reached to unbundle ZCCM (i.e. to sell its units separately). The first sale agreement relating to the purchase of Kansanshi Mine by the US company Cyprus Amax Minerals was signed in March 1997. This was followed by the sale of the Chibuluma Mine to Metorex Consortium and Luanshya/Baluba in October 1997. As debate went on over the disposal of the remaining parts, the donor community withheld the balance of its payment support in 1998 due to 'non-completion of the sale of ZCCM'. Further demand on Zambia to urgently dispose of ZCCM came from the delegates of donor countries at the May 1999 Paris consultative meeting. The donors argued that the sale would bring in the much-needed new investment and revitalize the whole economy. The remaining ZCCM assets were privatized by the year 2000.

Following completion of the process, however, two of the privatized units, RAMCOZ (Luanshya Mine) and Minerva, were placed in receivership while Anglo America, the buyer of Konkola and Nchanga Mines (KCM), announced on 24 January 2002 that it would extend no further funding to KCM beyond commitments entered into at the time of privatization. Its preferred option was an orderly closure of KCM's operations.

Benefits versus costs resulting from the privatization of ZCCM

By virtue of providing at least 80 per cent of Zambia's foreign earnings and being Zambia's largest single employer, ZCCM was undoubtedly the most important of the country's nationalized (and non-nationalized) enterprises. The manner in which the Zambian government implemented its sale aroused much concern and critiques the world over.

According to one analysis, the sale of ZCCM registered a number of positive results – for example, the sale mobilized the Zambian citizens, especially ex-employees of mining companies and industries that had provided social benefits, and created jobs and trading opportunities for local people. The potential of the mining sector was unlocked where the industry had previously suffered due to lack of investment and technological innovation. Quality and standards of Zambian copper increased on the global market, and the country saw a greater influx of capital from foreign investors. ZCCM's sale also reduced government expenditure and was considered, overall, to have brought Zambia into an 'era of economic resuscitation and investment opportunities'.

However, a 2003 editorial in *The Post*, Zambia's largest independent newspaper, asserted that privatization, especially that of ZCCM, had 'failed Zambia'. The Zambia chapter of Transparency International (1999) argued the sale 'was a looting exercise', a claim which may reflect the findings of a

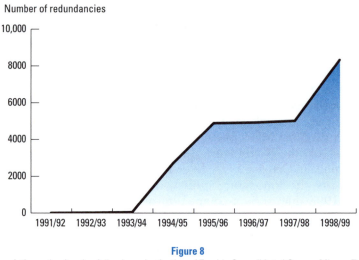

Figure 8
Cumulative redundancies following privatization of Zambia Consolidated Copper Mines. To make matters worse, social services (e.g. creches, hospitals) previously provided at the copper mines were discontinued.
Source: data from Kangwa, S (2001).

1999 survey of the local community on the privatization of ZCCM: the results showed that for the majority of Zambians, the sale of ZCCM had brought hardship and a decline in economic and social development.

Retrenchments and redundancies

Following negotiation, prospective mine owners agreed to provide employment to the existing labour force, avoid immediate redundancies and provide high-calibre management and training opportunities to employees. However, one of the most common characteristic of privatized mines was massive job loss as a result of retrenchment and redundancy programmes, as well as closures, as in the case of Minerva and RAMCOZ. In the run-up to the final sale of ZCCM, a total of 8329 employees were made redundant as of 31 December 1999 (see Figure 8). The Minerva closure resulted in the redundancies of all 150 employees, while the RAMCOZ failure affected more than 4000 employees.

Social services

The sale of ZCCM in units created adverse effects in the mining townships on service delivery in the run-up to the bidding period. During this time, potential new owners are said to have indicated to the government that they had 'no desire to be encumbered with the cost of providing social services'. The owners then developed a policy to hand over certain responsibilities to relevant authorities because they wanted to concentrate on their core business, which is basically mining (Phiri, 2000).

Thus, with the help of the World Bank, a holding company, Mining Municipal Services (AHC-MMS), was established to oversee the continued supply of water and removal of solid and liquid waste. At first, this included the management of storm water drainage that was later passed on to the local authorities who assumed responsibility for drainage, roads, markets and cemeteries. The Zambia Electricity Supply Company (ZESCO) took over the supply of electricity, with service to hospitals, clinics and schools and colleges either handed over to the government or privatized immediately. For obvious reasons, the new mine owners retained the fire-fighting infrastructure.

The transfer of social service responsibility to almost non-functional municipal councils resulted in a complete cessation of providing most services. Companies such AHC-MMS had facilitated a drastic shift of responsibility from mining companies to residents who were then required to pay huge sums of money for service. In addition, the same residents no longer had an income as the majority of them lost their jobs in the mines. The municipal authorities also clearly indicated that they had no alternative but to withdraw services to consumers who could not pay. Once rated as the fastest urbanizing area in the world, the Copperbelt, from the beginning of privatization, suffered a massive exodus.

The pulling out of KCM by Anglo America in 2002 did not bring an end to the retrenchment saga in Chingola. As the government took over, evidence appeared of plans for further restructuring and rationalization expected to affect significant numbers of the remaining employees.

In the meantime, the Zambian economy continued to worsen. As of December 2003, its debt to international financial institutions and bilateral creditor countries stood at Zambia's current debt of US$7.2 billion, reduced to US$6.49 billion in 2002 from US$7.12 billion in 2001. Debt-servicing each year amounted to more than twice the amount spent on health and education put together.

Conclusion

Undoubtedly, the re-privatization of the nationalized 'big brother ZCCM', which had provided for most social requirements in the local communities of mining areas and the Zambian economy at large, contributed to Zambia's social service problems. Advances in mining technology and the need for flexibility of supply in a climate of accelerated global competition and diverse corporate holdings had reduced the need for human labour in an impoverished land to a point below any threshold where demand would outstrip supply. Investment in the welfare of the labour force was never likely as a result of privatization in this situation. Yet, the state itself had never demonstrated great competency in delivering jobs or social services and had been weakened by a huge international debt burden. The aims, though, of re-privatization to bring freedom from mining company debts, diversified ownership, more Zambian involvement, capital gains and the retention of a minority interest did not address social provision or employment. Zambia would be left to restore employment and access to social services in its impoverished situation since the private sector had been allowed to avoid responsibility in these areas.

SAVING SIDEX GALATI STEEL MILLS IN ROMANIA

Black Sea University Foundation

The steel mills of Sidex Galati were the pride of communist Romania. The complex was one of the biggest ironworks of the world. However, when communism collapsed, it became apparent that under market conditions Sidex Galati was making heavy losses. By 1995 debts had accumulated to the staggering sum of 27,000 billion Romanian lei (approximately US$8 billion). The government wanted to sell and yet save the jobs of 28,000 steel workers. A buyer was found, namely LNM-ISPAT, an Anglo-Indian group, the world's number four steel-maker, owning mills in the US, Trinidad and Germany and generating a turnover of US$6 billion.

The pro forma sales price for Sidex Galati was US$54 million, apparently a steal; in reality, it was a high price since LNM-ISPAT also absorbed the huge debts and agreed to retain the labour force for at least five years, contributing US$130 million to a wage fund until 2006 to guarantee punctual payment of wages. Moreover, the new owners committed themselves to technological and environmental investments totalling US$350 million. Clearly, the alternative to this deal would have been to close the mills in order to end the run-away losses that amounted to 80 per cent of the combined sum of the losses of all Romanian firms.

After privatization, Sidex, renamed ISPAT SIDEX, increased production and sales by an impressive 30 per cent to more than 110,000 tonnes per month by May 2002. As of 2003, the company was paying its taxes on time (not a matter of course in Romania), and banks were eager to give credits for further expansion and modernization.

Indeed, ISPAT SIDEX was strategically increasing its quality, environmental standards and efficiency, with a view to meeting European Union (EU) standards at the time of Romania's accession to the union. ISPAT SIDEX aimed to become the largest iron and steel complex in Europe.

In conclusion, it can be said that all of those involved, including the new proprietors, saw the privatization of Sidex Galati as a true success story. An important element of the success was the state's hard negotiations in order to obtain commitments for thorough modernization and a high degree of job security. The high motivation of the workforce also certainly helped to overcome the miserable state of affairs that once existed at Romania's biggest industrial complex.

UNION MINIERE PIRDOP COPPER, BULGARIA: A CASE OF PRIVATIZATION AND THE ENVIRONMENT

Alexander Juras and Todd Schenk

Privatization was a centrepiece of the Central and Eastern European (CEE) region's transition from state-owned and centrally planned production to free-market capitalism. It was essential to the shift away from government command of the economic sphere, and few would disagree that some degree of privatization was necessary for the region to move forward. Privatization had powerful consequences, both positive and negative.

Privatization inevitably affected the state of the environment. The environment was rarely a priority for the governments of the CEE region pre-1990, which fervently developed heavy industries under state ownership and control. While the region has its share of pristine nature, the communist era left some major pollution problems.[1] The natural resources industries historically were particularly dirty.

The cyanide spill at a gold and silver mine operated by an Australian Firm in Baia Mare, Romania, during 2000 did not promote confidence that the situation would be better under the private ownership model of capitalism.[2] The privatized copper smelter and refinery in Pirdop, Bulgaria, may, however, serve as an example of how privatization in the natural resource industries can be beneficial for the environment when the conditions are right.

The UMPC copper refinery and smelter

The Union Miniere Pirdop Copper (UMPC) copper refinery and smelter in Pirdop, Bulgaria, was privatized in 1997 under an arrangement offering a 56 per cent stake to a single firm and placing 44 per cent on the stock exchange under voucher privatization.[3] The Belgian firm Union Miniere – which became Umicore – won the tender with a bid of US$80 million and a commitment to invest a further US$220 million in the operation (Nikolov and Jordanov, 2003). Incidentally, this was the second largest industrial privatization in Bulgarian history (Yonkova et al, 1999). By making a special offer to the other shareholders, Umicore increased its ownership and, by 2003, held a 96 per cent stake in the operation (Nikolov and Jordanov, 2003).

As of 2003, the UMPC operation produced 212,000 tonnes of copper anodes and 45,000 tonnes of London Metal Exchange (LME) grade copper cathodes per year. Forty per cent of the ore processed comes from surrounding mines and the rest is imported (Nikolov and Jordanov, 2003).

In 1997, the UMPC facility and surrounding vicinity were heavily polluted. Of particular concern to all, including Umicore, was the infamous 'blue lagoon', a reservoir containing 500,000 tonnes of arsenic and metal-tainted sludge, all held back by a rather weak dam (Synovitz, 2000). A breach in this dam would have devastated the region's agriculture and entire environment. Also of concern were toxic tailings and tainted soil around the plant, and the water pollution still occurring at that time due to the lack of a suitable production wastewater treatment regime.

Investment in the environment

According to Georgi Nikolov, director of legal affairs, and Peter Jordanov, manager of the Environmental Department at Umicore's UMPC operation, during an interview in July 2003, the UMPC facility was an appealing investment for Umicore; but the company recognized the problems and risks associated with the environmental situation. Subsequently, an agreement was reached whereby US$25 million of the US$80 million paid to the Bulgarian government[4] for the firm would be held by a third party, to be used for environmental remediation (National Trust EcoFund, 2000). The plan for the resulting remediation project was developed based on an environmental impact assessment (EIA) contracted by the Bulgarian government.

Umicore itself was responsible for the implementation of the remediation project, partially under the control of the National Trust EcoFund. The project consisted of two phases. Phase A focused on the 'urgent elimination of immediate environmental hazards'. According to the National Trust EcoFund, its targets were to prevent the collapse of the dam wall on the sludge settling pond (the 'blue lagoon') and to install new wastewater purification technology so that the pond could be bypassed from the process (National Trust EcoFund, 2000). In order to accomplish these targets the sludge pond was reinforced, its crest heightened and a monitoring system installed. An intermediate effluent treatment plant was also installed and dry residue storage basins were created. Phase B focused on 'environmental remediation and clean-up of past environmental damages'. It involved the encapsulation of the 'blue lagoon', the clean-up of approximately 400,000 cubic metres of contaminated waste and the rehabilitation of 7 million tonnes of old slag and 2 million tons of slag flotation tailings (National Trust EcoFund, 2000). According to Nikolov and Jordanov (2003), the environmental remediation programme was successfully implemented within the prescribed budget and timeline.

What is interesting about this situation is that Umicore itself insisted on having the remediation plan. Philippe Rombaud, executive director for Umicore in Bulgaria at that time, went so far as to say that his firm would not have purchased the operation without this kind of arrangement (Synovitz, 2000). It is important to consider the factors that contributed to Umicore's concern for the environmental problems at Pirdop; replicating these factors in the future can help to make privatization more environmentally sound (see Box 3).

Environmental legislation

The privatization agreement between Umicore and the Bulgarian government also included a clause that the operation would come into full compliance with all national legislation in the field of the environment within the subsequent five years (i.e. by 2002). Improvements necessary to reach this level were to be funded out of the US$220 million Umicore had committed to invest in

BOX 3 CONTRIBUTING FACTORS TO UMICORE'S CONCERN

Factors that contributed to Umicore's concern for the environmental problems at Pirdop, Bulgaria, included the following:

- Pirdop was known as a hot spot.
- Umicore self-image was as a reputable European company operating in compliance with existing legislation.
- Umicore staff were environmentally aware and sensitive.
- There was full commitment from top management to address environmental issues.
- A good local team existed.
- The European Union (EU) enlargement process stipulated the need that, sooner or later, firms operating in Bulgaria would have to comply with EU regulations.

Source: based on an interview with Georgi Nikolov, director of legal affairs, and Peter Jordanov, manager of the Environmental Department at Umicore's UMPC operation.

improvements. According to Nikolov and Jordanov (2003), the operation was most of the way there by 2003, but not yet fully in compliance.

Strong environmental legislation and enforcement are essential for a healthy environment. Private firms must be balanced by strong state institutions in order to protect the population and the environment. In the Central and Eastern European context, the spread of the European Environment Agency and compliance with the 'environmental accords' have been beneficial for ensuring that the environment is on the agenda. Bulgaria was anxious to join the EU, which acted as an impetus for it to work towards the EU's environmental standards.

Environmental management

Umicore brought with it a culture of environmental awareness and consideration in decision-making when it purchased the UMPC facility. An element of environmental concern (see Box 3), those working for the company perceived Umicore as a 'reputable European company that operates in compliance with existing legislation and is environmentally aware and sensitive' (Nikolov and Jordanov, 2003). As a result, Umicore established relatively ambitious environmental targets, plans to meet those targets and monitoring regimes to check their progress. Umicore also shares much of its monitoring results, even the bad news, with the public.[5]

Unfortunately, as the case of the cyanide spill in Baia Mare, Romania, and others seem to indicate, some firms moved into the region to escape stricter government requirements or public expectations that may have existed in their home countries. Civil society organizations, media and conscientious governments must play an important role in encouraging multinational corporations (MNCs) based in their countries to be good global citizens. Pressure from these groups is a powerful tool for encouraging multinationals to develop corporate social responsibility.

Other factors

The privatization of the UMPC refinery holds particular interest from an environmental perspective; but the process obviously also produced social and economic consequences.

A common reason for privatizing a firm is to make it more efficient. A negative consequence of the subsequent streamlining is the frequent lay-offs of employees. In the case of Pirdop, staff were reduced heavily, from 2600 to 1000 (Nikolov and Jordanov, 2003). Umicore did attempt to minimize the negative social impact on the community by providing compensation schemes for voluntary departure, and some new jobs were created by the environmental remediation programme and in new local businesses created to service Umicore. Local businesses benefited from Umicore's decision to outsource most non-core activities. However, unemployment has a negative effect on a community; all the more in countries in transition where unemployment insurance programmes are underdeveloped and weak.

One major criticism often levelled at multinationals is that they are not integrated within the local community. Decisions come from, and profits go to, far-off places with little concern for the local population. Umicore attempted to avoid such a situation by putting €150,000 a year into the community through its Corporate Social Responsibility programmes (Nikolov and Jordanov, 2003). Projects that it supported include the installation of energy-efficient street lights in the towns of Pirdop and Zlatita, renovations to the Pirdop hospital, and the covering of all costs for children registered with social services to attend 'Green school camps'.[6]

Conclusion

Private investors typically bring money, technology and an efficiency ethic that can be beneficial to the environment. They also bring a profit motive, which all too often promotes decisions that are not environmentally positive. Multinationals often have tenuous connections to the local communities whom they directly affect. In many cases, they also have experience of manipulating regulations in their interests. For these reasons, it is important that privatization is tempered by government regulations, the tools to enforce these and a well-developed civil society.

The privatization of the UMPC refinery serves as a good example of how privatization can be accomplished in conjunction with environmental remediation in a heavily polluting industry. The key factors that contributed to Umicore's concern can serve as guidelines for similar factors which could be sought out and developed in future cases involving the privatization of natural resources.

Other Resources

THE FIGHT AGAINST PATENTS ON THE NEEM TREE

Vandana Shiva and Ruth Brand

For centuries, certain parts of the neem tree have been used in India for cosmetics, medicine and pest control. The related knowledge has been transmitted from generation to generation. Indian farmers extract a particularly effective and ecologically safe pesticide from the seeds (Shiva, 1997). As this oil loses its effects comparatively soon after its extraction, and since it can be remade in India at any time, production matches actual need.

During the 1970s, some researchers became aware of the agricultural use of the plant and started developing a method to conserve the oil, allowing it to be sold worldwide. After successful tests of the product, they were granted a patent on the production technique and the product itself by the US Patent Office in 1992. Later, this patent was sold to W.R. Grace, a multinational US corporation (Shiva, 2000). Together with the US Ministry of Agriculture, the corporation also held a patent at the European Patent Office for a fungicide made from the neem tree extract (IFOAM, 2000b). Even if the content of the patent is not completely identical, the two products are, nevertheless, made from the same raw material: the genetic resources of the neem tree. This is true also of the further 90 patents on neem tree products existing in Europe as of 2000 (IFOAM, 2000a). The two patents held by the US corporation are particularly interesting because they were contested.

Patents, price escalation and protests

The privatization through patents of the neem tree led not only to a loss of property rights for the local population, but also to an enormous price on neem seeds due to the newly introduced competition: between 1980 and 2000, the price of neem seeds went up from 300 rupees a tonne to 3000–4000 rupees a tonne. The jump in price saw an often free resource become an exorbitantly priced one, with local users competing for seed with an industry supplying consumers in the North (Shiva, 2000). As the local farmers could no longer afford to purchase neem seeds while industry could, the diversion of the seed as raw material from the community to industry was expected,

Figure 9
Neem tree fruits.
Source: Gerald D. Carr.

ultimately, to establish a regime in which a handful of companies holding patents would control all access to neem as raw material and to all production processes.

The various patents on neem products held by multinational corporations in Europe, Japan and the US led to numerous protests by Indian farmers and non-governmental organizations (NGOs). A worldwide campaign against patents on neem products, aimed at protecting traditional knowledge and genetic resources in developing countries from resource piracy, was started in India in 1993 (Khor, 1995).

Successful patent challenge

In 1994, Magda Alvoet, former head of the Green parliamentary alliance, the Research Foundation for Science, Technology and Ecology and the International Federation of Organic Agriculture Movements (IFOAM) brought an action against the European neem patent (IFOAM, 2000b). Six years later, in May 2000, the patent was finally withdrawn from the US corporation by the European Patent Office. The reason for the withdrawal was the invention's lack of novelty because an Indian entrepreneur managed to prove that his firm had been producing an extract of neem oil designed for pest control, and had done so for 25 years (IFOAM, 2000b). In this way, the

Figure 10
Protest against neem tree fungicides extract patents in front of the European Patent Office (EPO),
Munich. Used for centuries in India for pest control and cosmetics, a fungicide made from Neem
tree seeds was patented in 1992 by a US corporation but later revoked.
Source: Petra C. Fleisser.

European Patent Office agreed with the scientists who had called the patent plagiarism and resource piracy. By 2003, it had not yet been decided whether the remaining 20 patents on neem products at the European Patent Office would be withdrawn. The action against the European Patent Office on neem products was the very first action against a patent on genetic resources held by a multinational corporation and resulted in the first withdrawal of a European patent on genetic resources of the South. Maintenance of the patent would have allowed the corporation to sell licences to Indian companies for the export of neem products.

Neem patent challenged in the US

In 1995, the neem patent granted in the US was contested by over 200 plaintiffs from 35 countries, mostly members of NGOS. As of the beginning of 2004, the case was still being examined. Since the product itself and the method of conservation were both patented, it is thought to be more complicated than the European case. There are also particular rules that probably only exist in US patent law: as of 2003, in the US, an invention was considered to be new even if it had been known abroad without being patented or described in a printed publication or publicly used. In the US, the patent remained valid in spite of the European Patent Office's decision, while in Europe the remaining patents on neem products were still in force. What is more, the case of the neem patent is a rare positive example. Usually, indigenous people or their governments have not even known that their traditional methods and plants have been stolen and patented by multinational corporations. Neither the international Agreement on Trade-related Aspects of Intellectual Property Rights (TRIPS), nor the EU Directive on Biotechnology (European Community, 1998) provides penalties for resource piracy.

Information as protection

In June 2002, a data bank designed to protect India's population against multinational corporation intentions was launched. The aim of the information system was to preserve the traditional knowledge of the people about plants and animals and about the therapeutic effects of natural substances. The data bank is designed to prevent further cases such as those of the neem patents.[1] It contains information about natural therapies whose effects are often superior to those of pharmaceuticals produced by big corporations. According to Ragunath Mashelkar, director general of the Council of Scientific and Industrial Research (CSIR) in New Delhi, India, a traditional medicament against gastric ulcers works twice as quickly as the best medicine designed in a corporate laboratory.[2] Mashelkar expects other countries soon to follow the Indian example in order to protect themselves, at least to a certain extent, from resource piracy.

Protections called for against public resource privatization

The case of the neem patent shows that a solution to the sale of natural heritage and traditional knowledge does not lie in protests against patents held by multinational corporations. It is too simple to distinguish between only multinational private corporations as the villains and rural people and states in the 'South' as the victims. Indeed, it was the US Ministry of Agriculture – a governmental institution – which held the neem patent besides W.S. Grace (Kein Patent auf Leben!, 2000). As of 2003, the only promising solutions seemed to be the strategic collection of data about traditional knowledge to prevent further cases in the same vein as the neem example, and changes in intellectual property rights laws to prevent bio-piracy. The latter is where the review of the TRIPS Agreement of the World Trade Organization (WTO) gains strategic significance since the withdrawal of one of the US-held European patents rested on proof of long-term production of neem products by an Indian entrepreneur. In a global market heavily weighted in favour of corporate players, the plaintiffs' victory showed that a private company in the South pitted against an alliance in the North (between the state and a private company) could make its case and win.

Strategic action to restore the neem tree and its derivatives as public resources seems wholly justified given the obvious failure of privatization in this case. State and private corporate gains, real and potential, from interests obtained without fair exchange, effectively eliminated balanced and non-exploitative local practices of cultivation and processing, as well as trade in a resource that contributes in a range of important ways to the health and general success of communities in India.

THE BASMATI PATENT

Ruth Brand

For many generations, basmati rice has been cultivated in Punjab, a region on the border between India and Pakistan. By 2003, this popular variety of rice could be found in virtually every supermarket, bringing US$277 million a year to Indian farmers. India always had the naturally exclusive right to deliver its basmati to the whole world, as this scented rice with special cooking qualities flourished only under the particular climatic conditions of the Himalayan foothills.

During the 1970s, the genetic information of about 90,000 different varieties of rice cultivated in Asia and Africa was collected in data banks.[3] A complete copy of genetic rice data was, and still is, stored at the US Department of Agriculture and included the information on basmati rice.[4] The data is accessible to research projects if a small sum is paid towards work aimed at guaranteeing the maintenance of the numerous rice varieties. Using information gained in this way, the International Rice Research Institute (IRRI) in the Philippines had developed new rice varieties that greatly helped to launch the 'Green Revolution'[5] during the 1970s (RAFI, 1998a). A study made by the International Food Policy Research Institute shows that the US economy realized up to US$1 billion through the use of improved rice varieties developed by the IRRI, whereas total US government support of the IRRI has only cost about US$63 million (Pardey et al, 1996).

A 'new' basmati rice?

Using new varieties as a base, the Liechtenstein firm RiceTec managed to breed a rice variety that looked and tasted very similar to the original basmati rice (RAFI, 1998a). It was striking that RiceTec used information originated by societies in the South and then wanted to patent it. Scientists, however, did not agree on whether the developed rice could be called a new variety. Many argued that it was the result of cross-breeding and therefore could not be treated as a novel invention (Erklärung von Bern, 1998). Nevertheless, RiceTec managed to obtain a US patent in 1997, arguing that the new variety could be cultivated outside Punjab and independently of the climatic conditions of that region – particularly in the US. From that time, RiceTec, protected by the patent, was free to sell its rice under the name of basmati, heavily cutting into the market for the original basmati (Business Line, 2001).

Challenging the patent

The Indian government brought an action against the basmati patent at the US Patent Office only in July 2000. Why not before? The government argued that the 20 different and individually protected qualities of the new rice and the complicated construction of the patent had made things difficult. However, another reason not mentioned by the government was the lack of documentation of the breeding undertaken by local basmati growers. This made proof of local breeders' work much more difficult (Devraj, 2001). But according to leading Indian anti-bio-piracy campaigner Vandana Shiva, the government did not even make an attempt to defend farmers' rights: 'Even in the debate in Parliament, the basmati issue has been narrowed to the issue of exports, and detracted from the large issue of bio-piracy, traditional knowledge and farmers' rights' (Shiva, 2001).

As a first answer to the action, RiceTec withdrew 4 of the 20 different aspects of the patent. But the main aim of the action against the basmati patent was the elimination of the patent as a whole. As a result of citizen pressure, the US Patent and Trademark Office cancelled 11 further claims (Business Line, 2001). The Patent Examiner also changed the title of the patent from 'Basmati Rice Lines and Grains', which included a broad generic claim to the invention of basmati. Ownership of the title became restricted to the specific breeding conducted by RiceTec, which the holder of the patent could not claim represented the unique qualities of India's traditional basmati, or bear the unique name 'basmati' (Research Foundation for Science, Technology and Ecology India, 2001).

By 1998, unexpected support for India's interests in the struggle against the US company came from the US itself. Members of the growing movement of the US Coalition against the RiceTec Patent did not want to be co-opted into exploiting people of the global South. The members boycotted RiceTec products and engaged in an international postcard and fax campaign to persuade RiceTec to give up all its basmati claims (RAFI, 1998b).

At first sight, the outcome of the patent issue appeared to be India's victory in the basmati battle as it ended RiceTec's use of the basmati name for the basmati-derived variety (Research Foundation for Science, Technology and Ecology India, 2001). The cancellation of most of RiceTec's claims prevented the potential use of the basmati patent against growing traditional basmati: in its original form, the patent would have allowed RiceTec to claim property rights.

Labelling concerns and protections

Indian food security expert Devinder Sharma calls the solution a basmati patent through the back door. According to the US Patent Office's new and corrected abstract, RiceTec's new breed of rice was 'a novel rice line, having characteristics similar or superior to those of good quality Basmati rice' (US Patent Office, 1994). This was the wording on the packaging found in supermarkets. If a label proclaims that a packet contains rice similar or superior to basmati, it is hard to consider the US Patent Office elimination of RiceTec claims a victory for India (Sharma, 2001).

A large proportion of true Indian basmati rice was sold in US and UK supermarkets. These became a target of RiceTec's sales strategy following the cancellation of most of its patent claims. RiceTec was already well known to US and UK consumers through its eye-catching, even mouth-watering, public relations campaigns. RiceTec paid supermarkets US$75 to $100 a month for the introduction of special stands where famous cooks invited consumers to taste dishes made from RiceTec products (RAFI, 1998a). Although the firm was no longer allowed to sell 'basmati' cultivated in the US, nothing could prevent the company from persuading consumers to change habits and switch to 'Texmati' or to the later product, named 'Bas 867', which, according to newly allowed labelling, had better cooking qualities than the real basmati from Punjab (Sharma, 2001).

The basmati patent issue is an example of the conflicts between North and South that have touched upon the TRIPS Agreement, designed to deal not only with patents, but also with labels identifying a good as originating from a special territory. The use of a certain label of origin might be forbidden if consumers were deceived about the real origin of a product. The problem in the basmati case was that protection could only be invoked if geographical labelling protections had been adopted in the country with a claim under the agreement. Unfortunately, India had failed to claim TRIPS protection for basmati rice, Darjeeling tea and other products (Devraj, 2001).

According to Pakistani anti-bio-piracy campaigner Uzma Jamil, RiceTec's claims were clear violations of the Convention on Biological Diversity (CBD), drawn up in order to recognize the sovereignty of a state over its natural resources (Devraj, 2001). Alas, the US has not ratified the convention[6] and does not seem to care about its rules! At present, nearly 50 per cent of the 4000 odd plant patents granted in recent times by the US Patent and Trademark Office pertain to traditional knowledge from developing countries such as India (Sharma, 2001).

Champagne and rice

A parallel case with a remarkably different outcome is the conflict over the name 'Champagne'. From 1908, already, the name could no longer be used outside the region of Champagne in France. Even wordings such as 'Champagne style' or 'according to the Champagne method' were disallowed.[7] Three differences arise between the cases of basmati and Champagne: first, the Champagne question was settled within the borders of the European Union (EU); second, no difficulty existed in providing documentation to prove that the product and related processes originated and were well established in the geographic region; and, third, TRIPS, the agreement on intellectual property rights, guarantees particularly strong protection for wines and spirits.[8]

The question can be asked: is it pure coincidence that it is regional labels from the wealthy states in the North, such as Scotch whisky or Bordeaux wine, which enjoy a label protection within TRIPS? Since ratification of the TRIPS Agreement is a compulsory requirement of WTO membership, any country that wishes to obtain easy access to the numerous international markets opened by the WTO must enact the very strict intellectual property laws mandated by TRIPS.

A case for prevention of plant privatization

The case of basmati rice shows the importance of preventing the privatization of plants, particularly those that play a large role in the welfare of a society. Respecting plants as a public resource protects agricultural, regional and sometimes even pharmaceutical independence. In this way, communities, at least in certain aspects, can remain or become sustainable. The privatization of plants creates avenues for wealthy and powerful corporations to wipe out markets for small traders and control the availability of products, even as they add to their diversity. The only advantages of the privatization of plants – potential new markets and profits – appear to lie with states and corporations that do not need them. The fashionable argument that new foodstuffs could result in products that could solve world hunger ignores the fact that the new foodstuffs would likely threaten local food production, that they would not have been tested for risks over the generations needed to produce a farmed hybrid, and that much food production for decades has been directed to excess consumption and waste in the North.

Plant privatization is questionable even as a concept when the scientific case exists that patented results of genetic manipulation represent only an accelerated method of developing hybrids. Nevertheless, patents have continued to be granted on plants. International agreements on intellectual property rights, labelling protection schemes, patent laws, grassroots action and basic documentation are the vehicles that countries and communities need to secure if they wish to protect the home-grown benefits generated by plants.

PRIVATIZING NATURE: PLUNDERING BIODIVERSITY

Aziz Choudry

Founded in 1987 and headquartered in Washington, DC, Conservation International (CI) claims to be an environmental non-governmental organization (ENGO). However, the Mexican NGO Centro de Analisis Politico e Investigaciones Sociales y Economicas (CAPISE) describes CI as a 'trojan horse' or corporate front group of the US government and transnational corporations.[9] CI's major corporate supporters include Cemex, Citigroup, Chiquita, Exxon Mobil Foundation, Ford, Gap, J. P. Morgan Chase and Co, McDonald's, Sony, Starbucks, United Airlines and Walt Disney.[10]

As I see it, CI's involvement in the Selva Lacadona rainforest in Chiapas, the southern-most province of Mexico, is deeply disturbing. In 1991, by brokering a US$4 million debt-for-nature swap between Mexico and the World Bank, CI bought the right to establish a genetic research station in the Monte Azules Biosphere Reserve in the Selva rainforest (Weinberg, 2003). This reserve was created by federal decree in 1978. Its status supposedly permits the use of land and resources only in a manner that maintains the area's natural character and biodiversity; but this overrides and violates the communal land

Number of patent applications per year

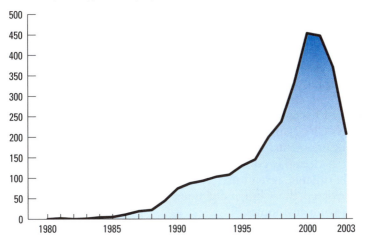

Figure 11
International patent applications on genetically modified plants per year. The number of new applications is shrinking since 2000 because of a lack of return on investment due to sceptical consumers.
Source: data from European Patent Office (2004).

and property rights of many indigenous peoples. Moreover, the government has encouraged logging, cattle-ranching, oil and resource exploration – and the establishment of military bases – within the reserve. And it has moved to privatize the region's rich biodiversity.

With the Mexican government already engaged in a repressive military campaign against indigenous peoples in Chiapas, especially supporters of the Zapatista movement, CI urged the government to forcibly evict certain indigenous communities in Montes Azules, accusing them of destroying the rainforest (Bellinghausen, 2002). The Selva is home to many Zapatista bases, as well as being an area rich in timber and biodiversity, as well as oil, petroleum and mineral resources. Since 1994, the heavy militarization of Chiapas has driven many people to seek refuge in the area. As part of Mexico's preparations to enter the North American Free Trade Agreement (NAFTA), a 1992 amendment of Article 27 of the Mexican constitution exacerbated the problem of landlessness by legalizing the private sale of communal (*ejido*) lands upon which millions of rural people (*campesinos*) depended for survival. The presence of the Zapatistas and autonomous indigenous communities in the region presents an obstacle to those such as the Mexican government and transnational – especially US – corporations that want to exploit these resources.

The Chiapas-based NGO CAPISE's June 2003 report[11] revealed that CI's programme of flyovers – part of their US Agency for International Development (USAID)-supported '*environmental monitoring*' programme – in planes that bore USAID markings, included areas occupied by Zapatista communities. In Chiapas, CI uses state-of-the art geographical information systems technology, including high-resolution satellite imaging. CAPISE charges that the images from this operation are made available to USAID and could be used to identify the location of natural resources of interest to commercial interests. CI has also given images to communities supported by the Mexican government as part of its campaign against the pro-Zapatista communities claimed to be destroying the forest. In the name of environmental protection, it pitted indigenous communities against each other, raising fears of conflict in an area already heavily militarized by Mexico's army. In March 2003, Global Exchange convened an emergency delegation to the area and, contrary to CI's claims, found the destruction most pronounced around military encampments, while the indigenous villagers accused of destroying the forest had outlawed slash-and-burn techniques and were practising sustainable organic agriculture.[12] In January 2004, Mexican armed forces violently evicted the Chol indigenous community of Nuevo San Rafael, burning down many homes.[13]

Between 1996 and 2000, the giant Mexican agribusiness/biotechnology corporation Grupo Pulsar donated US$10 million to CI-Mexico. Pulsar's claimed concern for ecology and biodiversity did not extend to its main activities, which included the promotion of monoculture in Chiapas, as well as the planned planting of 300,000ha of eucalyptus trees. The Chiapas-based Centro de Investigaciones Económicas y Políticas de Acción Comunitaria (CIEPAC) believes that:

> ... the Pulsar Group's 'donation' could more likely be a remuneration (but free of taxes, since it is a donation) for services lent by CI in bio-prospecting within the Selva Lacandona. Pulsar has the technology, the resources and the business knowledge to know that there are large rewards awaiting the 'discovery' of some medicinal property extracted from samples from the Lacandona. CI 'facilitates' the Pulsar Group's entrance; it helps orient its technicians in the prospecting, while at the same time pacifying local populations with programmes that promote the expansion of monocrops around the Selva, while projecting a conservation façade to the world' (CIEPAC, 1999).

CI's operations extend well beyond Chiapas in over 30 countries. They include numerous projects on or adjacent to major sites of oil, gas and mineral exploitation and extraction – for example, in Palawan (the Philippines), Colombia, West Papua, Aceh (Indonesia) and Papua New Guinea. In Panama, CI undertook 'ecologically guided bio-prospecting' for potential pharmaceutical and agricultural use with Monsanto and Novartis. In Surinam, it collaborated with Bristol Myers Squibb and Dow AgroSciences in a similar exercise. The organization's international track record suggests a motivation to conserve biodiversity for bio-prospecting for its private-sector partners rather than any concern for the rights of the peoples who are deeply connected to, and have long protected, the ecosystems in which they live. CI may claim that its corporate supporters share a concern in protecting the environment; but a more plausible explanation might be that when transnational corporations are confronted with global resistance and opposition to their activities, they seek to project a Green image of themselves. For example, CI's website boasted of its partnership for conservation with Citigroup in Brazil, Peru, and South Africa. Rainforest Action Network dubbed Citigroup 'the most destructive bank in the world', precisely for its role in financing the destruction of old growth forests.[14]

As seen in Chiapas, the management and privatization of natural resources designed to facilitate bio-prospecting has entailed social injustice, including human rights violations, by state security forces, political manipulation and environmental damage. CI's programmes offer ingenious ways of facilitating easier access to bio-prospectors for industry, and therefore easier privatization of yet more resources from the South at the expense of indigenous peoples and the environment. The role of such NGOs in an international climate of deregulation, privatization and liberalization deserves serious attention. In Chiapas and elsewhere, indigenous peoples are struggling for their rights to self-determination against a hostile, neo-liberal state, transnational corporate greed and a global landscape of free trade agreements, and international financial institutions such as the World Bank demand that they be entrusted with the management and preservation of their environment. In the guise of environmentalism, corporate NGOs such as CI advocate and thrive in a deregulated, neo-liberal climate, and ride roughshod over indigenous communities' fundamental rights. This commodification and privatization of life is being locked into place by national patent laws and intellectual property provisions of international trade and investment agreements, such as the World Trade Organization (WTO), NAFTA and many bilateral agreements. These facilitate monopoly rights to researchers and corporations, devalue indigenous peoples' knowledge and worldviews, and reduce biodiversity to a mere commodity to be owned, bought or sold for commercial gain. Where, as in Mexico's case, the state not only follows a neo-liberal model, but is a colonial occupier of indigenous territories, solutions to the plunder of biodiversity must go beyond mere calls for adequate state regulation and should be based on indigenous peoples' rights to self-determination – including traditional systems of environmental protection and the right to regulate access to their territories and all that lies within them.

PRIVATE FORESTS IN GERMANY

Ernst Ulrich von Weizsäcker

Forests have played a dominant role in German culture. Many fairy tales as collected by the Grimm brothers, such as 'Little Red Riding Hood' or 'Hansel and Gretel', play out in eerie forests. Less mysterious has been the role of forests over millennia as a source of energy and construction materials.

A wild, but rich, natural legacy, forests used to be the paragon of 'the commons', open to everybody for their daily needs. The situation became unsustainable during the 17th and 18th centuries when early metal, glass and construction industries, notably shipbuilding, led to more wood being harvested than was growing. Increasing shortages of wood resulted. This gave rise to the environmental concept of sustainability (in German: *Nachhaltigkeit*). The Prussian forest supervisor Georg Ludwig Hartig obtained royal agreement towards the end of the 18th century for a forest regime that did not allow more wood to be cut than naturally grew in each forest.

From commons to state and private property

Property is not well defined for the commons. In times of princely sovereigns, it was understood that princes had the ultimate say over the use of forests. They maintained hunting privileges, while commoners held well-defined rights to make use of forests without diminishing or damaging them. When the people assumed sovereignty through the ascent of democracy, some forests became state property, although private ownership was also widely accepted, mostly for farmers.

Today, private forests make up roughly 45 per cent of German forest acreage: some 20 per cent is in municipal (public) ownership and the rest comprises state forest. Private proprietors often have a greater propensity than the state to extract financial gain from their forests, although there is also a remarkable tendency among private German forest owners to consider their forest as the inter-generational source of income for the family, making overexploitation a rare exception. The state should be expected to acknowledge broader public goods functions for its forests, such as fresh air, good water quality, wildlife reserves and recreation for the urban population. These (public goods) functions are sometimes used as an explanation for the fact that state forests tend to be much less profitable than private forests. The discrepancy is illustrated in Figure 12 for the time span of 1980 to 2000.

This explanation, however, is a bit misleading. The poor economic performance of state forests, at least in part, relates to the fact that the state cannot lay off redundant workers and change policies in response to market signals as easily as private proprietors. The state can also use general revenues to compensate for losses, thus diminishing the need for profit-making. In social terms, though, the public benefit supplied by stable employment could be argued to offset the profit obtainable through workforce reduction. Nevertheless, the question remains: can state ownership safeguard certain public benefits at a tolerable price? One of the first questions that comes to mind in this regard is the ecological sustainability of forests.

Sustainable forestry: Public or private?

During the past, the prevailing belief for both private and state forests was that monocultures of fast-growing species such as spruce and firs were the most economically profitable option. By the 1990s, however, forest monocultures' vulnerability to disease and extreme weather conditions became obvious. Conversely, ecologically rich, multi-species forests with fewer human interventions were seen to be both more robust *and more profitable*. These

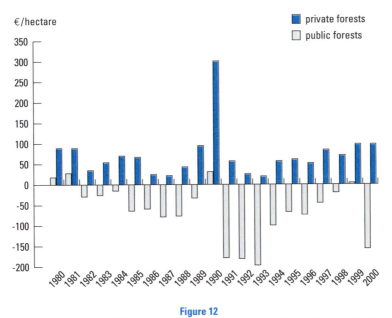

€/hectare

private forests
public forests

Figure 12
Net revenues or losses for West German public and (large) private forests. The great variance
over the years is mostly due to changes in supply and demand. Large-scale thunderstorms can
fell hundreds of thousands of trees and induce a collapse
of timber prices.
Source: Unternehmensinstitut e.V. (2003).

observations led to a growing acceptance among both private and state forest
owners of the ambitious Forest Stewardship Council (FSC) regime. The
ecologically sustainable practices advocated by the FSC originated in the
tropics as an answer to boycotts against tropical timber that was harvested
unsustainably at the expense of valuable and species-rich primary forests.
Where the FSC regime has been adopted, both profit and sustainability have
been secured.

The FSC regime recognizes biodiversity and long-term sustainability as
public goods and as necessary attributes for long-term financial profitability.
Such economic and social consideration leads to the notion that private and
public forests can be managed for the benefit of all. This holds not only for
tropical forests, but equally for European forests. The emphasis must be,
however, on *long-term* profitability. Short-term forest 'mining' can, of course,
yield huge profits; but by definition, it cannot be sustained.

The above snapshot shows that ecological sustainability depends upon
management regime, and that in Germany public owners have not been
noticeably better or faster at adopting sustainable management practices than
private owners. Privatization can be fully compatible with long-term public
benefits provided that sustainable management practices are applied and
monitored. Family ownership appears to be conducive to long-term thinking
and management and to the provision of related public goods. Better than a

fairy tale, given sufficient regulation and incentives with a regime such as that of the FSC, Germany's most recent forest story could hold a happy ending for all.

Energy

ENRON: UNREGULATED MASTER OF INFLUENCE

Matthias Finger

Enron is not an example of a privatized company. Rather, it is an example of an already private company, operating in and taking advantage of a market undergoing deregulation. By 2003, Enron, which went bankrupt in 2002, had indeed become known for its activities in the trading of energy (electricity and gas), as well as for its fraudulent activities. Most of Enron's top managers were eventually called to trial, accused of illegal financial manipulation.

Company evolution and scale

Enron is a case of a company from the old energy economy transforming, in less than 15 years, into an important actor in the new energy economy. The company was formed in 1985 as a result of a merger between a producer of gas and oil (Houston Natural Gas) and the owner of 50,000km of US pipeline (InterNorth). The new company rapidly became active in the trading of energy and bought up electricity producers (e.g. in California). Its acquisitions were generally financed by swaps in shares. This led to accumulated inherited debt, which was then transferred to new companies – companies that did not appear on the Enron balance sheets. In this way, Enron grew extremely rapidly, becoming, at the height of its success, the biggest energy trader in the US and Europe, accounting by itself for approximately 25 per cent of trading on both sides of the Atlantic. Within 15 years, Enron had also become the seventh largest corporation worldwide.

Energy trading

Energy trading goes hand in hand with the liberalization of the electricity sector both in the US and in Europe. Characterized by the unbundling of the functions of production, transport and distribution, liberalization created professions and markets in trading and brokering until then unknown in the energy sector. Where a broker focuses on the interface between client and producer, a trader focuses on time: energy (electricity and gas) is bought and sold in a market where producers and consumers try to hedge against the risk of price fluctuation. In other words, energy trading is not very different from trading on the financial markets. For this reason, it could be assumed that similar regulatory instruments would apply. However, this only came to be accepted over time.

Influence and unregulated practices

The 'success' of Enron appears to be the result of a combination of two factors. First, thanks to its previous involvement in oil and gas production, Enron had acquired significant expertise in political lobbying. This proved particularly useful in influencing political authorities, especially in the US, where Enron successfully managed to accelerate energy liberalization, while simultaneously fencing off interference by regulators, especially the Securities and Exchange Commission (SEC): the federal commission regulating the financial markets. Second, without being subject to financial regulation, Enron applied some very sophisticated financial instruments in its trading practices, and crossed what would have been regulated boundaries in the financial markets.

Lessons learned

The main issues raised by the case of Enron – by 2003 the biggest bankruptcy in corporate history – pertain to regulation. First, it became widely recognized that energy trading requires the same regulatory instruments and intervention as trading, in general. Second, the regulator must insist on a clear separation between trading and production since ownership of the production facilities encourages price manipulation. Third, since trading can endanger supply, particular attention must be paid to the issue of security of supply when it comes to energy.

THE PRICE TO PAY FOR DEREGULATION OF ELECTRICITY SUPPLY IN CALIFORNIA

Ruth Brand and Jürgen Scheffran

Power blackout in California

In June 2000, exceptionally hot weather and grid operational problems helped to cause power blackouts in the San Francisco Bay Area. The bay area's local utility, Pacific Gas & Electric (PG&E), was forced to interrupt service to 100,000 customers. Further blackouts occurred in January 2001 and then again in May. How could this happen?

During the early 1990s, energy prices in California were 50 per cent higher than on average across the nation, particularly due to cost overruns for nuclear power plant construction (*San Francisco Chronicle*, 29 December 2000a). Large customers, such as steel-makers, mining concerns and cement-makers, for which electricity costs make up 25 per cent of overhead, saw that independent power producers were offering power much more cheaply. They began to insist on change.

As a result, California embarked on a pioneering experiment: a new law allowed large users to buy power directly from independent producers and froze customer rates at artificially high levels so utilities could recover their investments in costly plants with those surcharges (The Foundation for Taxpayer and Consumer Rights, 8 December 2000). The law ended the monopolistic control held by utilities over both power production and supply by requiring them to sell off their generators. The system took effect in April 1998, and at first things seemed to work well. But power plant construction lagged while demand expanded. By early 1999, demand was skyrocketing, and no new significant generating capacity had been built in a decade. Independent investigations have even stated that, using the 1996 deregulation law, the energy companies were able to manipulate supplies and prices. In a report issued in July 2000, the California Public Utility Commission found: 'Sellers may have been withholding power from this market in order to drive up prices in other parallel markets' (Kahn and Lynch, 2000). The report also observed that investment in generation slowed when regulators put the risk for building generation on investors. Without more power, California was going to run out. But new power plant construction takes at least two years from start to finish. Another problem lay in the state's failure to push ahead on the conservation front. The 1996 deregulation law even froze energy conservation funding programmes. The California Public Utilities Commission then abolished them entirely (*San Francisco Chronicle*, 29 December 2000a).

During the early 1990s, California had enjoyed a power oversupply of 30 per cent. Consumption grew quickly, however, by 10 per cent in 2000 alone. Surrounding states, including Arizona, Nevada, Oregon and Washington, began to experience the same growth in demand. Since California imported as much as 25 per cent of its power from these states, the amount available quickly reduced by as much as half (*San Francisco Chronicle*, 31 December 2000b). Furthermore, the law had encouraged state utilities to sell their generators and existing electricity supply without guaranteeing access to affordable power. Following the deregulation law demanding the end of monopolistic control of companies over both power production and supply, the Public Utilities Commission had allowed the newly liberalized companies to sell half of their plants. But, instead, the two largest energy companies, PG&E and Southern California Edison, even sold all of their California fossil fuel plants. This prevented them from further price control for electricity generation. From that moment on, the two energy companies were forced to accept prices made by the new owners in the neighbour states – a fact that had not mattered as long as there had been enough electricity for sale.

When electricity wholesale prices exceeded retail prices, end user demand was unaffected; but the incumbent utility companies still had to purchase power, albeit at a loss. The debt load of PG&E and Southern California Edison began to balloon as they borrowed to pay for power. Barred from passing the

Costs per MWh

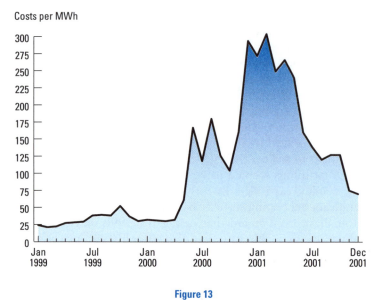

Figure 13
Prices on the wholesale electricity market for California. Prices peaked to their highest level in 2000. Following deregulation, no new significant generating capacity was built, despite the skyrocketing demand.
Source: data from California Public Utility Commission (2002); California Independent System Operator (2001).

cost on to consumers, the companies found that even the high frozen rates were not enough.

Who pays the price?

Governor Davis negotiated with wholesalers and electricity utilities to guarantee a stable price for the state's power supply. In February 2001, a new programme started which obliged the state to buy electricity from wholesalers and to deliver it to Pacific Gas & Electric and Southern California Edison at prices far below what the utilities had been paying on the short-term spot market at the time (*Associated Press*, 10 January 2001). The cost for the state of California mounted up to US$10 billion. As a long-term solution, treaties with various generating companies were negotiated, fixing the electricity price at a level of around US$60 per megawatt hour - approximately twice the level expected under usual market conditions (*Power Markets Week*, 29 April 2002). Those treaties obliged the state to buy electricity at fixed prices for a further ten years.

The central question then arose: who would pay the price for this expensive disaster – customers or the two big companies from past and future gains? Not surprisingly, PG&E proposed to pass the debts on to consumers, whereas consumer advocates challenged this plan, noting that the utility had also achieved windfall profits from selling electricity. For example, in the quarter covering the summer months when power costs first went haywire, PG&E's

profits amounted to US$4225 million, a 22 per cent increase over the same period in the previous year. As if the rate cap had not been their idea, PG&E and Edison launched a campaign to have the cap declared illegal. This would have enabled them to increase customer prices in order to recover the high costs of buying in wholesale power that they could not provide – the very risk they had accepted in exchange for the billions they had already pocketed from the high fixed prices. From September 2001 onwards, consumers were no longer allowed to change utilities. This was meant to keep them from fleeing utilities for lower-priced competitors, leaving the remaining customers to repay billions in debts acquired during the energy crisis (*The Los Angeles Times*, 24 January 2004). In May 2002 the higher costs were finally passed on to consumers, effectively charging them with the entire cost of overpriced contracts purchased throughout the state.

Opponents of such a solution say that the company's odyssey from one-time champions of deregulation to self-proclaimed victims of deregulation is a story of critical missteps and greed, including selling too many generator plants and underestimating rising electricity demands. (Public Citizen's Critical Mass Energy and Environment Program, January 2001) Some consider it an experiment in avoidance by corporations of responsibility for their own mistakes – and in how much the public can be forced to pay for those mistakes (*Associated Press*, 22 August 2002).

After consumer advocates had successfully defeated a legislative effort by Governor Davis to bail out Southern California Edison, a secret deal was made between the Davis administration and Edison, forcing consumers to pay off the company's US$3.6 billion in debts via higher tariffs. In July 2003, PG&E Corporation's National Energy Group declared bankruptcy. Three years earlier, the National Energy Group was thriving, thanks to the soaring wholesale rates for electricity triggered by the energy crisis (*San Francisco Chronicle*, 9 July 2003c). However, while executives of PG&E claimed bankruptcy, consumer advocates pointed out that PG&E's parent company, PG&E Corporation, saw its profits increase by 26 per cent in the third quarter of 1999 alone. Consumer advocates also note that PG&E Corporation has used billions from its utility subsidiary since deregulation to pay off debt and to repurchase its own stock on the market in order to make the parent company stronger for other ventures.[1]

A legislative effort to return California to the power system in place prior to the deregulation experiment failed at assembly committee level in July 2003. Although the chief provision ending big business's rights to cut direct deals with power producers had been removed, the bill had contained other provisions that would have restored California to a pre-deregulation power scheme. These included a provision that would have returned responsibility to the utilities for maintaining adequate power generation and supply for their customers and allowed them to recoup only reasonable costs (*San Francisco Chronicle*, 11 July 2003d). Ultimately, California's experiment with energy deregulation came at a staggering cost (*San Francisco Chronicle*, 27 March 2003a). In the words of Mindy Spatt, a spokeswoman for the Utility Reform

Network in San Francisco, it could be considered that 'This is one of the highest transfers of wealth from people in this state to those outside the state in history.'

In addition, bankruptcy created a boom time for some PG&E executives: the utility paid US$7.2 million in retention bonuses to more than 200 utility executives and managers. The bonuses were paid in addition to US$57.4 million distributed to about 6500 employees for meeting certain financial and operational goals. These payments came after the second anniversary of PG&E's bankruptcy filing; the first round of payments was made a year earlier (*San Francisco Chronicle*, 11 April 2003b). Further US$84 million were paid to 17 current and former executives in the beginning of 2004. During the same time, consumers learned that windfall profits are still flowing in PG&E's pockets two weeks after the California Public Utilities Commission voted to tap electricity customers for US$7.2 billion to bail out PG&E's bankrupt utility (*Contra Costa Times*, 3 January 2004).

The failure of liberalization caused by lax regulation of security of supply did not necessarily have to become such a mess. Rather, the state as a regulator failed also to oblige electricity companies to guarantee satisfactory maintenance of the grid via investment in infrastructure. At the same time, companies were allowed to sell power plants which brought down costs but also eliminated overcapacity, which could have served as a buffer for periods of increased consumption.

This dissatisfying solution of the California Energy Crisis from a consumer point of view was, by the way, not the end of insecurity in electricity provision in the US.

In the middle of August 2003, North America faced its largest power outage since 1965. Fifty million customers in the US and Canada were plunged into a blackout lasting up to a week (US–Canada Power System Outage Task Force, 2003b). Three generator shutdowns had triggered a cascade of thousands of transmission line failures, leading to a collapse that took just three minutes to complete (US–Canada Power System Outage Task Force, 2003a).

Most commentators agreed on the cause of the crisis, foreseen by various experts: it was again the deregulated electricity generation by the end of the 1990s. As private enterprises, the electricity-generating companies were striving to run the grid at a profit. One way to do this is to hold down capacity, which, of course, leads to the risk of shortages when consumption rises. The latter often occurs during daytime in hot summers when the use of air conditioners is high (*Süddeutsche Zeitung*, 16 August 2003a).

In a *New York Times* editorial, business expert Robert Kuttner wrote: 'Under deregulation, the local utilities no longer have an economic incentive to invest in keeping up transmission lines. Antiquated power lines are operating too close to their capacity. The more power that is shipped long distances in the new deregulated markets, the more power those lines must carry' (*New York Times*, 16 August 2003). Some experts even suggested that generating companies produce electricity shortages deliberately in order to maintain price levels.

A second way to keep costs low is to refrain from investment in infrastructure. This trend was reinforced with liberalization and led to a lack of grid infrastructure investment to the tune of US$50 billion. According to the US government, this sum should be invested now (*Süddeutsche Zeitung*, 1 September 2003b).

Though the origins of the California energy crisis and the August 2003 blackout in the north-east may be very different – the more recent blackout deriving from a chain reaction triggered by minor incidents on the grid – certain important similarities exist: the trend to deregulate electricity provision can lead to a lack of investment in parts of the system that produce no profit in the short run. The enormous financial damage caused, in both cases, was slated to be paid either by the state, via loss of tax revenue, or by consumers, via higher electricity prices and uncompensated costs of lost wages, sales and productivity (*The Daily News of Los Angeles*, 20 January 2001). Meanwhile, the high profits stayed in the pockets of the private electricity producers who remained without obligation to take responsibility for long-term investments.

Government, in introducing deregulation, ignored the need to provide for investment unprofitable under ordinary market conditions. This could have been covered by either the state itself or stipulated through clear regulation on an obligatory rate of reinvestment. Instead, the story of the decline of the condition of US electricity provision represents an example of failed deregulation of a common good on a for-profit basis.

Telecommunication and Postal Services

TELECOMMUNICATIONS IN MEXICO, URUGUAY AND ARGENTINA: A TALE OF CONTRASTS

Jochen Boekhoff

The telecommunications sector is often seen as a paradigm of successful privatization. Indeed, the typical evolution in this sector has been from clumsy, expensive public telephone systems to elegant, multipurpose, cheap and private systems offered by competing suppliers. According to standard economic reasoning, market forces are responsible for this desirable transition.

However, while markets have, indeed, accelerated the downward trend of prices for telephones and other telecommunication services, it cannot be denied that technological progress was the real driving force behind the trend of falling prices, and that much of that progress originated from military and other state-financed internet technology programmes, particularly coming from US defence research.

Moreover, privatization of telecommunication services did not always produce satisfactory results, as can seen by comparing the situation in three Latin American countries: Mexico, with a more or less a textbook evolution; Uruguay, with good results but no privatization; and Argentina, with privatization but very bad results.

The Mexican success story

Mexico was highly state centred from the early 20th century. State-owned companies, more than a thousand of which existed during the early 1980s, dominated the Mexican economy. During the 1980s, the international trend of privatization reached Mexico, and within ten years after 1982, more than 80 per cent of these companies had been sold (Botelho and Addis, 1997).

The biggest transformation was the privatization, in 1990, of Telmex, the Mexican telecommunications state monopoly. This was *preceded* in the years since 1982 by a period of heavy modernization, chiefly the introduction of digital technology. During this period, however, Telmex was short of financial resources and was unable to meet the soaring demand for telephone connections and for improved efficiency through digitalization. The state simply did not care much about customers' demand. The situation worsened with the 1985 earthquake which destroyed much of the infrastructure in Mexico City. But with the massive reconstruction period after 1995, the situation improved, and by 1990 already 29 per cent of the nation's telephone lines were digitalized. This fact and the foreseeable, near insatiable, demand for telecommunication services made Telmex an extremely attractive target for private investors and, hence, a prime candidate for privatization.

The road to modernization, however, had been rather bumpy. Earlier in the 1980s, Telmex went through major labour conflicts, which were appeased by a generous deal offering the workers a comfortable job guarantee against technological change. That deal, questionable in view of technological progress and rather poor service quality, eventually undermined the kudos of the workers' unions, which finally had to give in to further rationalization plans. On the other hand, there were solid expectations for a further expansion of telecommunication services so that redundant staff had good prospects of finding new jobs.

The need for major, and rapid, investment finally triggered the decision to privatize Telmex. A consortium of Southwestern Bell (US), France Telecom and Grupo CARSO (Mexico) acquired a share of 20.4 per cent of the company at a total price of US$1.76 billion, the largest sum ever paid for (parts of) a public company in Mexico.

Public regulatory control was to ensure improved services, modernization and certain workers' rights. Workers earned the right to purchase stocks with government-subsidized, low-interest loans, and were promised a seat on the Telmex board once they held 10 per cent of the shares. The latter never happened, however, because too many preferred to cash in by selling their stocks on the market.

Privatization certainly accelerated the process of making telephones available to a growing sector of Mexican society. Figure 14 shows the penetration of telephone lines in Mexico from 1975 to 2002.

But it was not solely the customers who benefited from privatization. Telmex's average revenue during the 1990s was sixfold its average revenue of the 1980s as a public authority (ITU, 2003).

Uruguay's public success versus. Argentina's private failure

The telecom situation in Uruguay squarely contradicts widespread belief in the superiority of the private sector. By 2003, penetration of telephone lines was highest in Uruguay when compared with all other South American countries. And yet the telecom sector remained entirely in public hands.

Neighbouring Argentina provides a stark contrast. The state-owned EnTel was entirely privatized in 1990. Two companies were formed, Telecom Argentina (with Telecom of France and Sted, Italy, as shareholders) and Telefónica de Argentina (with Telefónica of Spain as the main shareholder). International

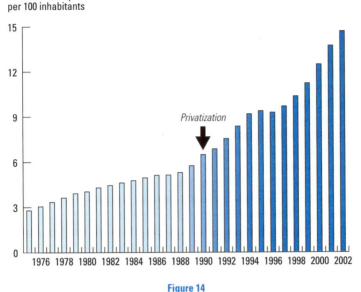

Figure 14

Number of main telephone lines in Mexico. The privatization of Telmex in 1990 resulted in a sharp increase in the number of main telephone lines.
Source: data from ITU (2003).

services were licensed to Starlet (owned by Telintar, Argentina), and cellular telephony outside the greater Buenos Aires area was licensed to Comprehensive Technologies, Inc (CTI), with GTE Corporation and AT&T as shareholders. Inside Buenos Aires, two other companies, CRM (owned by Movicom, Bell South and Motorola) and Movistar (owned by Telecom Argentina and Telefónica de Argentina) won the licence for the cellular network.

Despite the large number of companies, competition hardly occurred and investment declined somewhat after privatization. Until 1990, Uruguay had offered as many lines per inhabitant as Argentina, but left Argentina far behind in the run to 2000, establishing one telephone line per three inhabitants throughout the 1990s (see Figure 15). In 2002, in absolute figures, Argentina reached 22 lines per 100 inhabitants; Uruguay reached 28.

Correspondingly, the typical waiting time for telephone lines was shorter in Uruguay than in Argentina. While Argentina still had extremely long waiting lists during the early 1990s, Uruguay's public sector managed to cut waiting lists and eliminated them altogether from 1997 on. In Argentina, this nuisance still existed by 2003.

The picture for the price of cellular calls in Argentina was no better. Figure 16 shows that Uruguay followed the international trend of falling prices, while the private-sector companies in Argentina managed to maintain high prices using their respective geographical monopolies.

Not only were end users in Argentina paying the price of monopoly-based inefficiency, but investors in telecom services achieved much poorer results in

Number of telephone lines
per 100 inhabitants

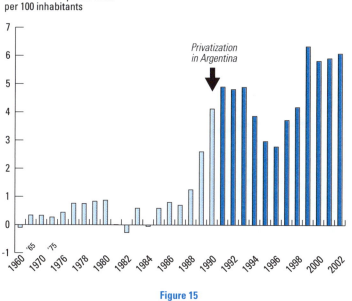

Figure 15
Uruguay's lead over Argentina in telephone lines per 100 inhabitants. Uruguay's public company
was speedier than private companies in Argentina in supplying telephone lines.
Source: data from ITU (2003).

Argentina than in Uruguay. While investors in Argentina 'earned' only US$4 revenue during the late 1990s per invested US dollar, Uruguayan investors reached values up to US$7.5 revenue per dollar (see Figure 17).

Conclusion

This snapshot does not allow for an in-depth analysis of the reasons for successes and failures in the three countries.

Mexico, surely, was a textbook example of how privatization can work. Investing in Mexico was attractive for foreigners. The North American Free Trade Agreement (NAFTA) made the northern provinces true boom regions. Although Telmex maintained near monopoly powers in many regards, not least the internet services, the mood of expansion was very strong, and the close ties with the US neighbours surely meant a high degree of quality demand and control on the part of business customers.

Argentina suffered from capital flight and the dollarization of the currency (which was meant to fight inflation and capital flight but created rigidity and was felt by the people as a harsh austerity measure) thus limiting the expansion of demand. The territorial and functional confines of the privatized networks were not designed to create competition, and no anti-trust laws were applied.

Uruguay, on the other hand, enjoyed a stable government aiming at rapid modernization of the country. Investments were done without hesitation by

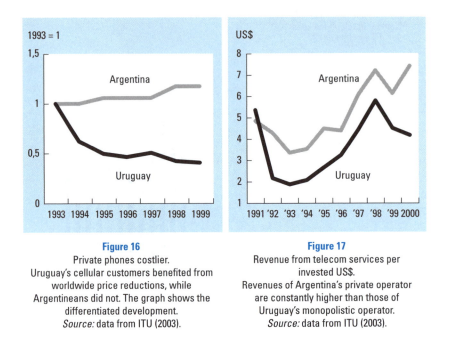

Figure 16
Private phones costlier.
Uruguay's cellular customers benefited from
worldwide price reductions, while
Argentineans did not. The graph shows the
differentiated development.
Source: data from ITU (2003).

Figure 17
Revenue from telecom services per
invested US$.
Revenues of Argentina's private operator
are constantly higher than those of
Uruguay's monopolistic operator.
Source: data from ITU (2003).

the state, and the country benefited from rapid worldwide modernization in the sector.

The most important conclusion is certainly that privatization is not by itself and by necessity superior to state management even in a rapidly changing high-tech sector.

PRIVATIZATION OF TELECOMMUNICATION IN JAPAN

Thomas Thümmel and Max Thümmel

Telecommunications is a global growth market. Annual revenues increased from US$700 billion in 1997 to about US$1 trillion in the year 2000. The US and Europe accounted for more than 50 per cent of the total; but the Latin American and Asian and Pacific markets had higher growth rates and almost doubled in size. As of 2003, Japan was Asia's technology giant and the world's second largest telecommunication market, totalling over US$100 billion (Hoover's online website, 2003). The Japanese market for infrastructure equipment, valued at US$433 billion, was expected shortly to grow into a US$1.23 trillion multimedia market, using the National Information Superhighway.

By 2003, Nippon Telegraph and Telephone Corporation (NTT) looked set to play a major role in this market. The question, though, was how big a role it should take as an actor whose formidable market dominance continued largely undiluted by privatization.

History of NTT

Until 1985, NTT was fully owned by the government (Kobayashi, 1997). In April 1985, the government partially privatized the company to promote competition (Onodera, 2003). But still more than 51 per cent of its shares were held by the government (Nambu, 1995). Then, in 1996, the Japanese Ministry of Post and Telecommunications (MPT), Japan's telecommunication regulatory agency, and NTT reached an agreement which went into effect on 1 July 1999 when NTT was split into two regional carriers and one long-distance/international carrier, all under a single holding company, again only partially privatized (Kawamura, 1996). This was seen as a stepping stone towards a complete privatization of NTT.

Were the goals of privatization achieved?

The declared goals of the privatization were simplification, improvement in management efficiency and increased transparency (Onodera, 2003). Improvements in efficiency were expected to be passed on, at least in part, to customers in the form of lower tariffs and charges (Raphael, 1998). The opposite happened. Charges increased for local calls, for the use of public telephones, for monthly contracts, for directory assistance and other services that used to be free, for telegrams, and a few other services (Iwasaki, 1998). In addition, wages of telecommunication workers fell, and 169,000 of the original 314,000 workers lost their NTT jobs (Iwasaki, 1998). Some 70,000 were absorbed by subsidiary companies; but many of these workers had to accept commuting times of more than one hour (Iwasaki, 1998).

However, as the worst result of the attempted privatization, the main goal to establish other companies in the telecommunication sector, and therefore to increase the competitiveness of the Japanese economy as a whole, failed (Kobayashi 1997).

Persistent monopoly structures

The 1985 restructuring of NTT as a pro-forma non-state company, and the opening of the market to newly founded companies, did not put an end to overarching monopoly structures (Nambu, 1995). Potential new competitors were eager to compete with NTT. They intended to supply own lines and, ultimately, to establish their own networks. However, the regional networks and subscriber lines remained entirely under the ownership of NTT, forcing potential new competitors to cooperate closely with NTT's regional networks. NTT remained so dominant that new companies could not compete as equals.

As of 2003, newcomers still had to search for niches not occupied by NTT in order to survive in the market. The most important business not by then covered by NTT was international calls (Kobayashi, 1997). These were the operating field of another monopolist, Kokusai Densin Denwa Corporation (KDD), which is now privatized. This dual monopoly structure stems from the market separation concept pursued by the Japanese government after

World War II (Gerstberger and Graack, 2003). KDD and NTT were established as two monopolists for two strictly separated segments of the telecommunication market (Gerstberger and Graack, 2003). KDD should solely serve the international market, while NTT should provide domestic telecommunication services. Liberalization removed that monopoly, owned by the KDD, by completely liberalizing the publicly leased public interconnections (*ko-sen-ko*) and excluding KDD (and also NTT) from the abolition of foreign capital regulations (Ministry of Foreign Affairs of Japan, 1999). But NTT, with all its power, was itself also entering this profitable market. As a consequence, KDD was transformed into KDDI, the second largest telecommunication company in Japan, due to a merger of three Japanese telecommunication companies, including DDI Corporation, KDD Corporation and IDO Corporation, in October 2000 (KDDI website, 2003). The merger was intended by the companies to compete more effectively against NTT (cms-info website, 2003).

NTT also remained the dominant player in the cellular phone business, although that sector, too, had been officially separated from the company. Originally a spin-off of NTT, DoCoMo was established in the infancy of the cellular phone business; but, by 2003, NTT still owned 67 per cent of its shares (Hoover's online website, 2003).

During the same year, NTT had maintained its dominance and control over the whole domestic telecommunications market in Japan, including mobile phones, and was strongly moving into the market of international calls. Hardly any benefits from market competition accrued to customers or to new entrants to the market.

Anti-monopoly measures

The Japan Fair Trade Commission (JFTC) decided this was unsatisfactory. In 2003, using anti-monopoly legislation, the JFTC proposed as a mere recommendation a number of steps to improve the situation, including:

- The NTT would no longer to have the right to refuse connection without legitimate reason.
- Entry into the market would be ensured by preventing actions that block or restrict market entry (e.g. by cartels).
- International competition would be promoted by enforcing the existing anti-monopoly or competition act.
- A stronger mandate for the JFTC would enforce the competition law.

From the time of privatizing the NTT until 2003, the government had sold 8.35 million NTT shares and obtained revenues of 13.55 trillion yen (Onodera, 2003). But limits were established to further sales under the NTT corporate law obliging the government to hold more than one third of the NTT shares. As of 2003, it held 45.95 per cent of the shares, compared to 51 per cent in 1985 (Onodera, 2003).

Questions arise as to whether the stipulation regarding state ownership is justified and whether or not it can serve as an anti-monopoly tool. As of 2003, it was still uncertain whether it would help or further hinder healthy competition considered necessary to benefit customers and to continue technological progress.

Conclusion

Privatization will not increase efficiency and reduce prices through competition if it leaves monopolistic structures and practices in place. Supervision and intervention by established supervisory authorities such as the JFTC must be provided for in privatization legislation. Given a watching brief and firm criteria by which to judge the success of any specific privatization, such an authority could act more quickly than in the Japanese case to remedy departures from stated aims of privatization.

It is important in the first place, however, to fully assess the likely share of the market of a company to be to privatized and its future role as a market player. In this way, a privatization structure can be designed deliberately to avoid market dominance by the privatized company. Regulation to enforce competitive practices, ensure technological advances and prevent market control needs to form part of privatization.

The question of state ownership share in any partial privatization requires careful analysis in terms of its potential role as either an anti-monopoly, pro-competition measure, or as a tool to ensure that social benefit provisions and commitments are upheld and not lost in the march to private profit.

By 2003, the case of Japanese telecommunications appeared to have raised such issues, but had yet to resolve them.

PRIVATIZATION IN OUTER SPACE: LESSONS FROM LANDSAT AND BEYOND

Jürgen Scheffran

Space privatization offers the promise of commercial cosmic markets that seem literally without limits. Originally, space programmes were largely driven by military interests and heavy governmental involvement, a situation that prevailed as of 2003. For the Bush administration, space is a battlefield in which the US should dominate to prevent a 'Pearl Harbor in space' (US Space Command, 1998; Hitt, 2001; Rumsfeld, 2001). Taking advantage of public subsidies, private actors have sought to commercialize the potentially vast resources of outer space, hoping for profits in commercial space launch and satellites, space tourism and entertainment, space solar energy, materials processing and even genetic engineering. Due to high costs, technical risks and long-time planning, prospects of space privatization still depend upon government funding. International law and ethical principles continued to restrain the appropriation and colonization of space, thus protecting the heritage of mankind.

Landsat: A difficult case of space commercialization

By 2003, the US government had made several attempts to commercialize the Landsat programme, a remote sensing satellite system that had generated global monitoring data for three decades (OTA, 1984; Cooper, 2003; Johnston and Cordes, 2003). A first attempt was undertaken during the early 1980s, driven by a constrained national budget and a trend towards cost reduction, assuming that outsourcing government functions to the private sector was economically more efficient. The Earth Observing Satellite Corporation (EOSAT) was selected to operate Landsat under a ten-year contract and to build two new spacecraft, with exclusive rights to market data and collect user fees. The US government was to provide US$250 million for spacecraft development over five years.

The 1984 US Land Remote Sensing Commercialization Act provided the legal framework, implementing Principle XII of the UN Principles Relating to Remote Sensing of the Earth from Space. Principle XII sees remote sensing as a public good, meaning that data is to be shared as openly as possible, on a non-discriminatory basis and at reasonable cost. This principle is clearly in conflict with commercial interests (Cooper, 2003). In subsequent years the Landsat programme was hampered by funding uncertainties, contract renegotiations and a lack of coherent government policy. Commercial success was prevented by financial barriers, such as high development costs, long construction times of satellite systems and high risks and costs in satellite launching and operation. Calculations of cost recovery were based on optimistic demand projections and inaccurate demand estimates for Landsat data. To compensate, the company raised prices; but this resulted in a significant drop of images purchased. Due to inherent technical and financial risks, continuous government subsidies were required to develop follow-on satellites and sensors. Few private operators were interested in competing with a federally funded monopoly, and those who did switched to low-resolution and low-cost data. At any rate, the government remained the largest customer.

In addition, remote sensing capabilities proliferated in Canada, France, Russia, India, Japan and Israel. From 1986, France's SPOT (Système Pour l'Observation de la Terre) satellite provided land remote sensing data with better spatial resolution at less cost than Landsat. In 1988, India launched the Indian Remote Sensing (IRS-1A) system and the competition intensified. New firms entered the market; but the demand for data did not grow quite as rapidly as expected. Aerial remote sensing remained a cost-effective and flexible competitor, finding a niche despite limited area coverage. As a result of these developments, the US lost its 1984 monopoly on land remote sensing with Landsat.

In 1992, the US Congress passed the Land Remote Sensing Policy Act, repealing the 1984 act and acknowledging that the commercialization of Landsat had not succeeded. Landsat was returned to government operations.

In March 1994 a Presidential Decision Directive (PDD-23) tried to balance US commercial and security interests. The Commercial Space Act of 1998 promised that the federal government would not duplicate commercial remote sensing and encouraged the acquisition and use of commercial data by government agencies. While the Bush policy was initially more favourable to private remote sensing, the emphasis on national and homeland security after the 11 September 2001 attacks on the World Trade Center in 2001 generated new restrictions.

A millionaire in space paradise: Holidays on *Spaceship Enterprise*

Despite the lessons from Landsat, expectations for space privatization jumped when Dennis Tito became the first space tourist. The 60-year old American multi-millionaire from Los Angeles enjoyed a trip on the *Soyuz* space taxi and an eight-day vacation on the International Space Station (ISS) in early May 2001 (see Figure 18). He described the journey to 'space paradise' as an excellent adventure and the most profound experience of his life, well worth his fare of US$20 million. Back on his home planet, he announced plans to promote the commercialization of outer space, encouraging further ventures for those with enough money to travel high in the sky. 'I think I can play a role as an intermediary between Wall Street and the space agency in getting that done', he said (Baker, 2001).

Worldwide attention to Tito's journey spurred the debate on space privatization. As of 2003, companies such as Space Adventures and MirCorp, which helped to broker the deal for Tito's private flight of fancy, continued to hope that space travel would become a money-maker. For Eric Anderson, president and CEO of Space Adventures, the international attention 'is testament to the fact that there are literally tens of thousands – millions – of people out there who want to experience space in some way'. In his view, 'Tito is no more a tourist than someone who spends months training to climb Mount Everest. He's an adventurer' (David, 2001). Together with other organizations, Space Adventures used the opportunity to push for vehicles capable of making suborbital flights, taking hundreds of passengers every year up to the edge of space, less than 160 kilometres away. And the US company Spacehab proposed plans, again after Tito's return, to build the Enterprise module, specially designed for sightseeing stopovers at a space station.

The Russian space agency, hoping to save the Russian space industry, eagerly accepted Tito's money and considered ten other paying customers. Jeffrey Manber, president of MirCorp, a joint venture with the builder of the Mir space station, RSC Energia, said: 'After Tito ... first we can see this market exists, and it must be nurtured as any new market needs a location, needs investments ... and there will be future customers... We are proud to have truly created this market and shown people that it is time to move beyond government controlled programmes.'

The Russian triumph in space was not well perceived by NASA, which tried to prevent the ride and questioned Tito's patriotism. Former US senator and

Figure 18
Entering new ground: Dennis Tito, the first space tourist.
Source: ITAR-TASS photo taken from screen/NTV channel.

ex-astronaut John Glenn called Tito's ride on a Russian spacecraft a 'misuse' of the basic research mission of space exploration. NASA grumbled because, again, Russia gained a first in space while its own efforts toward space tourism came late, despite the fact that the National Aeronautics and Space Act of 1958 already stated: 'The Congress declares that the general welfare of the United States *requires* that the National Aeronautics and Space Administration [should] seek and encourage *to the maximum extent possible* the fullest commercial use of space.' More than four decades later, these requirements had still not been met (Smith, 1999).

Some NASA officials see the entertainment and tourism industries as driving forces to promote government/industry partnerships in support of commercial space activity. A 1997 NASA study showed that about one third of American citizens were interested in taking a trip to space. According to the Space Tourism Society, every year nearly 100 million people attend space-related attractions (Terenzi, 2002). Space Camp California, a five-day educational children's camp which teaches math and science classes offers simulated space-flight demonstrations and introductory astronaut training courses.

What can the private sector do in space?

The enthusiasm over Tito's trip faded away quite quickly, and by 2003 no other space tourist had followed him into space. The Columbia Space Shuttle disaster in early 2003 and the lack of transportation for manned missions left the US space programme in deep crisis. Even though the private sector has been heavily involved in government-funded space programmes, there is little interest in paying the bill. If financial risks could be reduced by government support, private investors would be ready to take on a greater role in the privatization of space. They see the ISS as a trigger, and a number of commercial ventures have been suggested involving the partial privatization of the ISS and a space industrial park around it (Schuessler, 2001).

In the years leading up to 2003, NASA had shifted considerable resources into space privatization efforts. A 1998 NASA study to define 'Potential Pathfinder Areas for Commercial Development of the International Space Station' listed the following new opportunities: pharmaceuticals; biotechnology; materials; electronics/photonics; communications logistics; repair and maintenance; agriculture; imagery; education; entertainment; advertisement; manufacturing; and space technology test-bed operations (Schuessler, 2001). Space solar power could become one of the fields of great commercial prospects, providing energy supply for satellites and the space station. Another field is ageing-related research, studying the impact of space travel on muscles and bones, and the cardiovascular and respiratory capacity of astronauts, to better understand the diseases and weaknesses of aged people under highly dynamic circumstances.

A major field is materials science and micro-gravity research and production. Crystals grown in space could improve and help develop the next generation of computers and communications systems, such as light emitting diodes (LEDs), photo detectors, lasers and wireless devices. The University of Colorado, in collaboration with a pharmaceutical corporation, tested the effects of long-term weightlessness on antibiotic production aboard the ISS. Genetic engineering is supposed to be easier but also more expensive in the near weightlessness of space than on Earth.

In 2002, the company SpaceDev planned the first commercial space exploration mission, the Near Earth Asteroid Prospector (NEAP), which intended to use scientific instruments from NASA and other organizations to perform scientific, geologic and resource exploration of an asteroid (SpaceDev, 2002). SpaceDev intended to claim ownership of the asteroid and mine its resources on behalf of its shareholders in order to set a precedent for private space property rights. For Jim Benson, the founder of SpaceDev, 'Private property rights in space are essential to the rapid and orderly development of space' (Benson, 1998).

Space law and space ethics: Limits to exploiting the heritage of mankind

For the community of space enthusiasts, mankind's destiny is to conquer the high frontiers in space and exploit its supposed vast resources. At a time when the limits of planet Earth have become limits to economic growth, they promote space privatization as an infinite endeavour. Instead of sustainable development, they push for growth through space colonization. As of 2003, one of their targets was Mars, a whole planet subject to 'Terra-forming' (i.e. the idea of shaping a whole planet to make it liveable for an overflow of humankind emigrating into outer space; Cooper, 2003). Bush's Mars initiative of January 2004 further feeds such visions.

Contrary to both military and private appropriation of space resources, outer space is cast as a 'common heritage of mankind' which should not be subject to conflict or private ownership (Wolter, 2003). These principles are enshrined in the 1967 Outer Space Treaty (OST) in which parties agreed to keep space for peaceful purposes and defined the legal framework governing property rights in space. The exploration and use of space 'shall be carried out for the benefit and in the interests of all countries, irrespective of their degree of economic or scientific development, and shall be the province of all mankind'. Space, including the Moon and other celestial bodies, 'is not subject to national appropriation' (Schrogl, 2001). In addition, the Moon Treaty of 1973, which only nine nations have ratified, requires 'equitable sharing by all states' parties in the benefits derived from those resources'. Both treaties establish the 'rights of future generations', and they empower states as the principal actors in space, providing serious impediments to space exploration, colonization and mining.

The OST established a communal definition of global commons in space (*res communis*), in the same manner as for air, sea and sunshine. Environmentalists defend this principle because they are concerned that the extension of conflict in space and mankind's overconsumption of natural resources will result in the appropriation and 'fencing-off' of space and celestial bodies for colonization and resource depletion, duplicating conditions on Earth (Grossman, 2001). Despite their seeming infinity, space resources within reach are limited. This requires an environmental ethics for space which takes into account the societal context and human values, facilitated by a set of criteria, discussed in a public dialogue (Scheffran, 2001). As Ezio Bussoletti, who participated in a 2001 United Nations Educational, Scientific and Cultural Organization (UNESCO) report on space ethics, pointed out: 'This debate should be an open one, including all the appropriate bodies, space agencies, industry and other interested parties. It should analyse and consider potential risks, the management of risks and consequences of this activity. It should also be remembered that applications benefiting some members of society, impact adversely upon others' (Bussoletti, 2000).

TPG POST: A DUTCH PRIVATIZATION SUCCESS

Matthias Finger

By 2003, Royal TPG Post, part of the TNT Post Group (TPG), was the only privatized postal operator in the world. With over 163,000 employees and an annual turnover of €11.2 billion, although not the biggest postal operator, it was considered one of the most successful, along with Deutsche Post. Very efficient, highly automated and innovative, TPG Post owned operations in 59 countries and offered services in almost all countries of the world.[1]

Evolution of TPG Post

Like most postal operators, Dutch Post was originally part of a post and telecommunications (PTT) entity. However, the Dutch were among the forerunners in the liberalization of postal and telecommunication services. In 1989, the Dutch PTT organization was privatized in a step-by-step process that led to the separation of post and telecommunication services. Following privatization and separation from Dutch Telecom, Dutch Post transformed itself into a leader in the European mail, express courier and delivery logistics markets. The company's position was further strengthened when it acquired the Australian international express delivery company TNT, to become TNT Post Group or TPG.

TPG Post and European postal sector liberalization

The evolution and success of TPG Post must be seen within the context of the liberalization of the postal sector in Europe, where monopoly protection for national operators was being reduced to 350 grams in 1999, 100 grams in 2004, and 50 grams in 2007. In fact, the restructuring and privatization of Dutch Post preceded postal sector liberalization, thus giving it significant lead time over its competitors. Indeed, as a privatized operator, Dutch Post was able to take advantage of a weakness in the international postal system: it collected mail in high-price countries and delivered in low-price countries, reaping significant financial benefits from the operation. The financial returns were then used for acquisition. In these ways, when the European Postal market, as a whole, was being liberalized, Dutch Post had a significant advantage over its competitors.

Consequences of TPG privatization

As of 2003, the privatization of Dutch Post could be seen as a success story, at least when compared with most other postal operators, even in industrialized countries. Prices for basic (universal) services were low and quality was high. As an operator, TPG Post was very innovative and dynamic, both domestically and internationally. By expanding internationally, TPG Post was able to generate jobs, while at the same time maintaining high-level operations in The Netherlands. In addition, the historical postal system in Holland had undergone significant restructuring: for example, the Postbank was sold to ING, an insurance company, while the counters and outlets were franchised or sold. All in all, the transformation of Dutch Post into the TPG group is an example of successful privatization from the point of view of employees, consumers and the government as an owner.

By 2003, competitive pressure on all postal operators in Europe and worldwide was increasing. Ultimately, this was likely to lead to significant concentration in the sector. TPG Post, as subject to the dynamics of postal liberalization, had managed to take advantage of them, rather than becoming a victim, and looked well placed for continued success.

Transportation

BRITISH RAIL[1]

Martin Weidauer

The privatization of British Rail has become notorious for its lack of success. It is far from clear, however, whether the reasons for the debacle lie in privatization itself. According to Prime Minister Tony Blair 'Privatization was an important factor causing chaos in the railways, but the true reason was under-investment' (Mathieu, 2003). Indeed, the record shows the under-investment began well before privatization.

Prime Minister Margaret Thatcher made de-nationalization a top priority during the 1980s. Various sectors were affected, including telecommunications, water and transport. In the transport sector, the process started with British Airways, National Express Bus, urban bus operators, and the airports and maritime ports. The privatization of British Rail was introduced rather late, in July 1992, by John Major's government with the White Paper on 'New Opportunities for the Railways'. The bill was based on a bold interpretation of EC Directive 91/440 on the development of the European Community's railways. The privatization was completed only in early 1997, just before Major's Conservative party lost the general election of that year.

As is typical, the motives for privatization of the railway system were a desire for increased productivity and better services. It was believed these would result from more competition. Increased productivity was also meant to reduce the need for public subsidies.

Unfortunately for the rail system, subsidies had already been cut dramatically during the two decades before privatization, creating a trend of chronic under-investment in comparison to other countries (ECIS, 1996).

The fragmentation of British Rail

The 1993 Railways Act was not a simple affair. It involved a highly problematic fragmentation. The company Railtrack became one of the new owners and was exclusively responsible for the national infrastructure of tracks and stations. Initially, Railtrack was meant to remain in public ownership, but in a policy move to make privatization irreversible, its shares were ultimately sold to private investors in May 1996 (Böttger, 2002). Railtrack managed the tracks and coordinated timetables by allocating time slots to the train operators. Maintenance and renewal of the infrastructure, however, were sourced out to British Rail infrastructure service companies (BRISCOs). Adding to the complexity, the BRISCOs comprised seven maintenance companies, six track renewal units and seven design offices.

Leases for train operating companies (TOCs) to operate passenger rail services on a part of the network were put out to competitive tender. Bids were made on the 25 franchises carved out of the network. The franchises became operational in late 1996 and early 1997. Leases ran between 7 and 15 years and were conditional on investment in new rolling stock. Franchises were typically created as regional monopolies with few exceptions, such as the London to Gatwick Airport service where the need to gamble on which of different brands of train, with non-transferable tickets, will actually get you to your destination first continues to bemuse travellers to this day. Every TOC had an access agreement with Railtrack for the use of track, stations and other operating facilities. Setting up this intricate network of contractual relationships required vast amounts of technical, legal, financial and managerial advice and consultancy. The government's willingness to pay for this was contrasted unfavourably with its refusal to invest comparable sums in improving the railways.

The sale of British Rail rolling stock generated UK£1742 million for three rolling stock companies (ROSCOs). The ROSCOs leased the trains to the TOCs, competing for purchase. Only a few months later, all ROSCOs had been resold with enormous total profits of UK£910 million – private profit lost to the public sector.

Shortly after Railtrack was set up, an internal memo was leaked to the press in which Railtrack managers were instructed to use their company cars to travel between stations because this would be cheaper to Railtrack than paying train operating companies for rail tickets. The message this gave about fragmentation and conflicts of interest was a sign of worse to come.

Development of privatization

A positive development of the railway industry is seen in the growth in railway traffic and revenues from passenger operation up to the year 2000. This is explained, on the one hand, by marketing activities and increased frequency of trains and, on the other hand, by external factors such as economic growth and increased road congestion. For the TOCs, this improvement in financial performance was required to cover the decreasing level of the yearly subsidies written into the franchise contracts.

Difficulties resulted from the complex structure both of the contracts and of the responsibilities assumed by the companies. Railtrack's financial resources came mainly from track-access fees paid by the operators. A high percentage of the access fees had been set at fixed rates and produced a level of return such that Railtrack did not invest in expansion of capacity. Rail traffic

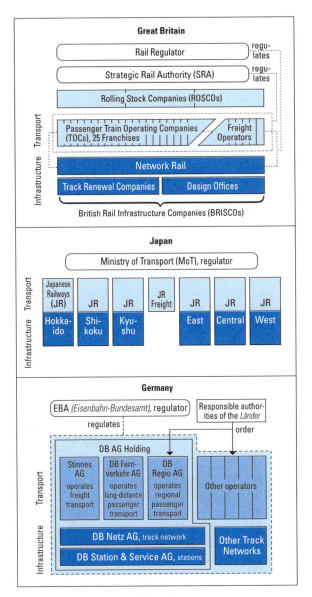

Figure 19
Different forms of railway structure in Japan, Great Britain and Germany. In Great Britain, infrastructure and transport are separated. Different private transport companies are partly into competition for passengers. In contrast, Japan's railway (JR) is vertical integrated with regional monopolies owning infrastructure and organizing transport. Germany's still public DB AG Holding owns nearly all of the infrastructure and provides transport service throughout the country. Other transport providers start slowly to play in the market.
Source: Martin Weidauer.

bottlenecks resulted and franchise incentive systems were not flexible enough to cope with an increasing transport volume. Indeed, the capacity of key bottlenecks, such as the approaches to the main London stations, went down after privatization because contractual entitlement to timed 'slots' prevented signal staff from using their skill and experience to squeeze extra performance out of the system by holding up some trains to secure the most efficient combinations of movements across junctions and shared tracks. The rigidity of the system of sale of timed slots also often worsened delays. If a train missed its 'slot' even by only a few minutes, it would have to wait for the next unreserved slot, since signal staff no longer had discretion to hold up other trains in order to allow the delayed one to make up time. Coordinated management to achieve the best overall result became impossible.

Despite some regulation by the state, the private Railtrack company could not be forced to invest in much-needed infrastructure renewal and safety. The failure to invest in new infrastructure resulted in poor service quality and a number of tragic accidents. In connection with accidents, systematic deficiencies became apparent in the management processes at Railtrack (Böttger, 2002). In the words of a former British Rail senior executive: 'Subcontracting maintenance and renewal work needs significant technical management and supervision that Railtrack did not have in place. While the physical work can be subcontracted, the responsibility cannot' (Bradshaw, 2001). In general, the need for Railtrack to invest in infrastructure conflicted with shareholder interest in dividends.

Crashes and poor service

A series of five fatal accidents occurred following privatization. Fifty-nine people died in dramatic collisions at Southall (1997), Ladbroke Grove (1999), Hatfield (2000), Great Heck (2001) and Potters Bar (2002). In the worldwide media coverage, the crashes were linked to reasons of privatization. This was an oversimplification. The overall figures for railway fatalities are not very different from those in other European countries, as can be seen in Figure 20. The Great Heck crash was caused by a road vehicle driver falling asleep, crashing off a motorway bridge into the path of one train and derailing it into the path of another, a sequence of events which even the most ferocious critic would have difficulty in blaming on privatization.

However, the investigations into several of the other accidents revealed contributory factors, such as inadequate maintenance, inoperative safety equipment, inexperienced and inadequately trained staff, disregarded operating and safety procedures, and muddled lines of reporting and responsibility which were related to privatization. Moreover, the paralysis and disorder that followed each incident, with no one able to formulate a sensible, coordinated and proportionate response on the part of the rail industry, and each company giving higher priority to avoiding blame and liability than to dealing with the problem, were widely blamed on privatization.

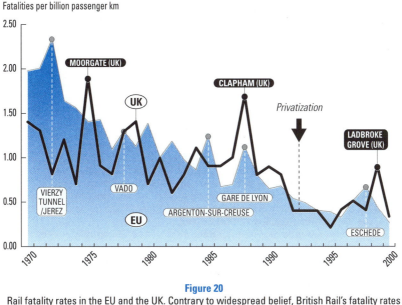

Fatalities per billion passenger km

Figure 20

Rail fatality rates in the EU and the UK. Contrary to widespread belief, British Rail's fatality rates
were not higher than those of the whole European Union.
Source: adapted from Hope (2002, p34); Rail Safety and Standards Board (2002).

Extreme weather events caused much worse breakdowns in rail services than comparable events had during the past. This, too, was widely blamed on privatization for having ended the 'over-manning', which, during the past, had provided reserve capacity for dealing with emergencies, and for erecting rigid contractual limits to powers and duties which prevented different parts of the industry from adapting resiliently to exceptional circumstances and doing what was needed to keep the trains running.

Consequences for customers proved highly significant. The Hatfield accident, in particular, led to hundreds of speed restrictions. The subsequent maintenance work carried out over the whole network led to the collapse of timetables (Hope, 2002) and, therefore, to penalty fees for Railtrack to be paid to the TOCs. As a result, the passengers lost time or stayed away. Revenues lost by the companies led to increased levels of public subsidy.

Other than an increase in the number of trains on busy lines between big cities, privatization did not bring many positive aspects for passengers. The chosen type of competition failed to produce expected cuts in railway fares. In fact, UK rail fares are the highest in Europe (Mathieu, 2003, p28) and made travelling by train much more expensive in relation to bus and air travel. Worse, perhaps, were the poor connections between trains operated by different TOCs and a morass of rules and exceptions for inter-ticketing between TOCs and between trains and buses. It is not surprising that the measured level of complaints reached very high levels, exacerbated also by increased numbers of delayed or cancelled trains and rush-hour overcrowding.

BOX 4 ECONOMICS OF TRANSPORT AND PRIVATIZATION

Felix R. FitzRoy

Political debate on transport and privatization generally ignores some of the basic economics of these issues. A key point is that rail systems involve large fixed costs of infrastructure and rolling stock, with relatively low operating costs. The marginal social cost of an additional passenger in a train or bus that is not filled to capacity is close to zero.

What does this mean for privatization? A common major objective is to reduce or eliminate subsidies, but if fares are set high enough to cover average total costs which include the fixed costs, then potential passengers who could have been carried at negligible social cost will be deterred. Most of them will probably switch to using private cars, generating huge external environmental costs of pollution, noise, accidents and congestion. Declining patronage on public transport then leads to reduction of service frequency and other aspects of quality in the name of cost-cutting, which leads to yet further decline in modal share.

There is equally little popular appreciation of the essentially inverted cost structure of private car use. The main cost item is the initial purchase price, a fixed cost that does not vary with use, while the marginal or operating cost of fuel and additional depreciation for any single trip is very small in comparison. However, the potential motorist will only compare the marginal, private cost of a trip (ignoring the purchase price and externalities) with the public transport fare that is usually much greater than the marginal cost of the service in order to cover at least part of the fixed cost.

There is thus a fundamental pricing bias against the use of privatized public transport, unless subsidies are explicitly maintained at a high enough level to cover fixed costs in a policy that is rarely observed in practice. Inadequately funded public transport suffers, of course, from the same problem, and this pricing bias adds to the distortion of modal choice generated by the familiar, large implicit subsidies offered to motorists through free access to congested roads (in the absence of road pricing), and fuel tax rates that are far below the marginal external cost of car use for many urban trips at least.

In recent years, car-sharing clubs, sometimes as part of new residential developments, have been growing in popularity in several countries. These clubs charge rates for use that cover fixed and operating costs in the same way as conventional car-hire, but at much lower levels which provide an attractive alternative to ownership for households that use cars only occasionally. The pricing bias is thus removed, and modes can compete on a more level playing field. Although the convenience of individual private car ownership is likely to remain dominant in most households, the pricing bias can actually be shifted to the advantage of public transport by the formation of 'clubs' whose members pay a fixed charge by purchasing a season ticket that entitles them to unlimited free or reduced-fare trips, for a given period of time. The crucial condition is that the price of the season ticket is set low enough so that most car owners will buy the ticket or 'join the club', and this will generally require subsidy.

In our study of season tickets and their effects in some European cities that have been most successful in expanding the use of public transport, it was shown that there are general welfare effects, and that the introduction of cheap, transferable season tickets played a crucial role in raising the modal share of public transport (FitzRoy and Smith, 1999). However, there are important complementary measures such as large-scale pedestrian zones in central city areas that encourage modal switch and make a major contribution to improving the quality of urban life. Crucially, congestion charging or road access pricing is also necessary in order to internalize negative externalities of road use and raise funds for public transport without distortionary taxation. London's pioneering congestion charging scheme introduced in February 2003 has reduced traffic by 30%, but widespread adoption still faces major political opposition.

Conclusion

The privatization of British railway was by far the most radical in Europe and can hardly be considered successful. Compared to other countries such as France, Germany or Japan, British railways are unsatisfactory in terms both of system quality and investment. But *why* did the British experiment remain so disappointing? It appears to have been a fundamental mistake to make railway infrastructure subject to the need to generate profits for shareholders. This systematically extended the period of under-investment. The UK government seemed to reach the same assessment when it decided, in 2001, to bring Railtrack under administrative supervision. A new not-for-profit company was formed, Network Rail, to run the track network. In 2003, it was decided that this company should also take over maintenance of the rail network and inherit a daunting task – getting the UK back on track. In this way, yet another phase began in an experiment with the privatization of British railways, leaving many feeling it might still be too much of a bad thing.

JAPANESE NATIONAL RAILWAYS

Martin Weidauer

Japanese railways are known for very high punctuality and reliable service. In the process of railway privatization, Japan managed to avoid mistakes made in other countries. By a number of measures described below, Japan avoided cherry-picking and unhealthy conflicts between performance and profitability. However, the state-of-the-art railway system remained a costly affair for the state, even after privatization.

The country and the history

Japan is a mountainous country. Seventy-five per cent of the area is more or less uninhabitable and unsuitable for agriculture. For a country with over 100 million inhabitants, this means enormous concentrations both of population and economic activity in the lowlands. This is seen predominantly in the Tokyo and Kansai (Osaka) agglomerations, but also between and beyond these conurbations. The topography lends itself well to mass transport. On average, the Japanese travelled 3100km per year by train in 1990 compared, for example, to the German average of 800km (Legewie, 1997; Mayer, 1995).

Since inception, Japanese railways were designed to be operated in part by the state and in part by private companies. In 1949, all state-owned parts were consolidated into one profitable public entity, the Japanese National Railways (JNR). Consisting of companies to run either highly efficient commuter lines or rural lines abandoned by JNR (only the latter with grants by municipal governments), the private sector was organized to serve more than 30 per cent of journeys.

Figure 21
The Japanese Shinkansen train.
Source: Heike Faul.

Financial troubles began during the 1960s, when JNR incurred huge infrastructure costs resulting from the political decision to create a new high-speed railway system. The first 'Bullet' train, the *Tōkaidō Shinkansen*, became operational in 1964. A construction company, the Japan Railway Construction Public Corporation (JRCC) was created to build new high-speed railway tracks. But JNR was obliged to buy and operate the expensive infrastructure. JNR tried to recover some of the cost by shedding labour; but strikes organized by powerful unions made that very difficult, creating a negative public image for JNR.

How JNR was privatized

The privatization of JNR took place in two phases and can be seen partly as a response to JNR's financial troubles and to its negative image. The first phase was only a nominal privatization since the shares of the companies were kept entirely by the state. A second phase began in 1993 with some of the shares of profitable segments sold on the stock market (for the following, see Koester, 1998).

Phase one started on 1 April 1987 with the split of JNR into six independent and regionally operated passenger railway companies and Japan Railway (JR) Freight. The JR Hokkaido, JR Shikoku and JR Kyushu on the smaller main islands, and JR East, JR Central and JR West on the largest island Honshu, came to own and operate infrastructure and trains in their respective territories. The high-speed infrastructure network was owned until 1991 by the Shinkansen Holding Corporation (SHC), which leased its very profitable lines to the three Honshu JRs. In 1991, the Honshu JRs finally bought the Shinkansen infrastructure, while the SHC was transformed into a state-owned Railway Development Fund, receiving continuous public subsidies for the further development of the rail infrastructure.

Also as part of the first phase, the JNR Settlement Corporation (JNRSC) was established in 1987 to free JNR from all earlier debts. JNRSC was instructed gradually to reduce these debts by selling off unused land. It was also supposed to find jobs for employees who would no longer be needed in a new system of profitable private rail companies.

JNRSC's job looked reasonably easy during the Japanese economic boom period, which lasted until 1991. During the ensuing period of stagnation and collapse of real estate prices, the reduction of debts by selling property became rather difficult.

The task of reducing redundant staff turned out to be easier. Many employees were laid off by JNRSC and, after review, rehired by the new JR companies. Workers failing to be re-employed were either placed elsewhere, accepted severance payments or were retired. Nationwide, it was regarded as a major success that only around 1000 employees had to be dismissed, which made it virtually impossible for the unions to oppose the process.

The development of the railway industry

Although Japan railways lost market shares to the road in the growing transport sector, privatization seems to have been instrumental in stopping the downward trend of JNR passenger numbers. Increasing labour productivity was achieved by technological innovation and continuous staff reduction. Such innovation included automatic ticket inspection at the access to platforms; improvement of information and service; flexibility to react better to regional needs; reduction of travelling time by new trains; and a tilting mechanism, as well as intensification of the train frequency to avoid massive overcrowding. Significantly, fares remained stable until 1996, trains remained highly punctual and train connections were optimized. All of this had a very positive influence on the opinion of Japanese rail-system passengers.

During the first decade of privatization, the three Honshu JRs made robust profits. They managed to surpass other private railways in both passenger numbers and productivity. The structural disadvantage of the island JRs was compensated for by government subsidies. In particular, the gigantic new train connections to the main island (Seikan Tunnel between Honshu and Hokkaido and Seto Bridge between Honshu and Shikoku, all projects initiated by the state) led to continuous losses converted only by subsidies into positive company balances. The situation of JR Freight is peculiar. Owing to the geography of the country where nearly all industrial sites are located close to the sea, coastal cargo ships dominate the mass transport market, while local distribution is increasingly road based. Only a very small share of about 5 per cent of the freight market is left to rail. Not surprisingly, JR Freight made losses. Economic stagnation and, in 1995, the Kobe earthquake worsened the picture. Some deficits in management and in innovation are also quoted as reasons for unsatisfactory results (Koester, 1998).

Rural rail services

Since 1980, a new law allowed JNR to abandon rail services with less than 4000 passengers per day. Most of them were transferred to a new type of 'third-sector' railway company, owned by local public authorities or by local private companies; but some lines were simply closed or replaced by bus services. The new rail operators were encouraged to increase efficiency and received state subsidies for the first five years. Only a few of the local companies became profitable, but in many cases obtained continuing subsidies from municipalities. Closures occurred due to a lack of local finance (Terada, 2001).

Preliminary assessment, 2003

After privatization, it was realized that measures were needed to share profits fairly among private companies in lucrative and less lucrative regions. First the island JRs were spared the old JNRs' debts. Honshu JRs were required to pay into a Management Stabilization Fund (MSF) from which the outer island JRs would receive subsidies. Rural services were subsidized by local public authorities, and the non-profitable JR Freight would pay only minimal infrastructure fees (Koester, 1998).

Competition between the different JR companies became barely possible, because they were all established to hold regional monopolies. Government regulation chiefly extended to safety aspects (the number of accidents going down since privatization). The second phase of privatization began in 1993 with the selling off of around 60 per cent of the shares of the three profitable Honshu JR companies (Terada, 2001). Their income was higher than forecasted and share sales helped significantly to reduce the debts of JNRSC. Notwithstanding this success, the debt burden of the JNRSC increased again and, by 1997, had reached levels attained by the old JNR in 1987, amounting to a deficit of nearly 28 trillion Yen (Imashiro, 1997).

All in all, the privatization of Japanese National Railways can be seen as a positive example. Nevertheless, it did not relieve the taxpayer from shouldering the cost of infrastructure.

REGIONALIZATION AS PART OF RAIL RESTRUCTURING IN GERMANY

Martin Weidauer

Regionalization was part of the reform of German railways and provides an example of a blend between private and governmental economies, seemingly offering some advantages of free-market competition.

German railway reform

As in other countries, the state-owned German rail continuously lost market share to road and air traffic both in passenger transport and in cargo from the 1960s. Deficits were high and growing; but, as part of the overall federal budget, they were not so visible. In 1990, after German unification, the West German Deutsche Bundesbahn and the rather run-down East German Deutsche Reichsbahn were merged. In an attempt to control debts through cost-cutting and de-bureaucratization, a private company was created in 1994, the Deutsche Bahn AG. In 1999, it was restructured as DB AG Holding, with four main subdivisions: DB Reise & Touristik, for long-distance passenger transport; DB Regio, for regional passenger transport; DB Cargo, for freight transport; and DB Netz, responsible for and owner of the track network. DB AG Holding remained owned by the state; but plans were made to sell its shares on the stock exchange as soon as it reached profitability.

Apart from a few branch lines, DB Netz owned the entire network as a monopolist, while the transportation market was opened to third parties paying track-access charges. Nevertheless, DB AG was vertically integrated as both the track infrastructure and much of the operations remained under single unit control. Many experts view this as unfair against third-party operators (e.g. Link, 2003).

Competition for profitable long-distance passenger lines had not opened up by 2003 because DB AG offered only empty slots to potential external operators, and there was no tendering for the highest network profit. New competitors would incur substantial risks due to high investment in the procurement of trains and to the non-availability of high-profit slots.

Competition in regional transport

A more open market was allowed at regional levels from 1996. Responsibility for regional passenger transport was transferred from the central government to the German *Länder*, which allocated an annual subsidy worth €6 billion (approximately €75 per person living in Germany) to finance regional train operation. The *Länder* were encouraged to initiate competition by tendering out services on single lines or small networks. Until 2003, around 40 non-DB AG operators had entered the market and were running regional passenger services. But only 10 per cent of the train kilometres had been tendered out. The low share of the market is explained because there was no invitation to bid for the commuter network services in the bigger conurbations. Since, on average, around 70 per cent of regional operators' income came from public subsidies, it appears that more competition may have been needed to raise efficiency.

However, a systematic increase in cost effectiveness was seen. While subsidies remained constant, ever more train kilometres are run. However, some loss-making tracks were closed down, shrinking the network system by 11 per cent (Link, 2003), most of the shrinkage occurring in East Germany.

Competition induced the various operators to improve services, with better timetables offering hourly services and faster trains. Again, much of the cost of new trains (up to 50 per cent) was covered by public subsidies.

Experiences were different in the various *Länder*. In Thuringia, powerful competitors to the DB AG were already running 25 per cent of the network. In Baden-Wuerttemberg, private regional operators reopened several lines formerly closed down. Often, the regional operators were actually created with the single purpose of reopening existing tracks (Schröder, 2001). By 2003, most of the new passenger services by non-DB-operators were running with an integrated fare system comparable to the one offered by DB AG.

Preliminary results

Competition in the German railway system was begun in only a small part of the service. Not surprisingly, but crucially, the DB AG monopolist was seen to fight hard in political commissions and in court to preserve its power (Hornig, 2003).

Meanwhile, customer satisfaction with railway performance decreased. The reasons, however, do not seem to relate specifically to regional private operators, but rather to a lack of punctuality, mostly on the part of DB AG long-distance trains. This, in turn, led to complaints about endless missed train connections. Furthermore, the new fare system introduced by DB AG in December 2002 was so complicated and unpopular that it had to be revoked altogether six months later.

In contrast to other sectors of DB AG, the volume of traffic for the DB Regio grew by more than 20 per cent in ten years, not including the train service of the other growing private operators. At the same time, public support was reduced to the level of 1993, since when subsidies had not risen. Overall, privatization until 2003 had produced a mixture of positive and negative impacts. But it should be noted that under the responsibility of regional institutions the regional train service developed very well when it allowed the *Länder* to manage its own affairs, including its finances. By 2003, results had yet to be seen from the plans to increase the private share of the public and private economies involved in the regionalization of German railways. Problems had been observed; but the question remained as to whether more privatization would prove to be the solution.

PRIVATIZATION OF THE TRANSPORT SECTOR IN ARGENTINA

Tim Gürtler

Economic, social and political background

Argentina's privatization programme was partly a reaction to the economic crisis at the end of the 1980s (Galiani and Petrecolla, 2000, p82). This reached its peak in 1989: foreign debt, negative growth, capital flight and hyper-inflation were higher than ever before (Saba, 2000, p258). As a consequence, the Unión Cívica Radical with Raúl Alfonsín as president lost the elections and Carlos Saúl Menem of the Peronist party took office in July 1989. He immediately initiated comprehensive economic reforms, which included massive privatizations of state-owned enterprises (SOEs). During the 1980s, there were approximately 900 to 1000 fully state-owned enterprises. In 1989, SOEs represented approximately 7 per cent of the gross national product, but 56 per cent of the fiscal deficit and 26 per cent of foreign debt (Valenzuela, 2003, pp101, 103.) The main objective of the Argentine structural reforms, including privatization, was to consolidate the fiscal budget by reducing the enormous expenditure (Llanos, 2002, p363).

Menem was able to form a coalition to back up his reform agenda. A majority in his own Peronist party, smaller conservative parties, some important think tanks, unions and important players of the private sector supported his reform plan. He also received support from foreign governments, the International Monetary Fund (IMF), the World Bank and the Inter-American Development Bank (Saba, 2000, p259). Additionally, most Argentineans were convinced that privatization was the only practicable way to get out of this disaster (Saba, 2000, p259). As early as 1989, Menem got the State Reform Act passed, providing the government with all necessary powers for privatization. Menem also fended off opposition to this reform. The Supreme Court, for instance, was considered as a potential opponent; hence, the administration increased the number of judges from five to nine and managed, in 1990, to appoint six pro-government judges, thus establishing a comfortable majority. (Llanos, 2002, pp60ff).

The process of privatization

In the public transport sector the government offered 40 per cent of the motorways, 85 per cent of Aerolineas Argentinas and 66 per cent of the freight transports of the National Railroad (Ferrocarriles Argentinos) to private investors.

Aerolineas Argentinas (AA)

In December 1989, the government offered 85 per cent of the shares for sale. Five per cent were retained for the state and 10 per cent for the employees. The total value of the enterprise was fixed at US$623 billion (85 per cent = US$529.5 billion). At least US$220 billion were required to be paid in cash, the rest as takeover of foreign debt.

To the disappointment of the government, only one expression of interest was received, from the Spanish trust already holding two other airlines, IBERIA and Cielos del Sur SA. Parliament tried to stop the sales process at this point, but was overruled by the Supreme Court. Opponents of President Menem interpreted this ruling as a further limitation to checks and balances. In November 1990, the privatization of AA seemed to be complete. But the consortium was not able to pay the price – as negotiated – of US$262 billion. Further negotiations were not satisfying, so finally, in 1992, the state was still in possession of 43 per cent of Aerolineas Argentinas (Valenzuela, 2003, pp119ff).

Motorways

At the end of the 1980s, only 30 per cent of Argentine motorways were in a good condition. As a result, the government planned to award about 10,000km to the private sector on the basis of a toll system. The 20 corridors were given to the supplier with the highest offer. One condition was to maintain quality standards. The award of contracts was criticized because only 29 enterprises took part and, as a consequence, there was almost only one offer per corridor. Moreover, the tolls increased by about 50 per cent during the first months. The government gave way and renegotiated the contracts. Hence, the planned revenues of US$890 billion were never realized. On the contrary, the state kept on giving subsidies and decreased the rate of taxation for the enterprises involved (Valenzuela, 2003).

Ferrocarriles Argentinos

In January 1991, the administration put up a plan, including the following key aspects:

- Two-thirds of the freight transport should be privatized by the end of the year.
- Profitable intercity connections should be sold, unprofitable ones given up.
- Staff numbers had to be reduced.
- Subsidies should be cut back to a level of US$160 billion (Valenzuela, 2003, p122).

The consortium of the Techint Group and Iowa Interstate Railroad put in the best offer for the freight transport system. Some parts of the rail network were offered to the provinces. However, only five of them accepted the offer; the others suspended the services. Concessions were also awarded for the public transport in Buenos Aires (Valenzuela, 2003). By the end of 1993, most parts of the railway was privatized, although the government still was in charge to regulate the rail system (Ramamurti, 1997, p1981).

Privatization results

As argued above, one of the intrinsic goals of privatization was to consolidate the state budget. During the 1980s, government expenditures for the railway sector surpassed US$1000 million per year (Ramamurti, 1997, p1985). Until 1995, subsidies were cut to an amount of US$140,000 (Ramamurti, 1997, p1985). With respect to Aerolineas Argentinas, the result is not that clear. Given the fact that the state still possessed 43 per cent of the airline, the goal of budget consolidation was not achieved to the same extent as with the railroads. This is especially the case since the takeover of foreign debt did not take place as intended. According to the government, taxpayers were positively affected by privatization outcomes due to reduced expenditures.

The government dismissed labour in large numbers. In July 1989, Ferrocarriles Argentinos employed 96,000 workers. In 1990, this number was cut by 11,000. When the government announced a further 27,000 dismissals, the labour unions organized a 60-day strike. But Menem did not give way. The strikes were declared illegal, staff numbers were cut and privatization accelerated (Valenzuela, 2003, p130). The government, however, did encourage employees to leave voluntarily. In the railway sector, about 46,000 workers left because of the economic incentives set by the administration. Furthermore, labour unions and employees were able to participate in the privatization process by obtaining shares on favourable conditions. Altogether, between 1989 and 1993, the number of employees in the public sector was cut by 119,018 (Valenzuela, 2003, p132). The crucial question is whether labour rationalization would have taken place in this dimension without privatization. An agreement between the Argentine government and the World Bank concerning Ferrocarriles Argentinos foresaw a cut of 30,000 employees, while a 1989 government blueprint indicated that about 50,000 workers were to be dismissed (Ramamurti, 1997, p1984). We can conclude that privatization had a huge impact on the number of dismissed employees.

Finally, looking at the utilization and the quality of services, the fleet of planes increased from 47 in 1991 to 81 in 1997, and the number of passengers rose during the same period of time by 120 per cent.[2] Rail passengers increased by 115 per cent, while rail cargo increased by 95 per cent. The punctuality of trains improved by 26 per cent (FIEL, 2002, p11). Hence, according to these indicators, the quality of service and utilization has improved. It remains uncertain, however, whether these improvements are related only to the privatization process. These findings could be approved affirmatively by the fact, that, although the number of passengers also rose on un-privatized rail lines, the amount of passengers on privatized lines rose much more (Ramamurti, 1997, p1988). A survey from 1995 confirms that more than 90 per cent of the rail passengers judged the quality of service as good as or even better than before privatization (Ramamurti, 1997, p1987). At the some time, fares did not increase (Ramamurti, 1997, p1987). Rail cargo prices decreased by 20 per cent between 1991 and 1994 – an effect that can be linked to more competition with trucks (Ramamurti, 1997, p1986). This finding underlines the positive role that privatization played with respect to service and prices. We have, at least, a strong correlation between improvements of service and privatization. Whether this is a strong causal relationship cannot be concluded within this snapshot.

AIR NEW ZEALAND

Diwata Olalia Hunziker

Air New Zealand began flying in 1940 as TEAL (Tasman Empire Airways Limited). It became a major regularly scheduled passenger airline based in New Zealand with a considerable international and domestic network. At the end of 1989, Air New Zealand was privatized through its outright sale to a consortium. In January 2002, the company was re-nationalized. As of June 2003, Air New Zealand's net profit rose to NZ$165.7 million, up by 152 per cent from the previous period, with a company workforce of more than 10,000 worldwide.

From TEAL to Air New Zealand

TEAL was registered as a company in 1940, flying from Auckland as a venture jointly owned by the New Zealand government (20 per cent), the New Zealand company Union Airways (19 per cent), the British Overseas Airways Corporation (BOAC) (38 per cent) and the Australian airline Qantas (23 per cent). In 1947, the New Zealand government formed the domestic airline National Airways Corporation (NAC). By 1953, the Australian government increased its share in TEAL to 50 per cent. The UK withdrew in 1954 and in 1961 the company was nationalized by the New Zealand government when it bought out the Australian share. The airline was renamed Air New Zealand four years later. Air New Zealand and NAC merged in 1978, forming the first New Zealand carrier to offer both international and domestic services. Privatization followed at the end of 1988, when Air New Zealand was sold for NZ$660 million to an international consortium.

Shifting gears: Consortium purchase

In 1984, the New Zealand government started to move from state intervention measures towards a market economy. Economic reforms then included abolition of capital controls, implementation of a floating exchange rate, abandonment of price controls, elimination of subsidies to industries and agriculture, introduction of labour market legislation and privatization of state-owned enterprises. In preparation for privatization, a constitution for the airline company was drawn up which permitted three kinds of shares. One of the shares, called a Kiwi Share, was held by the Ministry of Transport and entailed no dividends; instead, special voting rights allowed the ministry to veto changes in ownership or in the company's constitution. Before Air New Zealand's sale, the New Zealand government had allowed Ansett, an Australian airline, to buy 100 per cent control of a New Zealand domestic airline.

Air New Zealand's privatization in 1989 occurred by sale through public tender. The purchasing consortium was comprised of Brierley Investments

Limited (65 per cent), Qantas (19.9 per cent), and Japan Airlines and American Airlines (each with 7.5 per cent). Air New Zealand was accorded a major portion of 'A' shares, limited for sale only to New Zealand nationals. The initial public offering (IPO) was oversubscribed. Sale of 'B' shares (no restriction on nationality) followed in 1991.

New Zealand government steps back on board

Air New Zealand expanded its destinations and began acquisitions. In 1996, it announced a conditional agreement to acquire 50 per cent of Ansett Holdings, owner of the domestic airline Ansett Australia. Purchase of the remaining 50 per cent of Ansett Holdings was completed in June 2000, making it to the world top 20 airlines. By this time, the company had already entered into an alliance with various airlines (e.g. Canadian Airlines, Qantas and Scandinavian Airlines) and started adding airplanes to its fleet. The new organizational structure, however, kept the control of Ansett's management group, in this way preventing Air New Zealand from exercising significant influence. More importantly, the deal was concluded without the usual examination of Ansett's books. In the course of a few months, Ansett's accumulated problems led to the grounding of its planes in December 2000; a series of rescue packages were then negotiated to save Ansett and Air New Zealand. Qantas proposed a buy-in of significant shares from Brierley Investments and Singapore Airlines. At this point, the New Zealand government hesitated to allow control of Air New Zealand as its national airline to fall further into foreign hands. Negotiations failed and Air New Zealand decided to divest itself of Ansett. In September 2001, Ansett was placed into voluntary administration, becoming New Zealand's biggest corporate failure, with losses of NZ$1.3 billion. Recapitalization by the New Zealand government became the only realistic choice. Thus, in January 2002, 12 years after its privatization, Air New Zealand returned to the hands of the state.

An airline or more at stake?

It seems the failure of the privatization of Air New Zealand revolved around the acquisition of Ansett. The company neglected to plan properly and ensure sufficient equity to handle the risks involved. Considering the number of stakeholders involved, the management further neglected to provide the leadership needed to resolve the ensuing problems. Two words could best describe why privatization was unsuccessful: misjudgement and mis-management. The drive to create an international airline to compete in the world's top 20 over-reached the company's capacity and failed to address basic financial concerns related to Ansett Airlines and to fleet renewal. Although customer choice and service was increased by the acquisition, the improvement was not financially viable. As the New Zealand government had estimated, left to the market alone, Air New Zealand itself would likely have fallen prey to acquisition. In this case, intervention by the state demonstrates wider interests not typically encompassed by private ownership: the New Zealand government held national identity and national control of greater importance than financial return or market efficiency. With its bailout, the government showed a desire to ensure provision and management service to and within a group identified by its nationality rather than an ability to pay. The risk taken by the government may, in some measure, have been considered mitigated by the precedent of success under previous state ownership. In the case of Air New Zealand, the lure of greater profits in the international arena certainly seems to have been outweighed by national interest. Given the more complex stakeholder interests in a new period under mainly public ownership, it remains uncertain whether the resulting management would be able to achieve the success of a previous era.

SKYGUIDE: A CASE OF CORPORATIZATION

Matthias Finger

Skyguide was formed as a joint-stock company entirely owned by the Swiss Confederation. It was established in order to manage and monitor the civil and military air traffic in Swiss airspace and at the main civil and military airports. In addition, Skyguide was tasked with managing sections of airspace in France, Germany and Austria. By 2003, employees numbered 1400, with the majority of air traffic controllers stationed in Zürich and Geneva. Skyguide was set up under the supervision of the Federal Office of Civil Aviation to be the operational arm of a complex system of air traffic regulation.

The evolution of Skyguide

Skyguide's history goes back to the beginning of air traffic control during the 1920s. Air traffic control is usually considered a government responsibility, given that airspace is a scarce, public resource. In any given chunk of airspace – generally over a country – air traffic control is, furthermore, a monopolistic activity since no more than one operator can manage airspace without compromising safety.

Originally integral to the Federal Office of Civil Aviation, the operational part of air traffic control had already been assigned to an autonomous entity by 1933, and was transformed in 1988 into an organization named Swisscontrol. In 1996, Swisscontrol was officially incorporated, becoming a joint-stock company; it remained, however, 100 per cent owned by the Swiss Confederation. This was a somewhat rare arrangement since only a few air traffic control operators worldwide were joint-stock companies, even by 2003. As part of the corporatization process, a board was appointed by the government, composed of representatives of the main actors in Swiss air transport, including a representative of the former national, yet privately owned, carrier Swissair. Another substantial change occurred in 2001 as the military and the civil air traffic control operations were integrated within

Swisscontrol, which changed its name to Skyguide. As a result, the board was also changed in order to include a representative of the Swiss air force. This integration of military and civil operations in one entity constitutes a very original move, as Skyguide appeared, even by 2003, to be the only integrated air traffic control agency worldwide.

Despite an enormous increase in air traffic in Europe, especially in Switzerland, Swisscontrol, and later Skyguide, barely increased their personnel in the decade before 2003. This was mainly due to pressure from the operators in the various countries, Swissair in particular pressuring Skyguide via its representative on the board. Nevertheless, Swiss air traffic control became one of the most expensive worldwide, primarily because of high salaries (and living standards), and because approximately 30 per cent of the air navigation services above southern Germany are offered free of charge for political reasons (thus increasing the cost of other air services) in exchange for permission to use German airspace for traffic heading for Zurich. The Swiss government, as the owner of Skyguide, did not compensate the company for its activity over German airspace.

In other words, as a major consequence of the process of corporatization, Skyguide was forced to cut costs and, thus, to offer competitive prices for air traffic control. In this way, one of the main objectives of corporatization was accomplished.

The process of liberalization/privatization

Nevertheless, the process of Skyguide's corporatization needs to be set against the larger context of the transformation of air traffic control in Europe. Pressure on air traffic control stems from various sources: traffic increase, technological change and European integration.

The substantial increase in air traffic over Europe between 1988 and 2003 has increasingly led to delays and to demand for modernized air traffic control. The legal status of a stock-holding company, as exemplified by Skyguide, was regarded as suitable by the European Commission. Growing safety problems in European airspace also created concern. This was resolved through the separation of operational air traffic activities – designated for corporatization – and purely regulatory activities – to remain public. These changes were also actively promoted by the European Commission.

The pressure to corporatize and, perhaps eventually, to fully privatize is reinforced by technological change. Indeed, air traffic control is an information-intensive, technology-based activity, requiring heavy investment. Given financial and other restraints common to governments, a joint-stock company could offer improved possibilities to raise money for much-needed investment.

Finally, by 2003, strategically thinking air traffic control operators such as Skyguide already anticipated the European Commission project known as 'Single Sky'. This project aimed at restructuring European airspace with the ultimate goal of putting up newly designated sections of airspace for tender. A joint-stock company, which has itself already undergone substantial restructuring, could be well positioned in such a process. And this is precisely Skyguide's strategy.

Consequences of liberalization

Such liberalization and corporatization (or even privatization, as discussed in the UK) of air traffic control could be beneficial if the necessary regulatory mechanisms and institutions are put into place. Unfortunately, these were missing in the case of Skyguide. Due to a combination of stakeholder pressure via the board and a lack of regulatory supervision, Skyguide started to cut costs beyond a level acceptable from a safety point of view.

As a result, safety in Swiss airspace was compromised. For example, in 2003, air traffic control-related incidents in Switzerland were not only on the rise, but also above the European Union (EU) average. Worst of all, in August 2002 a series of Skyguide failures led to a mid-air collision in Swiss airspace over Überlingen, southern Germany, a highly unusual type of accident.

Issues raised by the liberalization/privatization of Skyguide

It would be unfair and simplistic to view the Überlingen accident and the numerous other airspace incidents as caused by the corporatization of Swisscontrol/Skyguide. But it is undeniable that this change has caused significant financial pressure on Skyguide, which can be linked to safety problems.

The case of Skyguide raises three types of issues resulting from liberalization and corporatization, namely:

1 *Pricing* of air navigation services: in a monopoly situation (like that of Skyguide), it is difficult to determine the exact price of such services. Pressure on these prices had primarily been determined by benchmarking principles (airlines can easily compare how much they pay for similar services across the planet); but it might well be that benchmarked prices can constitute a safety hazard in certain countries, where costs are simply higher due, as in the case of Skyguide, for example, to services rendered free of charge or to higher salaries, etc.
2 *Regulation*: if air navigation services are outsourced to a joint-stock company whose main objectives are efficiency gains, profit and expansion, there is an inevitable need to regulate the autonomous entity. Such regulation must primarily pertain to safety. In other words, the regulator will have to define acceptable safety levels, inspect the practices of the autonomous operators, and sanction non-compliant behaviour. However, in the case of Skyguide, the owner and the regulator were the same, and as the regulator did not undergo changes in parallel to those undergone by Skyguide, such regulation never happened. This is certainly one of the main, if not the main, reasons for Skyguide's low safety performance.

3 *Corporate governance*: this issue arises from that of regulation. Corporatization and, more generally, liberalization of air traffic control are processes where little historical experience is available. Intending to get the most knowledgeable people on board upon Skyguide's corporatization, the Swiss government actually made the mistake of putting the fox in charge of the chicken, thus opening the doors to cost-cutting in favour of the airlines, primarily Swissair, yet at the expense of safety. This seems to make clear the value of establishing separate entities with responsibility for regulation and operation, respectively.

Waste Disposal

NO TIME TO WASTE: HOW TO AVOID TOO MUCH OF A BAD THING (GERMANY, MALAYSIA)

Raimund Bleischwitz and Akira Proske

Waste has always been a by-product of human civilizations. What is new is the amount of waste produced by affluent societies and the potentially severe impacts resulting from hazardous substances. Globalization extends the pathways of production and consumption into every corner of the world. The distances that components of single products often cover by air are worthy of platinum frequent-flyer status. At the same time, space for disposal has become scarce, and waste treatment facilities have grown increasingly complex and expensive. Waste management tends to be a laborious process because the chain from the 'cradle' of resource extraction down to the needs of end consumers inevitably involves a multitude of actors and rule-making bodies. It is no wonder that waste ranks high on the agendas of both policy-makers and businesses. Problems relating to the issue are various:

- Negative *externalities*, relating to the use of services rendered by ecosystems, such as land, groundwater and air, can result when ecosystem capacities are overexploited. They can also arise in terms of pollution problems that, in turn, adversely affect human health.
- Problems exist in relation to the *scale* of activities, which may result from overexploitation of scarce resources or from the sheer amount of products available in affluent societies.
- Problems of *coordination* emerge where suppliers and commercial as well as private consumers have to direct efforts toward recycling, waste reduction, resource conservation, etc. Contrary to widespread opinion, downstream waste disposal policies do not sufficiently encourage upstream activities in recycling and waste reduction (Calcott and Walls, 2000; SRU, 2002).

Proponents of privatization tend to claim that public waste management is inefficient and leads to higher prices and lower standards of customer service (Shleifer, 1998; Lovei and Gentry, 2002). They believe privatizing waste management encourages efficient solutions, driving innovation and meeting customer demands. The way such a claim is reached, however, needs to be closely scrutinized. Incorporation of the principle of 'full-cost accounting' is essential. Fully accepted and implemented, it would force firms to think of services provided by the ecosystem as production factors to be included in overall cost calculation. But policies should do more than just 'get the prices right'. Our knowledge of the causes and effects of externalities is limited. Moreover, uneven emphasis on information about different factors (often called 'asymmetric information'; Faure and Skogh, 2003) can prevent appropriate action from being taken. Transaction costs (i.e. the cost of seeking, negotiating and implementing solutions) may well eat up any efficiency gains in production costs. For these reasons, waste management needs to be capable of reducing negative externalities, production costs *and* transaction costs. It also needs to generate new knowledge that helps to avoid waste production (Faure and Skogh, 2003).

Governments around the globe have begun privatizing waste management, providing good reason to review a few case studies. While Germany serves as an example for ambitious legislation in a country at the forefront of environmental policy implementation, Malaysia can be viewed as a newly industrialized country where, after a period of rapid growth, regulations dealing with negative externalities came to be introduced.

Germany

Germany began privatizing waste management during the 1990s in a bid to solve some specific problems. The Waste Avoidance and Recycling Act (*Kreislaufwirtschafts-/Abfallgesetz*) came into force in 1996. The new law was created against a background of increasing scarcity of disposal sites accompanied by growing environmental awareness. Both matters forced the government to reconsider the issues of recycling and waste avoidance. The new law establishes aims of waste avoidance and saving natural resources; it anchors product responsibility and establishes markets for industrial waste. At the same time, more specific legislation addressed packaging waste. Organized by a newly established industrial consortium, the well-known 'green dot system' (Duales System Deutschland AG) was launched late in 1990. Both the new legislation and the green dot system were supposed to encourage waste avoidance, recycling and, in general, more efficient waste management.

Some ten years later, however, success proves to be limited. The good news mainly relates to waste disposal. The overall volume was reduced significantly while high standards for health and the environment were maintained or even improved. A promising example is the recycling of plastic window frames, where recycling rates have reached about 90 per cent. By introducing specific mechanisms for meeting regulations on primary materials in the packaging sector, the green dot system achieved higher recycling rates than expected, but at high costs. The bad news concerns failures in waste avoidance and resource conservation – both top priorities in the legislation – and the high costs of running the system. The overall efficiency gains predicted by privatization proponents are hardly visible. Instead, monopolies and dependency on certain technology paths predominate. The German Advisory Council for the Environment points out in its 2002 report (SRU, 2002) that more flexible incentives for waste avoidance and resource savings have yet to be introduced. Overall waste figures hardly show an overall decrease (German Federal Statistics Office, 2003).

Obviously, some more specific constraints in the waste sector were either overlooked or not successfully tackled. An analysis by Peter Michaelis, member of the German Advisory Council for the Environment, raises some interesting points (Michaelis, 2001). He states the need to distinguish between competition *for* the market and competition *in* the market. Competition *for* the market, he says, makes economic sense where high fixed costs and the risk of losses due to high capital costs are evident. This is seen in the waste disposal sector and is clearly the case in the German waste incineration and packaging waste management system.

In the meantime, however, the downsides of competition for waste management markets have become apparent in the form of collusion, corruption and fraud among companies and the public sector. The city of Cologne and other German cities have been faced with corruption where a few incineration companies influenced public decisions to benefit their private interests, undermining competition and political credibility. In addition, most local governments subscribed to 'take or pay' contracts where quantities of waste to be supplied by the region are fixed for very long periods of time (e.g. 20 years). This is a definite disincentive for recycling and waste avoidance. The duration of most contracts is oriented to the investment cycle of general disposal or incineration facilities. This represents a major failure since the life cycle of waste can be open, instead, to more flexible options, such as material recycling, waste avoidance and resource efficiency. Such possibilities should also be analysed when concessions for the market are designed and offered by policy-makers.

The introduction of competition *in* the market for waste produced by private companies has also had negative side effects. Certified firms cannot compete with dumping offers from low-quality providers. In fact, 'good' recycling firms (e.g. for automobile recycling) have suffered while 'bad' firms operating in other European Union (EU) member states or accession countries have profited from lax controls. The German industrial association for recycling (Bundesverband für Sekundärrohstoffe und Entsorgung or BVSE) has bitterly condemned this state of affairs and called for better regulation of competition to generate conditions under which competition drives quality. Control and competition policies are crucial if high-quality standards are to be met and private firms are to receive incentives not to reduce their costs by exploiting externalization options.

The overall price level in German waste markets has been under pressure, caused by overcapacities in the incineration sector. Overcapacities in Germany, for instance, attracted waste from southern Italy, which was shipped across Europe. The overcapacities result from misleading estimates, the high level of fixed costs making a large facility more viable than a small one, and from political failures. In addition, the regulatory transition period for disposal of waste from private households ('*TA Siedlungsabfall*') was set to last until May 2005, giving an incentive to fill disposal sites at the lowest possible cost until that date. As a result, prices for filling had fallen, by 2003, below even normal total average costs. Because of these dumping practices, German disposal prices vary in the order of a factor of 20. They do not accurately reflect the scarcity of resources. They do not speak the economic truth.

The German Advisory Council (SRU, 2002) has pointed out that such ruinous competition means that private households end up subsidizing private firms. In some regions, waste prices for private households have quadrupled between 1992 and 2000, a curious effect that results from low prices being offered to a private waste-producing company. Competition in this sector is intense, whereas prices for private households are negotiated between waste companies and local authorities. Trapped in contracts with unfavourable conditions, public authorities with low negotiation skills all too often find themselves confronted with rising prices. The same amount of waste is priced differently and at the expense of private consumers – exactly the opposite of claims by proponents of privatization.

In the end, the German experience does not encourage any naive privatizing optimism. Privatization and competition are beneficial only if they are embedded in a sensible framework of regulations. Reform options discussed in Germany include competitive alternatives to the green dot system, improved cooperation among general disposal and incineration facilities (which would reduce regional disposal autonomy), and stricter liability in cases of non-compliance or corruption. Reformed regulations should definitely include economic incentives. These options by no means represent a backward-looking return to the 'good old days' of public provision. Instead, they may well lead to a waste management future where the positive effects of privatization and competition in the areas of recycling, reuse and waste avoidance are reconciled with public needs in the areas of disposal and public health.

Malaysia

In 1994, after years of successful economic growth, most disposal sites in Malaysia were full. Seventy-five per cent of landfills could no longer be used due to poor management during the past years. The areas were too small, compaction was badly organized and open burning was the order of the day. Only 4 of 83 landfills had acceptable standards even though some improvements had been carried out.

This was the situation in which the decision to privatize waste management was made. In October 1994, the Malaysian government initiated the privatization process by issuing a call for proposals. With a view to its Vision 2020 initiative – aiming to achieve fully industrialized country status by 2020 – the organization of the basic waste management infrastructure was perceived as a candidate for reform. A well-established Malaysian firm, HICOM Holdings Bhd, and Gartner Lee Keir Asia Inc, a Canadian company, formed a joint partnership that resulted in the formation of HICOM Environmental Bhd. This company developed a strategy for the privatization process and outlined goals and measures. The first step was to analyse the existing system by looking at waste streams, the former structure and resources (equipment, employees, etc.).

A major problem during these first years was the uncertain statistics on *real* waste volumes produced by the rural population and others outside the waste-collection system.

After years of privatization, however, the problems mostly remain unchanged. Both the rising (particularly urban) population and the increase in per capita waste rates result in ever-growing volumes of waste. By 2003, the capacity of disposal landfills had once again reached its limits. Industrial modernization, moreover, entailed increasingly complex waste qualities. 3R campaigns aiming at reduction, reuse and recycling had been initiated but showed no visible success.

The reason why privatization shows such poor results in this case may lie in the way that it was implemented. Seventy per cent of Malaysia's territory (Selangor, Pahang, Terenggana, Kelantan and the Federal Territory of Kuala Lumpur) was organized into four waste consortiums. Each holds a regional monopoly with a contract running from 20 to 25 years. As in Germany, such a system hardly offers incentives for more efficiency and waste reduction. In addition, monitoring of general disposal sites and incineration facilities is virtually non-existent. A Malaysian Nature Society position paper (MNS, 2001) urgently called for a reduction of emissions into the air and of pollution of soils and groundwater. The associated risks for public health and the environment are obvious, and the introduction of targeted regulations is imperative.

Emerging adverse effects of waste management make reform a true necessity. Options discussed by the Malaysian Nature Society and Environmental Technologies Industries include composting of organic waste, improved recycling and reuse, training, education and awareness programmes, as well as the establishment of environmental and eco-efficient industries. Monitoring and possible sanctions for non-compliance would be further options. Some progress may be expected as Malaysia strives to meet its goals for 2020.

Waste, corruption and illegal activities

Waste issues have entailed a surprisingly high level of criminal activities. In US states such as New York, waste was a 'mob' business (i.e. part of organized crime) until the late 1980s (Carter, 1997). Sources say that organized crime has had a strong voice in waste management in the highly industrialized country of Japan, (Fujii, 2001). The German state of North Rhine-Westphalia launched an official investigation into privatization processes of the early 1990s, when large incineration facilities were established with private investors. Illegal waste exports to developing countries are an issue dealt with under the Basle Convention (Johnston, 1998). And all of this is only the tip of the iceberg. The extent to which illegal activities are visible ranges significantly from 'ordinary' corruption to organized crime. It should also be noted that corruption has been widespread in the public sector. The lesson seems to be that privatization programmes must involve supervision of the structures created and of related risks. In the waste sector, the prevailing risks can be seen in:

- the high capital intensity of waste treatment facilities, in combination with their long lifetime;
- unbalanced flows of information ('asymmetric information') among facility operators, waste producers and public regulatory authorities; and
- a cognitive bias towards 'getting rid of waste', which leads to insufficient attention paid to the processes involved, as well as to aspects such as recycling, reuse and waste avoidance.

Conclusions and outlook

The example of Malaysia shows positive and negative effects of privatization. A look at other countries (e.g. the US, Japan, the UK, Sweden, India and Lebanon) reveals similar results. Despite some progress in terms of efficiency at the business level, overriding concerns should be the setting and monitoring of quality standards for waste treatment facilities; the design and monitoring of contracts between public and private actors; sanctions in cases of non-compliance and of corruption in cases of public procurement; and incentives for reuse, recycling, waste avoidance and resource savings. If these concerns are handled properly, markets in various forms can perform well. If not, the negative effects of privatization prevail.

Although economic incentives certainly have to play a role (e.g. in the form of fees for waste disposal and energy or resource taxes), the overall issue involves more than correct price-setting. A general shift towards waste reduction and resource saving requires legal incentives for producers to take responsibility. Governance must encourage cooperation among firms as well as among firms, individuals and the public. Concepts such as industrial ecology, eco-efficiency and 'Factor Four/Ten', (referring to an increase in wealth while reducing environmental pressure) provide tools that promote a new direction of technological progress (Bleischwitz and Hennicke, 2004). Incentives for learning how waste can be more efficiently recycled, reused and disposed of, or, better still, how material-intensive production can be avoided and shifted towards eco-efficient services and sustainable lifestyles altogether, are crucial. This applies to actors from and between all governance arenas. It is also relevant for research done by scientific disciplines. The contribution from engineering, jurisprudence, political science and economics will be all the greater if the relevant actors are enabled to use their knowledge in an integrated way. Privatization and competition provide advantages, but must be embedded in a civil society where legislation and politics provide quality standards and incentives to act.

Insurance

ABOLISHING PROPERTY INSURANCE MONOPOLIES IN GERMANY

Thomas von Ungern-Sternberg

When German Chancellor Helmut Kohl abstained from voting on the third European Union (EU) Non-Life Insurance Directive on 18 June 1992, he knew that this would help the directive to be adopted. This signalled the end of the 12 German property insurance monopolies then in existence. A year earlier, the German Bundesrat, the *Länder* Chamber, had unanimously voted to urge the federal government to vote *against* the directive in order to guarantee the monopolies' continued existence.

The EU justified its decision to open the property insurance market to competition by claiming that such a step would increase consumer welfare: 'Within the framework of an internal market it is in the policyholders' interest that he should have access to the widest possible range of insurance products available in the Community so that he can choose that which is best suited to his needs.'[1] The developments in Germany over the last ten years clearly seem to contradict this claim.[2]

Monopolies have lower costs and charge lower premiums

Until 1992, property insurance in Germany was characterized by a dual system. In roughly half of the country, there were no state monopolies and the property insurance market could be described as 'competitive'. In the other half, the market was controlled by local (state) compulsory monopoly institutions (CMIs), most of which were created more than two centuries ago.

A simple comparison of the premium levels and cost structures between the CMIs and the competitive insurance companies prior to 1992 should have been enough to convince the EU that introducing competition was unlikely to improve consumer welfare. In 1987, the average premium rate of the competitive insurance sector was 60 cents per €1000 of sum insured (SI). For the CMI, it was about one half of this amount (31 cents per €1000 SI). A large part of the difference in premium rates could be explained by the cost structures of the two systems. The competitive insurance companies spent 16 cents per €1000 SI on administrative and sales costs. The CMIs spent only 3.3 cents per €1000 SI on such costs (the cost differences between the state monopolies and the competitive insurance sector in Switzerland are of very similar orders of magnitude[3]). As a general rule, one can say that in competitive property insurance markets, between 30 and 40 per cent of premium income is regularly used to cover administrative costs and sales commissions. 'Sales rep competition' plays a much more important role in this market than the price competition that academic economists tend to focus upon.

This snapshot on the consequences of abolishing CMIs in Germany concentrates on three states – Baden-Württemberg, Bavaria and Hamburg – which were the most important in terms of premium income (and are also largely representative of the rest of the country).

As was to be expected, abolishing the monopolies led to a massive rise in administrative and sales costs and, consequently, in the levels of premiums (see Figure 22):

- In Hamburg, these costs increased from €6 million in 1992 to €17.5 million in 1998. Commissions for sales representatives increased from €0.7 million to €5.6 million. The premium rate increased by 35 per cent.
- In Bavaria, costs increased from €35 million in 1993 to €76 million in 1998. Commissions for sales representatives increased from €1 million to €10.5 million. The premium rate increased by 40 per cent. The Bavarian CMI was the first to anticipate the fall of the monopolies and most of the premium increases fell during the period of 1991–1994.
- In Baden-Württemberg, costs increased from €40 million in 1992 to €95 million in 1998. Commissions for sales representatives increased from €0.8 million to €30 million. The premium rate increased by 75 per cent.

In spite of these substantial premium increases, the CMIs lost less than 5 per cent of their initial customer base. This can be partly explained by the fact that their premium rates are still comparatively low. A further important cause is the fact that in property insurance customers switch insurance only very rarely.

Expenditures on prevention

In light of the premium increases, it seems very doubtful that abolishing CMIs was 'in the policyholders' best interest'. However the negative effects for property owners do not end here. As long as the CMIs enjoyed a monopoly status, they had a strong incentive to heavily subsidize the local fire-fighting organizations. The money they spent there helped to reduce the costs of claims. Integrating insurance and prevention can be seen as a classic application of the Coase theorem.[4] When the former CMIs had to share the benefits of their efforts for prevention with their competitors, their incentive structure radically changed. They limited themselves to paying the compulsory 'fire tax'. In

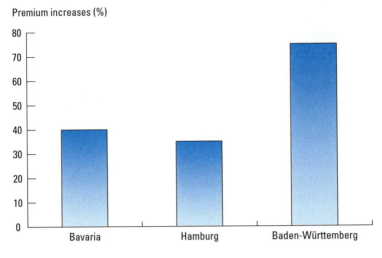

Premium increases (%)

Figure 22

Increase of premium levels for property insurance in selected German regions, 1992–1998. This price explosion can be explained by private insurers' high marketing and administration costs. *Source:* data from von Ungern-Sternberg (2004).

Bavaria, the contributions to fire prevention sank from €42 million in 1993 to €20 million in 1998. In Baden-Württemberg, the contributions for fire prevention sank from €30 million in 1993 to €9 million in 1998. The difference now has to be covered from general taxation.

Natural disaster insurance

One of the main advantages of having a state monopoly in property insurance is the fact that compulsory monopolies do not have to fear losing their good risks to competitors. They can engage in a certain amount of cross-subsidization. This is especially important in insuring against natural disasters such as floods or subsidence (when clay soils dry out they sink; the walls of houses built on them develop cracks and sometimes even collapse). Private insurance companies typically characterize such events as 'uninsurable', with the result that the property owners have to bear these risks themselves – or hope for public help if the event gets sufficient attention from the media.

The property insurance in Baden-Württemberg well illustrates the advantage of state monopolies when it comes to providing insurance against natural disasters. As long as it had its monopoly status, it could offer all of its customers comprehensive insurance cover against a wide range of elemental damages (including floods and earthquake) at a uniform premium. Only the rate for cover against earthquakes was slightly differentiated. When the market was opened to competition, it had hoped to be able to maintain this system. Given its initial market share of 100 per cent, it was in an ideal situation to succeed in this endeavour. Nevertheless, it failed. After a number of major floods in the years 1993 to 1995, it had the choice of either increasing its premium rate – and risk losing its better risks to competitors – or else finding ways of making bad risks pay more. It started sending all of those customers who had been victims of floods a letter of cancellation of their contract. It then offered to take them back, but only if they now accepted to pay the first €2500 of damage out of their own pocket. It did not fear to lose these customers to competitors because no competitor would offer contracts on these proven bad risks.

Outlook and conclusion

Since the beginning of the 1990s, Europe has witnessed a massive increase in damage from natural disasters. Political authorities begin to realize that they cannot just leave affected citizens alone, and that the current strategy of distributing state aid after the event is not a satisfactory solution. Both Spain and parts of Switzerland have public insurance monopolies which cover the population against damage due to natural catastrophes. Baden-Württemberg had such an institution and it performed admirably well until it was abolished as a result of the third EU Non-Life Insurance Directive.

It was easy for the EU to claim that 'it is in the policyholder's interest' to have the public monopolies abolished, especially if they knew nothing about the specificities of the property insurance industry. The developments on the German market over the last ten years have shown very clearly that the EU was wrong. We can only hope that the EU authorities and the national governments will admit their mistake and relax the regulatory framework and allow countries to return to well-designed state monopolies.

Culture and Media

PRIVATIZATION OF ITALIAN CULTURAL HERITAGE

Roland Benedikter

According to estimates by the United Nations Educational, Scientific and Cultural Organization (UNESCO), Italy holds approximately 30 per cent of the European cultural heritage. The Berlusconi government began privatizing part of it through its 'Law 112/2002'. By late 2003, 36 items, from antiquity to the 20th century, have been sold to international investment firms such as the American Carlyle Group and private investors, in most cases for amounts well below market value. As of 2003, hundreds more objects, among them temples, antique cities, medieval palazzos, archaeological sites, museums, beaches and islands, were waiting to be sold.

History, ideological influences and legal basis

Italy was described by the minister of cultural goods, Giuliano Urbani, as 'like a person with many houses, but also with many debts. So we have to look at which houses are dispensable.'

From the mid 1980s onwards, the growing influence of Thatcherism and neo-liberalism, combined with the inefficient and bureaucratic preservation of monuments, a chronic shortage of money in this field, the high maintenance costs of state-owned property and Italy's large budgetary deficit led to heated discussions about the privatization of the world-famous Italian museums. The rapid succession of different governments, though, allowed only small steps in this direction. In 1990, museum services were partly privatized through temporary licences; later, cultural instruction services and the organization of exhibitions followed. The adaption of various laws ensued during the 1990s, aimed at privatizing state-owned property, but with little effect. However, in 2002, Berlusconi's neo-liberal and second centre-right government, building on laws passed by former centre-left governments, introduced two important passages into the Financial Act. These later comprised Law 112/2002, which became known as the 'deficit-saver law' due to its drastic economizing measures:

- The state-owned company State Patrimony plc was founded and given possession of all state-owned estates, monuments, museums and cultural objects. Control of the company was vested with the Ministry of Economic Affairs, and a professional financial manager was hired as chief executive. Assigning de facto all cultural heritages to the Ministry of Economic Affairs was intended to improve the management of state property and to allow the use of infrastructure budget funds for preservation purposes.
- State Patrimony plc obtained the option to privatize (i.e. to sell certain listed objects in its possession) through the creation of another state-owned company, Infrastructures plc. Privatization was meant to lighten the load of the public budget, relieving it of maintenance and restoration expenditures. The conditions for sale were minimal: if the objects were under a preservation order, the Ministry of Economic Affairs, as well as the Ministry for the Protection of Historical Monuments, had to agree to the deal. For the rest, the law was rather vague, lacking clear statements about which objects may be privatized and which not. There were no additional criteria except one requiring the sale of groups of objects and not of individual objects in order to avoid too much cherry-picking, leaving objects of minor interest behind. Another problem arises with the fact that, as of 2003, there was no list encompassing all state-owned objects (estimated at 400,000), which would allow a well-planned, long-term overall sales strategy.

The situation in 2003

Based on this legislation, two major sales took place in February and April 2003, respectively. Among the 36 items sold were:

- Villa Manzoni, Rome (20th century);
- Manifattura Tabacchi, Florence (20th century);
- Archivio di Stato di Bari (19th century);
- Palazzo Correr, Venice (16th century);
- Palazzo Via dei Cambiatori, Reggio Emilia (1901);
- Palazzo Piazza del Monte, Reggio Emilia (1671);
- Palazzo Via Balbi, Genova (1677).

Significantly, not a single object was sold to a group engaged in the preservation of cultural heritage. The situation was also characterized by various other unfortunate facts:

- The incomplete list of state properties was haphazardly amended, often upon sales suggestions originating from the Ministry of Economic Affairs, as well as from regions and municipalities. No visible sales strategy was developed.
- Local proposals for a better use of state properties were usually ignored.
- Published sales lists seem intentionally lacking in transparency with regard to stipulations on cultural preservation. The *Gazzetta Ufficiale della Repubblica Italiana* (no 183, 6 August 2002) has an 800-page supplement

Figure 23
Palazzo Correr, Venice (16th century). Heavy investments in restoration awaiting the new private owners.
Source: Tobias Schäfer.

(no 163) that gives no concrete guidelines on what the relevant Ministry of Cultural Goods considers of historical importance. Therefore, it became particularly difficult for the media, for citizens and for Parliament to check the regularity of the sales operations. Senator Giovanna Melandri asked all of the right questions on 3 March 2003, about conditions, value, price and catalogue listings, but had not obtained any satisfactory answers (Melandri, 2003).

• Prices were consistently low, with properties sold even below their real estate value and at the very lowest advance price estimates of the state. It became an embarrassment that the former Minister of Culture came to serve as adviser to the Carlyle Group, which picked up the major part of objects sold so far at a give-away price.

Public sales also raised suspicion because Infrastructures plc created subcontractors, which in turn maintained close ties with international real estate firms. Furthermore, in order to accelerate sales, democratic control has been undermined. Law 112/2002 does not:

• allow the State Council to formulate restrictions;
• allow conservation stipulations to have any effect on sales;
• give any restrictions for resale to the new private proprietor.

Examples of privatized assets

A few illustrations from the diverse range of items sold in the 2003 sales help to assess the results of privatization.

The Villa Manzoni near Rome was built in 1928 for the family of count Manzoni by the internationally renowned architect Armando Brasini on the remains of an antique roman villa near the grave of Emperor Nero. The 9ha park surrounding the building of 3000 square metres was often considered to have been transformed into a public park. The price secured by the Carlyle Group of €230,000 was ridiculously low, far below its real estate value. It barely compared to the price of an apartment of 120 square metres in the popular Roman Centocelle not far from the site.

One of the best preserved industrial complexes of the architectural 'rationalism' of the 1930s, the Manifattura Tabacchi in Florence encompasses 15 factories with a total of 0.5 million cubic metres. It was sold to the Fintecna investors group, which intended to divide up the ensemble to resell at a handsome profit. International tobacco manufactures and private investors expressed interest. It seems inevitable that the historical structures will be destroyed as they do not correspond to modern concepts of manufacturing rationalization. A rescue by the city of Florence looks possible but is unlikely, involving purchase (and, thus, reversal of privatization) of the monument. Fintecna is almost certain to ask a considerably higher price of the city, making privatization, in effect, a drain of money from public to private hands. The Manifattura Tabacchi sale has been considered an example of a major failure of Italian public policy, where no mechanism had been established to distinguish between what could be sold from what had to be preserved.

No less disturbing is the case of the archaeological site of Alba Fucens of Massa d'Albe in southern Italy (Abbruzzo), an ancient city from the fourth century BC. The site includes an amphitheatre, a spa complex, a market forum, a town hall and a large sanctuary dedicated to Hercules. This site has been called one of the most important ancient Roman outposts in central Italy. The whole ensemble was offered for a price of €40,615, which was an insult according to Mario Parlati, mayor of the neighbouring city of Massa d'Albe.

But this is only the tip of the iceberg. The *Gazzetta Ufficiale della Repubblica Italiana*, which publishes objects for sale, is an 800-page document that lists some worthless old barracks and offices, but also jewels such as the Palazzo Barberini, a Baroque masterpiece that houses Rome's National Gallery of Art. The list also contains a number of islands, such as the Tuscan islands of Gorgona and Pianosa, the Villa Jovis, a huge complex of the Emperor Tiberius, sited on the island of Capri (for a mere €90,000), and 150ha of coastline on the Costa Smeralda. More catalogues were in the pipeline.

Pros and cons

The fact is that the Italian state lacks the money to properly care for its treasures. Italy has an abundance of valuable objects, including some 30,000 palazzi, villas, churches and monasteries, of which only 10,000 are well documented. Prime Minister Berlusconi and the responsible minister, Urbani, vowed not to sell any object 'of national interest'. But there was no definition available for what constitutes national interest, and some of the examples sold seemed to be of obviously high national interest.

The government's hope is that private owners would invest money and time to look after the objects. But as of 2003, many of those who expressed interest immediately disclosed that they intended to keep the objects for just a few years before selling them at a profit. The question, essentially, is whether the state will be willing to impose restrictions, including certain obligations to keep important sites accessible to the public or at least to art historians. What is more important are firm long-term rules and well-policed compliance on the maintenance of the architectural and artistic character of the sites. On the other hand, it remains highly controversial that the state should allow private owners (such as the Carlyle Group) to make profits from public goods originating from the rich Italian tradition. State President Ciampi called publicly for great caution in selling Italy's state-owned buildings and sites.

Finally, whether or not its aims could be achieved and, if so, whether or not at reasonable cost, a fundamental legal question arises concerning the premise of privatizing Italy's national treasures. Renowned Academician Giorgio Oppo, professor of law, expressed the opinion that the whole law was a spectacular expression of a lack of imagination regarding future global developments, including the growing importance of local cultural heritage, on the part of the Berlusconi majority of legislators. He, like others, raised serious doubts about the compatibility of Law 112/2002 with the Italian constitution. At the time of writing, it was uncertain if such doubts would or would not prevent the privatization of cultural heritage already under way in Italy.

THE SALZBURG FESTIVAL, AUSTRIA: AN EXAMPLE OF PUBLIC RESPONSIBILITY AND PRIVATE MONEY

Raffaela Kluge

When it comes to the pros and cons of privatization, the arts world takes a special category. As a rule, arts institutions are not self-sufficient; they depend to varying degrees upon public or private support for their subsistence.

The Salzburg Festival is known to be one of the most prominent art festivals in the world. Over the 80 years of its existence, it has done justice to its reputation by the extraordinary number and the unmet quality of annual performances – be it concerts, plays or operas. Its mixture of private and public funding could represent one possible model for contributing to a lively artistic landscape in Europe. This is not, however, an example of full privatization. As the public share may be further reduced in the future, the arts may eventually have to be financed to a greater extent by private money, as well as by the immediate beneficiaries: the spectators.

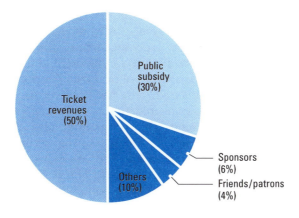

Figure 24
Breakdown of budget sources for the Salzburg Festival (2003). The festival's success
demonstrates how private and public resources can facilitate high-quality arts.
Source: Salzburg Festival.

Funding the Salzburg Festival

As a public institution, the Salzburg Festival Fund has a governing body that
comprises representatives of the city, regional and federal governments, and
the board of tourism. As one of the most prestigious and renowned arts
institutions in Austria, the Salzburg Festival has become, over the years, a very
important arena for political representation.

An astounding 50 per cent of the budget comes in through ticket sales,
some 6 per cent from private sector sponsors, 4 per cent from several friends
of the festival associations and private donors, and the remaining 10 per cent
from rentals, co-productions and TV rights (see Figure 24). Compared to
continental European standards where most arts institutions draw around 90
per cent of their budget from public subsidies, financing more than 70 per
cent independently is exceptionally high. Bearing this in mind, it is surprising
that sponsors, patrons and donors – the third most important source of income
– are not represented on the festival governing body. In the US and the UK,
private benefactors are usually well represented in arts institutions. Given the
increasing importance of private money, the Salzburg Festival might have to
adapt as well.

The state, nevertheless, remains – by law – the ultimate guarantor for the
festival, through the Salzburg Festival Fund, in case of urgent financial needs.
However, the governing body has successfully matched income and expenses
every year, so it never had to make use of this privilege.

High-class standards and audiences

One of the reasons for the success of the Salzburg Festival lies in its ambition
to continue providing top-quality culture. Salzburg has set artistic standards

and staged historic performances; but it has also, from time to time, provoked scandals with innovative and avant-garde productions.

High quality justified very expensive tickets, affordable only by the wealthy. Thus, Salzburg has become a 'must' for the rich and the beautiful from all over the world, a cultural, social and political meeting point, and also a platform for the business community. Salzburg has, however, set up a youth programme that offers low-price, sponsored tickets to young people who could not otherwise afford to attend. This programme also aims to educate future generations of audiences. As of 2003, the sponsor of this particular programme was Nestlé, one of the festival's main sponsors and one of the biggest global players in the food sector. This is a case where private money has taken on public tasks and social responsibility.

Future prospects

The Salzburg Festival has taken a road similar to the one most arts institutions in the UK were forced to take since Prime Minister Margaret Thatcher pushed her policies of slimming the public sector. Other European countries experiencing hard times in public finance look likely to be forced to follow the same example. Europe would then need a new culture of giving where citizens and corporations take direct responsibility for their arts institutions and thus contribute to the continuing development of Europe's rich cultural landscape. However, even if private-sector involvement in the arts were to grow, it appears necessary for the state to continue to be a guarantor as in the case of the Salzburg Festival.

THE GLOBAL MEDIA MONSTERS: PRIVATE MEDIA DOMINATE THE WORLD'S PUBLIC SPHERE

Dušan Reljić

The youngest of the ten global 'media monsters', a phrase coined by the London *Economist*, was about to be born in the fall of 2003. French company Vivendi Universal and General Electric (GE) Co of the US announced talks to merge the French conglomerate's entertainment assets with GE's NBC television station. The deal, considered to be worth up to US$40 billion, was the latest in a spectacular series. Staggering deals in the global media industry had peaked in January 2000 with the creation of the world's 'mega media monster', AOL Time Warner, a deal estimated to be worth US$350 billion.

Merger mania

The acquisition of Vivendi's entertainment operations – which included the Hollywood movie factory Universal Studios, cable channels such as USA and SciFi, as well as theme parks – would enhance General Electric's NBC position as a major US provider of media content. Other operations were MSNBC, a cable news channel jointly owned with Microsoft, the world's biggest software company; CNBC, a financial network jointly owned with the US business news publishing house Dow Jones; Bravo, an arts channel; and Telemundo, a US Spanish-language television station.

The US-led merger mania in the media industry during the late 1990s caused worldwide concern. In February 2000, after the AOL Time Warner integration, Walter Cronkite, the grand old man of US journalism, expressed his criticism 'of the direction that journalism has taken of late, and of the impact on democratic discourse and principles'. He thought the mergers had been 'diluting standards, dumbing down the news and making the bottom line sometimes seem like the only line'. 'We all know that economic pressures and insecurities within news organizations have reduced the scope and range of investigative reporting', Cronkite said and warned: 'In a healthy environment, dissent is encouraged and considered essential to feed a cross-fertilization of ideas and thwart the incestuous growth of stultifying uniformity' (Cronkite, 2000).

Convergence, concentration and control

Globalization of telecommunication, harnessing technical advances of mind-boggling speed, have not led purely and simply to access by more and more of the world to new sources of information and entertainment. Media markets themselves have evolved with great speed, facilitated by innovation arising from digitalization and by convergence. The effect has been a growing concentration of ownership both over the global communication channels and the content transmitted through them. The crucial trend is vertical integration, or conglomeration, of media ownership. This process originated in the US and moved on to encompass all countries that are part of the world market. In a reaction to the overwhelming expansion of privately owned media industries and their push for further liberalization on the media markets, the Council of Europe (COE) adopted on 27 January 2004 a resolution in which it called on governments to reaffirm their commitment to maintain 'a strong and vibrant independent public service broadcasting whilst adapting to the requirements of the digital age'. The argument brought forwarded by the COE, and shared by the European Union (EU), as well as many non-governmental national and international actors, is that public service broadcasting is distinguished from commercial media by its specific remit to act independently of economic and political power.

Technical convergence primarily concerns the possibility offered by digital technology. Products such as newspapers, films, and CDs, traditionally sold as physical products, are now 'dematerialized': with the help of computers, they are converted into digital data and transmitted to any spot in the world which can be reached through telecommunication. Digital technology also opened the way to multimedia – for example, the combination in a single product of voice, picture and text.

Economic convergence during the last two decades of the 20th century led to media companies moving with great speed towards concentration. The mergers were usually explained by the necessity of concentrating financial resources to cover ever-increasing production costs, particularly in the audio visual sector. Only large companies could afford to pay – for instance, the high cost of broadcasting rights for the soccer World cups and similar events that attract worldwide attention. More and more companies that traditionally operated in separate segments of the market, such as television and telecommunications (or, indeed, toy manufacturing or even the textile industry), began to unite to create a coherent 'value chain'. This could be seen, for instance, in Walt Disney Inc's production of animated cartoons, its management of theme parks based on the cartoon characters, and its sale of merchandising rights for children's clothes featuring images of the cartoon characters. Vertically integrated companies can be in a position to exploit their products at every level of the value chain.

Big players

In 1983, 50 corporations dominated the US market and the biggest media merger in history was a US$340 million deal (Bagdikian, 2000). Only four years later, the number had shrunk to 29, and by 1990 to 23. In 1997, the biggest firms numbered ten and involved the US$19 billion Disney–ABC contract, at the time the biggest media merger ever. Finally, in 2000, the creation of AOL Time Warner was more than 1000 times larger than the biggest media ownership transaction that had occurred up to 1983. The leading global 'media monsters' had annual revenues that surpassed the gross national product (GNP) of countries in the developing world and in poorer parts of Europe.

Germany's Bertelsmann, positioned at the beginning of the 21st century as the world's number four media conglomerate, was the only non-US competitor among the seven largest media holdings in the world (see Figure 25).

As of 2003, 40 to 60 national, regional or smaller global corporations occupied the second echelon of global media players. Most of them – such as Dow Jones, Reuters, Havas, Mediaset or Westdeutsche Allgemeine Zeitung (WAZ) – come from Western industrialized countries. But some from elsewhere, especially South America, were also considered important regional players – for instance, Globo, (Brazil), Clarin (Argentina) and Cisneros (Venezuela). Media markets in former communist countries of Eastern Europe represented a strong presence of foreign ownership in the media industry, particularly in the press sector. In this segment, West European companies, largely from Germany (WAZ, Bertelsmann, Springer, etc.), achieved a dominant role.

Concern over consequences

However, fewer and fewer domestic and transnational players featured in the media field. This resulted in the possibility of less diversity and reduced quality

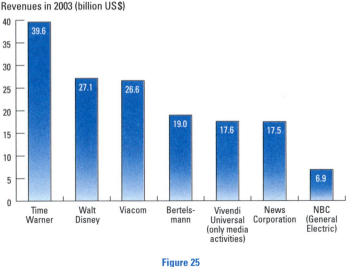

Revenues in 2003 (billion US$)

Figure 25
The seven leaders of the global media industry, 2003.
Source: Company annual reports.

in journalism. Expanding on Walter Cronkite's concern over journalistic standards, media critics point out that when there are few media owners in the mainstream, the diversity of issues and perspectives risks being reduced and political influence and interests from a few can affect the many (Shah, 2003). Excessive media concentration can have a distorting impact on the democratic process, and on broader social, cultural and economic activities. Once powerful media corporations are established, it becomes almost impossible for public authorities to reverse the development and limit the economic and often political power wielded by the 'media oligarchs'. The Campaign for Press and Broadcasting Freedom (2001), a UK non-governmental organization (NGO) working to promote plurality in mass communications, offered this description of how Rupert Murdoch, owner of News International, had used his influence on the government:

> *In the UK we have seen how such a powerful group, News International, was allowed, and indeed encouraged, to grow. In part, this was a reward for the support Rupert Murdoch gave to successive Conservative governments under Mrs Thatcher through his newspapers (the acquisition of the* Times *and the* Sunday Times *was not the subject of a referral to the Monopolies and Mergers Commission, for example). Also, the satellite service, Sky, was exempted from regulatory and other limits placed on other UK broadcasters and the newspaper publishers under the 1990 Broadcasting Act and then allowed effectively to take over its rival, BSB.*

It is worth noting that Murdoch's Fox News enthusiastically supported the US military interventions in former Yugoslavia in 1999 and in Iraq in 2003, as well as siding with much eagerness with the US government's introduction of controversial new security laws after the terrorist attacks in New York on 11 September 2001.

Gatekeepers, sources and paths

Pundits perceive three controversial issues of global competition arising from convergence and strongly affecting the freedom of choice in European media markets (Pereira, 2002). The first is the so-called gatekeeper role that companies play if they predominantly control a certain technology required to access a market. Such a company can dictate conditions and prices to competitors. This situation came up in the course of the AOL/Time Warner merger, as AOL was the leading internet access provider in the US and the only provider with a presence in most EU countries. The second issue of source in the media industry pertains usually to a company manufacturing an audio visual product and holding the copyrights. As of 2003, AOL/Time Warner possessed one of the biggest music libraries in the world and through preferential ties to Bertelsmann, another music library giant, could establish an overwhelming control of what people worldwide might read, watch or listen to. The third issue involves the possible control of 'paths' or distribution channels of media industry products. Traditionally, media industry products were sold as concrete material products such as books and CDs, or were distributed by analog terrestrial television broadcasting. New distribution forms included first the internet, but also mobile telephony, digital satellite broadcasting and similar advanced platforms. Again, AOL/Time Warner is a good example: AOL had more than 34 million subscribers worldwide who were also potential customers of movies, music and other media content produced by Time Warner.

Encourage and curb: Contrasting government acts

Concern seemed also to be growing in the US about the power of large media companies. On 3 September 2003, a US federal court blocked the controversial new Federal Communications Commission (FCC) media ownership rules pending a full judicial review. The proposed rule changes were backed by media giants, including News Corp's Fox Television News. The new rules, adopted by a 3:2 vote in June 2003 after vehement criticism from consumer advocates and other public protests, would allow a single media company to reach 45 per cent of the national television audience through local TV station ownership – up from 35 per cent. Companies would be able to own both newspapers and broadcasters in the same markets.

The European public and law-makers at the European Parliament were also engaged in a debate on the integrity of the media, which was felt to be threatened by growing concentration in the industry. In 2004, the European Parliament was due to debate a complete overhaul of the European Community's 'Television without Frontiers' directive. The directive was expected to take account of technological developments and changes in the structure of the audio visual markets. To prevent the monopolization of the global media market through increasing convergence, the EU embarked on a policy of imposing conditions on market players in order to ensure access to competitors. No company should be able to dominate the market through a technological gatekeeper role, or through control over production or distribution paths. It remained to be seen whether, together with anti-monopolistic acts of national governments, the EU's competition policy, as well as other instruments such as a revised 'Television without Frontiers' directive, would provide sufficient corrective to the evidently harmful monopolization of world media markets.

Health

PARTIAL PRIVATIZATION OF HEALTHCARE IN CHILE

Olaf Rotthaus

In 1981 the Chilean healthcare system was caught by the massive wave of privatization that flooded the country after military dictator General Augusto Pinochet orchestrated a coup in 1973. A group of highly trained economists, disciples of Milton Friedman at the University of Chicago, the so-called 'Chicago Boys', were in the centre of all efforts to transform both Chilean state and economy under the premises of neo-liberal ideology (Holst, 2001a, p16). After the military coup, they joined the government and were promoted in top positions (Gonzalez-Rossetti and Chuaqui, 2000, p3).

Following the ideas of Friedman and Hayek, they planned to transform the Chilean society and economy on the following principles:

> Freedom to choose *goods and services and to engage in any economic activity;* subsidiary role of the state, *which should limit its intervention;* the principle of economic non-discrimination *or the non-discretionary character of the law and of regulations; the principle of* equality of opportunities, *where the role of the state was constrained to satisfying basic needs in order to eliminate extreme poverty; and, finally,* the technical character of public policy-making (Gonzalez-Rossetti and Chuaqui, 2000, p69).

In 1979, the government started reforms in various public fields, such as labour relations, pensions, education, agriculture, regional administrative organization and healthcare. Minister of Labour José Pinera, with a degree not from Chicago University but from Harvard (but, nonetheless, a crusader for neo-liberal ideology to this day, at the CATO Institute), referred to these reforms as such:

> *The ... modernizations seek to introduce margins of personal freedom unknown for the Chilean people to contribute to the necessary equalization of opportunities, to give dynamism to economic development, to value the voice of experts in decisions adopted by governments which are eminently technical, in sum, to transform Chile into a modern nation where reason prevails over*

prejudice and dogmatism, and where individual freedom becomes the general rule and state intervention the exception (Gonzalez-Rossetti and Chuaqui, 2000, p71).

And with special regard to the reform of pension funds and healthcare, Pinera stated: '"Solidarity" should not continue to be the excuse for the fact that certain state monopolies are not accountable for the mandatory savings they require from workers' (Gonzalez-Rossetti and Chuaqui, 2000, p71).

After the privatization of the Chilean pension system in 1980 under these conditions, the economist-run reform agenda by the military regime focused on healthcare in 1981. Until then, healthcare in Chile had been basically the responsibility of the state. The 1952-founded national health service, Servicio Nacional de Salud (SNS), covered healthcare for blue-collar workers and provided an extended infrastructure of medical units and hospitals all over the country. White-collar workers were covered by the Servicio Medico Nacional de Empleados (SERMENA), created in 1942 by a unification of several social insurance funds. The SERMENA insured received medical care either in SNS institutions or, since 1968, also as an option by private providers. The system was accompanied by public health-oriented legislation since the 1930s, including a disease prevention act in 1938 and several successful programmes to fight communicable diseases (Holst, 2001a, pp12–16).

The 1981 reform consisted of three main measures:

1 the decentralization of the SNS into 27 (now 29) regional SNS;
2 the restructuring of the public health insurance system by establishing the Fondo Nacional de Salud (FONASA);
3 the introduction of private insurers, the Instituciones de Salud Previsional (ISAPREs) (Holst 2001a, pp12–16).

This last measure, the part-privatization of health insurance, was the decisive factor. The goal was to establish competition between the ISAPREs themselves and between ISAPREs and FONASA. According to neo-liberal ideology, competition leads to more efficacy and efficiency, and, thus, in the health sector leads in the end to a better healthcare for the insured. It has to be mentioned that the members of the military and the police, along with a few other public servants, were exempted from this competition. They could stay in their own public health funds. All other employees and pensioners were obliged to be insured either by FONASA or by one of the ISAPREs. Contribution was first set to 4 per cent of gross income, and from 1986 until the present to 7 per cent for both FONASA and ISAPREs. Contributions are only paid by the employees: the former parity between employers and employees in paying contributions was abolished.

From the beginning of the reform, ISAPREs were guaranteed ideal market conditions. No governmental regulations existed besides the 7 per cent contribution. ISAPREs are not required to accept any applicants, but FONASA is. As a result, ISAPREs can choose their insured. They 'cream off'

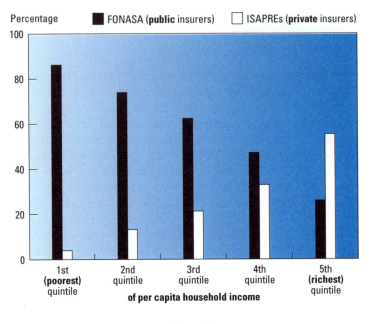

Figure 26
Health insurance coverage in Chile by household income, 1998.
Private insurers 'skim the cream' by focusing on high-income, low-health risk groups.
Source: data from Barrientos and Lloyd-Sherlock (2000).

the high income and low risk. 'The ISAPREs focus on providing insurance cover for high-frequency, low-cost services for high-income, low-health risk groups. Their marketing efforts are aimed at these groups' (Barrientos and Lloyd-Sherlock, 2000, p421). FONASA has to contract everybody else. ISAPRE premiums vary in relation to age, gender and former illnesses. Because of high co-payments in relation to risk (i.e. contributions that insured people still have to make towards treatments, up to 75 per cent of the costs for medical care), only the healthy and wealthy can afford an insurance by an ISAPRE and get high-level medical care by private providers. For example, young fertile women have to pay the highest co-payments. ISAPRE contracts frequently also include stop-loss components that limit the risk of the insurer to a certain amount. Above this amount the insured has to cover all expenses. (Jack, 2000, p39). As an analyst to the World Bank points out: 'This feature is perverse' (Jack, 2000, p39). Co-payments rise so rapidly above the age of 50 that only 4 per cent of those aged over 65 can afford private insurance (Holst, 2001a, pp16–18). Under these conditions, ISAPREs recorded rapid increases in members until the mid 1990s. By 1999, the ISAPREs insured just under a quarter of all insured, while the percentage of the FONASA insured decreased from 84 per cent in 1983 to 59 per cent in 1999.

In 1998, 55.4 per cent of individuals in the top household income quintile belonged to ISAPREs, but only 4 per cent of the lowest quintile did so. FONASA has retained the low- to middle-income groups in the formal sectors; but it also covers the overwhelming majority of the lowest two quintiles (see Figure 26).

In 1998, ISAPREs insured 27.2 per cent of those aged 25 to 49, but only 6.7 per cent of individuals aged over 65. FONASA had to insure 80.4 per cent of this age group, while the coverage between the age of 25 to 49 was 56.5 per cent. Barrientos and Lloyd-Sherlock sum up:

> *The failure by the private sector to provide health insurance cover for low-income groups, and for old-age-related and catastrophic illnesses, concentrates high health risk groups within FONASA, reinforcing service demand pressures on the publicly funded sector. Improved provision in the public sector directly undermines the ability of the private one to attract and retain affiliates* (Barrientos and Lloyd-Sherlock, 2000, p421).

In 2001, former Chilean Minister of Health Michelle Bachelet Jeria judged the consequences of the healthcare reform by the 'Chicago Boys': 'Since healthcare is determined by affiliation to a health insurance, there is injustice in access to most of all health services... Private insurers pick the young, the healthy and the well to do. Without adequate regulation there is no chance to avoid such problems, which in the end result in inefficiency, injustice, fragmentation and social splitting' (Holst, 2001a, p3).

As a result, improvements to the healthcare reform in Chile are now in progress. Remarkably, this started with the last legislative act that the military regime announced just two days before its end. An authority was established, the Superintendencia de ISAPREs, to register and control ISAPREs and their contracts and to provide information to the public (Holst, 2001a, p21). The democratic governments since 1990 have continued in this direction by widening the responsibilities of this authority and by reinforcing public health programmes, providing better access to medicine for the poor. However, the governments have faced strong resistance by private insurers, who represent an influential economic sector, since they recorded the highest returns on investment of all economic sectors in Chile.

The 2000-elected President Lagos proclaimed top priority for healthcare reform with the national healthcare objectives plan, AUGE (Plan de Acceso Universal con Garantías Explícitas). The plan includes focusing on prevention, better quality and access in ambulatory and primary healthcare and modernizing the regulations of the system (e.g. establishing a risk structure compensation between private and public insurance). Furthermore, there 56 diseases have been identified that will receive prompt attention by all parts of the healthcare services prioritized on their urgency. These diseases include cancer, cardiovascular conditions and AIDS. Patients with any of these and other severe diseases will not have to pay more than 20 per cent of co-payments; if they cannot afford to pay, they will be subsidized by the government, via a proposed solidarity fund, set up by an increase in alcohol, tobacco and fuel taxes.[1]

HEALTHCARE IN THE US

Kai Senf

The US spends more than any other country on healthcare. In 1999, total expenditure was US$1200 billion, about 12.6 per cent of gross domestic product (GDP) (in 2002, total expenditure amounted to 14.6 per cent of GDP), and this is estimated to rise to US$2000 billion by 2007. Drug prices are among the highest in the world, and spending on pharmaceutical products is expected to increase by 15 to 17 per cent per year (Cap Gemini Ernst & Young, 2002, p22).

At the same time, approximately 44 million individuals are not covered by health insurance, and it is estimated that about as many people are only inadequately insured (Friedrich Naumann Foundation, 2001). The US is the only developed country that does not offer extensive social protection against the risk of illness. The world's 'wealthiest' country is heading towards medical poverty. How come?

The American health system is primarily market oriented and dominated by private actors. This leads to two major problems (Fein, 1998a, p71):

1 funding of medical costs, especially for an increasing number of individuals who are uninsured, underinsured or otherwise unable to meet the high costs of medical care; and
2 the organization of care delivery and, especially, its growing emphasis on for-profit organizations.

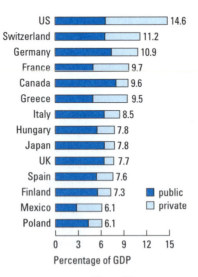

Figure 27
The US spends a higher proportion of GDP on health than any other country. It is also the only Western country where private expenditure (light shaded) exceeds public (dark shaded).
Note: data for Japan from 2001.
Source: OECD (2004).

Funding of medical costs

The health insurance of most Americans is tied to the employer. National care systems for socially disadvantaged (Medicaid) and older people (Medicare) exist and it is possible to become insured privately; but around 60 per cent of the population, and 85 per cent of American employees, are insured via their employment. Loss or a change of work results in a loss of insurance coverage before a new contract can be signed – often on worse conditions (Deppe, 1993, p43).

Up to 70 per cent of the insurance fees are paid by the employer, who decides about the type and level of employees' health insurance. Employers tend to try to minimize the costs. Smaller businesses often do not take out health insurance for employees at all because of the cost. Affected employees, unemployed and self-employed people can only take out private health insurance. This is expensive, excludes important benefits, and is not available to people already affected by illness (Jost, 1998, p47).

The proportion of wages used for health insurance increased from 20 per cent in 1977 to 27 percent in 1998. At the same time, weekly wages for privately employed workers dropped 11 per cent. As a result, younger and lower- and middle-income people tend to save money on health insurance. Millions of people who are living above the poverty level and are being excluded from national aid programmes are not, or are insufficiently, covered by health insurance.

This situation is aggravated by increasing health expenditures and restrictive social politics. Reforms during the mid 1990s restricted access to the state-run Medicaid programme. At least 675,000 individuals were expelled from the programme and now have no health insurance. It is estimated that each percentage point increase in health costs results in 300,000 more uninsured people. Some analysts forecast 54 million Americans without health insurance in 2007 if economic growth continues as during the 1990s. According to the National Coalition on Health Care, this figure could rise to 61 million people in 2009 if there is a period of economic slackness in the meantime.

The following example illustrates another problem. The chairman of a major US auto company proudly announced that his enterprise has stabilized its health insurance fees and healthcare costs. He attributes this success to hard bargaining with the hospital sector. He implies that employers who do not cut costs are irresponsible and profligate. The chairman is followed by the head of the hospital in a community where the auto manufacturer is the dominant employer. The doctor speaks about the impact of the enterprise's 'success' on the ability of the local hospital to take care of uninsured people. In striving for the 'best deal' he could cut, the manufacturer had withdrawn the 'extra' funds that helped to subsidize the care of those not fortunate enough to have insurance coverage. Unwilling and, by the way, also legally unable to turn uninsured patients away, and not ready to close services that attract non-paying patients, such as outpatient and emergency care, the hospital was eating into its endowment and would soon face bankruptcy. Cost-containment efforts had not reduced the costs of necessary care. Instead, they had saved money for one employer by withdrawing funds that provided care to a significant part of the community (Fein, 1998a, pp69–70). This story can be repeated across the US.

Organization of care delivery

In reaction to rising costs, US insurers began to use the new system of managed care to control costs and benefits. The most famous and frequent form of these managed care organizations (MCOs) are health maintenance organizations (HMOs). The managed care insurances conclude contracts with insurers and other providers of benefits in the health service. Today, approximately 80 per cent of the US health service follows the managed care principle.

Managed care is a system of integrated medical care for insurants and patients. Its major elements include the control of quality and costs, the contribution and coordination of all suppliers of health benefits, and the specific support of prevention and compliance by patients. The idea was that everybody could win if, in a three-way partnership, all parties behaved responsibly and cooperatively. Customers would take personal responsibility for minimizing their risks of illness through adopting healthy lifestyles. Doctors and hospitals would offer only necessary and appropriate treatments without 'gold plating'. Insurers would pay a reasonable rate for whatever treatments patients actually needed. As a result, customers would be assured of the healthcare they need at the lowest feasible price, healthcare providers would be able to make reasonable profits out of giving good and appropriate care, and the HMOs would advance in the market by being able to offer a better product at a lower price than conventional insurance. Over time, competition would force the rest of the market to follow suit, driving quality up and prices down.

Unfortunately, the system has not lived up to its promise because the private-sector partners have continued to put cost-cutting first. More than two-thirds of all HMOs are for-profit organizations. Their emphasis is on 'managing costs' rather than 'managing care'. They have tended to keep costs down by excluding or rationing more expensive treatments. Achievements in efficiency have not led to lower insurance fees or better medical services for customers, but only to higher shareholder value. For-profit HMOs are more expensive and offer lower quality than non-profit ones (Families USA Foundation, 1997). A 1999 study of HMOs, for example, found that: 'investor-owned HMOs are associated with reduced quality of care. Although total costs are similar in investor-owned and not-for-profit plans, the latter spend more on patient care' (Himmelstein et al, 1999). Administrative expenses of for-profit HMOs are higher than those of non-profit insurances, as well. For some organizations, overhead costs reach 25 to 33 per cent – money diverted from medical care. A 1996 survey of patient satisfaction by the Consumer Union, furthermore, showed that the 11 top-ranked HMOs were non-profit plans, while the lowest-ranked HMOs were for-profit plans (*Consumer Reports*, 1996).

The critical point of view on the ability of private health insurance companies to provide high-quality medical care for the people is perhaps best expressed by the following experts. Paul Ellwood – one of the men who coined the term HMO during the 1970s, promoted HMOs as an alternative to national health insurance and founded the influential pro-market Jackson Hole Group – came to the conclusion that it is time to discard the concept of managed competition as ineffective therapy for access, cost and quality problems of US healthcare (Fein, 1998b, p32).

Rashi Fein, professor of the economics of medicine at Harvard Medical School, says: 'Many of today's problems derive from an ethos in which healthcare and policy decisions are driven almost exclusively by competitive cost-cutting and economic consideration — and by the fact that for-profit firms have imposed their behaviour patterns on the healthcare field' (Fein, 1998b, p36).

The example of the US shows that there are limits to a privatization of the healthcare system. Regarding the suppliers of medical services, competition and market are very useful instruments to increase quality and the efficiency of costs. However, on the demand side (insurer and insurants), privatization leads to negative socio-political effects, particularly the exclusion of large numbers of the population from healthcare.

Making protection depend upon ability to afford insurance privatizes health risks. This kind of privatization has led to an insecure future for a significant number of Americans and to the danger of slipping into poverty through illnesses. This effect has been intensified by the dominance of private market-oriented insurance companies. Competition between private enterprises has not led to a higher level of quality, lower costs and less bureaucracy, as had been widely hoped for and predicted, but to exactly the opposite (see Butzlaff et al, 1998, pp279–282; Jost, 1998, p49; Deppe, 1993, pp41–46).

HEALTHCARE REFORM IN ZAMBIA

Brighton Lubansa and Brenda Mofya

An ambitious privatization/liberalization programme was launched in Zambia in 1991 by the Movement for Multiparty Democracy Government. The party had just been elected on a liberal economy ticket, and privatization and liberalization formed part of structural adjustment programmes imposed by the Bretton Wood institutions. This resulted in the transfer of ownership of many state-owned enterprises into private hands. Like many African countries, Zambia yielded to pressure to accept such programmes as a pre-requisite for much-needed aid to cushion its foreign debt burden.

Principal elements of reform

The privatization/liberalization process aimed to improve the efficiency of companies and service providers, and to turn them into more viable economic entities. The process started with the 1992 Privatization Act.

While incentives were put in place to encourage private investment in the health sector, such as the opening of privately owned hospitals and clinics, major reforms were implemented: health boards were established; regional authorities were decentralized by increasing responsibilities and participation at district level; and, most notably, user fees were introduced in government-owned hospitals. Previously, state-owned health institutions provided services with minimal or no charges.

By 2003, while some improvement in the sector had been recorded, concern continued to grow that the provision of healthcare services to the mostly poor majority of Zambians had deteriorated. It is interesting to note that despite concern and debate, the World Bank concluded that 'the health care reforms in Zambia represent an ideal model for Africa to follow' (Lynas, 1999).

Consequences of reform

A study conducted by Ngulube and Mwanza in 1995 for Zambia's Centre of Health, Science and Social Research Institute revealed that three years after the introduction of health reforms in the country's Eastern Province,[2] there was an overall drop in the provision of healthcare services. District hospitals and 15 other health facilities were studied, producing the following findings: performance by health facilities of immunization rates at only 79 per cent; poor access to health facilities; lack of laboratory diagnostic facilities; continuous shortages of medication; poor training of health workers; and a lack of knowledge by health workers of some diseases and their treatment, as, for example, with malaria (Ngulube and Mwanza, 1995). The study concluded that the implementation of health reforms in the province had not been successful due to the lack of coordination and cooperation among health services and the community, as well as a lack of coordination of the reforms themselves.

Deterioration was not limited to the Eastern Province, but extended also to the capital, Lusaka. The University Teaching Hospital (UTH) provided a clear picture of the consequences of health sector reforms. In 1999, journalist Mark Lynas found most of those unable to afford the expensive, high-quality private hospitals went to UTH. There, wards were crowded and patients received very little medical attention, some dying from easily cured conditions. Tuberculosis patients were housed close to women giving birth. Many patients could afford neither treatment nor medication (Lynas, 1999).

The healthcare situation was aggravated by the privatization of the backbone of the Zambian economy, Zambia Consolidated Copper Mines (ZCCM). Private owners, in a bid to maximize profits and increase the cost efficiency of the ZCCM, made thousands of workers redundant. The sale of ZCCM also affected the provision of social services, particularly healthcare, which used to be provided by ZCCM in every Copperbelt town. Mine hospitals offered very good health services to miners and their families, as well as to non-miners (Kangwa, S., 2001). Roan Antelope Corporation of Luanshya, which under ZCCM owned two hospitals, Roan Antelope and Luanshya, provides an example of the effects of privatization. Rather than run it as a private concern, the new owners handed over one of the hospitals to the government. In addition, the mine operated clinics in all of the townships, most of which the new owners decided to close, arguing that certain responsibilities were handled best by relevant authorities such as the Ministry of Health. Accordingly, it was claimed that this 'helps the mining companies to concentrate on their core business, which is basically mining' (Mofya, 2000).

By 2003, the private sector in Zambia seemed to have focused only on urban areas, which provided lucrative markets. Rural health centres had received little attention in the reforms, which led to their closure or complete neglect. Consequently, in order to receive healthcare, the rural populace had to travel at great expense to urban areas. Thus, health reforms for these people reduced their access to healthcare (Ngulube and Mwanza, 1995).

The HIV/AIDS crisis in Zambia had several impacts on the economy, as a whole, and on the provision of healthcare services, in particular. An estimated 1.2 million people were living with HIV/AIDS in Zambia by 2003. This created a high demand for healthcare services and a need for high-quality provision. Unfortunately, the HIV/AIDS impact on the adult productive population[3] reduced the number of potential taxpayers, thus reducing government revenues. This, in turn, affected the government's ability to provide the much-needed high-standard healthcare services.

Nevertheless, there was some noticeable improvement in the provision of healthcare services for those able to afford the fees. This could be seen at UTH where, in 1999, the fee-paying section achieved higher rates of survival for patients who could afford the deposit fee of 100,000 Kwacha (US$40). Fee-paying patients received better treatment and were kept in clean and spacious hospital rooms (Lynas, 1999).

In the case of private clinics, which mushroomed in urban Zambia due to the liberalization of the health sector, those who could afford the high-required fees continued to receive the best service. Healthcare providers in this arena, in the same vein as retail shops, competed for clients. Quality of service was cultivated in order to retain current 'customers' and to attract new ones.

Conclusions and recommendations

The Zambian reforms came at great expense to the recipients of healthcare services and benefited only a wealthy or privileged few. Although the market was liberalized and many private healthcare providers were established, the fact remains that the private sector's *raison d'être* was to make a profit without obligation or commitment to cater to the poor and rural population. As of 2003, healthcare facilities continued to worsen, as did access to health facilities for the great majority. Acute shortages of drugs and health workers continued to be poorly trained and equipped. Zambia may have received a round of applause from the International Monetary Fund (IMF) and the World Bank for its reforms, but these organizations cannot have grasped the true effects of the policies imposed on this poverty-stricken African country.

A rush to reform under pressure caused real damage to Zambia's vital social sector. Health reforms may have been more successful if delayed in order to analyse the results of privatization in other sectors. This would also have given more time to prepare the population for change. More importantly, increased provision of social services by the private sector might have been balanced with regulation to prevent profits gained at the expense of the health of the poor.

PHARMACEUTICAL RESEARCH AND DEVELOPMENT FOR NEGLECTED DISEASES: MARKET FAILURES AND THE CASE OF SLEEPING SICKNESS

Tobias Luppe

By 2003, the situation in pharmaceutical research and development could be described as a fatal 90:10 imbalance: 90 per cent of health-related investment is directed towards only 10 per cent of the world's population. Not surprisingly, this investment focused on the needs of people living in the US, Europe and Japan.

Direction and results of private-sector influence

Over the last decades of the 20th century, pharmaceutical research and development was increasingly financed by private companies. Using patent legislation as the primary incentive for investment, governments gradually withdrew from the pharmaceutical sector with the aim of introducing competition as a dynamic force into the market, fostering the development of innovative drugs.

Thus, potentially live-saving drugs became commodities, having to prove their added value in cost–benefit calculations rather than in health benefits. Consequently, research and development of medicines came to be steered by expected profits, rather than by a drive to meet needs and improve health (see Figure 29). Subject to fierce competition and shareholders' scrutiny, pharmaceutical companies have been forced increasingly to 'rationalize' their activities (i.e. interrupting unprofitable research activities or closing down production lines of unprofitable medicines). Moreover, in their search for profits, companies have become increasingly interested in sectors that are not strictly medical, such as fitness, performance and beauty. These changes helped to create a situation where the health problems of the majority of the world's population came to be ignored and their diseases neglected.

R&D spending (billion US$)

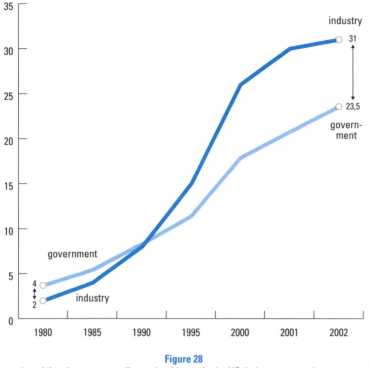

Figure 28
Research and development spending on healthcare in the US. Industry overtook government in
the early 1990s.
Source: data from National Sciences Foundation (1999, p20); PhRMA (2004, p39).

With companies increasingly dependent upon the enormous revenues generated by very few blockbuster drugs, no capacity was left for research and development (R&D) into diseases that primarily affect the poor. As one strategy in the search for alternatives to blockbusters whose patents expire, big companies turned to mergers, resulting in an increasingly centralized market and the repetitive review of R&D portfolios. As research showed in 2000, of the top ten companies, occupying 48.5 per cent of the world market, two were not producing any medicines for tropical pathologies and six had no research activities in this field. Strikingly, it was predominantly European companies that remained concerned with tropical diseases – a legacy from colonial times. In time, these efforts, too, will inevitably cease (Drugs for Neglected Diseases Working Group, 2001, p12). R&D into sleeping sickness, as well as production of therapeutic tools against the disease, represents an example of such fatal change.

Sleeping sickness: An unprofitable disease

Sleeping sickness (Human African *Trypanosomiasis*) is a parasitic disease endemic on the African continent. The disease derives its name from its

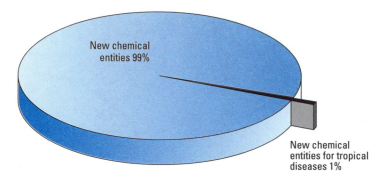

Figure 29

Lack of research and development for tropical diseases. Only 1% of all new chemical entities are used for therapeutic innovations on tropical diseases.
Source: data from Trouiller et al (2002).

classical symptoms: in the second stage of the disease, the parasites cross the blood-brain barrier, causing sleep disturbances that progress into coma. If not adequately treated, sleeping sickness is 100 per cent fatal. Sixty million people were at risk of the disease worldwide by 2002 (Stich et al, 2002).

For decades, private pharmaceutical companies have not found it profitable enough to invest in new sleeping sickness drugs. Existing medicines began long ago to lose impact due to parasite resistance. Moreover, the toxic and sometimes lethal side effects of the medicines used to treat the second stage of the disease made them an unbearable choice for doctors. The drug melarsoprol, used as a first-line treatment, kills 1 in 20 patients through its side effects (Legros et al, 2002, p439). The substance contains arsine, making the solvent to be injected aggressive enough to melt plastic syringes so that it can be administered only in glass syringes. Doctors knowingly intoxicate their patients hoping that the parasites will die first! Patients describe the feeling of a melarsoprol injection as 'chilli going up the veins'. Side effects, treatment failure and fear of death cause a highly tense atmosphere in treatment centres using melarsoprol. Pushed by additional epidemiological factors, by the late 1980s, the number of cases was back up to the extremely high 1940s level (see Figure 30). Doctors in Central Africa were faced with a devastating public health problem almost empty handed.

An unprofitable treatment

The early 1980s brought a glimmer of hope for the 500,000 people making up the annual statistics of those infected with sleeping sickness. A French pharmaceutical research institute developed an anti-cancer drug, eflornithine, which was found to be effective against sleeping sickness. Although not easy to administer, it had far fewer side effects than existing medicines. Furthermore, it was potent enough to cure even comatose patients. It soon became known as the 'resurrection drug'. For the first time in 50 years, doctors

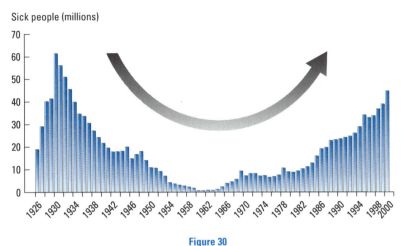

Sick people (millions)

Figure 30
Incidence of sleeping sickness over time. Sleeping sickness comes in very long cycles. The recent uprising of the epidemic was accompanied by an embarrassing absence between 1995 and 2001 of the relevant drug production because companies saw no profits.
Source: WHO (pers. comm.).

had a new weapon to fight the disease. It comes as no surprise that the drug was a by-product rather than the outcome of a guided research effort into this tropical disease. Yet, high hopes were crushed by the forces of the progressively competitive pharmaceutical market. In 1995, after merging with the original producer companies, Hoechst Marion Roussell stopped the production of eflornithine. The reason: a lack of return on investment. The patent was handed over to the World Health Organization (WHO) (Sjoerdsma, 2000).

As stocks gradually ran out, the WHO and Médecins sans Frontières (MSF), an international medical relief agency involved in fighting sleeping sickness, desperately searched for a new production site for eflornithine. Given the toxicity of melarsoprol, growing resistance and empty research pipelines, eflornithine was the only effective and responsible treatment left for the increasing number of sleeping sickness patients. At the beginning of the new millennium, this resulted in a seemingly paradoxical situation: although demand for the drug was higher than ever before, no supplier could be found. Unfortunately, this demand arose from an unprofitable market. The patients were simply too poor to be cured. Increasing competition, mergers and cost–benefit analysis in the pharmaceutical sector had left no place for poor patients.

At the end of the year 2000, the pharmaceutical company Bristol-Myers Squibb (BMS) surprised the medical world by bringing eflornithine back into production. However, this move was not designed to help the 150,000 patients who would die from sleeping sickness that year. Vaniqa™, an eflornithine-based cosmetic lotion, targeted a much more affluent population: female Americans seeking a depilatory facial treatment. Hair removal as a potential effect of eflornithine had been discovered by the company in collaboration with Gillette. At US$100 per month and patient, Vaniqa™

promised a far higher return on investment than the drug produced for African patients trying to live often on less than the equivalent of US$50 per month. This time, small demand from a very profitable market pushed companies to engage. Patients in Africa were dying of melarsoprol-resistant sleeping sickness in large numbers while the component necessary to save their lives was only available as a cosmetic cream for the market of the rich.

Intense pressure from the WHO and organizations such as MSF – which had started its worldwide Access to Essential Medicines Campaign in 1999 – led to a surprising change in 2001: the company Aventis (the result of yet another merger between several pharmaceutical companies, and the successor to Hoechst et al) signed a deal with the WHO to restart the production of eflornithine for the treatment of sleeping sickness patients. Aventis guaranteed the substance's availability for a period of five years. BMS also did its modest part by financing the first year of production. Since 2001, eflornithine was available again and has been used successfully by MSF and other organizations in Africa.

Despite this good news, as of 2003 problems remained: MSF and the WHO were still looking for a company willing to produce eflornithine once the production period guaranteed by Aventis expires in 2006. So far, anything beyond this date is still uncertain. Furthermore, new research and development was desperately needed into innovative treatment options since eflornithine is difficult to administer and might soon become ineffective due to drug-resistant strains. Private company research pipelines were still empty.

Conclusion

The story of eflornithine exemplifies some consequences of the privatization and liberalization of the pharmaceutical market and potential ad hoc remedies. Research and development into new medical tools have accelerated dramatically, resulting in almost 1400 new chemical entities marketed since 1975 (Trouiller et al, 2002). This could be regarded as a positive effect of privatization. But, as in the case of eflornithine, it is highly questionable whether privatization and the competition it brings really result in medicines needed by the majority of the world's population. Charities such as MSF cannot do much but point out the consequences of market failure. The interim solution to the eflornithine shortage, like similar ad hoc measures, lacks the global vision and sustainability needed to tackle the situation. Intervention by governments could correct the fatal imbalance and create a global system that takes into account the social, as well as the economic, dimension of pharmaceutical research and development. The existing system, relying heavily on patents and competition, yields a number of shortcomings which are fatal to millions of human beings in developing countries every year.

Education

EDUCATION IN CHILE

Ernst Hillebrand

Out of the blue, Santiago de Chile students took to the streets in May 2002, in wild protest against plans to raise the prices of preferential student tickets for public transport by 10 per cent. The entire nation was flabbergasted by the evening news showing their sons (and a few daughters) running amok, attacking policemen, demolishing street signs and smashing traffic lights. The state struck back relentlessly. 'If youngsters want to shorten their lives by spending up to ten years in prison, they may go on like this', was the reaction of the deputy home secretary in his first public comments – strong words in a country relatively lenient towards horrifying crimes committed by the Pinochet regime. A deeper cause than ticket prices must have been behind the demonstrations. According to close observers, the main reason for the outcry lay in a deep frustration with the educational system which appears to have become a costly dead end for many young Chileans.

Privatization of the education system

Much of the educational system, like other sectors of the Chilean economy, had been privatized and de-nationalized on the advice of the neo-liberal 'Chicago boys'[1] called in by Augusto Pinochet during the late 1970s. Based on the belief that education is a service sector like any other, where the market would ensure the best delivery, the educational system was structured in three segments: an expensive elite private education, from kindergarten to university; a state-subsidized, but church-dominated, segment; and public education run and financed by municipalities. Most young Chileans find themselves stuck in the latter. Here, financial conditions remain poor, infrastructure bad and failure rates high. The lack of educational achievement contrasts greatly with the private segment. This is largely due to the fact that private schools offer, over the whole schooling period, 40 per cent more lessons than public ones.

At university, the picture is somewhat different. Here, the mix of private and public institutions sees a number of public or publicly subsidized universities maintaining international prestige and attracting the elites from Chile and abroad. Notably, the Catholic University of Santiago and the Universidad de Chile, where the best students receive stipends from the state, are known as two of the best in Latin America.

Private universities were introduced during the Pinochet period, with a view to catering to the wealthy and academic elites, further educating them for the competitive world and in the Catholic values of the ruling system. A conspicuous case in point is the Universidad de los Andes, located in an exclusive suburb of Santiago and run by Opus Dei, the ultra-conservative Catholic organization. But competition also reigns in this area, and so Opus Dei – which expanded its operation to several colleges and two universities in Chile – has to compete with a still more fundamentalist organization: the Legionarios de Christo, itself overseeing at least two universities.

However, the bulk of the private university sector makes offers to weaker students and students from poorer and lower-middle classes who cannot afford the high tuition fees even of the good public universities. Enrolment at these private universities, offering a wide variety of courses and qualifications, soared by 450 per cent within ten years from the early 1990s. Yet, in order to afford the fees, students, as a rule, have to work, often at night, creating conditions not exactly the best for academic success.

Consequences of privatization

It is not easy to evaluate the Chilean experience. Compared to the 1960s, when only 0.2 per cent of the population made it to a university degree, the situation improved dramatically. The economic stabilization of the late 1980s and the boom years of the 1990s fundamentally improved the country's situation, including its education sector. During that decade, 25 per cent of those leaving Chile's schools got a chance at university, and 70 per cent of those entering university in 2003 came from families with no academic tradition. Much of the educational progress was made in the post-Pinochet democracy years, with a tripling of public expenditure on education since 1990, while the Pinochet regime cut university spending by 40 per cent.

But there are clear signs of what even liberal economists should see as market failure: between 1996 and 2002, the cost of a university education increased by an average of 41.7 per cent (34.9 per cent in public universities and 44.1 per cent in private universities). The average tuition fees in Chilean universities exceeded the Latin American average. This situation generated a high dropout rate, ranging from 30 to 50 per cent of students who enrol. If a middle-income family had to pay 30 per cent of its income for higher education in 2003, the projection, according to specialists, is alarming. By 2020, this figure could rise to 66 per cent – for just one child. During the 1990s, the country became flooded with social science and economics graduates, more cheaply trained, surviving as taxi drivers or accepting unpaid internships with very vague hopes, ultimately, of a decent job. In the meantime, there persists a shortage of academics trained for a technology-based, rather than a resource-based, economy. Poor families, especially those of native Indian origin, still have very poor prospects. Ernesto Schiefelbein, former education minister, concluded that Chile's education system 'is bad and unjust'.

COMMUNITY-MANAGED BASIC EDUCATION IN GUATEMALA: A SOLUTION FOR THE POOR?

Sabine Speiser

Basic education is a human right and a public commitment, stressed repeatedly since the United Nations Educational Summit of 1990 and during the international 'Education for All' campaign launched in 1998, but still not achieved.[2] Guatemala, the country with the largest population in Central America, ranks among the least developed Latin American countries in terms of basic education. Annual dropout rates average 11.4 per cent and are highest in the first grade at 17.3 per cent (World Bank, 2001b). These, and low enrolment rates, particularly affect the Maya population, which represents around 60 per cent of the national population. While the United Nations Development Programme (UNDP) reports an average share of 2.8 per cent of gross domestic product (GDP) for education in countries with a low Human Development Index, Guatemala, at 1.7 per cent, ranks far below its Latin American neighbours (UNDP, 2003). The high numbers of bilateral and multilateral development projects after the Peace Treaties of 1996 were unable to substantially influence this standing.

Figure 31
A community school in Guatemala.
Source: Antje Begemann.

There are two exceptions: one is completely private schools, where the upper class can purchase a better education for their children with relative independence from the public education system. The other is PRONADE (Programa Nacional de Autogestión para el Desarrollo Educativo), the subject of this snapshot. PRONADE is a community-managed primary education programme which deserves analysis as a particular non-profit form of privatization. It was designed to focus on those excluded from the education system: the rural, mainly indigenous poor in remote areas. The programme was established in order to increase enrolment, especially during the first years of primary education.

In Guatemala itself, PRONADE is controversial and widely discussed as a specific model for decentralization[3] which, together with general education, is one of the basic agreements in the Peace Treaties of 1996; as a privatization that weakens the trade unions of teachers, who are the main opponents of the programme; and as a way of achieving universal primary education.

How PRONADE works

PRONADE is delivered through a new network of local education committees (*comités educativos*, or COEDUCAs) that manage community schools (*escuelas de autogestión comunitaria*, or EACs). The Ministry of Education contracted institutions for educational services (*instituciones de servicios educativos*, or ISEs), usually non-governmental organizations (NGOs), to identify, organize, legalize and support COEDUCAs, and to train the teachers and prepare information material about schools and communities. At the national level, a specialized technical unit was established to work closely with the minister of education.

COEDUCA members were primarily rural people who took charge of school management, contracting teachers, the management of infrastructure and equipment and the provision of lunches. As of 2003, PRONADE was active in 4162 communities with 12,644 teachers and 386,038 students, and still with planned expansion ahead (Departamento de Informática de PRONADE, 2003).

Consequences of community management

PRONADE definitely opened and widened access to primary education in rural areas: nearly 400,000 additional children were enrolled from 1995. It is unlikely that the Ministry of Education would have succeeded to the same degree by establishing 'normal' schools in the rural and distant areas targeted by PRONADE. The programme enjoys substantial support from the World Bank, the German KfW Bank for Reconstruction and others; but 88 per cent of its overall costs are covered by the national government of Guatemala. Whether such external money would have been equally successfully applied if it had been targeted at the established education system remains an open question.

Obviously, every child attending school is one child less without basic education, and this is valuable and a step towards implementing the internationally agreed Millennium Development Goals (MDGs) and the commitments to Education for All. However, by 2003, it was still not possible to guarantee the necessary quality of basic education through PRONADE structures.

Adults with little or no formal education themselves represented the majority of COEDUCA members. They were doing very well in providing necessary support to the formal education of their children by managing the schools. But it would be difficult or even impossible to expect them to supervise the quality of education in their schools.

Due to the control of teachers' work by regular COEDUCA visits to schools, students' school hours are increasing, which is likely to have a long-term effect on achievements. This has been the experience at least within a similar programme, EDUCO, in neighbouring El Salvador (World Bank Group, 1998). It is also a good example of how close contact between organized parents (clients) and teachers (providers) can improve school services and how accountability works in the direct relationship between clients and providers. However, the question remains as to whether these positive results are influenced or not by the other tasks given to COEDUCAs, such as the financial management of their community schools.

Clear standards and regulations for educational quality at the primary level were not in place by 2003. Parents did not have the technical competence to set and enforce educational standards, and Guatemala's NGO sector, employed as ISEs, did not have sufficient capacity to assume the task of educational quality control and improvement. There is, therefore, a need for the conventional educational system to help supervise and raise the standards of community schools – even though the 'normal' public schools also need to improve.

Usually, privatization is expected to increase efficiency. PRONADE schools and teachers do not seem to be cheaper for the state, but the ministry's calculations do not allow for any further conclusion on this matter. The bilateral and multilateral development institutions have substantially supported the PRONADE system as a way of making up the lack of educational services in rural areas, which is in line with the donors' focus on poverty alleviation. But the evaluations available do not yet yield clear assessment of the efficiency of the system.

The indigenous Maya people, as the majority of the country's population, especially in rural areas, are still marginalized and discriminated against. Generally, the Guatemalan educational system has been slow to recognize rights to bilingual and intercultural education, and the PRONADE schools are no exception.[4]

Little is known about PRONADE's impact on gender equality in a country where the majority of families still prefer their sons to be educated if the resources are not sufficient to send all of their children to school. But PRONADE provides an important element for female education – namely, neighbourhood schools – at least during the first school years. In terms of teachers, the programme does not show much of a gender balance; usually, women are neither eager nor able to take jobs in remote areas.

In a country like Guatemala with a long oligarchic and centralistic tradition, the fact that the population, particularly the poor Maya population, has an opportunity to participate actively with regard to their own public services is progress. The qualification gained by COEDUCAs to manage small schools, including the financial aspects and organization, created steps towards participation in local democratic control and the development of the necessary competences. The opportunity constituted an advantage for local people, even if their willingness to participate was limited by the harsh experiences of the long civil war. But, by 2003, it was still an open question as to whether the very poor Maya population in remote areas would succeed in moving the government to a pro-poor orientation.

Community management of education: The best solution for the poor?

Community-based school management is a specific form of privatization. Strictly speaking, it is not a shift of property and property rights or user rights from the public to the private sector since private enterprise is not involved. Basic education for poor populations is not a sector where money can be made, but rather an area of social responsibility. Although COEDUCAs could be considered analogous to non-profit organizations, their funding is guaranteed by the Ministry of Education, removing any responsibility to establish income sources even while external financing supports public funding. 'Private' in this sense, then, means civil, largely supported by national government funds, and self-managing, and as such offers an extension of the meaning of privatization.

Community-based education, as shown in the example of PRONADE, should be seen as a specific type of public–community partnership between the government (via the Ministry of Education), the community (via its COEDUCA) and organized civil society (via the ISEs, usually NGOs, participating as an intermediary between them). The government subcontracts services with two different institutions: COEDUCAs for local school management and ISEs for their support. In this way, two public governmental tasks of the education system are passed on to civil institutions, while only the task of financial distribution remains with the ministry.

Conclusion

Who wins and who loses? At first glance it seems to be a win–win situation, with the community obtaining education for its children, ISEs contracted, and the ministry achieving higher enrolment rates, especially of the poor, the indigenous and the most marginalized children. However, as already mentioned, teachers and their unions are concerned about loss of employment rights and weakening of the unions. PRONADE teachers are contracted by the COEDUCA for one year at a time, without sickness insurance or the job security enjoyed by teachers contracted for the public schools, who are employed as civil servants until retirement by the national government.

It can also be argued that the children – especially rural poor and Maya children – do not win enough. PRONADE schools were not able to offer the full cycle of nine years of basic education, and the necessary reforms of the educational system were not in place by 2003. PRONADE's genuine success in extending basic education to a further half a million children by 2003 has improved the ministry's record in relation to the Peace Treaties of 1996 and its international reputation. But this may have taken pressure off the ministry to make progress on broader reforms of the education system, which have been under discussion for years. On the other hand, it would be unfair to expect the PRONADE system to reform the whole education sector in Guatemala. It may be a model adaptable to certain circumstances, but it can improve its outcomes only if the public education structures in place fulfil their tasks and support basic standards, especially for quality and equality.

Models such as PRONADE may have a positive effect on access to primary education, but are not designed to cover issues of quality and equality. In 2003, risks remained of deepening the divide between groups in society, especially along ethnic lines. While the debate in Guatemala compared normal public schools with PRONADE schools, the only academically good education was still beyond both of these systems and in upper-class private education, where education had become not only a good but also a business.

THE INCREASING PRIVATIZATION OF UNIVERSITIES IN TANZANIA

Verdiana G. Masanja and Michael von Hauff

Following Tanzania's independence in 1961, the tertiary education sector, which also includes its universities, expanded rapidly and also changed structurally. It should, however, be noted that these changes did not speed up appreciably until the 1990s, when the programme of liberalization began.

In 1961, the University of Dar es Salaam (UDSM) was the only institution of higher education in Tanzania, and it still remains the country's flagship university to this day. By June 2004, UDSM had three campuses with 16 faculties, 5 institutes and 1 bureau. It was only in 1984 that UDSM was split into two; the then Faculty of Agriculture at Morogoro Campus became autonomous and was named Sokoine University of Agriculture. These were the only two public universities until 1991, when the policy of liberalization started and the government allowed privatization of higher education.

Trends leading to liberalization

Pre-independence, university education in East Africa was given at Makerere in Uganda, then a college of the University of London. The Royal Technical College (RTC) in Nairobi (later the University of Nairobi), in Kenya, was established in 1956. As Tanganyika[5] was gaining independence in 1961, the

University College of Dar es Salaam was established as a constituent college of the University of London. The three, Nairobi, Makerere and Dar es Salaam, formed the University of East Africa in 1963, which in 1970 became autonomous national universities in each of the three countries, Kenya, Uganda and Tanzania. At independence, in 1961, the enrolment of Tanganyikans in schools and higher education institutions was very low: less than 200 students attended a university (out of a total population of 10 million) and only 0.2 per cent of the population of Tanganyikans were enrolled in primary schools, even less in secondary schools (URT, 1998, p20).

Even though the population of Tanganyika was larger than those of the two other East African (EA) countries, Tanganyika lagged behind in participation rate in higher education in terms of enrolment rate, institutional development and proportionate representation. Such a trend has been maintained (URT, 1998, p48).

Immediately after independence, Tanganyika worked towards the Africanization of the high-level human resources in key government positions. Among others, Tanzania implemented the Education for Self-reliance (ESR) policy in 1974 that attempted to move away from a Eurocentric education system to one that was relevant to the rural livelihoods of most of Tanzanians. Under the ESR, universal primary education (UPE) was implemented as of 1977 and led to great achievements, where the nation attained nearly 100 per cent gross enrolment ratio in primary education by 1980 (Masanja et al, 2004 p2). Concerted efforts were also made to localize higher education and make it relevant to the circumstance of the country. Students would be admitted into higher learning institutions after two years' work experience. This resulted in a decade (1974–1984) of under-utilization of university education by more than 25 per cent, with women mostly affected and a predominantly older student population. This led, in 1984, to a revision of the 1974 ESR policy; students could get admitted directly. Applicants began to surpass enrolment capacity and the student population age profile became younger. The demand for higher education also became increasingly high.

Under ESR the philosophy was to have a restricted higher-level education to match the available employment positions, while attaining UPE. Until 1992, higher education in Tanzania remained largely public and quite small, expanding from 12 institutions in 1972 to 16 in 1992 (URT, 1998, pp27–30). Until 1992, only Nyengezi Social Training Institute (established in 1960) was non-governmental, belonging to the Catholic Church.

Resulting from a run-down economy and social sector, mainly due to the oil crisis and the war with Idi Amin of Uganda, structural adjustment programmes (SAPs) were introduced to make the country eligible to borrow from the International Monetary Fund (IMF) and the World Bank. The SAPs introduced cost-sharing in social services. This contributed to almost a decade of continual decline in government allocations to education, resulting in the deterioration of education provision and reversed the gains Tanzania had made by implementing the 1974 UPE framework. Due to lack of funds for an expansion of public universities, Tanzania yielded to pressures to allow private higher education.

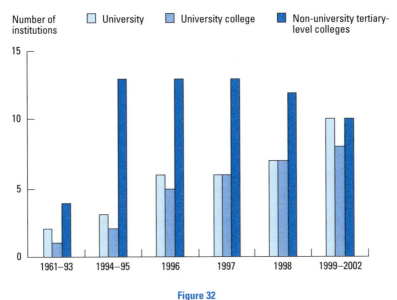

Figure 32
Numbers of tertiary education institutions in Tanzania. Liberalization led to an expansion of tertiary-level institutions in Tanzania. Since 1997 the number of universities has increased due to upgrades of non-university institutions by private investors.
Source: von Hauff and Masanja (2002).

Tertiary-level expansion

Liberalization then led to the expansion of the university sector, although this did not really take hold until 1997. Rather than a process solely of expansion, it also involved upgrading (and consequently re-naming) non-university tertiary-level colleges to the university status (see Figure 32).

Six non-university-level institutions were upgraded to university status by June 2004, including the Ardhi Institute, which became the University College of Lands and Architectural Studies (UCLAS) of UDSM. The Tanzania School of Journalism became the Institute of Mass Communication of UDSM, the former Nyegezi Social Training Institute (NSTI) was re-instituted as the St Augustine University of Tanzania, the Institute of Development Management was upgraded to university level and renamed Mzumbe University and the Kunduchi Marine Institute was upgraded to be the Faculty of Aquatic Sciences of the University of Dar es Salaam. By June 2003, eight new universities were established, of which only one is owned by the government – the others by religious organizations (five by Christian organizations, one by a Moslem organization and two by Indian organizations). Non-university-level institutions numbered 13 in 2003.

By 2003, two trends looked set to continue: the increase in the number of private universities and the shift away from the non-university tertiary sector to the university sector. Other non-university tertiary-level institutions were expected to soon gain university status. A further nine institutions had applied for accreditation, although these applications were still at a very preliminary stage. The number of institutions applying for accreditation was predicted to increase by more than ten within a few years.

Such changes have to be seen against the background of a national economic crisis and a resulting crisis in the tertiary education sector in Tanzania. The crisis in higher education took hold during the late 1980s. In response, the government began to look for the best strategies to ensure financial sustainability. Task forces were formed to advise on short- and long-term developments. The crisis had manifested itself in a wide range of problems, including budget cuts, low enrolment figures, poor infrastructure, and poor teaching and learning conditions. Many of the problems had resulted from the global economic crisis, which caused Tanzania's external debt and debt repayment obligations to increase, which, in turn, meant that Tanzania (like many other African countries) was unable to provide adequate funds for tertiary-level education. Tanzania already lagged well behind other sub-Saharan African countries with regard to the percentage of population enrolled in tertiary education (i.e. 0.27 per cent university-age cohort participation rate; see von Hauff and Masanja, 2002).

In 1999/2000, a total of 6214 high school graduates qualified for university study; but the state universities could cater for only 3069 of them. In other words, 3145 could only attend other tertiary educational institutions or study at private universities. This prompted Tanzania to intensify efforts to provide tertiary-level education despite the financial crisis. Privatization seemed like a practical way of increasing investments in the tertiary sector. The price was the introduction of private institutions which charge tuition fees and private candidates in public institutions who are charged tuition fees.

Consequences of tertiary-level expansion

The increasing privatization of the Tanzanian education system seems to have contributed to increasing social inequality. This appears to be despite the fact that liberalization and structural reforms led to a remarkable reduction of inflation, from 33.4 per cent in 1994 to 5.9 per cent in June 2000. The country also enjoyed increased economic growth, reaching 5.5 per cent in 2001, from negative growth several years earlier. For 2003, growth was expected even to reach 6 per cent. However, while the lower inflation rate has contributed to certain income stability, especially in the lower-income groups, lower-income groups have barely participated in economic growth. Since the mid 1980s, the number of people living in poverty has risen and by 2003 it was more than 50 per cent (von Hauff and Masanja, 2002).

The growing disparity in incomes and the increasing number of families living in poverty led to an income-dependent process of selection in school and university education, as well as other sectors. Since the privatization of education, it is young people from households with higher levels of income who are increasingly enjoying quality education and, hence, have a better chance of benefiting from university education. This process could be alleviated if universities offered scholarships and loans to students from lower-income groups. However, by 2003, there were only a few scholarship programmes in Tanzania, and this situation will not change appreciably in the short term. In June 2004, the government passed a bill on student loans which has raised substantial controversy with regard to the terms and conditions not being pro-poor.

Conclusion

From the second half of the 1990s, Tanzania's policy of liberalization allowed private universities to come into being, creating additional university places that were urgently needed. Yet, the private universities supported only a student body drawn mainly from affluent families. As the proportion of people living in poverty increased dramatically during the 1990s, a considerable section of the young population remained excluded from university education, particularly as financial contribution at public universities was also introduced as a result of international pressure. By 2003, there were no schemes in Tanzania sufficient to provide a lasting solution to this dilemma.

Pensions

A WEAK SPOT IN THE US PRIVATE PENSION SYSTEM

Beate Klein

Robert Thornton thought he had it made. The 55-year-old field technician was planning to retire from Lucent Technologies last year with US$263,000 in his 401(k)[1] plan. Then the telecom giant tanked, and his nest egg disappeared. 'I had all of my plan invested in Lucent', he laments. By the end of 2000, Lucent was down 80 per cent. Thornton, who now works for Avaya, a Lucent spin-off, has postponed his retirement for another five years (Braham, 2001)

This 2001 *Business Week* report highlights a plight common among middle-class US workers caught in a trap of dependency on company pension plans. By 2003, given the poor future predicted for already meagre social security, the potential risks of private plans came increasingly under the spotlight.

The structure of US private pension plans

In the US there are two main types of private pension plans offered by employers: defined benefit (DB) plans (often called 'traditional') and defined contribution (DC) plans, of which the most common is the 401(k). As social security[2] replaces only 41–47 per cent of a worker's pre-retirement income (about half of what is needed) (Economic Policy Institute, 2003), private plans are a way of providing an additional pension.

Defined benefit plans guarantee a set level of retirement income usually based on salary and years of service. Contributions to a pension trust are made by the employer. The employer bears the risk of stock market difficulties: if a trust is under-funded, the employer is obligated to fill up its pension fund (General Motors, for example, in 2002, had to pay US$2.2 billion into its fund) (Bigler, 2002). In addition, DB plans are insured: 'If a defined benefit plan terminates with insufficient assets to pay promised benefits, the Pension Benefit Guaranty Corporation (PBGC[3]) provides plan termination insurance to pay participants' pension benefits up to certain limits' (GAO, 2002a).

Defined contribution plans, by contrast, shift the risk of investment from employers to employees. With DCs, employees contribute defined parts of their salary into an individual account; but the value of their retirement benefits depends upon stock market success and upon their own knowledge of investing, which a lot of employees do not have. Companies typically offer a menu of investment options, usually including their own stock, which company employees can choose as their major fund for retirement, instead of diversifying their savings. Companies also often match their employees' contributions with company stock. Such additional stocks usually cannot be sold before the employee's 50th birthday.

From paper gains to painful losses

Robert Thornton is not the only one who had to change plans for retirement. With the crash of Enron, WorldCom and others, workers lost billions of dollars with their 401(k) plans. The combined loss of thousands of Enron employees alone totalled nearly US$1 billion. More than 60 per cent of the assets held by Enron's 401(k) retirement plan were shares of Enron stock. When the company's difficulties became known, most of the employees were not allowed to sell their stocks and upon Enron's bankruptcy lost what they had hoped would fund their retirement. For most workers in this situation, this meant that they would have to work much longer than originally planned and try to make up for the losses sustained. For older employees, it brought the possibility of having to continue to work for a living even when officially retired.

There has been a shift over the past 20 years from defined benefit plans to defined contribution (especially 401(k)) plans, both of which are offered by employers. 'The extended bull market helped popularize 401(k) plans, which happened to be introduced just as the long boom began in the early 1980s' (Hechinger, 2002).

By 2003, after long believing themselves on the losing side, many of those who chose the traditional pension scheme seemed to be far better off than even some of their own family members:

'I don't want to flaunt it', Mr O'Connor, 51, says. 'I remember when everyone was building up millions in their 401(k)s. I thought: "My god, how good they had it." Now they're going to struggle for I don't know how long. All of a sudden, I'm the guy who looks like he's got the bull by the horns.' Mr O'Connor's cousin, Mr Lassandrello, 50, like most employees of private companies, has long relied on a 401(k) retirement plan. When the stock market soared, his nest egg seemed destined to provide more comfortable retirement than his cousin's pension. But in the market tumble of the last two years, Mr Lassandrello's retirement savings plunged 30 per cent. If he stopped working now and wanted to be sure he wouldn't outlive his money, he could just draw US$28,000 a year. His cousin, Mr O'Connor, would be able to retire at 51, expecting to receive US $54,000 a year (Hechinger, 2002).

But Mr Lassandrello would still be quite well off: despite the fact that as of 2003, social security would provide retirees with an average of only US$800 per month, many American workers did not have any private pension scheme offered by an employer at all. Social security still provided 31 per cent of those aged 65 and older with 90 to 100 per cent of their income (AARP, 2003). According to the US General Accounting Office (GAO, 2001), of all workers earning less than US$40,000 per year, only 38 per cent had a private pension plan. Half of working men participated in a pension plan, but only 44 per cent of working women:

> *Among the reasons for low-income workers' lower pension plan participation rates are that low-income workers are more likely to work for small employers (who are less likely to offer pension plans than larger employers), are more likely to work in part-time positions (which are less likely to be covered by pension plans than full-time positions), are less likely to be able to afford to save for retirement through employer-sponsored plans, and depend more heavily on social security as a source of retirement income (GAO, 2001).*

It is clear that even today, and especially considering the demographic development, social security alone is not sufficient for a dignified retirement life. But is the right way a private pension scheme where employees are expected to make investment decisions and bear the risk alone of stock market failure? And what should be done about those who do not earn enough money to afford a pension scheme?

What the future could hold

After the crash of Enron and others, politicians began trying to enhance employee protection. On 14 May 2003, the House of Representatives passed a bill 'that would allow financial services companies to sell investment advice to workers in 401(k) retirement programmes, while also giving the workers the ability to sell company stock in those accounts sooner than they can now' (Leonhardt, 2003).

Private pension schemes like defined benefit plans, where the state provides certain security against financial market risks and 'limits the amount of employer stock to 10 per cent of plan assets' (CRS, 2002) – or the above-mentioned bill – may solve the problem of risks taken by the employee, but does not offer retirement solutions for the growing stratum of low-income workers in the US.

At 72, Elizabeth Shubert was working three days a week in a supermarket – for US$5 per hour. '"Social security is just enough for food, beverages and a few clothes", she reports' (Cohausz, 2001). Will US residents have to become accustomed to older people forced to work to finance the last years of their life? This could well be the prospect for American society and an unfortunate consequence of a private pension system which, by 2003, still included a potentially enticing but limited and risk-based option without any guarantee of provision. What's more, the system and its options remained unaffordable or unavailable to a sizeable portion of the US workforce, who would likely face a bleak future based on public provision of an increasingly insecure social security.

THE SWISS THREE-PILLAR PENSION SYSTEM

Geneviève Reday-Mulvey

Switzerland's pension system is a very interesting example of complementarity between public and private schemes. Over recent years, it has aroused much interest in international quarters. Indeed, most international experts agree that the Swiss three-pillar pension system is a balanced one and, given similar if not identical demographic challenges, one that will remain in better shape than the systems of most European Union (EU) member states (see Sommer and Gerber, 2001).

The three-pillar pension system

Switzerland can be compared to continental European countries such as Germany, France, Austria and Belgium, where public pension schemes are provided by social contributions shared between employers and employees. But, unlike these other countries, contribution and benefit rates under the first pillar system are fairly low. On the other hand, the second pillar has been made compulsory since 1985 for almost all wage earners (although optional for the self-employed). Switzerland was the first Organisation for Economic Co-operation and Development (OECD) country to introduce a mandatory privately funded and managed second-pillar scheme (Queisser and Vittas, 2000).

First pillar. This is a compulsory public social insurance scheme called the 'AHV/AVS' (Old-age and Survivors' Insurance), set up in 1948 and designed to cover basic material needs. It is financed from worker–employer contributions and by government. The contribution for wage earners is currently 8.4 per cent of income (from any paid work) with no upper limit and a state subsidy of 20 per cent is added. Wives and those without paid work are also covered by this pillar. It is based on a well-established principle of solidarity, there being no ceiling for contributions and the maximum pension being limited to no more than twice the minimum pension amount. Old age and survivor benefits accounted for more than 7 per cent of gross domestic product (GDP) in 1998 (Queisser and Vittas, 2000).

Second pillar. The first pillar is supplemented by a private occupational pension scheme. The system is designed to allow retired persons to maintain the living standards they enjoyed prior to retirement. Contributions are paid on a compulsory basis by workers and employers, with both a ceiling and a floor on income (in the year 2002, the floor was 25,320 Swiss francs a year). In 2003, under pressure from trade unions, the floor was decreased to 18,990 Swiss francs. The revenue from contributions is invested in pension funds supervised by the public authorities. Coverage is estimated to be about 74 per cent of the labour force (Queisser and Vittas, 2000). Two labour-force categories (part-timers and female workers), however, are still more often than not ill served by the second-pillar scheme. About one third of all employed women earn less than the minimum income requirement for compulsory coverage. About 45 per cent of self-employed individuals under 60 years are currently covered by the second pillar.

Third pillar. This was established as a private provision in the form of pension savings and life insurance contracts. Its purpose, encouraged by tax incentives, is to provide for supplementary needs. By 2003, about 1.5 million individuals under the age of 60 were members of a third-pillar scheme, which corresponds to about 50 per cent of all employed individuals in this age group. Coverage among men was about 10 per cent higher than among women (Sousa-Poza, 2003).

Together, the first and second pillars currently yield about 60 per cent of income before retirement. A number of retired persons receive a first-pillar pension only; if they do draw a second-pillar pension, it tends to be a small one. The reason for this is that second-pillar pensions were not compulsory until 1985 (and, even then, only concerned workers whose annual income was above the floor). In such cases, the first-pillar pension can be increased by a cantonal supplementary benefit which, especially for older persons in retirement homes and other pensioners on low incomes (in particular, single women), constitutes a substantial resource.

Recent reforms

The first-pillar system (and, to a lesser extent, the second-pillar system) is subject to regular revision. Rather than passing drastic reforms as in other European neighbouring countries, the pension system in Switzerland is being adjusted step by step.

The tenth (1997) revision, for example, overhauled the entire system, bringing two of the most notable changes:

1 Provision was made for a gradual rise in the retirement age for women aged between 62 and 64 years (set at 65 for men).
2 A 'splitting' arrangement was introduced for couples, providing entitlement to an 'individual spouse pension' where both spouses could draw a benefit based on one half of the combined income of the couple received during the time of marriage, with an addition to cater for education and childcare.

An 11th revision, adopted by Parliament in 2003 and rejected by popular vote in spring 2004, had two objectives:

1 to strengthen arrangements for financing the AHV/AVS with additional resources, derived from value-added taxes, in order to make the state pension sustainable until 2015; and
2 to equalize the age of retirement for both women and men at 65 years.

Earlier proposals regarding the need to encourage flexibility and 'à la carte' retirement were reserved for the 12th revision.

Benefits and limits of privatization

The stength of the Swiss approach is mainly that the three pillars, and in particular the first two, function as parts of a single system.

Therefore, limits to the potential for further privatization can be observed not only in the second pillar itself, whose management is under constant public scrutiny, but also in the very strength of the social principles upon which the first-pillar public system is based: 'It fully reflects the solidarity between the generations, income groups, sexes, single and married people, regions, and urban and rural areas' (Queisser and Vittas, 2000).

The Swiss system is a good example of a situation where considerable non-governmental involvement in the past effectively precludes further involvement by the private sector in the future. Rather than investigating whether further market efficiencies could lie in increased private involvement, the current debate currently concentrates, instead, on the impact of recent negative market returns and the wisdom or otherwise of reducing the legal guarantee on a nominal rate of return.

The main limitation where the second private pillar is concerned is that the self-employed, the unemployed and disabled workers, as well as workers on short-term contracts are not required to participate. Moreover, workers earning less than 18,000 Swiss francs in 2004 will still not be required to contribute. This means that only 77 per cent of the labour force was covered by 2003 (Sousa-Poza, 2003), although the proportion of 'eligible' workers is probably closer to 90 per cent (Queisser and Vittas, 2000). A substantial proportion of women, constant over the 1990s, is not covered. However, the recent decision to lower the floor as of 2004 was, doubtless, set to improve the system.

Another problem is the high degree of fragmentation of the second pillar. In 1996, it comprised about 11,600 institutions, 60 per cent of funds being made up of affiliates with less than 100 members each, and 87 per cent each with less than 500 members. This dispersion results in high administrative costs and relatively low investment returns. The large number of small institutions makes supervision and transparency difficult without offering any real benefits to workers. Furthermore, employees do not have any choice in selecting pension funds and in placing their investments (Queisser and Whitehouse, 2003).

Although the Swiss three-pillar pension system, in its entirety, is both balanced and robust, fully capable of fulfilling its function of providing old-age financial security, the non-universal coverage of the second pillar has been a focus of political debate (Sousa-Poza, 2003). It is perceived by many as the major drawback of the private system. Observers of Swiss pension arrangements are unanimous, however, about their overall success – something that makes further reform problematic and further privatization much less likely.

Police and Security

'RENT A SOLDIER': THE PRIVATIZATION OF SECURITY AND WAR AND THE CASE OF MERCENARY COMPANIES IN AFRICA

Thomas Thümmel, Fabian Fechner and Jürgen Scheffran

Privatization of security is not a new phenomenon, but a new trend. East Indian companies employed up to 300,000 mercenaries at a time to support and secure their exploitation and trade from the 17th century through the early 19th century, until India and other parts of Asia were colonized and mercenaries were gradually replaced by colonial troops (Lock, 2001, p209). Nearly 200 years followed during which military and police forces were primarily controlled by the nation states. By the 21st century, however, a re-emergence of widespread, large-scale mercenary employment had become evident.

The international context of security privatization

The long period of mainly state-controlled military forces drew to a close around 1990, with the end of the Cold War. After the fall of the Iron Curtain, hundreds of thousands of soldiers lost their jobs, and huge arsenals of weapons were no longer needed for the balance of deterrence. It turned out to be impossible to disarm all of the unemployed soldiers, scrap their weaponry and reintegrate them into their respective societies. Thus, they became ready to offer their services to anyone willing to 'rent a soldier' (Wulf, 2003). Demand for private-sector soldiers was particularly strong in 'failed states' in which the army or the police were not willing or unable to secure public order. The growing 'tendency of individuals, groups, and organizations to rely on private security forces rather than on the state's police and paramilitary formations' (Klare, 1995), by 2003, was shaping current conflicts, as well as conflict resolution. This was especially the case in many parts of Africa where violent conflicts provided fertile grounds for private military companies.

Mercenaries and private military companies in Africa

Africa is a continent with a high conflict potential, much of it of colonial origin and often relating to local and international fights for dominance over rich natural resources. Many African states with borders of colonial origin, disrespecting tribal and cultural traditions, have lacked the financial resources to maintain an effective police force and a reliable army. In fact, some have lacked a functioning state. Ethnic, and in some cases religious, rebellions have challenged the powers of central governments, which have then been tempted to seek support from private professional soldiers. Rich mineral resources and relatively scarce fertile soils have tended to be the focus of interest of governments, of rebels and of international companies. Deals have been made between relatively weak governments and international companies to offer mining rights to the latter in exchange for mercenary security support.

Mercenaries are often organized as private military companies (PMCs). South African Executive Outcomes (EO), founded in 1989 in Pretoria, represents one of the most prominent examples. After the apartheid regime, the new company recruited its employees (around 70 per cent black) predominantly from a former South African elite unit, the 32nd Battalion of the South African Defence Force, and from the South African Police. In addition to offering traditional services of war planning and operations, EO ran its own commercial air company (Ibis Air International). While EO officially ceased operations on 31 December 1998 – supposedly due to large financial losses – the EO subsidiary Sandline International (SI) continued the business with a similar strategy. Other internationally operating PMCs include Military Professional Resources Inc (MPRI), Gurkha Security Guards, Defense Systems Ltd (DSL), Levdan, Silvershadow and Vinnel. MPRI was founded at the end of the 1980s by highly decorated US military personnel with good connections to the Pentagon. Other companies also rely heavily on retired US, and sometimes other, military staff, of whom some also served in executive ranks of private firms.

Sierra Leone and South Africa provide instructive cases of PMC activity (Mandel, 2000). Since May 1995, Executive Outcomes assisted the government of Sierra Leone in fighting the rebel movement led by the Revolutionary United Front. President Valentine Strasser faced a desperate situation. The national army was small, hastily recruited, corrupt and without professional skill. Over the four-year war, 1.5 million people had become refugees and over 15,000 killed. Within months, EO had trained local self-defence units to replace the government army and removed rebels from the capital and the principal diamond mining areas. It attracted other foreign investors in the mining industry owing to an 'unofficial alliance' between EO and the UK-based Branch Energy Company, now owned by the Canadian mining company DiamondWorks. Although fostering short-term stability, this intervention could not prevent some long-range problems: Sierra Leone became subject to extensive influence by foreign mercenaries and developed a potentially permanent need for protection. While Sierra Leone's 1996 democratic elections went well, the new government continued to rely on EO for security. The new regime, though, was overthrown by a coup in May 1997 following the end of dependence in February of the same year.

In South Africa, after the apartheid era, all unemployed soldiers were registered and had to return their weapons, but then turned heavily to privatized domestic security. South African private security firms employed 130,000 guards and earned almost US$1.5 billion in 1997, more than three times as much as in 1990. As of 2003, there were ten times more private than public police in South Africa. Both blacks and whites became disappointed in what the government could provide and did not trust the police to maintain law and order. The government police could not do the job required due to low pay, widespread corruption, restrictions on police powers, and friction between veterans of the old apartheid police and new recruits from the former guerrilla army of the African National Congress (ANC). Private security guards became ubiquitous, watching cars for shoppers, patrolling malls, keeping banks and mining houses safe, and guarding houses and neighbourhoods. Although crime decreased, the private security forces did not all have proper training, some were accused of irregular behaviour, and private protection was not affordable to many of those who most needed it.

Consequences of privatized armies

The privatization of war is not just a resurrected form of warfare, but a form with severe consequences for society, as well as for the individual. By transferring the means of violence and the instruments of war – the ultimate symbol of the sovereignty of a nation – into private hands, the monopoly over legitimate force by the state is at stake. As Jessica Mathews of the Carnegie Endowment for International Peace notes: 'The steady concentration of power in the hands of states that began in 1648 with the Peace of Westphalia, is over, at least for a while' (Mathews, 1997).

Some of the firms involved developed into globally operating businesses, offering a variety of services, including direct military operations, military advice, logistical support and reconstruction after a conflict. By privatizing security services, the firms have been able to directly pursue the interests of their customers, independent of government control. To anyone who could afford and wants to use force in conflict they could offer to train a complete army or to recruit the soldiers themselves. For governments overstretched by the security tasks entailed in protecting their country and inclined to reduce costs by transferring some duties, it has often been cheaper to hire soldiers on demand at low salaries than to maintain expensive standing national armies. Theoretically, by transferring some duties to private companies, governments may concentrate their efforts on other core missions, such as the economic and social development of their country.

The weaker a state – in terms of military training or social and economic development – the greater the danger for that state of losing control of the process and becoming dependent upon private mercenaries who offer a comprehensive service. One of the societal implications of this process is the possible loss of a guarantee of security for the population. Personal security transforms from a universal human right into a commodity distributed and traded on markets for a price that the poor cannot afford.

The anti-mercenary resolution of the UN

In 1989, the General Assembly of the United Nations adopted the resolution of the International Convention against the Recruitment and Training of Mercenaries. It was a prophetic resolution for the decade to come, but did not receive the political support it deserved. By 2003, it had been ratified by only a few states and therefore had not come into force. Even major countries, such as Germany, which officially ban mercenaries had not ratified the resolution.

However, most of the real problems of weakened states did not exist or were not visible when the resolution was drafted. Faced with such problems and the need to protect citizens, public institutions and private trades, an incapacitated state may find it easier than other options to rely on privatized forces. Similarly, in a poorly functioning state, wealthier individuals and businesses may themselves prefer to undermine public provision by turning to privatized security. Transition strategies are needed in order to regenerate states so that they can effectively handle security problems. The role of the democratic state as the only legitimate holder of police and military forces needs to be widely accepted since the limits to privatization are particularly visible and important in the fields of the police and military sectors.

PRIVATIZATION OF POLICE SERVICES IN FRANKFURT, GERMANY

Tonia Sophie Müller and Simon Stähler

The privatization of security services is a worldwide phenomenon (James, 2002). By 2003, more and more fields were seeing a shift from a monopoly of state police to private security services. Clients for such services are individuals, local neighbourhoods, private firms and even public entities, such as municipalities. Worldwide, the public has shown a feeling of insecurity, which may be partly induced by the media's preference for covering crime and violence (Obergfell-Fuchs, 2000, pp24ff). Another motive for the privatization of police services, particularly the simpler ones, is a desire for lower costs.

The situation in Germany

In Germany, the market for private security increased steeply from 620 enterprises in 1984 to 1800 in 1996 (Obergfell-Fuchs, 2000, p16), and to 2500 in 2000 (BDWS, 2003). By 2003, the private security workforce had reached half the size of that of the state police (see Figure 33). The rapid increase in employees looked likely to lead to a situation similar to that in the

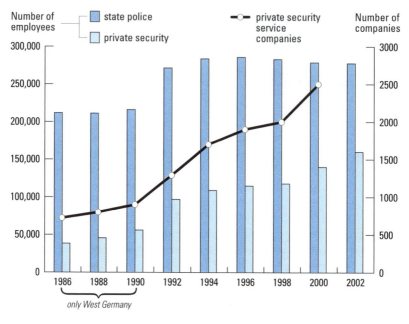

Figure 33

The development of added security in Germany: A growing trend towards private security firms carrying out police duties (e.g. street patrolling). Workforce of state police compared to private security. *Source:* data from BDWS (2003); Ottens et al (1999, p185); German Federal Bureau for Statistics.

US where private security services had surpassed state police forces, building a workforce of roughly 1.5 million (Obergfell-Fuchs, 2000, p32).

In Germany, the legal status of private security was not clearly defined until 2002. Security firm staff had – like every other citizen – the right to use force only to defend themselves or others in an emergency, or to hold back fleeing offenders caught in the act. Any further police rights were strictly reserved for public officials by the constitution (Article 33, IV Basic Law). A legal amendment of July 2002 defining private security service rights did not really change the situation.

The Frankfurt experience

In 1999, 80 security companies with a total of 3000 employees were registered in Frankfurt. At that time, the state police staff numbered 3600. In June 1999, the city signed a cooperation agreement with nine local companies for security in trains and subway stations. Another firm had been charged with more basic services, such as local parking, including the collection of parking fees, since 1995.

The public police gave private security staff the status of a subsidiary police with rights to control illegal parking. This move took its legal basis not in federal but in state laws, and raised serious doubts among lawyers (Huber, 2000, p92). One question concerned the private company's uniforms, which were not easy to distinguish from official ones worn by the town's traffic control. Some 93 per cent of Frankfurt citizens surveyed wanted private security staff to be distinguishable.

In September 1999, the city council of Frankfurt decided to terminate the agreement, effective from 2002, and return to state employees for the job as none of the expected advantages had materialized (Göpfert, 1999). The private security workers were inexperienced in dealing with citizens. Some blundered over licence plates, the electronic registration system or even traffic signs, leading to anger and high refund costs for the city. In the end, the privatization of this public duty cost the city some 10 per cent more and was generally seen as a failure.

The situation was much better regarding private security services for private clients. City shops hired security firms to patrol the inner city. The same service was contracted for the main railway station. In both cases, the patrolling staff enjoyed no extra rights. Contrary to popular belief, private security staff were not entitled to chase homeless people away from public spaces, or to take offenders into custody or note down their names. They were employed only for personal security and the protection of private property.

How did the police react?

Not surprisingly, the state police were rather hesitant about the massive presence of private security. However, there were some fields in which cooperation between public and private security came to be seen as useful. For example, private services could observe hot drug-dealing spots. At mass events involving strong emotions, such as soccer games, private guards could mingle with groups of fans and help to keep order, not as representatives of the state, but, in certain cases, maintaining a connection with the police.

In cases of shoplifting, the experience was not so positive. Offenders occasionally complained about excessive use of force. A policeman gave evidence in a case where a citizen complained about injuries suffered from a private security employee; the latter retaliated and sued the plaintiff. Many policemen doubted the competence of private security employees in the de-escalation of tension or in their behaviour towards certain people, for example mentally disabled, inebriated or threatening individuals. They especially criticized the lack of training and self-control required for such critical tasks (Obergfell-Fuchs, 2000, pp307ff).

From 2003, a new federal law required a much longer training time for private security and order-keeping services than was required before. But many policemen feared that, due to the profit orientation of security firms, guidelines were in danger of being ignored or stretched, so it remained doubtful whether this would lead to improvements. Heinrich Bernhardt, then Frankfurt's chief constable, expressed worries as early as 1996 about a massive presence of private security forces in the city and other public places. He strongly felt that the state's monopoly of force should not be undermined. He foresaw the danger of a 'law of the jungle' situation, resulting from privatization and a business orientation for police forces. Because of a lack of direct control over the companies, misuse and undesirable developments within the business were unlikely to be controlled or stopped (Bernhardt, 1996, p58).

And the citizens?

An opinion poll conducted during the period of major privatization did not produce any surprising results. Most people in Frankfurt sometimes noticed the private security staff but had no real knowledge of their work. Only 8 per cent said they had been in personal contact with a security company during the previous 12 months (Obergfell-Fuchs, 2000, p130).

This may indicate a certain lack of transparency and engagement in the work of private security services regarding their tasks and rights. In contrast to the state's approach to crime prevention, the private security staff did not seek any social relations with the people.

The most important result of the poll related to 16 possible private services tasks. Among the people interviewed, there was not a majority in favour of completely turning over any of the tasks to private hands. Task-sharing between state and private services was advocated in the fields of patrolling malls and city centres, personal protection, event management and traffic control. Respondents felt that all other tasks should remain with the state police. Among these tasks, some were already carried out mainly by private companies. These included guarding hazardous transports, deportation of rejected asylum seekers and answering private alarm system calls. The study also showed widespread fears that privatization might lead to a 'two-class' security: 69.4 per cent of those interviewed agreed with the statement: 'Private security serves and protects only the rich' (Obergfell-Fuchs, 2000, p160).

Conclusion

The Frankfurt experience shows that most positive expectations for privatization were unjustified. People seem to show no desire for the privatization of traditional police tasks with a few exceptions, such as in the areas of site protection, money transport escort and personal protection. No confirmation could be found for the main argument in favour of privatization – namely, lower costs. Indeed, it can be the case that costs are even higher.

From a broader perspective, the privatization of police tasks touches fundamental questions about the functioning of the democratic system. The police as an executive power play an important part in the concept of power-sharing in a democratic state. Private security companies are not directly subject to democratic control: they seek profits and they may be subject to concentration trends that dominate the market economy.

The fact that in many countries private security staff are poorly paid may cause concern (Beste, 1996). In the UK, security guards typically earn only half the average national industrial wage. Kevin McMahon, an Irish union representative, declared: 'In our experience, self-regulation has proven to be a completely inadequate means of either protecting or raising industry standards.' In 2002, even Thomas Berglund, the head of SECURITAS, market leader in Europe, demanded regulations for higher wages and better working conditions to improve the standards (James, 2002). Thomas Berglund's call for regulation seems wise given the need to guarantee proper conditions, both for security staff and for their clients. The development of using underpaid private security guards to protect the property of the wealthy is also problematic as it might be seen as a symbol of social injustice. For the clients, especially the public, but also the private ones, careful scrutiny of the performance, social consequences and cost effectiveness of private security services appears essential in every case.

PRIVATE PRISONS IN THE US

John Züchner

In the US, in 2004, an increasing number of prisons were being built and operated by private companies. The trend began during the mid 1970s following the passage of harsh drug laws in the state of New York. Many people received prison sentences instead of a fine or community service. In 1982, Mario Cuomo, then governor of New York, turned to the Urban Development Corporation, a public agency funded to build housing for the poor, to construct new prisons. Other states, due in part also to harsh legislation, such as California's 1994 Three Strikes Law, also saw a steady increase in the number of inmates and a commensurate need for more prisons.

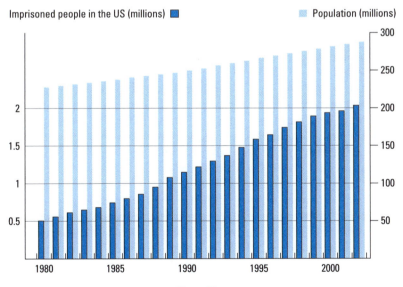

Figure 34
Imprisoned people in the US. From 1980, the US inmate population rose by 300 per cent whereas the population increased by 26.6 per cent.
Source: data from US Department of Justice (2003); US Census Bureau (2003).

Faced with the problem of overcrowding and insufficient financing, several states started to privatize their prison systems. Privatization in other domains encouraged the thinking that privately owned companies could operate more cost effectively than those in public ownership.

Public versus private prisons: Pros and cons

Comparing 13 empirical studies of private and public correctional facilities in the US, Culp (1997/1998) found that private prisons did 'generally appear to be operating more economically than public facilities'. According to the analysis, privatization can save 4 to 14 per cent of annual operating costs. Costs are reduced through outsourcing, reducing fringe benefits, hiring fewer personnel, and by setting aside government bureaucracies.[1]

However, unleashing market forces in such a sensitive area also creates many problems. In 1991, the state of Texas launched a massive project to build new prisons using inmate labour. An additional capacity of 100,000 public prison beds was created in just a few years. As a result, the private prison industry in Texas was confronted with a shrinking demand for prison beds. 'Bed brokers' provided the answer. A new service was created to bring in convicts from overcrowded prisons in other states. The bed broker received a commission, and the county conferring legal status on the prison got a smaller fee. Both were paid per person and per day. The prisoners were then transported to the designated prison. Consequences for the prisoner could be severe when travel distance was increased for visiting relatives or friends, and this, in turn, could reduce the chance of reintegration within society.

A company in the prison industry aims to make the highest possible profit. Privatization leads to a 'market' logic that creates a 'demand' for prisoners as a means to generating profit. As privatization began, there was a large supply of prisoners. Prison administrators had an incentive to keep inmates for the longest possible time, an action that could be facilitated by improper denial of parole. From 1993 to 2000 in a time of increasing privatization of prisons, time spent in prison rose on average from 12 to 17 months.[2]

The aspect of increased time served prompted concern from several quarters, including the American Civil Liberties Union (ACLU): 'The most extreme sanction the state has against the individual, short obviously of the death penalty, is imprisonment, and that should not be turned over to an organization whose primary concern is the profit of its shareholders' (ACLU, 1997).

Moreover, a whole 'service' industry evolved, from phone company competition to install public phones in prisons, to the sale of prison products made by inmates, to trade shows, etc. The phrase *'prison-industrial complex'* was coined (e.g. Schlosser, 1998), echoing the Eisenhower term 'military-industrial complex'.

Problems also arose with prison labour. As of 2004, prisoners worked for an hourly wage ranging from 16 US cents for simple tasks up to 50 cents for skilled jobs. Private companies made use of this cheap labour. American

Airlines, for example, used prison inmates as call centre agents. Such a situation raises a moral issue and the question, as posed by David Shichor, of the consequences of a foreign company takeover of a corporation involved in the management of US prisons: 'Is it acceptable that a foreign corporation handle and will have a certain degree of authority over American prisoners and will make a profit from it?' (Shichor, 1995).

Legal issues and corruption

As of 2004, private prisons also faced legal issues:

- *Use of force*: by law, restrictions on the use of force were greater for a private security guard than a police officer. For instance, a private guard was not normally allowed to use deadly force to put down a riot. Legislation on this point was fragmentary; yet, private prison guards potentially faced situations daily where the use of force might be considered necessary.
- *Legal liability*: the government remained liable for claims made by inmates, raising financial risks that could reduce monies saved through privatization.

In addition, with the aim of full prison occupancy, private companies hired lobbyists to gain the support of politicians and officials for stricter laws and further liberalization of the prison market. Linkages formed in this way between private prison companies and the criminal justice system potentially create highly problematic conflicts of interest.

In September 1997, the state of Montana cancelled its contract with the Bobby Ross Group after three Dickens County Prison inmates escaped and one was killed by a fourth inmate. A month later, the same prison received the highest possible ratings from an inspector for the Texas Commission on Jail Standards. The inspector also worked as a consultant for the Bobby Ross Group, earning US$42,000 per year.

Even more striking is the case of J. Clifford Todd. Mr Todd received about US$200,000 from the chairman of US Corrections, one of the largest US private prison companies. In return, Mr Todd sent prisoners to US Corrections in his capacity as a county correctional official (Schlosser, 1998).

Rehabilitation without regulation?

Prisons are part of the judicial system and partly serve a public safety function. They are considered a place for punishment, but also for rehabilitation. Without regulation, however, a private company has no interest in engaging in the latter since profits are generated when an inmate either stays a long time or – once released – receives another sentence.

Public interest or private profit?

In theory, for privatization to work, consumers express their preferences and make a choice, thus setting free-market forces into play. In the case of prisons, however, such forces do not always result in adequate provision of service in the public interest. Operation of the market in the field of prisons has produced improved conditions and lower costs. However, improvements have come at the price of longer prison terms; displacement of liability; security questions; moral issues of cheap labour; doubt over rehabilitation; corruption on at least some occasions; and the potential for unfair consequences for inmates for undue private influence on a public service and for foreign control of a judicial function. Hence, it appears that privatization should be chosen as an instrument in this sector only with strong regulation in place to counter the negative effects shown to arise.

PART III

Privatization in Context

INITIAL REMARKS

Oran R. Young

Privatization does not occur in a vacuum. Each case unfolds in a broader social context, encompassing the mindsets of key actors, the institutional setting and the distribution of power in the relevant society. Both the material setting (e.g. the state of a society's economy) and the intangible setting (e.g. expectations in the minds of key policy-makers) shape the course of individual episodes of privatization. In this part of our book, we endeavour to set privatization in context in three domains.

To begin, we place privatization in a broader *historical, intellectual and global context*. The historical background shows a paradigmatic shift in the allocation of tasks between the public sector and the private sector. The new paradigm or mindset is fundamentally economic. It follows the 'Moral Syndrome A' according to Jane Jacobs's (1992) entertaining dialogue between the 'merchants' and the 'guardians'. The 'guardians' of the non-economic values of 'Moral Syndrome B' have suffered a decisive blow, it seems, from the triumphant merchants or economists. The so-called Washington Consensus emerging during the mid 1980s reflects that paradigm shift for the development and poverty-reduction agendas. Government and market successes and failures are now seen in a new light. The neo-liberal mainstream assumption about market failures asserts that they result from a *lack* of market functioning or else from too much regulation. We assume a more balanced view and look at the need for control both for the state and for the firm. Of particular importance for the context of privatization are questions of governance, especially global governance. We devote a separate chapter to this topic.

Next, we compare and contrast experiences with privatization in a variety of *regional settings*. We consider the North/South debate about the results of privatization in the advanced industrial societies of the northern hemisphere (e.g. privatization in the G7) in contrast to various developing societies. But there is more to the issue of regional settings than this. We pay special attention to economies in transition, especially Eastern Europe and the successor states to the former Soviet Union. We also consider the role of culture in explaining variations in the outcomes of privatization. We ask whether cultural factors influence the results of privatization in distinct regions such as Africa and Latin America.

Finally, there are broader forces that may influence the course of privatization and that require consideration in any effort to foresee the probable consequences of experiments with privatization in *specific cases*. Does it matter, for instance, whether multinational corporations become major players in the privatization process? Does the involvement of intergovernmental actors such as the World Bank make a difference? Are services different from normal goods when it comes to anticipating the consequences of privatization? Does it matter whether a given economic sector is heavily affected by corruption or features a large black market? Issues of this sort often play a prominent role in determining the results flowing from specific cases of privatization.

The General Context

POST-WAR HISTORY: THE UPS AND DOWNS OF THE PUBLIC SECTOR

Ernst Ulrich von Weizsäcker[1]

Globalization is new but not the 'end of history'

Privatization is part and parcel of a major historic trend. The trend may be characterized by the increasing dominance of the markets over state affairs, or else of the private sector over the public sector. Some call it the neo-liberal revolution. Others call it 'globalization', and with good reason. The overwhelming strength of the markets is derived from the fact that they are global, while state affairs remained local.

It can be argued that this new trend is mostly a pendulum swing back from earlier state domination. Let us take a look at both: the earlier dominance of the state and the emergence of the new trend. It may help us to better understand where and how the balance between public and private affairs could be restored again.

Let us go back in history to the dramatic days of the end of the Cold War. Francis Fukuyama (1992) called it the *End of History*[2] And it *was*, indeed, a historic watershed:

- The end of the Cold War freed all people from the spectre of an atomic world war.
- Democracy, free speech and free press spread throughout most of the world.
- The neo-liberal revolution, which had begun in some parts of the world during the 1980s, was extended globally and began to bear fruit. Global firms flourished, acquisitions and mergers skyrocketed, and so did foreign direct investments.
- Stock markets reflected this optimistic economic feeling and soared, allowing market capitalization of the world's total stocks to triple within ten years (see Figure 35). Hundreds of millions of new participants were attracted to the stock markets and many more thousands of start-up firms were created worldwide.

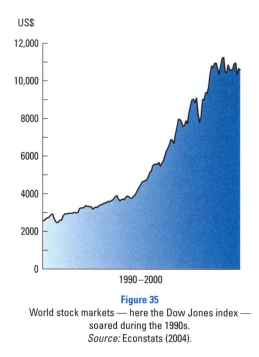

Figure 35
World stock markets — here the Dow Jones index —
soared during the 1990s.
Source: Econstats (2004).

- Perhaps the most prominent reason for global firms to invest in foreign countries was outsourcing into low-wage areas in order to gain competitive cost advantages. This kept consumer prices low and helped to develop the emerging market economies. Furthermore, it greatly helped to decrease inflation rates to their lowest level since the early 1960s.

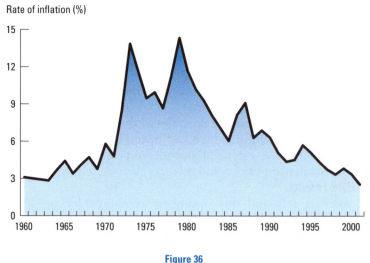

Figure 36
Inflation is worldwide at its lowest level since the 1960s.
Source: data from World Bank (2003a).

Number of internet hosts worldwide (millions)

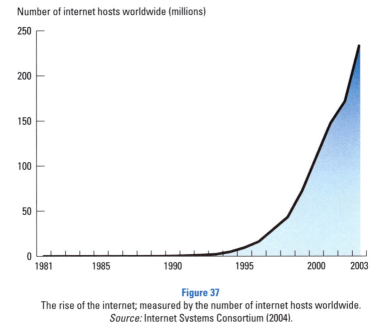

Figure 37
The rise of the internet; measured by the number of internet hosts worldwide.
Source: Internet Systems Consortium (2004).

- The internet became an immensely powerful tool of worldwide communication. It made the truly global firm possible and it signalled a new state of mind for the global young generation – until it was also discovered by the elderly (see Figure 37)!

All in all, it can be said that a euphoric feeling was dominant in many parts of the world, most notably, perhaps, in the US and in China, but also among those who were participating in the world capital markets. To Fukuyama, this euphoric feeling also signalled the end of a type of history that was characterized by ideological and territorial conflicts, often ending in violent wars. There was no need, so it seemed, to ever fight ideological battles again. The good empire had defeated the evil one. The subsequent events of 11 September 2001 and its aftermath have shown that there was more 'history' to come even in Fukuyama's sense. But let us for a moment stay with the 1990s and the decades before.

The global reach of all the exciting phenomena mentioned gave rise to a new and paradigmatic term, *globalization*. Figure 38 shows its career during the 1990s in the German language, which was representative of other languages.

The paradigm shift from state to private had also had a massive impact on the then ongoing Uruguay Round of the GATT (General Agreement on Tariffs and Trade). The round had a rather bumpy start after 1986. Significantly, it was only after 1990 that the round accelerated. The most sweeping decisions ever with regard to trade liberalization were taken in 1992 and 1993. For the

Usage frequency of the word 'globalization'

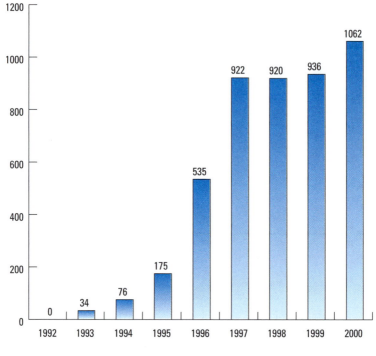

Figure 38
Occurences of the term '*Globalisierung*' (globalization) in a German newspaper.
Source: adapted from German Bundestag (2002); data from *Frankfurter Allgemeine Zeitung*.

first time, the international trade regime began to set rules for what used to be *internal* affairs of the state. Public services, patents and public investments were included in the trade regime, through the GATS (General Agreement on Trade in Services), TRIPS (Trade-related Intellectual Property Rights) and TRIMS (Trade-related Investment Measures) agreements, respectively. Such proposals had long been on the wish list of free traders; but their swift and unanimous agreement had been inconceivable before 1990.

The outcome of the Uruguay Round was not welcomed by all. Many developing countries felt uneasy but did not dare to block the agreement. Globalization and trade liberalization were not, in fact, advantageous for all. There were many losers, not only among the former communist states. There *are* major downsides to globalization. These are also related to the end of the Cold War. *They all relate to a significant weakening of the nation state and, counter-intuitively, of democracy.*

The new weakness of public affairs and of the democratic state is a central focus for critics of privatization.

Remember the early days of the Cold War!

In order to understand the dynamics of the chain of events around 1990, let us look closer into the history of the nation state. The nation state enjoyed an unquestioned authority since the early 18th century. The concept of parliamentary democracy that emerged since the late 18th century was built around the nation state. State authority was as good as total, particularly during war times. That was the 'natural' situation until and during World War II.

The Cold War setting around 1948 reinvigorated the nation states in the West. They were seen indispensable as shields against expanding communism. And everybody at the time saw communism as aggressive, owing to the fact that its 'holy scripts' spoke of an historical 'necessity' of capitalism collapsing under its own internal 'contradictions'. Accordingly, the Soviet Union saw it as her mission to expand communism and to support communist movements worldwide.

There was a formidable momentum behind the commitment (see Figure 39). Shortly after the war, Mao Zedong's communist movement celebrated its complete victory in mainland China. In Czechoslovakia, a progressive and communist movement was successful in 1948. North Korean communists invaded South Korea in 1950 and were forced back to their pre-existing borders by an international coalition under the US flag. The Soviet Union attained the technology of atomic weapons, including the hydrogen bomb. In Vietnam, the anti-colonial Viet Minh movement turned more and more openly communist and finished more than 100 years of French dominance. And the communist ideology dominated liberation movements in virtually all remaining colonies, most visibly, perhaps, in Algeria and the Congo. In India, the communists became so strong that Prime Minister Jawaharlal Nehru had to concede to them the defence portfolio, which some Western observers saw as the beginning of the end of democracy in India.[3]

Later, the communist 'bacillus' crossed over to the Western hemisphere. All Latin American countries had their communist movements combating feudal structures and dictatorial regimes. Much to the distress of the US, the first country to fall was its close neighbour, Cuba, where Fidel Castro's communist revolution toppled the bloody and corrupt Batista regime. In the wake of this blow, the Soviet Union moved to install missiles on Cuba, causing a crisis that nearly triggered World War III.

It was the time of the 'domino theory' (where one domino topples the next). The way to deal with the threat was called the *containment strategy*. It was meant to merely thwart further expansion of the communist block, and nothing more.

Military containment seemed a frustrating and insufficient strategy, especially after the experiences of the Korean and French Indochina wars. The Soviet Union seemed unbeatable for all practical purposes. From the outset, it was clear to the West that the Cold War in its core was an *ideological* war and that perhaps the best containment strategy would be the proof that capitalism had a better recipe than communism for offering *mass prosperity*. Thus, efforts

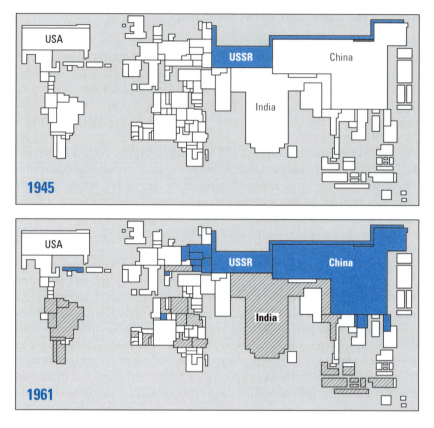

Figure 39
The expansion of communism after World War II. The top picture shows the communist area of
influence in January 1945, the bottom picture shows it in 1961, with some 'uncertain' countries
shaded. To accentuate the strength of the movement, countries are represented in proportion to
their population.
Source: Martin Stürmer.

were made to develop an economic and social strategy of containment. The
idea of *capitalism with a social and human face* got the upper hand. Strong,
prosperous and democratic states were seen as reliable bulwarks against
communism. And the best bulwark, so it appeared, was the *welfare state*
reassuring the poor that capitalism was better than communism even for them
(see, for example, Walker, 1994, pp137–138; Painter, 1999, p35).

In West Germany, the pro-American Adenauer government developed the
Social Market Economy, masterminded by its minister of economics, Ludwig
Erhard. Similar developments went on in the other five countries that formed,
since 1957, the core of the European Economic Community (EEC). Its
earliest pillar, the European Coal and Steel Community, enshrined a far-
reaching model of co-determination between capital owners and workers.

At the same time in the UK, Australia and New Zealand, social inclusion,
and socialist ideas of nationalized core industries, dominated political debate

and government action. Japan had a clause in her new constitution excluding the existence of an army; hence, economic and social success seemed the only strategy available of fending off communist infiltration. Finland, Sweden and Austria; India, Indonesia and Burma; Egypt, Algeria and Tunisia (to name but a few countries from different continents) tried other paths of developing a healthy middle way between capitalism and communism. In each case, the *state* maintained the central powers for both social equity and major economic decisions.

Even in the US, after the confrontational days of Eisenhower, Dulles and McCarthy, social equity became a national goal. During the Kennedy/Johnson period, *affirmative action* laws were introduced on equal opportunity employment for races and gender. School buses were ordered to end racial discrimination at the level of primary education. Several equity acts were actually induced by Supreme Court decisions taken during the Eisenhower years! Social security systems were created or expanded, and affordable mortgages were supplied by the state-subsidized company Fannie Mae. At the same time, many US analysts felt alarmed by the sudden strength of economic competitors in the Far East and in Europe and observed, with a degree of envy, how these competitors managed to create synergies between a strong state and their industries. 'Japan, Inc' was seen as an extremely successful model, with much stronger state powers than were allowed in the US by its constitution. At the time, even business leaders in the US saw the state hardly as a nuisance, let alone an enemy.

Capitalism with a human face also accompanied the period of decolonization. The former colonial powers and the US made it their official policy to help the new states with money and expertise. All Organisation for Economic Co-operation and Development (OECD) states joined in the building-up of a system of bilateral and multilateral official development aid (ODA). A fairly generous ODA goal was defined of giving 0.7 per cent of the rich nations' gross domestic product (GDP). And the main focus of ODA was the construction and modernization of the public sector. ODA and a mutually profitable North–South trade seemed like a good recipe against communist infiltration into the 'Third World'.

The Third World? Yes, that was the new term for mostly developing countries which had joined in a group of 'non-aligned' countries between the first (Western) and the second (Eastern) worlds. The movement was created as early as 1955 by three charismatic and rather leftist, but anti-Soviet, leaders: Tito from Yugoslavia, Nehru from India and Nasser from Egypt. Later, as the movement expanded, it christened itself the Group of 77 or G77.[4] The West, despite considerable suspicion, made its peace with the G77, partly because there was no other choice and partly because the group *did* serve as a tool against communist expansion (see Williams, 1991, pp17–39).

The Soviet Union also attempted to win sympathizers and allies among the non-aligned countries, but her chequebook was thinner than the Western ones and the authoritarian (and, in some regards, outright racist behaviour of the Soviet leadership) was not exactly appealing to the developing countries. So

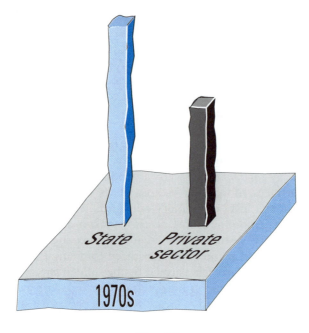

Figure 40
The post-war situation until the 1970s: The state is dominant, but business is happy.

the 'Three Worlds' situation was reasonably satisfactory for the West, at least with regard to the containment of communism.

During all of this early post-war period, the state had an extremely comfortable bargaining position towards its private sector and international capital. It was the state, after all, which set the rules for inclusive capitalism and with democratic legitimation. As a result, the state or public sector remained dominant over the private sector. The private sector, on the other hand, considering the communist threat, did not protest against this dominance. Moreover, it was a period of high growth rates, which left the private sector ample space for making good profits. Figure 40 symbolizes this state of affairs, which Social Democrats (in the US: Liberals), in particular, remember as their happier days.

A new issue entered the scene during the 1960s and more prominently during the 1970s: *environmental pollution*. When pollution reached scandalous dimensions, severely affecting public health and aquatic wildlife, public protests spread and a new type of civil society groups emerged. In response, the state moved towards strict pollution-control laws. Pollution control, too, was a public-sector affair. The history of environmental legislation, and enforcement, provided additional evidence for the superiority of the state at the time.

Third World euphoria and sudden misery

The stable Three Worlds situation did not last very long. The first big change came in October 1973, with the *oil shock*. The oil-exporting countries had managed, in 1960, to form a cartel, the Organization of Petroleum Exporting Countries (OPEC), which – on the occasion of the Yom Kippur War – rose to political strength and punished Israel's friends, and thereby the entire OECD, by dictating a quadrupled price for crude oil and threatening not to sell oil at all to the closest allies of Israel. Jahangir Amuzegar (1999) estimates that the accumulated OPEC gains had exceeded over US$1200 billion until 1985. Thus, OPEC managed to extract many times more dollars from OECD countries than were thus far allocated for ODA (US$398 billion from 1960 to 1985, after World Development Indicators: see World Bank, 2003a).

Even while many of them suffered, the developing countries and, with them, the global left rejoiced at first. The reason? OPEC showed that developing countries were able to get a 'fair share' of the world incomes by 'collective self-reliance'. Along this model, commodity-rich developing countries dreamed of their own cartels (e.g. for copper or coffee). Suddenly, the day of truly closing the gap of wealth between the rich and the poor countries seemed near. The goal was the New International Economic Order (NIEO), involving fair trade and a strong G77-dominated UN system – financed by the rich countries. In particular, the United Nations Conference on Trade and Development (UNCTAD) had become the G77's counterweight to the 'rich man's club' of the GATT (see Bhagwati, 1977, pp6–7; Rothstein, 1977).

The West was partly paralysed at the time by a phenomenon called 'stagflation', a very uncomfortable mixture of economic stagnation and inflation (see Bruno and Sachs, 1985). Frustration was spreading about unfulfilled promises of the dominant left, both domestically and globally. Islamic fundamentalism re-emerged in Iran. Public opinion in the West turned more and more openly against the UN. The business sector was getting tired of state dominance, with its bureaucracy and the cost of the welfare state. The pendulum began to swing back from national and global generosity. Two emblematic victories for conservative leaders, Margaret Thatcher in the UK and Ronald Reagan in the US, marked the change. Tax cuts, deregulation and privatization became the key words of the new 'neo-liberal' agenda. Regarding privatization, the promise was that the private sector would do the same job just more efficiently – to the benefit of both the clients and the taxpayers.

In the meantime, the rest of the world also underwent major changes, which rapidly destroyed the earlier 'Third World' euphoria. High oil prices were good for oil exporters but awful for everybody else, especially the poorest countries. The Soviet Union became entangled in an increasingly hopeless adventure in Afghanistan and was struggling with major internal weakness and massive self-doubts. Communism rapidly lost its earlier magnetism. Even in China, new pragmatic leaders defeated the ultra-communist 'gang of four'. The G77 could no longer play the convenient 'umpire's' role between East and West. Massive explorations of oil and gas resources yielded unimagined quantities of the fuel, which eventually cut OPEC's market dominance down to size. The dreams of a coffee or copper 'OPEC' never materialized. The G77 gradually lost its strength and self-confidence.

Apart from the G77 weakening, the developing countries were also to be hit very badly by another development from 1979 onwards. The US Federal Reserve Bank under Paul Volcker sharply raised interest rates on the US dollar to peak levels above 20 per cent. Developing countries, mostly indebted in the US currency, were suddenly confronted with huge burdens of debt servicing. This marked the beginning of the debt crisis (Gyohten and Volcker, 1992, p198).

A large number of countries had to turn to the international financial institutions (IFIs), notably the International Monetary Fund (IMF) and the World Bank. Bank loans to developing countries increased by more than 50 per cent in three years to more than US$362 billion at the end of 1982. However, the tide had also changed in the IFIs. The 'Washington Consensus' emerged between the US Treasury and the IFIs (e.g. Stiglitz, 2002). This was a neo-liberal agenda consisting essentially of strict budgetary austerity, liberalization (i.e. letting foreign competitors enter the markets), and privatization, thus widening the scope for competition from abroad.

The effects of the Washington Consensus were mixed, at best. Some successes were achieved in combating inflation, and some superfluous bureaucracies had to go. A few countries were able to build up an export-led economic recovery. But millions of people in the developing world lost their livelihoods and fell back into poverty and destitution. In Latin America, which had been reasonably well off in earlier times, the 1980s were referred to as *'the lost decade'*.

The new weakness of the public sector

Now we are back at the point where we left Fukuyama. Capitalism has won the Cold War. The private sector, enthused by its new global freedom, but worried about the upcoming, relentless global cost competition, felt that the priority homework for the state was now to reduce bureaucratic costs and the tax burdens on capital, high achievers and private firms. Some neocons (neo-conservatives) went so far as to argue that the welfare state had done its duty and should now be slashed down to the mere essentials of survival.

Investors and wealthy taxpayers threatened to leave countries that, in their opinion, were too 'expensive', and they meant it. Countries were thereby forced to compete against each other by reducing tax rates for the corporate sector and for the rich. Figure 41 shows the dynamics for corporate tax rates from 1995 to 2004.

Reducing state spending has been a priority of most governments since the 1990s. The demographic transition to growing elderly populations with higher public service demands dramatized the situation. Nation states, provinces and municipalities have become ever more tempted to sell remaining assets to private investors (i.e. to accelerate privatization) – not necessarily because they saw privatization as desirable, but because of the sheer need of cash.

Percentage of average corporate tax rates

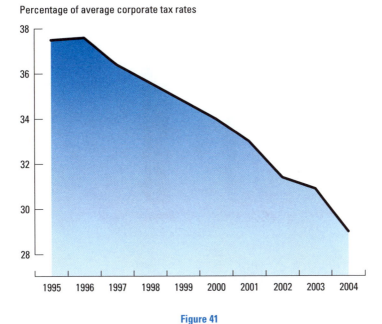

Figure 41
Average corporate tax rates in OECD countries. Tax competition leading to a systematic decrease of corporate tax rates.
Source: OECD data, adapted from: KPMG (2004, p2).

Many see the state as miserably weakened. And privatization has become the most visible symbol of that weakness. Surveys in Chile show that 80 per cent of the population disapproves of privatization, and 90 per cent in Argentina (quoted from Kessides, 2004)!

During the 1970s, the state and the public sector dominated over the private sector. Today, the situation is completely reversed, as Figure 42 demonstrates in a caricature fashion.

What does this mean for *democracy*? Citizens can influence the democratic state by voting, participating in party politics and through advocacy, lobbying and pressure groups. They have little experience and extremely little power to influence the giants of the private sector. This erosion of democracy is perhaps more dangerous than the weakening of this or that public good through the process of privatization. Noreena Hertz (2002) goes as far as calling the process *The Silent Takeover: Global Capitalism and the Death of Democracy*. She gives ample evidence, including from the privatized media, of how the private sector has systematically undermined public interests and democracy.

The euphoric mood of the 1990s may turn to its opposite *unless we manage to rebalance public and private interests* and somehow reinvigorate democracy.

Figure 42
Globalization has caused the (international) private sector to dominate over the
state and public sector.

Global governance

Clearly, the next question is how to approach this new situation. One part of
the answer is a radical and unbiased empirical assessment of the benefits and
costs of privatization. This is a major motive for our book. Other studies may
deal with the pros and cons of *liberalization*, of global *homogenization* (e.g. of
cultures) or of the post-Cold War *US unilateralism*, so candidly described by
Kagan (2003). In addition to this empirical analysis, it may be useful to draw
some theoretical conclusions and add further considerations for political action
(see Part V of this book).

One of the central messages is that capitalism needs a reliable frame. It
means that the trend since the late 1970s of weakening the state must come to
an end and should be reversed. However, we cannot return to the geographical
limits of nation states. To a considerable extent, state regulation that protects
public goods must be agreed on internationally, or at least regionally.

It may be useful at this juncture to draw an historical parallel. During the
19th century and earlier, small dukedoms or states joined into larger nation
states. In retrospect, this was not only politically reasonable but facilitated the
division of labour and the economies of scale. Many losers were left on the
economic battlefield: those whose technology and marketing were unfit for
the larger scale. This was the concern of the Luddites who wanted to reverse
the wheel of history. The larger economic entities were more or less successful
in creating and sustaining the division of labour. At the same time, the nation

states worked hard or were forced to do so by the workers' movement to create a sense of fairness by distributing the benefits gained from the enlarged entity. Regardless of any social or moral motives, this was extremely useful in the period of building the nation states.

However, the 19th-century nation states became obsolete. After brutal wars fought by the nation states, most notably in Europe, the time was ripe for larger entities. For this step, there were strong political motives, and again the intensified division of labour inside the EEC yielded enormous benefits from the economies of scale. On the one hand, the creation of the common market meant a continuing liberalization of markets, including the privatization of large parts of the public sector.

On the other hand, the larger entity in Europe ensured that the losers of structural change were at least partly compensated and socially integrated. Moreover, the European Community systematically began to create a reliable frame of regulation and European law (including a European Court of Justice), harmonized standards for consumers and the environment, common rules on taxation and fiscal rules for contributions to the community or the European Union (EU), and, finally, a common currency. Last, but not least, a European Parliament was created and was given increasing powers in EU affairs. In this way, the EU, as a new larger entity, could strengthen the economic cooperation of its member states and prevent them from, for example, harmful tax competition. Furthermore, it is big enough to engage with transnational corporations. Despite its well-publicized defects, internal tensions and contradictions, the EU might therefore become a supranational guarantor for a healthy balance of public and private goods.

The historic lesson seems to be that keeping this balance and maintaining democratic controls is beneficial for all. This is the case for *global governance* (see Part IV).

But democracy is not only about keeping public goods intact. It is also, essentially, about participation. It has been difficult enough to secure a degree of participation at the level of a nation state of 10 million or 100 million people. This is exceedingly difficult for Europe, notably after its recent enlargement. It seems nearly impossible on a world scale. New methods that invite ordinary citizens to participate in global affairs have to be invented and developed further. One hopeful approach is the systematic recognition of the civil society organizations (CSOs) in the political arena and in the global private sector. We shall come back to examine this approach in the chapter 'Escaping Pernicious Dualism: Civil Society between the State and the Firm' in Part IV.

BOX 5 ON MERCHANTS AND GUARDIANS

Ernst von Weizsäcker and Maria Gordon

'Merchants' and 'guardians' can be seen as the two paradigmatic ends of the political and economic spectra. Merchants view privatization as a good thing, while the guardians of higher values regard it as suspect.

Merchants dislike restrictions on their trade from ideological rules established by 'guardians' of often questionable higher goals.

Jane Jacobs, the grand old dame of urban studies, wrote an entertaining book, published in 1992, on the divide between the two antagonists. Entitled *Systems of Survival: A Dialogue on The Moral Foundations of Commerce and Politics*, the book relates a series of fictional conversations mediated and arranged by a retired publisher. He invites an academic, a lawyer, a crime novelist, a loan officer and an environmentalist. The sharp intellectual exchange sees the group divide into two camps, one on the side of a merchant syndrome of moral attitudes, the other defending more traditional guardian values.

Moral syndrome A (merchant)	Moral syndrome B (guardian)
Shun force	Shun trading
Come to voluntary agreements	Exert prowess
Be honest	Be obedient and disciplined
Collaborate easily with strangers and aliens	Adhere to tradition
	Respect hierarchy
Compete	Be loyal
Respect contracts	Take vengeance
Use initiative and enterprise	Deceive for the sake of the task
Be open to inventiveness and novelty	Make rich use of leisure
Be efficient	Be ostentatious
Promote comfort and convenience	Dispense largesse
Dissent for the sake of the task	Be exclusive
Invest for productive purposes	Show fortitude
Be industrious	Be fatalistic
Be thrifty	Treasure honour
Be optimistic	

The two syndromes relate to *two different systems of survival* found in human history (lacking the ability to trade, animals use just *one* syndrome). The two systems classify moral activity only in relation to making a living, and thus confine the scope to economic and political life.

Merchants consist of traders and people engaged in commercial activity. Guardians include Plato, religious leaders, aristocrats, nationalists and socialists. The dialogue suggests that the two syndromes arose when past tyrants met defiance from those who wished not just to speak out freely, but also to trade freely. History constitutes a series of successful fights for freedom won by trade champions from wayward guardians as the two groups strove to survive. Guardians tend to appropriate and misuse commercial morality, while merchants act from a neutral and functional basis. Guardian morality trespassing into successful commercial worlds fosters the authoritarian state. The ensuing web tangles badly, until the necessary reassertion of trading values. When merchant morality pulls society back from overreaching guardians, the world sees welcome events, such as the fall of the Berlin Wall and the collapse of the Soviet Union.

It follows from Jacobs's book, then, that it can be only a matter of time before trader survival systems, through mechanisms such as privatization, break the hold of the haywire guardian morality behind the problems of the modern industrial and technological age.

Unfortunately, however, Jacobs's characters probe to polite depths only. The success of Israeli Kibbutz people stems not from the Marxist principle behind their operation, but from their behaviour as perfect merchants, innovating and respecting contracts. Deceptive corporate lobbying, ostentatious executive perks, corporate largesse, and so on lurk outside the cosy, insulated intelligence of the dialogue. Yet, in 1992, the author reflected a dominant view. The book surely served as a deliberate antithesis to the work of the notorious German writer Werner Sombart. Sombart's writings included a shocking World War I pamphlet on 'Merchants and Heroes', dedicated to the German soldiers fighting heroic battles for the good cause against the British 'merchants'. Well known as the author of *Modern Capitalism* (1902) and *The Jews* (1911), he described and deplored, in the former, the rise of profit-oriented capitalism and the corresponding decline of craftsmen and peasants modestly oriented to their daily subsistence. The Jews, according to Sombart, dominated the capitalist side together with the Britons and destroyed the virtues of the old society. Sombart's absurd but dangerously influential thinking helped to pave the way for the Nazi tyranny. Today, no inclination exists anywhere to follow his bizarre worldview.

Yet, no matter how entertainingly and temptingly presented, an opposing view biased in favour of a merchant syndrome necessarily excludes complex realities. If 'merchant' and 'guardian' are useful categories, does either type, in pursuit of a living, really operate on the basis of an exclusive system of moral values? Do prowess, discipline, tradition, loyalty, largesse and honour always lead to authoritarian behaviour? Are such characteristics absent from boardrooms? Do guardians such as politicians or religious leaders act, for instance, without voluntary agreements, thrift, initiative or enterprise? Can moral attitudes seriously be separated into the universal and those displayed only in economic and political arenas? Whatever the answers, in matters concerning privatization, individual players, in all categories, and their observers need to examine the moral basis of their actions in order to avoid both Sombartian absurdities and Jane Jacobs's chattering shortsightedness.

THE GLOBAL CONTEXT: PRIVATIZATION IN A GLOBALIZING WORLD

Oran R. Young

Introduction

Globalization makes domestic systems more sensitive to events beyond their borders. Privatization that occurs largely within societies cannot be understood without taking into account the forces of globalization. This section situates the trend toward privatization and deregulation within the overarching processes of globalization and addresses the challenges of governance arising from the combined effects of privatization and globalization.

Globalization and the demand for governance

Globalization has various strands, including the growth of international trade and financial flows, a weakening of the democratic nation state, the movement of human populations across borders, and the onset of global environmental changes. Together, these processes have created or intensified a range of collective action problems or, in other words, situations in which what is rational for individual actors produces socially undesirable outcomes.[5] In the process, they have dramatically changed the setting within which specific experiments in privatization/deregulation occur.

Three developments of this sort stand out as both important in their own right and relevant to the limits to privatization:

1 instabilities arising from the institutional architecture of global trade, financial flows and monetary arrangements;
2 increases in disparities between the rich and the poor, both within and between countries;
3 threats to the planet's life-support systems.

Globalization in the form of increases in international trade, transboundary flows of capital and reliance on global monetary systems (see Figure 43) has produced undeniable gains in terms of overall increases in gross world product. But these processes have led also to increasingly serious instabilities arising from linkages and chain reactions in the global economy (Soros, 2002; Stiglitz, 2002), including massive unregulated flows of capital from one country to another and business cycles that spread throughout the global economy as a result of rising interdependencies. The financial crisis beginning in Asia during 1997 and spreading to Brazil and Russia is an example. In a sense, the global economy stands today where national economies stood at the onset of the Great Depression in 1929.

We cannot turn the clock back in an effort to lower interdependencies and to insulate national economies from the impacts of outside forces. Rather, we

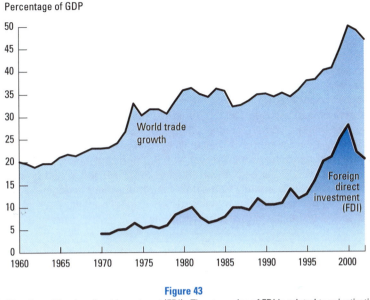

Percentage of GDP

Figure 43
World trade and foreign direct investment (FDI). The steep rise of FDI is related to privatization and coincided with the emergence of the term globalization (see Figure 38).
Source: data from World Bank (2004).

must improve the global economic architecture, with financial institutions featuring anti-cyclic mechanisms that can replicate at the global level the most successful efforts launched during the 20th century to control economic instabilities at the national level.

The growing gap between the rich and the poor at both global and domestic levels leads to a collective action problem that is different in character from the institutional instabilities described above, but no less troubling (see Figure 44).

At first glance, increasing inequality might not seem a cause of concern for winners in the global economy. The rich can insulate themselves from the poor under many circumstances, and justify their position with the comforting idea of trickle-down economics and the proposition that a rising tide floats all boats.

Quite apart from its questionable ethical character, however, this perspective is shortsighted. Rising inequalities cause alienation and even hatred in many quarters, a fact we ignore at our peril under conditions of widespread and escalating terrorism. Growing populations of poor people tend to overwhelm the capacities of governments to deal with a variety of problems, eventuating in the dangers associated with failed states. Situations of this kind breed corruption, and, at a minimum, slow the emergence of growing groups of consumers with the resources to purchase the products of advanced industrial systems. What may seem acceptable to the winners in the short run is therefore apt to give rise to growing costs (including opportunity costs) for all over time.

BOX 6 THE 1997–1998 EAST ASIAN CRISIS

A sudden 25 per cent decline in the value of the Thai baht in July 1997 triggered massive shifts in foreign direct investment, along with currency speculation that hit Indonesia, Korea, Malaysia and the Philippines and spread, ultimately, to Russia and Latin America. What 'started as an exchange rate disaster threatened to take down many of the region's banks, stock markets and even entire economies' (Stiglitz, 2002, p89). While the crisis is over now, its impacts proved severe and lasting. During 1998, Indonesia's gross domestic product (GDP) fell by 13.1 per cent and Thailand's by 10.8 per cent. By 2001, 'three years after the crisis, Indonesia's GDP was still 7.5 per cent below that before the crisis, Thailand's 2.3 per cent lower' (Stiglitz, 2002, p97). It would be a mistake to attribute this crisis entirely to a single factor. But there is general agreement that massive unregulated flows of investment capital constitute a major source of this sort of instability in the global economy.

Although many countries are making gains in controlling local pollution, the combination of rising human populations, growing affluence and new technologies is now threatening to overwhelm or severely disrupt the planet's life-support systems. This has produced serious collective action problems involving the thinning of the stratospheric ozone layer, the onset of large-scale climate change and an unprecedented rate of loss of biological diversity (see Figures 45 and 46).

Additional threats of this sort include growing shortages of freshwater, problems arising from agricultural uses of genetically modified organisms (GMOs) and the consequences of increasing human intervention in the planetary nitrogen cycle.

BOX 7 THE GROWTH OF INEQUALITY

Although poverty has become a focus of renewed attention at the international level, there is no consensus regarding the actual numbers of people living in poverty. Using the familiar US$2 a day criterion, the World Bank has estimated that 2.718 billion people were living in poverty in 1990, a figure that had risen to 2.801 billion by 1998 (World Bank, 2002c). Sala-i-Martin, by contrast, argues that the correct figure is less than 1 billion and that the US$2 a day criterion is misleading (Sala-i-Martin, 2002). But there is no doubt that inequality measured by the gap between those at the top and the bottom of the economic pyramid is growing both domestically and internationally. Thus, 'recent data show that the world's richest 50 million people earn as much as the poorest 2.7 billion' (Rischard 2002, p214). Income inequality between the richest and the poorest countries 'has doubled to 40 to 1 over the last four decades (Rischard, 2002, p31). In the US, 'the ratio between the income of the top one fifth of the population and that of the bottom one fifth jumped from 18:1 in 1990 and 24:1 in 2000' (Rischard, 2002, p31).

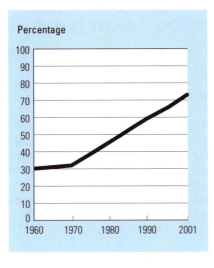

Figure 44

Growing inequalities. Ratio of incomes of the richest fifth of the world population to the poorest fifth.
Source: UNDP data, adapted from German Bundestag (2002b, p55).

What is common to all these concerns is the emergence of human-dominated ecosystems in a setting where social institutions are unprepared or poorly designed to exercise effective control over human actions that affect the planet's life-support systems (Vitousek et al, 1997). Concerted efforts to control ozone-depleting chemicals on a worldwide basis show that meeting such demands for governance is possible (Parson, 2003). Yet, there has been little success, to date, in efforts to create effective governance systems to address many other threats to the planet's life-support systems.

Governance without government

Whatever the merits of creating centralized public authorities or governments to address demands for governance arising at the local and national levels, we cannot rely on this option as a means of supplying governance at the global level.

There is nothing remotely resembling a global government in existence today (Suganami, 1989). Despite high hopes in some quarters and endless proposals for reform, the United Nations is, ultimately, a consortium of states that have no intention of relinquishing sovereignty over matters within their domestic jurisdiction and little willingness to give up their right to refuse to accept decisions that they have not consented to explicitly.[6]

Despite the emergence of promising developments in some issue areas (e.g. the creation of the International Criminal Court and of the Financial Stability Forum in the wake of the Asian currency crisis), this is unlikely to change significantly in the foreseeable future.[7] Proposals for 'world peace through world law' (Clark and Sohn, 1958) remain as utopian today as they were throughout the 20th century.

BOX 8 RAPID CLIMATE CHANGE EVENTS

Recent studies of the palaeo-climatic record have revealed that the Earth's climate system has experienced sudden and sharp changes occurring over periods of years, rather than decades or centuries (Alley, 2000; Mayewski and White, 2002). These abrupt changes or rapid climate change events (RCCEs) are the results of non-linear processes involving occurrences such as the 'switching off' of the Gulf Stream or a sudden rise in sea levels of 5 metres or more. Some climatologists now argue that RCCEs, which may increase or decrease mean surface air temperatures by as much as 5° Celsius, can occur within a period as short as a decade or less. The social impacts of RCCEs would be entirely different from those of gradual changes. Social systems that have a well-developed capacity to adapt to gradual changes can prove quite brittle in the face of RCCEs.

Nor is it clear that a world government would, on balance, be a good thing – even if we were able to create one – given the dangers of anti-democratic or authoritarian behaviour on a global scale made possible by advances in technology.

Accordingly, a growing interest in the idea of governance without government (Rosenau and Czempiel, 1992) is not surprising. This idea distinguishes governance treated as a social function, involving the search for solutions to specific collective action problems, from government construed as a structural option relying on a certain kind of organization to supply governance.

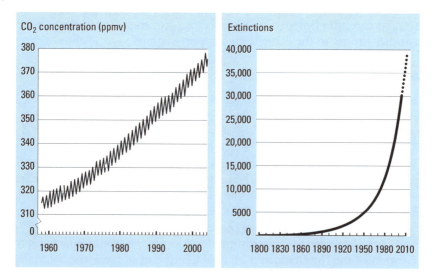

Figure 45
Atmospheric CO_2 concentrations.
Source: data from Keeling and Whorf (2004).

Figure 46
Species extinctions since 1800.
Source: Whole Systems Foundation.

Separating governance from government allows us to see that many mechanisms other than government in the ordinary sense have been and are being used to supply governance in a variety of settings and at different levels of social organization. Small-scale societies, for instance, regularly develop decentralized and often informal social practices to avoid the ravages of collective action problems such as the tragedy of the commons (Ostrom, 1990; Ostrom et al, 2002).

How far such mechanisms can supply governance applicable to the collective action problems under consideration here is a matter to be addressed through systematic research. But, encouragingly, it is already clear that the creation of a government does not constitute a necessary condition for meeting the demand for governance in a variety of settings.

At the international and, especially, the global level, interest in governance without government now focuses on the roles played by issue-specific institutional arrangements or, as they are widely known, regimes defined as sets of rules, decision-making procedures and programmes that define social practices, assign roles to participants in such practices and regulate interactions among the occupants of these roles (Young, 1999).

Such regimes have emerged in response to the demand for governance in numerous international issue areas. The world trading system and the global monetary system are both regimes in this sense. The arrangements dealing with the proliferation of nuclear weapons and the control of chemical weapons are prominent security regimes. The ozone regime, the climate regime and the regime dealing with biological diversity are all global arrangements that address environmental issues. In the environmental realm alone, there are currently between 150 and 200 regimes addressing large-scale or global issues, along with many more on matters that cross national boundaries but are less than global in scope (Weiss and Jacobson, 1998).

As the ozone regime shows, some of these arrangements have proven quite effective. Seasonal thinning of the stratospheric ozone layer will continue for some time to come because of ozone-depleting chemicals already resident in the Earth's atmosphere. But production of these chemicals has declined sharply worldwide since the signing of the Montreal Protocol in 1987 (see Figure 47).

The General Agreement on Tariffs and Trade (GATT)/World Trade Organization (WTO) system has performed well on its own terms, but has produced unintended side effects whose consequences have proven to be profound. The volume of international trade, not only in absolute terms but also as a proportion of total economic activity, has increased sharply during the lifespan of the international trade regime (see Figure 43). But we are now increasingly preoccupied with a range of issues, including the links between trade and the environment, the problems associated with trade in services, and the controversies over the TRIPS (Trade-related Intellectual Property Rights) Agreement that were all unforeseen at the time of the negotiation of the GATT in the late 1940s.

How can we maximize the success of regimes in solving the problems they are created to address, while minimizing unacceptable side effects? This is the

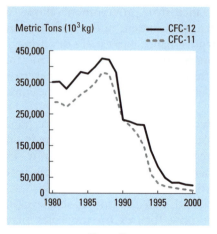

Figure 47
Decreasing production of chlorofluorocarbons. Chlorofluorocarbons are mainly responsible for the thinning of the stratospheric ozone layer.
Source: Alternative Flourocarbons Environmental Acceptability Study, Rand Environmental Science and Policy Center.

critical question for global governance today and in the years to come. The outcomes of efforts to solve these global problems will have critical consequences, as well, for many initiatives involving privatization at the domestic level.

We already know some relevant things. Stakeholder engagement and a sense on the part of individual actors that the provisions of regimes are fair, for instance, clearly make a difference. But there is much more to be learned before we can design governance systems to deal with specific concerns with confidence that they will contribute to progress and not cause side effects worse than the initial problems.

Harmonizing the three pillars

Most studies of governance without government treat regimes as devices for solving collective action problems and focus on arrangements that are embedded in formal or legally binding agreements among states (Krasner, 1983; Rittberger, 1993; Simmons and Martin, 2002). For the most part, they assume that the behaviour of states is the proper area of interest for those concerned with global governance.

This perspective is understandable for those steeped in the assumption that the world is organized as a society of states (Bull, 1977). But it obscures some fundamental realities that must be taken into account today. Progress on governance at the global level depends upon forging appropriate and effective links among (mostly national) governments, the private sector (including multinational corporations, or MNCs), and global civil society (including a wide range of non-state actors).

Sophisticated accounts of the supply of governance at the domestic level have long recognized the need to harmonize the efforts of these three pillars.[8] It is difficult for governments – and largely impossible for democratic ones – to solve collective action problems in the absence of a civic culture that supports legitimate interventions by public authorities to meet the demand for governance. Business practices that ensure high levels of compliance with public regulations covering everything from accounting procedures to environmental impacts are also important.

This is why recent studies which suggest that we are witnessing a decline in civil society in the US and elsewhere, in the advanced industrial world, are being taken so seriously (Putnam, 2000). It also accounts for the profound concern that has accompanied recent revelations in the US and elsewhere regarding business practices that are often fraudulent and certainly violate the spirit of various regulatory systems.

The three pillars also need to be harmonized at the level of global governance. Despite the prominence of realist arguments emphasizing the central role of state power (Grieco, 1990; Gruber, 2000), evidence regarding the limits of these arguments is growing. Recent studies pointing to the emergence of a global civil society and providing new insights into the role of norms at the transnational level have revealed influential forces at work at the global level (Finnemore, 1996; Wapner, 1996; Keane, 2003). There is growing interest, as well, in the emergence of voluntary regulations on the part of leaders of MNCs in such forms as the development of the ISO 14000 standards and the creation of the Marine and Forest Stewardship Councils (Haufler, 2001).

These efforts to raise the profile of global civil society and to benefit from the emergence of self-regulation on the part of MNCs should not blind us to the continued importance of power at the international level. Any effort to understand the protracted conflict in the Middle East or the shifting international role of China without taking into account changes in the nature and distribution of power, for instance, cannot succeed. Similar remarks apply to the role of the US as a laggard in efforts to address the problem of climate change.

Yet, meeting the challenge of global governance will depend fundamentally upon our ability to find new and effective ways of harmonizing the contributions of government, the private sector and civil society. A key point of departure in addressing this challenge is the observation that recent trends toward privatization have produced a troublesome imbalance among the three pillars. The appropriate response to this situation is not merely a matter of reallocating tasks between the private sector and the public sector. What is needed is a proper balance, including civil society as well as government and the private sector (see the schematic three pillars in Figure 66, page 327).

The role of democracy

Important as it is to find effective ways of meeting the challenges described in this section, we have an additional concern that seems essential to this analysis of limits to privatization. It is not sufficient simply to solve collective action problems; it is important to do so in a manner that conforms to basic norms and principles of democracy.

Avoiding economic instabilities and protecting the Earth's climate system are important goals. But solving these problems in a manner that gives rise to authoritarian practices would amount to trading one set of problems that require innovative solutions for another set of problems that impose costs associated with supplying governance in a manner that is illegitimate and unacceptable on ethical grounds.

Democratic procedures may also play a role in meeting the challenge of global governance. Actors – often called stakeholders in this context – who are able to participate in deciding how to meet the demand for governance in specific settings often regard the results as legitimate and feel an obligation to live up to their commitments in the absence of coercion or the threat of sanctions. In effect, they pay more attention to the logic of appropriateness in contrast to the logic of consequences than their counterparts, who have had no voice in deciding on responses to collective action problems (March and Olson, 1998).

Democracy is compatible with a variety of political institutions. There is no reason to conclude, for instance, that parliamentary systems are more or less democratic than presidential systems, or that centralized political systems are more or less democratic than federal systems. Nor does the provision of opportunities for citizens to vote offer any assurance that a system will meet the test of democracy. We are only too familiar with authoritarian systems in which over 90 per cent of eligible voters regularly and dutifully cast their ballots for a dictator.

What is essential to democracy is a meaningful opportunity for stakeholders or those who will be affected by collective decisions to participate, and to have their voices heard, in the decision-making process (Dahl, 1989). Democracies do not guarantee individual stakeholders a veto over collective choices that they dislike. On the contrary, those who have had a full and fair opportunity to participate are expected to acquiesce in the will of the majority (within limits) once a collective decision has been made.[9]

In domestic settings, we have considerable experience with efforts to structure institutional arrangements in such a way as to ensure that they conform to the requirements of democracy. In general, the challenge is to steer a course between the twin dangers of paralysis in systems that provide too many guarantees for the individual stakeholder and authoritarianism in systems that do not provide adequate safeguards for the rights and interests of individual stakeholders. Getting this balance right is a perennial topic of interest in democracies.

No system is perfect; 'the price of democracy is eternal vigilance'. The challenge at the global level arises from the fact that much of our experience with domestic systems is not applicable to meeting the growing demand for governance discussed earlier in this section.

Box 9 The International Monetary Fund and the democracy deficit

In democratic systems, the effects of inequalities in economic power are mitigated, however imperfectly, by the operation of political arrangements that are based on the principle of one person, one vote. At the international level, however, even this highly imperfect method of offsetting the effects of inequality is missing. In the International Monetary Fund (IMF), for instance, the US is the dominant member, with 17.11 per cent of the votes, while the weakest members have 0.01 per cent of the votes and several dozen have 0.10 per cent or less.[10] And there is no way to redress the impact of this striking inequality in the content of decisions arrived at through the countervailing influence of other, more democratic, institutions. Small wonder, then, that many countries do not accept the actions of the IMF as legitimate and are bitterly opposed to what they understandably regard as the anti-democratic and colonialist character of this international institution.

We know, for example, that the concerns of some stakeholders are being ignored or dismissed lightly in the context of the operation of the global trade and monetary systems (Stiglitz, 2002).

Yet, the fundamental idea of a social contract is applicable at the international level, just at it is to solving collective action problems at the national and local levels. In effect, states and other powerful actors must accept some limitations on their sovereignty or freedom of action in order to solve large-scale problems such as the onset of climate change or the eradication of poverty, even when the solutions feature various forms of governance without government.

Finding ways of making the climate regime more effective, for instance, is undoubtedly important. But a concern for democracy at the global level would require paying increased attention to issues of human health and food security. Although most agree regarding the importance of climate change, it is understandable that many developing countries concerned about matters of safe drinking water and food security are not prepared to place climate change at the top of their list of priorities.

Back to privatization

What is the connection between the onset of globalization and the limits to privatization? Although individual situations vary greatly, the fundamental answer to this question lies in the growth of interdependencies between domestic activities and the forces at work in the outside world.

Specific cases illustrate a variety of mechanisms that play a role in this context. Countries facing currency crises and applying to the IMF for help must yield to pressures for privatization arising from the Washington Consensus, which calls for reducing the size of the public sector and stimulating the growth of free markets. When the privatization of waterworks leads to ownership and control on the part of MNCs, countries are vulnerable to the withdrawal of suppliers who claim that such enterprises are unprofitable. There is no escaping the pressures to conform to international standards that apply to services such as telecommunications and air traffic control.

The point is not that the impacts of these linkages are always bad from the perspective of individual countries. Rather, those advocating privatization and endeavouring to design effective institutional arrangements to go with it must understand that the outcomes in specific cases will be determined, in considerable measure, by outside forces that they have little power to control.

Several general themes emerge from this analysis. Recent trends towards privatization within countries constitute understandable responses to past problems. Yet, the limits to privatization are becoming increasingly apparent. Private actions at their best cannot solve collective action problems in the absence of rules of the game that are widely understood and generally regarded as legitimate. Overarching problems, such as instabilities in global trade and financial regimes, the growth of disparities between the rich and the poor, and the onset of global environmental changes, will profoundly affect the consequences flowing from domestic initiatives involving privatization and deregulation. For the most part, individual countries will not be in a position to solve these global problems. But ignoring them in efforts to make use of privatization successfully at the domestic level can, and often will, lead to disaster.

The Regional Context

PRIVATIZATION IN G7 COUNTRIES

Matthias Finger

This section considers the phenomenon of privatization in the G7 countries (i.e. the US, Canada, the UK, Japan, France, Germany and Italy).[1] It shows that privatization varies significantly from country to country, but especially between industrialized and developing countries. With the exception of the UK, and to a lesser extent Italy, privatization is not (yet) a significant phenomenon. Furthermore, the US must be treated separately, as well as Canada (although to a lesser degree), which displays some similarities with France, Germany and Italy.

Overview

The term 'privatization' was popularized by the sale of British Telecom in 1984, and became quite mainstream throughout the rest of the decade. The process began during the late 1970s, with the Thatcher government in the UK, and spread across countries and continents. From 1977 to 1999, 2459 deals in 121 countries with approximately US$1110 billion worth of proceeds of sales were reported (Siniscalco and Fantini, 2001). Of the 34 countries studied for the 1977–1999 period, Sri Lanka is the only country which never implemented any major privatization, while the UK leads the ranking with 169 operations. Turkey leads the less developed countries, with 60 operations.

Organisation for Economic Co-operation and Development (OECD) data shows that the infrastructures generated most of the privatization proceeds between the aggregate period of 1990–1999, with the peak in 1997, and Latin America leading. As for the G7 countries, Figure 48 indicates that Italy is the biggest privatizer during the 1990s, followed by France and the UK if Germany is left aside.

Let us now look at each of the G7 countries in more detail.

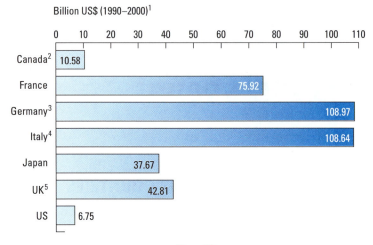

Figure 48

Value of assets privatizatized in G7 countries 1990–2000. Germany is first because of the sudden and massive privatization of East German assets in 1992.

Notes: [1] The amounts shown are gross proceeds from direct privatizations. These do not necessarily correspond to the net amount available to the government. The figures are on a calendar year basis and they may not add up to published budget figures. [2] There were no federal privatizations in 1997, 1999 and 2000. Provincial data are currently not available. [3] Up to 1997, information on trade sales is not available. [4] Including indirect privatizations since 1996–2000 raising million US\$ respectively 2325; 2018; 3235; 5791; 9244. [5] Debt sales for years 1990–97 (fiscal years) amounting to £5347 million, £7924 million, £8189 million, £5453 million, £6429 million, £2439 million, £4500 million, respectively. All the figures are provided in fiscal years.
Source: data from OECD (2002).

UK

The UK pioneered privatization during the early 1980s. While the UK was not the first to undertake large-scale privatization (Chile had a significant programme during the late 1970s), it seems to have been the most widespread and advanced of any in an OECD country. As of 1999, 119 public enterprises have been privatized or sold off. Apart from the postal service (Royal Mail), practically all public enterprises have been privatized. The main driver was ideological and political, in particular neo-liberal ideology (embodied by the Thatcher government), the need to compensate for reduced taxes and the desire to weaken the unions.

In 1979, public enterprises in the UK accounted for 8 per cent of employment, 10 per cent of output and 16 per cent of total gross domestic fixed capital formation (see Pollitt, 1999). By 1992, after a decade of privatization schemes, the comparable figures were 3 per cent of employment, 3 per cent of output and 5 per cent of gross domestic fixed capital formation. During the Conservative administrations of Margaret Thatcher (1979–1990) and John Major (1990–1997), large-scale privatizations of many of these enterprises took place. By 1998 only a few public enterprises remained, most notably the Post Office, and even the Post Office has been the subject of proposals for privatization.

Privatization in the UK can be classified into three stages according to the administration under which they were undertaken. During the first Conservative administration in 1979–1983, only companies which were already listed on the stock exchange (e.g. British Petroleum) or which operated in competitive markets (Amersham and Associated British Ports) were sold off. The second administration of 1983–1987 started privatizing major utilities with British Telecom (BT) in 1984, then the world's largest public offer for sale, and British Gas in 1986.

The third Conservative administration during 1987–1992 privatized the water and electricity industries, the privatization of electricity involving horizontal and vertical separation of state-owned companies and the creation of a power pool. The fourth Conservative administration of 1992–1997 privatized some companies previously thought to be un-sellable: British Coal, British Energy (which owns the newer nuclear power plants) and British Rail.

While all of the major privatizations of telecoms, gas, water, electricity and railways were opposed by the Labour opposition at the time, the post-1997 Labour government of Tony Blair had no plans to reverse these privatizations and, indeed, continued feasibility studies of the privatization of remaining state-owned enterprises. However, political resistance led the government to prefer 'public–private partnerships' to outright privatization and the continuing crisis on the railways has forced the government, against its will, into what amounts to a piecemeal partial re-nationalization.

US

There has been little privatization in the US because, at the federal level, much is already in private hands. There are hardly any public assets at the federal level, with the exception of the postal service, which is the biggest employer in the world. At the state level, there are some public assets, such as power plants and distributors, as well as educational and health institutions. There are more public assets at local or city level, including public transport, energy, health, education and water. There has been more outsourcing or contracting-out than privatization in the strict sense, especially at the state level.

Canada

In terms of public ownership, Canada is more like Europe than the US. There are significant public assets, most at state and local levels. At the federal level, little privatization has taken place, except Air Canada. At the state level, there has been some corporatization and subsequent floating of some shares at the stock market, especially in natural resources (mining) and energy (Hydro Québec and Hydro Ontario). Almost no privatization has taken place at the local level.

State-owned enterprises have been used as vehicles to implement public policy in Canada for many decades. For example, federal Crown corporations such as Canadian Arsenals, Air Canada and Petro-Canada promoted government policy in national security, cross-Canada transportation, and the domestic oil industry. However, owing to fiscal constraints, increased concern about the efficiency of public ownership, changing conceptions of natural monopolies, and the availability of other options to meet public policy objectives, governments in Canada began to privatize their corporate holdings in the mid 1980s.

The Canadian federal government began privatizing the delivery of public services only recently. For example, the upkeep of national parks was contracted out in 1997. Other levels of government have been widening the range of services that they contract out for more than a decade. Some provincial governments introduced competitive bidding for services such as highway maintenance and computer support during the 1980s. Hiring private firms to collect waste, remove snow and provide many other local services has been a common practice in municipalities for many years.

The largest and most prominent privatizations in Canada have involved public share offerings in Crown corporations. The federal government's initial public offering (IPO) of shares in Canadian National Railways (CN) in 1995 was the largest stock market flotation ever undertaken in Canada. While large Crown corporations are usually privatized through public share offerings, most privatizations in Canada during the 1980s and 1990s were arranged as sales to existing private businesses. Such trade sales typically fetch a higher price than IPOs because the purchaser acquires control of the enterprise. The privatization of Crown corporations can bring substantial sums of money to governments. Between 1986 and 1996, proceeds from the ten largest federal privatizations totalled Cdn$7.2 billion. In 1995 alone, the federal government raised more than Cdn$3.8 billion from the sale of shares in CN and Petro-Canada. Half was received in 1995, the rest in instalments in 1996 and 1997. Over the past decade, provincial and municipal governments have also raised large amounts of money through asset sales. The sale of shares in Alberta Government Telephones raised the most, Cdn$1.7 billion, followed by the flotation of Manitoba Telephone Systems (MTS) in 1996 for Cdn$860 million (see www.bankofcanada.ca).

Japan

As in most countries, public enterprises in Japan were originally part of the state administration. Some of them were transformed into autonomous entities, such as the Japanese National Railways in 1948 and the Nippon Telegraph and Telephone in 1952. The Post Office (comprising a significant banking activity), however, remained a government department. At the local level, there are thousands of local public corporations (approximately 10,000 in 1995), mostly utilities.

Privatization in Japan started quite early in 1981 with the creation of the Provisional Commission for Administrative Reform (PARC), calling for the privatization of the main public enterprises. Three public enterprises were to be privatized – namely, the Japan Tobacco and Salt Public Corporation (JTSPC), Nippon Telegraph and Telephone (NTT) and the Japanese National

Railways (JNR). In the JTSPC the government ultimately only sold a minority of shares. The sale of shares in NTT was slow; but the government finally only retained one third of the shares. JNR, in turn, was split up into seven companies: six passenger companies and a freight company. The huge debts that had accumulated over time were passed on to the freight line and three passenger lines, while the other three companies were totally freed of debt. These three railway companies, all located in mainland Japan, are now fully privatized, while the government still holds a majority of shares in the four others (see www2.jftc.go.jp/eacpf/03/privatization.pdf).

As of August 2004, the Japanese government has announced a plan to transform the Post Office (including the Post Bank) into a shareholding company, to split it into four independent businesses (i.e. mail, postal savings, life insurance and management of the network) and to privatize each of these four entities. This announcement is likely to trigger negative reactions, especially from the unions.

All in all, therefore, full privatization in Japan remains a quite limited phenomenon and is limited to the three main railway companies. Furthermore, no privatizations have so far occurred at the local level, involving the numerous utilities.

France, Germany and Italy

France, Germany and Italy are, to a certain extent, similar. The European Commission is indeed driving the liberalization process, which, in certain sectors, may lead to privatization. The rate and extent of liberalization differ from sector to sector and depend mainly upon the various sector directives, as elaborated by the commission. Indeed, in each of the sectors, the European Commission elaborates so-called Green or White Books (non-binding) and directives (binding), leading to a step-wise opening-up of the various infrastructures markets. Liberalization is thus most advanced in the telecommunications sector (Germany, Italy and, partially, France have all privatized their telecommunications operators), followed by air transport, post, electricity and gas, railways, broadcasting, higher education and water.

There are significant differences. Italy is probably most advanced in liberalization; yet, there is little privatization so far except of telecom and electricity.

In *France*, privatization must be seen within the context of nationalization during the 1980s. Many previously nationalized companies were privatized during the late 1990s, especially in banking, oil (TotalFinaElf) and insurance. There is also partial privatization of Air France and France Telecom, but not much beyond that. Water and wastewater have always been private in France (see 'The top public service transnational corporations' on page 239, on the rise of public service transnational corporations). The role of the state in the French banking industry increased at the beginning of the 1980s, when prominent commercial banks were nationalized. This was reversed during two periods of privatization during the late 1980s (Société Générale, Crédit

Commercial de France and Banque Indosuez) and the 1990s (Banque Nationale de Paris was privatized in 1993 and Crédit Lyonnais was sold in 1999).

Privatization is even more evident in the water sector. Water provision in France is the responsibility of municipalities. These franchises – also called 'delegated management contracts' – have existed since the late 19th century. Today, two companies – Suez (now called Ondeo) and Vivendi (now called Veolia Environment) – hold two-thirds of the franchises.

Italy's ambitious privatization programme accelerated during the second half of the 1990s under the Berlusconi government, and had averaged proceeds of some US$12 billion a year during 1992–2000. In 2001, proceeds dropped to US$2.6 billion, one of the lowest since the launch of the programme. The decline in activity was due, in part, to unfavourable equity market conditions, leading to postponement of planned transactions, such as the sale of further stakes in ENEL (Ente Nazionale per l'Energia Elettrica), the electricity company whose privatization had begun in 1999. Italy's privatization programme has covered a wide range of sectors, such as banking, insurance, energy, manufacturing, telecommunications and electricity. In 2001, the single most important sale was the US$2.5 billion public offering of a 6 per cent stake in ENI (Ente Nazionale Idrocarburi), the Italian oil and gas company. Other transactions were very small and included financial-sector assets such as Banca Nazionale del Lavoro and Mediocredito Centrale S.P.A.

Official sources report 592 sales worth US$65.2 billion during the period of July 1992 to December 1997. Forty-nine major deals amounted to US$60.1 billion, approximately 92.1 per cent of the total revenues. In the banking industry, state involvement was very important at the beginning of the 1980s, but declined significantly from the mid 1990s, with the privatization of several institutions. Despite the privatizations, the state retained an indirect influence on many banks via its role in the so-called '*fondazioni*' (joint stock companies holding stakes in several banks). The most prominent privatized banks were Banca Commerciale Italiana, Credito Italiano and Istituto Mobiliare Italiano. The privatization wave followed the adoption of the 1993 Banking Law, which allowed banks to pursue market objectives as opposed to social functions (OECD, 2002).

Germany is probably more advanced in the overall privatization process if one includes regional (state) and local levels. At the federal level, we have, so far, the partial privatizations of telecom and postal services, as well as the corporatization of the railways. At the *Länder* level, there has been some privatization in energy: one must note the privatizations of Veba (electricity) and VIAG (aluminium, glass, chemicals, logistics, etc.) and their merger into E.On, which is now one of the two major energy players in Europe (besides Electricité de France (EDF) from France). At the local level, there are new forms of corporatization and delegated management, especially of the *Stadtwerke* (i.e. the local utilities). Indeed, at the local level, a lot of creativity was needed in order to balance the budgets. Subsequently, some cities sold their *Stadtwerke*. In some cases, the cities maintained the ownership of the infrastructure but offered delegated management contracts to private operators, many of them French.

Other notable transactions included some capital-increasing activities: the flotation of Fraport AG (Frankfurt airport) shares on the stock market was intended to raise funds for the investment in the airport, and it did not involve the federal government's 18.4 per cent stake holding in the company. This was the first time that the shares of a German airport were being offered on the stock market. The other capital-increasing activity was Deutsche Telekom's issuance of new shares to purchase Voice Stream/Powertel. This transaction reduced the government stake from 42.8 per cent to 30.9 per cent. Other notable transactions involved the sale of shares in the Juris GmbH (information services), reducing the government stake to just over 50 per cent, as well as the full privatization of DEG (Deutsche Investitions- und Entwicklungsgesellschaft mbH) (financial services). The government plans to take further steps in privatizing Deutsche Post AG and Deutsche Telekom AG when capital market conditions are more favourable (OECD, 2002).

Conclusion

Apart from the UK, privatization in the G7 countries is not a phenomenon on a scale comparable to developing and Eastern European countries. This can be explained by the fact that the financial pressures upon the state were smaller and, at least in the case of Europe, liberalization is driven but also structured by the European Commission, which has never said anything about privatization. As a matter fact, the European Commission's main idea is competition (even among public operators), not privatization. The question, however, remains as to whether further liberalization will lead the G7 countries to more privatization.

PRIVATIZATION IN LATIN AMERICA

Jorge A. Schiavon

Privatization has been one of the central components of the neo-liberal structural reform process in Latin America over the last 20 years. Nearly all the countries in the area – except for Cuba – have implemented market-based policies, among them privatization, to transform their economic structure and development strategy from inward-looking, state-dominated import substitution industrialization (ISI) towards outward-looking, market-dominated, export-led growth. However, privatization has varied dramatically in its timing, pace, depth, scope, breadth, ideological support and level of commitment between countries, sectors and industries, and even within single countries over time. However, several common causes and consequences of the privatization process in Latin America can also be underscored. This section describes and explains the common causes of the privatization of state-owned enterprises (SOEs) in Latin America, the wide variation of the national privatization processes, and the shared short-run and long-term consequences of these endeavours.

Latin American countries implemented privatization programmes between 1985 and 2000 – Chile as early as 1974 – because they shared an almost identical international environment and very similar domestic macro-economic constraints. Neo-liberal market-based solutions to rebuild national economies and stimulate sustainable growth became desirable as the result of several factors: first and foremost, the economic and debt crisis of the 1980s, which most political actors believed to be a consequence of the exhaustion and crisis of the ISI state-dominated development strategy; second, the successful example of the Chilean and East Asian experiences; third, advice and pressure from the international financial institutions (e.g. the International Monetary Fund, the World Bank, and the Inter-American Development Bank, basically through conditionality mechanisms in their loans); fourth, the collapse of the Soviet Union and the central planning or socialist option; and, finally, the empowerment of domestic pro-reform coalitions within governments. Furthermore, the lack of investment in state-owned enterprises during the years of the debt crisis – combined with the technological change which made some of their production processes archaic – reduced the quality and quantity of goods and services produced by public firms. Against a background of region-wide dominance of the 'Washington Consensus' ideas – the pre-eminence of private-sector actors, the role of market forces to promote economic efficiency and sustainable growth, and the implementation of prudent macro-economic policies, trade liberalization and free-market capitalism – these factors made privatization attractive as a mechanism that would generate efficiency gains in production, reduce fiscal deficits and the burden of the external and internal debts, and send a clear signal to the international markets about the commitment to neo-liberal reform in the region.

Between 1985 and 1995, all of the Latin American governments publicly announced their intention to implement privatization programmes. However, the capacity of these governments to enact privatization varied substantially from country to country, and even within the same country between different administrations. Chile started as early as 1974, and Bolivia and Mexico followed until 1985, while Brazil and Ecuador waited until 1995 to seriously promote privatization; the rest of the countries in the region started between 1985 and 1995. Argentina and Chile followed a radical shock strategy, while Brazil and Colombia preferred gradualism. Argentina, Chile and Mexico enacted deep privatization policies, selling the vast majority of their SOEs, while Colombia and Venezuela only sold a reduced number of public firms. Argentina, Chile and Peru privatized enterprises in practically all of the economic sectors; but other countries reserved some strategic sectors to public ownership: Brazil (oil and strategic public utilities), Mexico (oil and electricity), and Venezuela (oil). Brazil (under Collor de Mello) and Chile accepted payment for state-owned enterprises in domestic and external debt

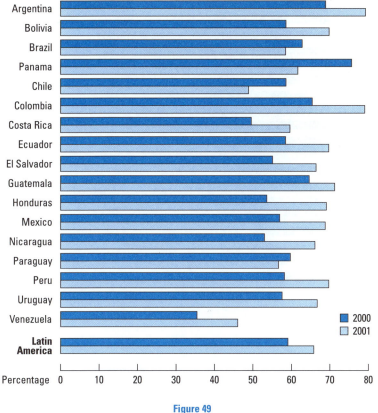

Figure 49
Percentage of population disapproving of privatization.
Source: data from Inter-American Development Bank (2002, p2).

instruments, while Caribbean countries and Peru accepted only cash; Argentina, Brazil (under Cardoso), Mexico, and Venezuela received both cash and debt bonds. Finally, in terms of ideological support and level of commitment towards the privatization process, disapproval rates were higher in Argentina and Colombia, and lower in Chile and Venezuela (see Figure 49). In Argentina, Bolivia, Colombia, Mexico and Peru, privatization was supported by some sectors of the economic and political elites led by Menem, Paz Estenssoro, Gaviria, Salinas and Zedillo and Fujimori, respectively, and questioned by the opposition and considerable sectors of the population.

The privatization programmes have also varied dramatically within single countries over time, depending upon the preferences of the administration in office. A very clear example of this is Brazil: Sarney (1985–1990) could not initiate privatization due to lack of domestic support; Collor de Mello (1990–1992) tried to implement broad and deep privatizations, but was stopped and impeached by the opposition in Congress; Franco (1992–1994) understood the public sentiment against privatization and did not pursue it; Cardoso (1995–2003) restarted the privatization process, but limited it to

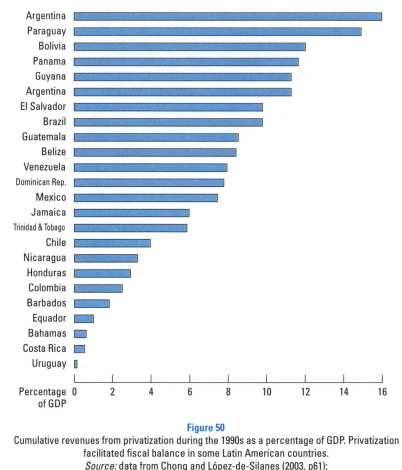

Figure 50
Cumulative revenues from privatization during the 1990s as a percentage of GDP. Privatization facilitated fiscal balance in some Latin American countries.
Source: data from Chong and López-de-Silanes (2003, p61);
Lora (2001).

steel, petrochemicals, fertilizers and other non-strategic economic sectors; and, most recently, Lula da Silva (2003) has brought the process to a complete stop, with no clear signs of reactivation in the near future.

Even if the results of privatization in Latin America are mixed in terms of success within countries, sectors and industries, all of the privatization programmes in the region share the same basic results. In the short run, revenue generation was positive for all countries, generating some external and domestic debt relief, relaxing short-term cash constraints, and facilitating fiscal balance in the years in which the flow of resources was greater (see Figure 50). In the longer run, privatization had a substantial impact by functioning as a credible commitment signal to domestic and international actors of the seriousness of the neo-liberal structural reform process of the country in question. The impact on attraction of foreign investment and return of domestic capital flight was directly proportional to the depth and breadth of the privatization programme.

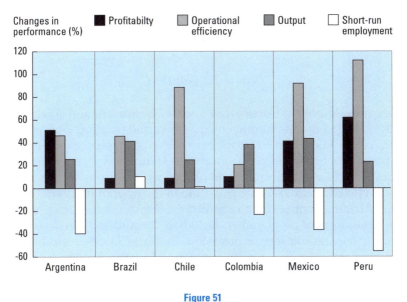

Figure 51
Costs and benefits of privatization in Latin America.
Source: data from Inter-American Development Bank (2002, p1).

In purely macro-economic terms, privatization was, almost without exception, positive because it increased operating efficiency, productivity, profits, and the quality and quantity of goods and services produced. This positive impact was higher when privatization was conducted in more market-oriented and competitive economies through coherent, well-designed, competitive and transparent programmes, and where suitable regulation and monitoring procedures for the privatized firms were implemented by the government. However, in micro-economic terms, with the notable exceptions of Brazil and Chile, privatization was accompanied in the whole region by reductions in employment, stagnation or reduction in wages and living conditions for middle- and lower-income classes (see Figure 51), and an increase in income distribution inequality.

In sum, even if the privatization programmes in Latin America varied dramatically in many ways, they share similar domestic and international origins, and have very similar economic and social consequences, both positive and negative. In the course of the next years, the degree of positive macro-economic and negative micro-economic impacts will be directly and inversely related to whether the privatization programme is inserted in a larger, coherent, transparent, popularly accepted and institutionalized structural reform process. In the near future, we can expect Chile to continue to be successful, while Brazil, Colombia, Mexico and Peru will make very few additional advances, and Argentina and Venezuela might even witness some reversals in the road of structural reform and privatization.

LIBERALIZATION OF SERVICES: EXPERIENCES OF AFRICAN CONSUMERS

Nessie R. Golakai

Services include physical necessities such as healthcare and water supply, banking and telecommunications, entertainment and tourism. They contribute significantly to production costs. For example, in Mali, services account for up to 70 per cent of production costs for goods. Consumers therefore have much to gain or lose from the liberalization of services, directly as service recipients and indirectly as service costs are passed on in the price of products.

Many African countries have reformed the services sector under economic structural adjustment programmes, including deregulation, privatization and private participation in service provision. Public utilities – including water, telecommunications and electricity, banking and financial services, health and education – have been commercialized. Private companies, including big foreign multinationals, have secured key interests in these sectors. The trend towards liberalization of services is set to be consolidated through the General Agreement on Trade in Services (GATS), which seeks further progressive liberalization in the service sector.

Will consumers gain or lose?

In theory, consumers should benefit from increased competition that further liberalization of trade in services can bring about. More competition should lead to improved productivity and better service delivery, reduce excess profits and limit the market power of firms. In turn, this should lead to improved quality and lower cost. However, evidence to date has shown that liberalization can directly threaten the protection and promotion of consumer interest, particularly for poor consumers who cannot afford services provided on a purely commercial basis.

Introduction of user fees and dollar-linked costs

The reform of the services sector has seen the introduction of user fees and cost-sharing mechanisms. Previously in many countries, healthcare was provided free of charge. A 'cash system' was introduced at government-operated hospitals and clinics, which requires patients to pay hospital and consultation fees and sometimes even buy medication, such as injections, before being treated. This has placed considerable strain on workers and the poor. In Mozambique, for example, malaria treatment costs increased from the equivalent of U$10 before health sector reform to U$40 afterwards.

At the same time, the cost of services such as hotels and telecommunications are increasingly dollar linked. Depreciation in the local currency leads to an almost automatic increase in charges. It should be noted, though, that in the few cases where local currencies appreciate, there is no commensurate decrease in charges.

Increased access limited to urban areas

Since the introduction of reforms in the telecommunications sector in Ghana, there has been a rapid increase in the number of fixed and pay phones in the country, from 3166 in 1996 to 191,380 in 2000. Three providers of cellular phone services have over 45,000 subscribers, and the internet and data service providers have approximately 100,000 subscribers (ISSER, 2002, p132). However, in the rural areas, the telephone operator Capital Telecom has only been able to provide approximately 500 lines to individuals in rural areas.

Limited regulatory independence and autonomy

In Mali, the production, distribution and billings of water and electricity are the sole responsibility of La Société Energie du Mali (EDM-SA). The government owns 40 per cent of the shares. French multinational Saur International owns the remaining 60 per cent.

One of the stipulations of the reform process was to set up an independent regulatory authority; but this has, to date, not been done. As a result, EDM-SA has been serving as a de facto regulator in the sector. This position does not guarantee the interest of consumers against abuses. Litigations are frequent between users and the contractor, EDM-SA.

In Kenya, the Communications Commission of Kenya (CCK) gave a directive ordering all private courier service providers to adjust their prices upwards to levels higher than the rates that the Postal Corporation of Kenya (PCK), a government-owned company, charges. The CCK also granted monopoly rights to Telkom Kenya Ltd for fixed-line telephony in Nairobi and the national internet backbone. This has had negative implications for the quality of internet access: service providers have no influence over quality because of the monopoly of the national carrier.

Impact on consumers

Choice. In some sectors choice has improved. In the telecommunication sector, for example, there is greater choice for consumers to access telephone services either through landlines, cell phones, pay phones, the internet or paging facilities. But public utility services such as water and electricity have merely changed from public monopoly to private monopoly.

Redress. Privatization and commercialization have preceded the establishment of effective regulatory authorities. These regulatory bodies remain weak. Hence, consumers have witnessed a change from public to private monopolies with no improvement in their ability to obtain redress.

Representation. Consumer representation in regulatory boards will need to be enhanced either through formal representation or through the setting-up of formal mechanisms for dialogue if they are to fulfil their aim of ensuring consumer welfare.

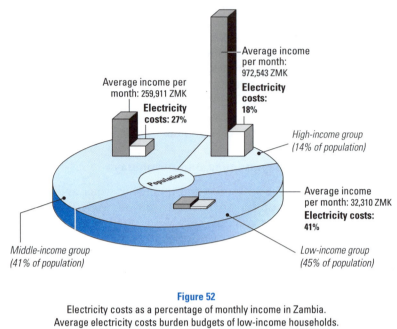

Figure 52
Electricity costs as a percentage of monthly income in Zambia.
Average electricity costs burden budgets of low-income households.
Note: 100 Zambian kwacha (ZMK) = approximately US$0.20.
Source: Zambian Central Statistical Office (*CSO Priority* and *Living Conditions Monitoring Surveys*
1991–1998).

Access. Service expansion has mainly benefited urban and middle-class customers. Rural areas and low-income urban fringe districts have lost out due to low expected returns.

In Mali, EDM-SA has not invested in the expansion of electricity or water services. Since the privatization of water and electricity, neither consumer protection nor levels of access to water and electricity were improved. Tariffs are set up according to different levels of consumption. Users consuming more water and electricity have to pay more. At first sight, this rule seems to favour vulnerable consumers. In reality, this policy affects poor families negatively, forcing them to drastically reduce their consumption of water and electricity and allow EDM-SA to service more consumers without additional investments. This policy, far from protecting the vulnerable consumer, aims, rather, to compensate for insufficient investments in the sector.

Affordability. With the linking of costs to the US dollar and cost recovery, many poor and rural consumers can no longer afford some services. In Zambia, electricity charges for the newly commercialized electricity supplier in Zambia have meant that most low-income households cannot afford to meet their energy needs (see Figure 52).

Figure 52 shows that, on average, monthly electricity cost for the lowest income group as a percentage of total monthly income is 41 per cent, 27 per cent for the middle-income group and 18 per cent for the higher-income group. A large share of household income that would be devoted to energy costs could indicate that the economic burden of meeting energy requirements would be too high. This has implications on affordability of electricity, especially for the low-income group, which represents 45 per cent of the population in Zambia.

Conclusion

The cases discussed above indicate that liberalization of services has been a mixed bag. Universal access to essential services such as health and water is hampered by limited investment and a focus by privatized service providers on areas of high return. Affordability has become an issue, particularly for poorer consumers who now have to pay out more of their meagre incomes to receive the same level of service. Liberalization has not assured consumers of better service delivery, either. In Mozambique, 10 per cent of consumers interviewed have had equipment damaged by power surges without compensation by the electricity company.

All of this points to the need for a strong and effective regulatory framework. Regulatory mechanisms have been set up for most commercialized/privatized service sectors; but their institutional capacity to enforce standards, review proposed tariff rates and arbitrate consumer complaints in their sector remains weak. Regulatory bodies need to be independent in order to effectively establish clear guidelines and standards, and have the power to enforce them. Consumer organizations have a key role to play in this process in order to ensure that liberalization is balanced and takes into consideration the needs of consumers within a developing country context, where the majority of people live on less than US$1 a day. Formal mechanisms of consultation and input need to be established in order to ensure that customers have a voice.

NO LIMITS? PRIVATIZATION IN CENTRAL AND EASTERN EUROPE

Zsolt Boda

Privatization, together with liberalization and macro-economic stabilization, is an essential element of the economic transformation that Central and Eastern European (CEE) countries have undergone during the past decade. Moreover, the speed and depth of privatization has been regarded by many experts as the key measure of economic success or failure. It has been assumed that the higher the share of private enterprises in the economy, the more successful the country is in this painful transition process. The importance attached to privatization is understandable given the specificity of the centrally planned economies, where almost all productive assets were in the possession, or under the tight control, of the state, and official ideology did not question the predominance of collective ownership.

Privatization in the CEE countries is unique in many respects, not 'just' because of the political importance assigned to it. The quantity of the assets that changed owners is huge and touched upon almost all sectors of the economy. The speed of the process, especially in countries leading the reforms, such as Hungary, has also been extremely high if we compare it to Western European examples. The privatization process is also unique because it has happened in a dynamically changing environment. In Western Europe, privatization is somehow defined by the existing legal, political, cultural and economic conditions. But in Central and Eastern Europe, these social framework conditions were not well defined. Laws and institutions regulating the privatization process itself, as well as the functioning of a market economy, had to be created; capital markets did not exist, and in general the demand for assets has been weak; political support for privatization and private ownership has been very different from country to country and has changed considerably over time; economic recession appeared to be deeper and its social costs have been higher than expected before; and a hostile mentality towards the market system or the lack of personal and social entrepreneurial skills have also been important in many countries. These conditions have significantly affected the methods of privatization in the different countries. But let us first look at the motives behind privatization and the expected outcome of it for social conditions.

Clearly, some of the motives were directly political. Privatization has been regarded as a political act to definitely put the communist system to an end. Furthermore, it was used as a means by new political elites to deprive the old communist nomenklatura from the economic basis of its power, as well as to try to create a new middle class and national bourgeoisie. It must be noted that these objectives could not easily be reached: in all of the CEE countries, many of the members of the communist nomenklatura could preserve their position in the elite by transforming their political and network capital into an economic one. They were in a good position even for successfully participating in the privatization process, either as buyers or as middlemen, mediating between the state and foreign investors. And the new national entrepreneurial classes are being formed only slowly under the pressure of increased global competition of the multinational companies, on the one hand, and the lack of management and marketing knowledge as well as capital, on the other.

Another political motive was to create social support for economic changes. Hungary, and to a lesser extent Poland, already experienced some economic reforms during the 1980s. Therefore, general attitudes towards market-oriented changes were more or less supportive there. However, practically in all of the remaining CEE countries public opinion was distrustful about radical economic reforms. The functioning of the market was not familiar to people and nobody could realistically evaluate the depth of economic problems to be faced. That is why in most of the countries politicians hesitated to take radical policy measures and made concessions to public opinion. For instance, CEE countries – except Hungary – considerably limited the entry of foreign companies during the first half of the 1990s. However, some forms of privatization, such as mass privatization schemes (which means a free distribution of shares of the state-owned companies to people) and the restitution of previously nationalized property seemed to be a good means of creating individual interest in, and political support for, market-oriented economic changes. This strategy apparently worked out because countries, such as the Czech Republic, Bulgaria and Romania, which undertook only relatively slow reforms during the first half of the 1990s could speed up liberalization at the end of the decade. Mass (or voucher) privatization and/or restitution of some of the property (mostly lands) nationalized during the communist era happened in all of the countries. This created a moral basis for the new market system and provided people with some, though mostly very limited, assets that could alleviate the dramatic social effects of the economic recession.

Other reasons for privatization were obviously of an economic nature. Hungarian economic thinkers, for instance János Kornai or Tibor Liska, pointed out already during the 1980s that soft budget constraints of the state-owned companies, as well as the lack of real ownership, were the main reasons for the inefficient functioning of the communist economy. Therefore, several reform proposals were developed about how to simulate the logic of the market, and how to create the responsibility and the motivation that is supposed to characterize the business decisions of a real owner (in Hungary, this topic could be dealt with in academic circles, which was not the case in most of the other CEE countries). Thus, privatization promised to increase efficiency through the creation of real ownership. In other words, privatization was taken to be the key factor in creating a healthy economy with competitive companies which provide jobs for people and pay taxes, instead of depending upon state policies and subsidies – which was the case of many of the old socialist, state-owned firms. Looking back to the history of 14 years of transition, we can conclude that privatization was not the only factor and measure of economic success, and many other conditions influenced the development path of different countries. Furthermore, privatization in itself proved to be a necessary, but not sufficient, condition for creating efficient corporate governance. The resulting ownership structure, as well as state policies, or the surrounding social and market environment (including the quality of the legal system, and the mentality and quality of the human resource) are factors that have also influenced the emergence of competitive firms.

Finally, a very important motive for privatization was the necessity of increasing budgetary income. This seems to be a short-term goal. However, the methods, the speed and the depth of privatization have been largely influenced by it. Hungary had the most pressing macro-economic problems during the early 1990s and it was the first country in CEE to undertake privatization measures and to create the proper legal environment for private businesses, as well as for the entry of foreign direct investment (FDI). Until 1995, half of all

FDI in CEE came to Hungary! Hungary is also leading in privatizing the utilities and public services (water, energy and the healthcare system), and privatization campaigns have always come in times of economic recession and deteriorating macro-economic conditions. The other countries were privatizing at a slower pace, turned to mass (voucher) privatization schemes, and limited considerably the role of foreign companies in the economy. However, after 1997, macro-economic problems, like the growing deficit of the current accounts, forced these countries to speed up privatization, as well as to give up the absolute preference for local owners in privatization policy and for inviting foreign investors. After 1997, FDI-friendly policies were introduced in Bulgaria, the Czech Republic, Poland and Romania, among others.

Privatization, especially the sale to foreign investors, can generate a considerable amount of budgetary income. This money can finance short-term deficits, but can also be used to fight inflation (as happened in Poland and some other countries) or to reduce the external debts of the country (as in Hungary). In these latter cases, privatization revenue contributed to the macro-economic stabilization of the country (i.e. it served longer-term objectives). Studies about the amount of privatization revenue demonstrate that the privatization method is clearly important: domestic sales (especially to employees) are only possible at a relatively low price, while higher revenue is to be expected from sales to foreign investors. But, again, we should put privatization in context. Privatization revenue depends upon many general economic and social factors, such as the overall development level of the country, the quality of the infrastructure or political risks. For instance, the Czech Republic outperformed Hungary in raising privatization revenue, despite the fact that the latter has been leading in terms of the scale and speed of privatization, including privatization to foreign investors.

Let us now turn to the privatization methods that have been used in CEE countries. These methods include:

- 'spontaneous privatization';
- small-scale or pre-privatization;
- mass (voucher) privatization;
- management buy-outs;
- employee ownership programmes;
- transfer to social security;
- restitution of physical property (houses, land, etc.);
- privatization sales to local strategic or institutional (financial) investors;
- privatization sales of at least 10 per cent of equity to foreign strategic or institutional (financial) investors.

Each of the CEE countries used a specific 'mix' of these methods. In addition, privatization policies have changed considerably over time. Later in this section, we will offer some comments about the limits and merits of the most important privatization techniques. But let us first have an overview of their shares in different countries' privatization policies (see Figure 53).

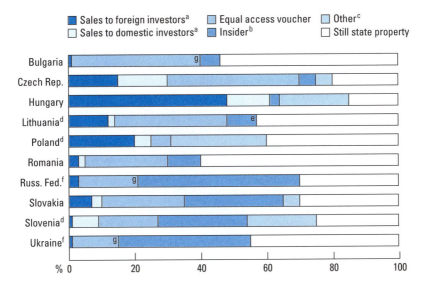

■ Sales to foreign investors[a]   ■ Equal access voucher   □ Other[c]
□ Sales to domestic investors[a]   ■ Insider[b]   □ Still state property

Figure 53

Distribution of enterprise assets between privatization methods in selected Central and Eastern European countries, up to 1998.

Notes: a: Includes both direct and portfolio sales.
b: Management buy-out and employee share ownership programme. c: Leasing, debt-equity swaps, restitution, transfer to social security funds and local organizations and liquidation.
d: Data available from the privatization agencies, up to end-1998. e: This share of employee participation is also included under the voucher data as employees acquired voucher shares of their companies. f: Up to end-1997, based on unweighted averages.
g: Data on equal access vouchers include also sales to domestic investors.
Source: Kalotay and Hunya (2000, p41).

'Spontaneous privatization'. This term does not refer to the outcome, but to the process of privatization. It has only historical relevance. Spontaneous privatization is the process through which state-owned firms gained growing autonomy from the central authority; at one point they transformed into private companies, making use of the unclear legal environment. In a general sense, the spontaneous privatization began during the 1970s and 1980s in Hungary, Poland and Yugoslavia, where market-like economic reforms were introduced. These reforms gave much more autonomy to the firms in making their own business decisions. This autonomy was then used and abused by the management in 1988–1990 when they privatized the assets of their company, either buying it for almost nothing (a kind of management buy-out) or selling it to other local or foreign investors. Spontaneous privatization is believed to have been characterized by deep corruption and individual rent-seeking behaviour. It was ended by the privatization laws of the countries. According to estimates, in Hungary one tenth of the state-owned company assets were privatized 'spontaneously' (Voszka, 1998). It is to be noted that, according to evidence, the overwhelming majority of spontaneously privatized firms either went bankrupt or were bought up by (foreign) strategic investors.

Small scale and pre-privatization. Pre-privatization refers to two phenomena. One is the possibility offered by new legislation at the end of the 1980 in some of the CEE countries, such as Czechoslovakia, Hungary, Poland and Yugoslavia, to create small firms (which sometime were not private formally, but gradually became so) or begin some kind of entrepreneurial activities. The other is the sale of the shops of huge state-owned retail companies to individual entrepreneurs. Foreign investors were excluded because the aim was to strengthen the national entrepreneurial class. The philosophy of this small-scale privatization is still relevant in the case of land. The ownership of land is basically reserved for individuals in CEE countries (i.e. not only foreigners, but even local companies are excluded from it). This became a major issue during the accession negotiations between CEE countries and the European Union (EU) – EU members of CEE countries must give up this policy.

Mass (voucher) privatization occurred in almost all CEE countries; exceptions are Hungary and Macedonia. The details of the method (e.g. the criteria of eligibility and the quantity of the shares assigned) have been somewhat different from country to country; but the idea is the same: the free distribution of state-owned company shares. The merits of the method are obvious: it made privatization an easy and speedy process and, at the same time, responded to concerns for social justice. As mentioned above, it certainly had the double positive effect of providing some assets to people in times of serious economic depression and creating social support for market institutions. However, mass privatization generally did not lead to efficient ownership and better corporate governance. Access to capital and new management practices was not secured either. Fairness considerations have also been limited by the fact that the huge amount of equities distributed among the populace led to a fall in their price, and the shares occasionally landed in the hands of clever businessmen. At the beginning of the 1990s several theoreticians cherished the idea of some kind of 'popular capitalism' based on the free distribution of shares. Now it seems that mass privatization could not fulfil all of the hopes that were attached to it. It has been a very important part of privatization in CEE, but its significance is clearly diminishing, giving place to direct sale methods and to the emergence of real owners.

Employee ownership programmes figured in the privatization policy mix of all CEE countries. Just as voucher privatization, its possible role in creating a 'popular capitalism' has also been the subject of theoretical reflections. The ideology of employee ownership and collective auto-regulation has particularly been strong in Poland (due to its great trade unionist traditions) and the former Yugoslavia (where it had already been part of the official socialist ideology). Its merits and problems are similar to those of mass privatization: it is easy to put into practice and it is popular; at the same time, it does not bring benefits in terms of additional investments, marketing knowledge and managerial skills. Several studies tried to explore whether companies owned by their employees are less competitive than others (Kovách and Csite, 1999; see also Kalotay and Hunya, 2000, pp45–46). Results are somehow ambiguous; but it seems, indeed, that firms with foreign or even local owners are more competitive than firms privatized through the voucher system or given to employees. However, even if this is true, we should keep in mind that typically the already better-performing companies could be sold directly to either local or foreign buyers. In many instances, employee ownership came only as a last resort when privatizing a given company.

Restitution of property has been limited to certain assets such as land or buildings, and to certain former owners (individuals and churches in most countries). Compensation schemes have also been developed, for instance in Hungary, through which people were given vouchers or equities for their losses during communist times. Nevertheless, the overall economic significance of restitution and compensation has been limited.

Sales to local and foreign strategic or institutional (financial) investors. Direct sale of firms is a relatively slower process because it needs complex legal and institutional guarantees, as well as time for negotiations. However, it has several positive effects. Unlike voucher or employee ownership programmes, it raises revenues for the budget which then can be used for achieving either macro-economic stabilization or social policy goals. That is, if used for the benefit of the society, this revenue also meets fairness claims. Direct sales to investors create better corporate governance and therefore enhance the competitiveness of the firm. This effect has especially been observed in the case of companies sold to foreign owners. A comparative study across the CEE countries made by United Nations Conference on Trade and Development (UNCTAD) (see Kalotay and Hunya, 2000) demonstrated that privatization to foreign investors led to a generalized improvement in almost all of the economic performance indicators of the companies. Output, capital investment, research and development expenses, domestic market share for lead products, and productivity increased.

There is a general belief that foreign companies are, first and foremost, gaining their markets through buying local companies which are then closed in order to enable the foreign company to import its own products. This belief cannot be justified as a general rule, although it is indeed sometimes the case. Another general belief is that privatization, and especially the sale of firms to foreign owners, contributes to the decline in employment. True: employment declined faster in the rapidly privatizing Hungary than in the Czech Republic during the first years of the 1990s. However, the survey shows that employment decrease in the companies privatized to foreign investors was small compared with a generalized decline in employment in the given countries. Again, we should put privatization into context: privatization has been just one element of a painful transition process. It is not privatization in itself that causes the growth in unemployment, but the restructuring of the inefficient centrally planned economies.

The recognition of the positive economic effects of FDI, as well as the pressing macro-economic problems, have forced practically all CEE countries to try to attract more FDIs in recent years. Still, many practical and more general questions remain about the use and role of FDI. For example, should privatization favour minority or majority foreign ownership? Should it favour strategic or institutional (financial) investors? Should privatization contracts focus first and foremost on getting a good price, or should social and environmental criteria also be included, even at the expense of achieving only a lower price (evidence shows that these additional criteria are difficult to enforce)? And, most importantly, should some strategic companies or economic sectors be excluded from privatization to foreign investors? Finally, is there an optimal level in the share of foreign ownership in an economy?

A special case in the region is Hungary, where the share of foreign capital in the industry is one of the highest in the world (around 65 per cent). Moreover, Hungary opened practically all sectors to strategic foreign investors, including banking, telecommunication, energy (electricity generation and distribution, as well as gas distribution), water and, recently, healthcare. The privatization of higher education is also being considered. The question is: how far will the other countries follow Hungary's path, which consists of privatizing almost everything and relying heavily on foreign investments? The fact is that policy measures and proposals of this sort are being developed in the other countries as well.

In summing up, 'spontaneous privatization' was a phenomenon of the early transition years; employee ownership programmes and mass or voucher privatization also had their peaks during the first part of the 1990s. Apart from some ongoing legal disputes, restitution of property is generally finished. We can say, as a general rule, that in recent years direct sales to local or foreign investors have dominated privatization. This means without any doubt an impoverishment of privatization techniques, but at the same time signals a 'normalization' of the situation (the development of capital markets and other market institutions). Many innovative privatization techniques that could be observed in Central and Eastern Europe have been the fruits of the pressing necessity of transforming the economy, on the one hand, and the lack of well-functioning market conditions, on the other. But the relative decline of their relevance also signals the fall of alternative development paradigms, such as that of a 'popular capitalism', and the triumph of liberal economic order in the region.

PRIVATIZATION IN SOUTH ASIA

Joachim Betz

South Asia was a latecomer in divesting public-sector enterprises and still accounts today for only around 4 per cent of total privatization proceeds of developing countries. Privatization has taken various paths: Sri Lanka started first (in the context of a much earlier programme of liberalization and deregulation); India, Pakistan and Bangladesh followed in the wake of a severe balance of payments and/or budgetary crisis. India, the largest economy in the region, had the greatest proceeds from privatization by a wide margin,

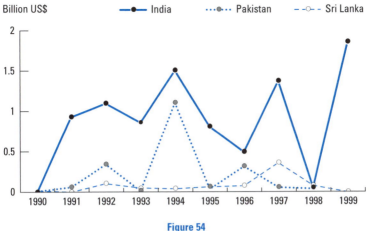

Figure 54
Proceeds from privatization in India, Sri Lanka and Pakistan.
Source: World Bank (pers. comm.).

followed by Pakistan and Sri Lanka. Bangladesh and Nepal had privatization programmes which brought heavy employment losses in the former state enterprises but not much state revenue.

Privatization was pursued in South Asia for the same general reasons as everywhere: to reduce budgetary deficits, increase economic growth, widen the space for private initiative, develop capital markets and improve services. Divestment in South Asia was motivated primarily by fiscal reasons, accelerating after a further increase of already high budget deficits in the region during the early 1990s, and also by mounting subsidies for loss-making public enterprises and services. The moderate level of realized privatization proceeds hardly helped to bridge the deficits. Privatization in South Asia proceeded in a gradual way (in contrast to Latin America) as unions were quite strong; the public sector accounted for a considerable part of employment in the formal sector and included at least some profitable enterprises.

Sri Lanka, Bangladesh and India

In *Sri Lanka* – where economic liberalization started in 1977 – privatization had to be delayed due to political instability until 1987. To reach popular (i.e. labour union) acceptance, the process was called 'peoplization', boiling down, in practical terms, to the handing over (free of charge) of 10 per cent of shares to the workers in former state units. In most cases, 51 per cent of total shares were offered to strategic investors on open bids (to secure transfer of technology and attract new investment); the rest was offered to the general public (to develop the capital market). In the first phase, only 43 'easy' units were sold that did not produce essential items; loss-making enterprises and state plantations were left out. The latter were merely brought under private management (on five-year contracts) which did not encourage new investment.

After this first boom, the process slowed down as responsibility for privatization was shifted from one agency to the next, often with overlapping mandates and by interference of line ministries. In 1996, after a new unitary agency for the privatization process (the Public Enterprises Reform Commission) was established, the process gained considerable momentum, especially after the country had signed structural adjustment agreements with the Bretton Woods institutions. By the end of 2002, 86 companies were privatized (leaving 70 units in the public domain), usually by selling the majority to a strategic investor (Salih, 2000; Knight-John, 2002).

In *India*, the privatization process was even more spread out as most governments did either not command a majority or depended upon unreliable coalition partners, sceptical of the merits of privatization. Until the mid 1990s, only 5 to 20 per cent of shares in 31 public-sector undertakings were divested by (bundled) selling of shares to public financial institutions. After criticism of undervaluation and poor receipts earned by this method, a disinvestment committee was established in 1996 which recommended strategic selling to individual owners or companies. Even now this meant only divesting, at most, 49 per cent of shares in 39 units. Shares were overwhelmingly bought by mutual funds and financial institutions, and political interference hardly decreased. After 1999, the process accelerated because of rapidly increasing internal debt and a changing intellectual climate (favouring market-oriented reforms), as well as the negative side effects of earlier deregulation on state enterprises. As most formerly restricted sectors were opened up to private investment and imports from 1991 onwards, the public sector subsequently had to become more competitive or else perish. During the late 1990s, up to 74 per cent of shares were sold (after 2000, a few cases of complete sell-out occurred) and management control therefore shifted to the private owner. This definitely increased share prices during divestment (Gupta, 2002; Kapur and Ramamurti, 2002). After the May 2004 electoral success of the Congress party and its allies, which was due to a certain extent to perceived lop-sided effects of market-friendly policies, the privatization policy of the new government was pursued more selectively.

In *Bangladesh* the reform of the overstretched public sector (due to the takeover of abandoned factories after partition of Pakistan in 1971) began during the 1980s and gathered momentum after 1993 in tandem with liberalization. Direct sale of state enterprises has been the dominant method. Political discord between the alternating parties in power, opposition by trade unions, lack of investor interest and absence of a sufficient legal framework limited the exercise.

Effects and regulation

Privatization was certainly a success in reducing the financial burden of the states in question, although budget deficits did not diminish very much. The financial benefits were due mostly to the partial elimination of subsidies to former state enterprises (subsidies to Sri Lanka's state units came up for 10 per cent of gross domestic product (GDP) during the mid 1980s) and the high interest cost of public loans in deregulated markets. In India, receipts were far behind targets and below 0.3 per cent of GDP per annum for 1991 to 2002. In Sri Lanka, gross proceeds ranged between 0.2 and 2.5 per cent per annum, with net proceeds (deducting privatization expenses) between 0.1 and 1.25 per cent.

Privatization proceeds were generally not used to upgrade social infrastructure. In Sri Lanka, they went into a privatization fund and were practically spent for current expenses, including defence. After 1995 they also served to retire foreign debt, leading – among other causes – to a marked improvement of debt indicators. In India, privatization income was used to finance current expenses. Later, an effort was made to link it to public debt reduction.

Success of privatized companies in South Asia was mixed. Plantations in Sri Lanka saw a spectacular turnaround in terms of profits, production, exports and investments. Profits and investments increased also in other companies after divestment, but only to a limited degree. Six companies went bankrupt and had to be re-nationalized, leaving the workers without compensation. In India, turnover and profits of divested companies also went up (by 22.6 per cent and 59 per cent, respectively); share value also improved, whereas the proportion of public credits in working capital went down. In the difficult production environment of Bangladesh, nearly 50 per cent of small privatized units had to close down, and large units showed mixed results, at best. The enterprises remaining in operation could increase profits and even diversify production. In Nepal, privatized companies enlarged capacity and showed some increase in labour productivity. Profits, however, remained modest.

Effective regulation of private companies in sectors hitherto served by public monopolies should precede privatization; in this respect, the record is less encouraging in South Asia. Regulation was (and remains) weak in Sri Lanka and was first left to market competition alone. Private bus transport was not regulated at all, although public regional transport boards (plagued by overstaffing, an outdated fleet and forced subsidies for the transport of school children, etc.) had to compete against private companies able to operate only the attractive lines since 1987. In 1987, a Fair Trading Commission was established to obstruct anti-competitive behaviour, while consumer protection was left to a different agency. This separation of functions proved counterproductive and gave way to the merging of the two bodies recently, although the new agency was stripped of its powers to look into monopolies and mergers.

Regulation is better in the financial sector, where the Central Bank or the Insurance Board is responsible, and in the telecom sector. The Telecom Regulatory Commission is responsible for granting licences; but prices are determined by the market only. Even in this case, regulation did not stop interference and malpractices (obstruction to interconnections) shielding dominant providers against competition. In December 2001, an agency for the regulation of all sectors except bus transport, petrol and telecommunication was established. In addition to deficient regulation, the government of Sri Lanka, in order to entice private buyers, gave temporary monopoly rights to some companies (e.g. Shell) for up to ten years in some operations – with negative distributional consequences (Knight-John, 2002).

In India regulation was introduced long before privatization of the relevant sector. Agencies, however, could not operate without government interference. The regulating authority for telecommunication (TRAI) was set up while the public Department for Telecommunication (DOT) was responsible not only for making telecom policy, but also the main supplier of services. Private operators were struggling with unrealistic licence fees; the regulatory authority was locked in legal disputes with the government for granting licences and fixing of tariffs. Eventually the deadlock was solved by better separating the functions of TRAI and DOT (Gupta, 2002; Baijal, 2002).

Effects on consumers were mixed. Waiting times for new connections and prices for long-distance calls fell dramatically in South Asia, while the quality of service improved (Srinivasan, 2003), accompanied by higher charges for basic services (to the disadvantage of the relatively poor). Prices of other services sometimes shot up; this, however, rarely discriminated against the poor since services were hardly ever accessible to the poor anyway. In Nepal, product prices of divested companies went up by 50 per cent, reflecting unrealistic pricing policy.

Shares were first offered at rather low prices in Sri Lanka with the objective of broadening access. However, many workers quickly sold their shares in the market to raise income, and they were mostly acquired by more prosperous groups. In terms of reducing income inequality, this process was, therefore, a failure.

As mentioned earlier, quite a few former state enterprises had to close down in Nepal and Bangladesh. This led to the immediate loss of 3200 jobs in Nepal, although some workers were re-employed on a contract basis. In Bangladesh, privatization led to an aggregate downsizing of the labour force of the enterprises affected by about 25 per cent. In Sri Lanka, the figure was 17 per cent. Retrenched employees in South Asia usually received compensation payments ('golden handshakes') or made use of voluntary retirement packages (*before privatization*), which were rather generous, including up to two months' salary for each year of service, plus provident fund and accrued interest. In Sri Lanka, several companies operated with ad hoc solutions, which, depending upon the relative strength of local unions, meant even more generous packages. These came as a windfall gain to qualified employees (who quickly found re-employment), but left the less qualified with no sustainable living basis. In India 230,000 employees were offered compensation packages at an average value of 130,000 rupees, benefiting mostly senior workers near the retirement age. This whole exercise had questionable distributional consequences and came at a huge cost to the public exchequer. In Pakistan, almost a quarter of the bid value for privatization was utilized for payment on golden handshakes (see Joshi, 2000).

Retraining and redeployment of employees was marginal. In India, a National Renewal Fund for these objectives had already been established in 1992, financing practically mostly voluntary retirement packages. In Bangladesh retraining of jute mill workers was supported by the World Bank, but met only limited interest of targeted beneficiaries because of the long gap between job loss and inception of the training programme. In 1998/1999 a Special Workers' Fund was set up, financed adequately to retrain 15,000 workers per year. Unfortunately, here and in other South Asian countries this was not accompanied by supportive labour market policies.

Salaries generally did not deteriorate after privatization. In Sri Lanka, some companies registered significant improvements (also in fringe benefits). Workers, too, realized some windfall profits by selling their shares. In India, remuneration improved after privatization. Labour productivity, which was extremely low in former state units in South Asia, definitely increased.

Conclusion

In sum, privatization in South Asia, because of its moderate scale, did not deliver very much in terms of growth, employment generation or economic democracy. It helped to contain budget deficits and to finance current state expenditures. As mostly relatively sound state enterprises were privatized, they could often be turned around in terms of profits and productivity. Workers did not suffer much by privatization, in general, while consumers only drew moderate benefits. The weakest spots in the exercise were regulatory deficiencies (favouring some happy few), and very poor efforts to retrain retrenched employees and to develop active labour market policies (including some form of unemployment insurance).

Special Issues

ESSENTIAL SERVICES: SHIFTING THE BURDEN OF PROOF

Tim Kessler and Nancy Alexander

A tougher test for private provision

Private provision of essential services bears a heavier burden of evidence than public provision.[1] Essential or basic services include those needed for livelihood, health and dignity, especially water and sanitation, electricity and healthcare. Given the unique social contribution of essential services and the considerable risks involved in privatization, evidence of public-sector failure is not, by itself, sufficient justification to adopt private provision. Privatization advocates should therefore make an empirical case that the conditions for controlling market failure and promoting equity are actually in place before adopting private provision policies.

The privatization of basic public services has become a dominant issue in policy discourse in developing countries. For example, in the water and sanitation sector, public–private partnerships (PPPs) – an increasingly common form of private provision – have grown worldwide from almost none in the early 1990s to more than 2300 today. Moreover, major global institutions such as the World Bank, the International Monetary Fund (IMF) and the Organisation for Economic Co-operation and Development (OECD) are aggressively promoting private provision and greater private-sector participation in every essential service sector.[2]

Why is the private provision of essential services a problem?

While external pressure is an important element of controversy, citizen opposition to private provision of essential services also arises from what many perceive as unique characteristics of this policy area. What makes essential services so special?

Public goods

First, essential services are public goods (see Box 2 in the 'Introduction'). As such, their benefits, such as public health and economic productivity, extend well beyond the particular individuals who consume them. As the 2003 *Human Development Report* states, governments have traditionally provided essential services because 'their market value alone would not capture their intrinsic value and social benefits' (UNDP, 2003, p111). A common argument for private provision is that essential services are a drag on budgets. However, while governments should address fiscal strains by improving efficiency and levying higher tariffs for those who can afford them, the budget itself is not a legitimate reason to privatize. There is broad consensus that citizens should collectively pay for 'pure' public goods such as national and personal security (military and police) and environmental protection. One never hears complaints that such services 'run losses' – even though they are financed entirely by tax revenue – because their social benefit is so obvious. Although infrastructure and social services differ from pure public goods because they are excludable, they are no less important for promoting broad social benefits.

Poverty reduction

A second reason that essential services are special is their central role in poverty reduction. The world's governments recently committed themselves to achieving the Millennium Development Goals (MDGs). Essential services are widely acknowledged as the principal means through which these goals can be achieved. Because private provision is typically accompanied by increased tariffs, many have voiced concern that poor people will either be unable to afford services, or left with subsidized but poor quality government services.

The cases in the 2003 *Human Development Report* and the 2003 *Social Watch Report* identify numerous examples of price increases and social exclusion resulting from privatization (as well as the implementation of cost-covering user fees, often an initial step towards private provision). The privatization of infrastructure often combined profit-maximizing incentives with monopoly power. During the late 1990s, the privatization of electricity in Brazil led to a 65 per cent increase for residential consumers, far higher than the rate of inflation. In Peru, privatized electricity companies raised real prices by a factor of 14 between 1992 and 2002. In Bulgaria, the privatized water monopoly raised prices twice within three years despite a contract stipulating stable prices during that period.

Private provision of key social services has also resulted in increased costs for public providers and, ultimately, to taxpayers. In Malaysia, privatization of essential medical services such as drugs and hospital supplies led directly to increased costs for government provision of healthcare without improvements in services. The 1996 privatization of support services, such as maintenance, equipment and cleaning, increased operational costs four to five times. There is also widespread evidence that private healthcare provision leads to higher costs through induced consumption and the absence of government intervention to inform or protect consumers. For example, 'With limited access to professional services and aggressive drug production in an unregulated market, the result is irrational drug use – particularly among poor people' (UNDP, 2003, p114).

Privatization proponents commonly argue that while prices may increase under private provision, the hikes are justified by improved service and access for the poor. Unfortunately, extensive cross-sectoral evidence casts doubt on this claim. In the social services, the expansion of private-sector participation leads to 'cherry-picking'. Private providers have strong incentives to serve primarily people who are able to pay commercial prices, and who enable firms to minimize overhead costs. In Chile, research by the Inter-American Development Bank (IDB) shows how health insurers attempt to exclude people who become ill. This finding is reinforced by the Social Watch country report for Chile, which states that commercially priced health insurance for women of child-bearing years is three to four times higher than for men in the same age bracket (Arteaga, 2003). The 2003 *Human Development Report* reveals serious problems with private health insurance schemes in Latin America: 'And because managed care organization attract healthier patients, sicker patients are being shifted to the public sector' (UNDP, 2003, p113).

Expanding the choice of providers invariably draws better-off consumers into the private sector. Those who are unable to afford commercially priced private services remain with the state, thus creating a segregated 'two-tier' system based on income. Among countries which had promoted private participation in healthcare and education, Social Watch reported the emergence of 'two-tiered' services in Costa Rica, Malaysia, Nepal and Uganda, as well as wealthy countries such as Germany, The Netherlands and the US.

But the most dramatic evidence of private providers circumventing the poor is in water, the most essential of all services for those in poverty. According to International Rivers Network, 'Water multinationals have little or no interest in rural drinking water systems. Corporations are rarely able to profit from poor and dispersed rural populations, who mainly depend on local water sources such as wells, springs and streams' (McCully, 2002, p2). Even small businesses appear hesitant to invest in the areas that need it the most. As a WaterAid study of rural water reform in Uganda explains: 'communities that are disadvantaged by the terrain in their locality – where the more expensive technical options are required – are unlikely to benefit from [private-sector] projects... Contracts to the private sector avoid expensive deep drilling operations' (WaterAid, 2003). The investment prospects for rural water service are particularly discouraging. As former UK Environment Minister Michael Meacher put it:

> *Private sector finance will certainly be important, but it will generally not be used for basic services. Thus, the World Bank's database on private participation in infrastructure, whilst it shows that private investment in water and sanitation in developing countries, to date, totals US$25 billion, also reveals that none is in South Asia, and almost none is in Africa. Yet these are the two regions in the world without adequate water and sanitation services. This indicates that private sector investment is, at present, insignificant at providing basic water and sanitation services to the very people who most need it'* (Meacher, 2001).

These are not merely the opinions of advocacy organizations. They are on public record by privatization enthusiasts and major private-sector players. For example, the World Panel on Financing Water Infrastructure, chaired by former IMF Director Michel Camdessus, promotes private capital investment, but also concedes that 'Compared with other types of infrastructure, the water sector has been the least attractive to private investors, and the sums involved have been the smallest' (Winpenny, 2003). In a meeting on water policy in Uganda, staff from the French multinational Vivendi stated that the imperative of making a reasonable profit limits investment to larger cities with sufficient per capital income (Bayliss, 2002).

Similarly, the CEO of another French water multinational, Saur, articulated what he characterized as unreasonable demands on the private sector in developing countries, such as universal provision requirements. Noting a 'marked increase in risk for the private operators, particularly in developing countries', he lamented the 'emphasis on unrealistic service levels [which leads to] limited interest in the market'. He concluded that investment requirements cannot be met by the private sector and that 'Service users can't pay for the level of investments required, not for social projects... The scale of the need far out-reaches the financial and risk taking capacities of the private sector.'[3]

Financial incentives

As investors become increasingly unwilling to take on risky projects in developing countries, it is increasingly common for the public sector to provide them with lucrative – and costly – financial incentives. In its effort to attract private firms to basic infrastructure sectors, for example, the World Bank is promoting a range of 'fiscal support', including commercial guarantees, tax breaks, grants and direct subsidies (Irwin, 2003).

Examples abound throughout the developing world. Pakistan was only able to lure private investment into its energy sector through an incentives package that included price indexation for fuel prices, US and Pakistani inflation, as well as exemption from corporate income tax, customs duties, sales tax and other surcharges on imported equipment, as well as permission for power generation companies to issue corporate bonds and shares at discounted prices (Augustus, 1997). In 2001, the Kenyan government suspended a water contract with a subsidiary of Vivendi when it was revealed that the company would invest nothing except a billing system over ten years, despite earning 15 per cent of total collections over that period. In addition, the local water department would reimburse the company for hardware after ten years, without even discounting for capital depreciation (the contract was later revised) (Bayliss, 2002). In South Africa, a power consortium led by UK's BiWater provided only about a quarter of capital investment in upgrading and expanding service in the Nelspruit municipality. The majority of capital for this private venture was supplied by the South African Development Bank (Smith et al, 2003). In Honduras, the US-based energy corporation AES obtained exemptions on all taxes and charges as a condition for building an 800 megawatt power plant in Puerto Cortes.

Governments also attract investors to essential service sectors by agreeing to assume virtually all financial risk in expensive operations. These can create enormous 'off-budget' liabilities that can become more onerous than debt itself. In the power sector, the 'power purchasing agreement'(PPA) is one of the most notorious instruments that corporations use to ensure profit at the expense of consumers and taxpayers. In the Indian state of Maharashtra, a US$3 billion Dahbol power plant was touted as the country's largest foreign investment project. However, over a decade after investment began, the state's electricity board claimed that the Enron-led consortium had manipulated prices through the PPA and was charging over double the rate of comparable publicly owned generators. After the board called a moratorium on payments, Enron shut down operations and initiated litigation.

In Uganda, AES negotiated a PPA for the Bujagali hydroelectric project that was later shown to be excessively expensive. The government had little experience with such contracts, and relied on World Bank advice in setting up the PPA provisions. An independent review by an Indian energy consulting firm concluded that not only were capital costs the same as other power plants with twice the generating capacity, but the PPA imposes excessive payment requirements and restricts the government's ability to sign other agreements that could reduce its fiscal exposure (Prayas Energy Group, 2002). The PPA has been suspended. Long-term power contracts have generated numerous disputes with governments which accused companies of extracting excessive financial benefits through high prices or selling unneeded energy. In addition to the cases described above, such contracts have been renegotiated or cancelled in Pakistan, Croatia, Indonesia, Hungary, Costa Rica and the Dominican Republic (Corral and Hall, 2001).

The unwillingness of private firms to invest in low-income people has led much of the development community not to rethink privatization, but rather to rethink how to *finance* privatization. The influential 'Camdessus Report', *Financing Water for All* (Camdessus, 2003), specifically recommends greater use of multilateral guarantees for private investment – yet another off-budget liability – as well as direct use of development assistance to 'facilitate water projects managed by private operators under public control' (Winpenny, 2003). The global development institutions have increasingly turned to financial incentives to attract private providers into otherwise financially unattractive investments.

The use of such mechanisms to attract private financing underscores an apparent double standard. When governments run losses to subsidize publicly delivered services, conventional wisdom is that such arrangements are not financially sustainable. However, when funds from the same public sector (or lending institution, which must be paid back eventually) are used to finance private provision of the same service, the arrangement is characterized as an innovative approach to poverty reduction.

The salient point is that government must engage in some form of social redistribution when poor people cannot afford basic services. From a financial perspective, the main question in considering the choice of provider is: which is likely to cost the government more money? In many cases a public service may require significant subsidies, especially if it has to reach a lot of poor people. These 'loss-making' enterprises are one of the main justifications for bringing in private firms. But if governments have to offer major financial incentives to succeed in attracting more private capital, policy-makers need to ask how high that price is, and if it justifies a major policy change.

Market logic

Finally, even mainstream economists have questioned privatization of essential services because of the distinctive market logic in these sectors. Network-based infrastructure, such as water systems and electricity transmission, are often natural monopolies. In most settings, there can only be one energy grid or centralized water system. Formally 'connected' households are likely to be served by a single entity, regardless of whether it is public or private. Where competition is thus constrained, effective public regulation becomes the key to assuring affordable access to quality services.

Barriers to entry in social services are much lower than for infrastructure. Many have argued that increased private provision in these sectors brings benefits of competition. In the healthcare sector, in particular, the multilateral development banks (MDBs) increasingly promote deregulation and help finance private providers. However, healthcare is also subject to significant market failures. According to an IMF researcher:

Allocation cannot be based solely on cost effectiveness, which focuses on efficiency, but ignores equity. Markets alone cannot produce efficient outcome in the healthcare sector, which suffers serious [market] failures due to asymmetry of information, imperfect agency relationships, barriers to entry and moral hazard.

Because patients know far less than physicians about how to 'consume' healthcare, doctors have tremendous power to induce consumption (Hsiao, 2000, pp7–11).

Proponents of private provision are likely to respond that keeping services also entails serious risks, including the continuation of fiscal losses, poor quality and exclusion of the poor. We do not deny the reality of these risks in many countries. However, we do maintain that the risks of reforming poor government services may be less than those in privatizing them. In this regard, proponents of private provision confront important questions about the role of the states and citizens. The decision to privatize public services often carries implicit – and contradictory – assumptions about government.

One assumption is that poorly performing public services, characterized by corruption, low capacity or political capture, cannot be reformed sufficiently to deliver quality services. However, another assumption is that, given the requirement of effective public regulation in preventing market failures, the (same dysfunctional) state will take the leading role in monitoring and disciplining private providers. Solving the 'privatization paradox' requires evidence that suggests how market failure and equity issues will be addressed through private provision.

Privatization advocates are aware of this challenge, and there is considerable agreement about appropriate steps towards more effective regulation, which include greater regulatory autonomy and authority, adequate financing, as well as full transparency and legal recourse for consumers. While not all developing countries have poor regulatory capacity, the problem is common enough that governments should have to demonstrate adequate capacity to monitor and sanction private utility providers before undertaking private provision.

The MDBs now provide technical assistance and financing for institutional 'capacity-building', which often includes the hiring of foreign consultants in so-called 'twinning' arrangements. But it is patently implausible for any government to claim that such stop-gap measures will enable it to effectively monitor and enforce compliance from highly sophisticated corporations – literally overnight.

Conclusion

Proponents of private provision of essential services often assume a 'counter-factual of inaction'. They compare best-case private provision scenario with continuation of failing public service. The implication in much privatization literature is that government is simply beyond hope. Yet there are often viable options for reforming the public provision of essential services, especially by increasing accountability to citizens, and making budgets more progressive. In many cases, the constraints on these options are starkly political, while in others the need is for greater technical capacity or better organizational incentives. Before committing to private provision, especially with weak regulatory capacity, governments should compare the difficulties of 'doing privatization right' and undertaking meaningful public-sector reform.

Importantly, there are real alternatives to private-sector provision. Pace and sequence are critical. Experience with 'big-bang' structural reforms has been disappointing because the institutions required to make them work are usually not in place. A gradual, cautious approach can help governments to avoid big mistakes and also enable learning that translates into subsequent policy action. In the case of essential services, full private-sector management (or ownership) of service delivery may suddenly give government new responsibilities that it is not willing or able to fulfil.

Private provision contracts need not delegate wholesale management of complex services to a single provider. Within the private sector, large corporations contract out specific tasks to smaller firms in order to increase efficiency or production flexibility – while maintaining full control over finished products and services. Similarly, governments may continue to provide essential services directly while using contracts to produce important inputs into final service delivery – for example, construction, installation of utility connections, lab tests and bill collection.

There is an important distinction between a service contract, which assigns responsibility for isolated tasks, and management contracts, which transfers full management authority to a firm. The more isolated the task, the less risk the private firm is expected to assume. Privatization advocates point out that service contracts under weak public management are unlikely to result in significant improvement (Marek et al, 2003). However, by the same token, where regulatory capacity is weak, governments are unlikely to enforce private-sector compliance with terms of complex and sweeping management contracts.

Weak states therefore present obstacles to both public and private service delivery options. The challenge for policy-makers is to determine how to structure and sequence reforms in order to enhance the government capacities needed to make chosen reforms effective. As they begin the reform process, governments can harness the efficiency and incentives of private provision without taking big risks. For example, private firms may bid on delivering specific elements of service delivery to government buyers, rather than delivering the entire service to households.

Particularly where regulatory capacity is weak, governments as customers are likely to have far greater ability to hold private firms accountable than individuals. Greater efficiency achieved through private-sector participation – as opposed to broad management or control – may help to improve service quality or financial sustainability, thereby contributing to effective public-sector reform. Alternatively, as government learns how to monitor and regulate limited private provision activities, it may become better prepared to move on to more advanced stages of private provision.

PRIVATIZATION OF THE INFRASTRUCTURES

Matthias Finger

Within the overall context of liberalization, deregulation and privatization, infrastructures such as telecommunications, postal services, energy (electricity and gas), railways, air transport and water have distinctive technological and economic characteristics. Liberalization can be partial, at most, because parts of infrastructure (e.g. railway tracks, electricity grid, etc.) are natural monopolies. Infrastructures involve heavy technologies so they require substantial investments, as well as guarantees by governments. Unlike social services, for example, many infrastructure services are commercial in nature and are sold on the market even before liberalization.

Privatization

Privatization of infrastructure in the narrow sense of selling assets to the private sector has been practised only by a very few industrialized countries, namely the UK and New Zealand during the 1980s. It was, however, widely practised in the developing countries and in Eastern Europe, mostly as part of the structural adjustment policies imposed by the World Bank and the International Monetary Fund (IMF). The forces pushing for such privatization are mainly ideological in nature, grounded as they are in neo-classical economics, and provide a very simplistic view of infrastructures. Many privatizations of this kind face serious technological, economic and political obstacles, and have had to be scaled down, subsequently restructured or even reversed.

Deregulation and unbundling

Liberalization, meaning the introduction of competition into at least parts of infrastructure services, has been much more significant as a means of privatization than asset sales. Competition can take the form of either 'competition *in* the market', where different organizations compete for customers, or 'competition *for* the market', where monopoly rights for a defined set of services, geographical area and time period are put up for tender. Liberalization is a form of *deregulation* because it requires changing the infrastructures' competition rules so that competition can occur.

Liberalization often requires *unbundling*, which means splitting different stages of service delivery into different organizations, so that the parts suitable to be exposed to competition are separate from the non-competitive (monopoly) elements of any given infrastructure. What actually can be unbundled and submitted to competition varies widely between sectors:

- In the *telecommunications* sector, such unbundling has already largely occurred, the last remaining monopoly being the so-called 'last-mile' (i.e. the local telephony network). However, it is already technologically possible to also unbundle the last mile, notably by means of wireless telephony.
- In the *postal* sector, unbundling has so far not yet really occurred, even though total unbundling is technologically possible between collection, transport, sorting and distribution. Competition can take place in all four of these segments of the value chain.
- In the *electricity* and *gas* sectors there is unbundling between production, high-voltage transport and local distribution; but competition can, and increasingly does, occur only in the production segment of the value chain.
- In the *railways*, unbundling can take place between the rail infrastructure and train operations. Consequently, competition can be introduced in the transport segment.
- *Air transport* has always been unbundled between airports, airlines and air traffic control. Competition is already well developed in the airlines segment. Competition in the airports sector is possible where there are practicable alternative airports that serve the same population centres: the rapid growth in 'low-cost' airlines in Northern Europe has been greatly supported by smaller and more basic regional airports offering cheaper deals to compete against traditional international hubs.
- In the *audiovisual* sector, unbundling has, to a certain extent, already occurred, distinguishing between content, on the one hand, and the

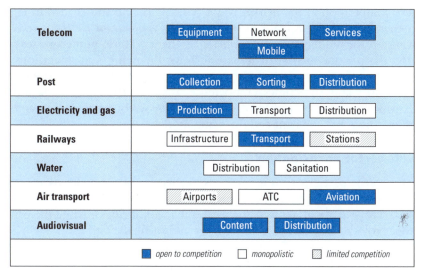

Figure 55
Potential for unbundling and competition in different infrastructure sectors.
Source: Matthias Finger.

distribution of the content, on the other. Moreover, competition can actually be introduced in both segments.

- Finally, in the *water* sector (water distribution and sewerage), unbundling does not really make sense, even though there is already significant experience with competition for the market.

Figure 55 presents the theoretically possible unbundling. Blue indicates the segments of the value chain, which can be exposed to competition, while white indicates the segments that will remain monopolistic even after liberalization. Shading indicates segments where limited competition is possible.

Wherever *competition in the market* is theoretically possible (blue in Figure 55), one will generally not observe privatization, but rather the emergence of private competitors to the historical operators, called the incumbents. The forces pushing for such unbundling and, subsequently, for competition are:

- technological changes (particularly in telecommunications and electricity);
- internationalization and industrial strategies, which led to a growing search for competitiveness and, therefore, of cost control by all economic and financial companies;
- diversification of needs and of demand whereby users demand innovation;
- failure of public management; and
- in Europe, the European Commission, which is driving unbundling and subsequent introduction of competition, motivated by the desire to create a common market for infrastructures and the need for greater efficiency.

Where competition in the market is not possible (white and shaded in Figure 55), there is still the possibility to introduce *competition for the market* by putting up for tender the monopolistic segments. Here, numerous ways of having the private sector participate in both financing and operations are possible (see the following section). Driving forces here are primarily lack of public money and, sometimes, competence, as well as the World Bank and the IMF, which have actively promoted such private-sector participation and the corresponding management and financing models.

Private-sector participation

Private-sector participation is often also called 'public–private partnership' (PPP). Under PPPs, the infrastructure usually continues to be owned by the public sector (national, regional or local public authorities), while the private partner provides management, technology and/or financing.

Private-sector *participation in management* can take several forms. The World Bank developed a French water sector approach and recommended it to (or imposed it upon) many developing and Eastern European countries as part of a larger structural adjustment package. Here, the private sector takes over the relationship with the customers and provides services to the owner of the infrastructure. One can distinguish between three levels of services, depending upon the risks the private operator is willing to take:

1 In a *management contract* – generally, between one and four years – the private company takes over the management (usually the upper management layer) of the infrastructure operator, but does not provide any financing or pay for small investments. The private operator is paid from the fees charged to the customers and pays some of this money to the infrastructure operator for the right to manage it.
2 In a *lease contract* – generally, between 4 and 15 years – the private company takes over not only the management of the infrastructure operator, but also some of its operations and pays for running investments necessary for the daily operations.
3 In a *concession* – generally, between 10 and 45 years – the private company basically takes over the infrastructure operator, the public sector retaining only legal ownership. The private company pays for all investments, including major ones.

Intermediary models are possible. Both the public authorities and the private company take the most risks in the last model.

Private-sector *participation in financing* is different, though linked with private-sector participation in management, especially when it comes to recouping investment costs. Again, the model is originally French, though the World Bank, and especially the IMF, have substantially refined it. Three common models are:

1 Build-own-operate-transfer (BOOT): the private operator builds the infrastructure and remains the owner of it during a certain period of time (i.e. generally during the duration of the concession, for example, 10 to 45 years). After that, the infrastructure becomes public, and the private operator generally loses the concession.
2 Build-transfer-operate (BTO): the private operator builds the infrastructure and hands it over to the public sector. In exchange for the investments, the private operator receives a concession (or ocasionally a lease contract), during which he has the right to appropriate the user fees.
3 Rehabilitate-transfer-operate (RTO): this is like BTO, but is based on rehabilitating existing infrastructure, rather than building new. The duration and type of the contract primarily depends upon the amount of money that the private operator had to put up for the rehabilitation.

Conclusion: Problems

Different models can each raise different problems:

* *Asset sale*: this is the least widespread model. Its main problems are the prices and the quality for the consumer, public-sector dependency on private operators and, more generally, the issue of security of supply.
* *Deregulation*: the introduction of competition into segments of an infrastructure value chain is probably the model with the least number of problems. Nevertheless, one must mention here the problem of cherry-picking (private operators are only active in the most lucrative markets, thus leaving the non-lucrative markets to the public operators and handicapping them), as well as the problem of weakening the system's integrity.
* *Private-sector participation*: this is also potentially problematic, creating problems of public-sector dependency and instrumentalization, corruption and asymmetry of information.

Strong and effective regulation can help to address all of these problems (see the chapter on 'Regulation' in Part IV).

THE TOP PUBLIC SERVICE TRANSNATIONAL CORPORATIONS

Matthias Finger

One cannot talk about privatization and liberalization more generally without simultaneously discussing the rise of transnational corporations (TNCs). Indeed, there is a whole set of companies whose business it is to provide public services in the areas of water, energy and transport, as well as in health, catering, etc., and who have significantly grown precisely as a result of the various forms of privatization. This snapshot briefly describes what a public service TNC is, presents a few selected examples, highlights the public service TNCs' strategies, and evaluates the phenomenon in the context of privatization.

What is a 'public service TNC'?

Public service TNCs are corporations that make the majority of their turnover and profits from providing what were traditionally called public services. We also define public service TNCs as companies that offer more than just one public service (e.g. telecommunications and broadcasting). For example, they distribute water, clean wastewater, deliver electricity and gas, offer public transport by rail or bus, broadcast information, provide education, health and hospital services, and deliver social services and even security (e.g. policing, military protection or imprisonment). In short, they are active in the areas where the public sector was traditionally active at national, regional or local levels. The term 'TNC' refers to the fact that these corporations now spread beyond the local and even the national levels and provide such services across national borders.

At first, there appears to be opposition between public services and TNCs. While public services traditionally emanate from one public authority and are aimed at citizens, TNCs exist across countries and are there to satisfy customers and make profits. Some of them even have become more powerful than governments. However, with liberalization and privatization, this contradiction seems to disappear somewhat: there is an increasing number of TNCs that provide public services in lieu of public entities.

Essentially, there are two models of emerging public service TNCs:

1 The traditional model is of French origin and consists of private companies offering services instead of the state or local government. This is typically the case of the French water TNCs – such as Vivendi or Suez – which have started out by providing drinking water and sewage services to French municipalities since the beginning of the 20th century. In the same category one can mention French (e.g. Bouygues) and US (e.g. Bechtel) construction companies. These TNCs, particularly because of their privileged contacts with the political authorities, have managed to either buy public service operators or obtain concessions for providing public services. This is, for example, the case in road building (e.g. toll roads) or in broadcasting or mobile phones. Basically, there are two ways of making money here. First, the TNCs obtain a concession from the public authority which allows them to charge fees to users. Second, the TNC obtains a subsidy from the public authority and, in exchange, provides the public service (e.g. in the case of security services). There are, of course, combinations of these two approaches.

2 The second model is of a completely different origin: here we have (generally local) public operators (so-called 'public enterprises' that previously remained confined to their geographical borders), which, as part

Box 10 RWE

Founded in 1898 as Rheinisch-Westfälisches Elektrizitätswerk Aktiengesellschaft (RWE), Essen.

Core business areas: electricity, natural gas, water, waste management and services.

Major companies: RWE Power; RWE Rheinbraun; RWE Trading; RWE Net; RWE Plus; RWE Solutions; Innogy Holdings; Harpen; RWE Gas; RWE Dea; Thames Water; American Water; RWE Umwelt; Heidelberger Druckmaschinen; Hochtief.

Number of employees worldwide (2002): 131,765.

Number of countries: 22.

Annual revenue 1996/1997: €36.9 billion.

Annual revenue 2002: €46.6 billion.

Source: www.rwe.com

of their corporatization or even privatization, seek to diversify and expand beyond traditional local, regional or national borders. Some of these companies actually continue to be publicly owned, yet behave on the international scene like any other transnational corporation. It is obvious that the bigger the original public enterprise, the bigger the chance of becoming a public service TNC once unleashed. A typical example here is Electricité de France (EDF), the French electricity giant, or the Dutch Postal Service (TPG) (see 'TPG Post: a Dutch privatization success' in Part II). Often, these types of public services TNCs are even actively supported by their respective governments. Another example is RWE, originally a municipal company that has managed to become one of the biggest public service TNCs worldwide in just a few years.

Overall, it is interesting to note that this phenomenon of public service TNCs is primarily a European and not an American phenomenon. Indeed, most of the currently most powerful public service TNCs are of European (particularly French and German) origin, a phenomenon which is still reinforced by current European Union (EU) liberalization policies and practice. These European companies are trying to make inroads into the US market. US companies that can be qualified as public service TNCs in the broad sense are mainly limited to the military and security sectors (e.g. Halliburton, military contractors and companies operating prisons).

Based on the above definition, there are numerous TNCs that qualify as public service TNCs. Figure 56 indicates their name and the diversity of their activities.

Box 11 Electricité de France

Founded in 1946 to supply fossil-fuelled power to help rebuild France.

Core business areas: energy generation and trading, distribution, supply and retail, water.

EDF Group companies: 73 companies in total; includes London Electricity Group; EnBW (Germany); Demasz (Hungary); SME (Czech Republic); SSE (Slovakia); Estag Group (Austria); Electricité de Strasbourg, SIIF Energies and TIRU (France); Semobis (Belgium); BERt and Demasz (Hungary); Eck, ECW, Kogeneracja and Rybnik (Poland); EDF Energy (formerly London Electricity Group) (UK); Fenice (Italy); Graninge* (Sweden); Port Said et Suez (Egypt); Azito (Côte d'Ivoire); Edenor and Edemsa (Argentine); Light and Norte luminense (Brazil); Central Anahuac, Saltillo and Altamira (Mexico); Figlec and Synergie (China).

Number of employees worldwide (2002): 172,000.

Number of countries: 24.

Annual revenue 1997: €29 billion.

Annual revenue 2002: €48.4 billion.

Note: * An agreement reached on 14 August 2003 provides for the sale of EDF's interest in Graninge AB to EON Group's Sydkraft AB, subject to the approval of the European Commission competition authorities.

Sources: EDF Group Annual Report, EDF Group Annual Results and *EDF Group Financial Statement* (1997 and 2002) (see www.edf.fr)

Box 12 Bechtel

Founded in 1898 as a railroad construction company.

Core business areas: civil infrastructure; development, financing and ownership; industrial, mining and metals; petroleum and chemicals; pipelines; power; telecommunications; US government services.

Number of employees worldwide (2002): 44,000.

Number of countries: 60.

Annual sales profit 1997: US$11.4 billion.

Annual revenue 2002: US$11.6 billion.

Sources: Bechtel Report (2003) and *Bechtel Global Report* (1999) (see www.bechtel.com)

Company	Main Business	Home Country	Sector														
			Ca	Cl	Co	Cp	Cs	Ed	En	Ev	He	Hg	M	P	SP	T	W
Bechtel[1]	Construction	USA			•		•		•						•	•	•
Bouygues	Water	F			•		•		•	•				•			•
Electricité de France (EDF)	Energy	F							•	•							•
Endesa	Energy	E			•				•	•							•
Group 4 Falck	Security	DK													•		
ISS	Cleaning	DK	•	•							•						
P&O	Shipping	UK					•							•		•	•
Serco	Defence	UK			•	•	•	•		•		•		•	•	•	
Severn Trent	Water	UK							•	•				•			•
Sodexho[2]	Catering	F	•				•	•	•		•				•		•
Southern Company	Energy	USA			•				•								
RWE[3]	Energy	D			•[4]		•		•	•							•
Suez[5]	Water	F			•				•	•							•
Tyco	Security	USA			•					•			•		•		•
United Utilities[6]	Water	UK			•				•	•			•	•			•
Veolia Environment[7]	Water	F			•				•[8]	•						•	•
E.On	Energy	D			•				•								•
WMX	Environment	USA							•	•							•

Figure 56
Top public service TNCs.
Key: Sectors: Ca=Catering; Cl=Cleaning; Co=Communications; Cp=Computers; Cs=Construction; Ed=Education; En=Energy; Ev=Environmental; He=Health; Hg=Housing; M=Manufacturing; P=Property; SP=Security and Prisons; T=Transport; W=Water.
Home countries: D=Germany; DK=Denmark; E=Spain; F=France; UK=United Kingdom; USA=United States of America.
Notes: [1] Includes International Water. [2] In January 2000 Sodexho Alliance, world's leader in food and management and Universal Services, world's leader in remote site management, announced their merger and became Universal Sodexho.
[3] Acquisitions in 2002 in electricity and gas, and in water in 2001 (Thames and American Water) have made RWE a leading TNC in the utilities industry. [4] Print media. [5] Includes Ondeo/United Water, Sita and Tractebel. [6] Includes North West Water and Welsh Water, among others. [7] In April 2003 Vivendi Environment became Veolia Environment, with the gradual withdrawal of Vivendi Universal from its capital. [8] In partnership with Dalkia/EDF (34%).
Source: Company annual reports.

Selected cases

Public service TNCs – also called 'multi-utilities' – expand into other sectors and by doing so grow. Such expansion generally takes place via acquisitions, leading, not astonishingly, to a significant concentration process. Already today, a few public service TNCs dominate the public service market. The most important ones are, not astonishingly, French. Among them, we find Suez Lyonnaise des Eaux (now called Ondeo), Vivendi Environment (now called Veolia Environment), Bouygues and the German RWE. All four companies have undergone, over the past years, substantial expansion and restructuring. Such restructuring has been heaviest at Vivendi, which has actually separated its communications business from its multi-utility business.

Public services TNCs' strategies and business model

When talking about the strategies and business model of these public service TNCs, one needs to distinguish between the strategies up to 2001/2002 and more recent evolutions. Indeed, until approximately 2001, these public service TNCs appeared to be on a process of steady expansion into other sectors and countries, characterized by business growth and concentration (mergers and acquisitions). In doing so, they were taking advantage of (quite limited) economies of scale and scope. Their main competitive advantage, however, appeared to be the growing asymmetry of information between themselves and the (mostly local) public authorities whose services they were providing. Indeed, as these companies became ever bigger and more experienced, their information (e.g. about costs) was ever increasing, thus making them better able to negotiate. Simultaneously, and thanks to parallel policies of decentralization, the negotiation of public service contracts was shifted down to regional and even local levels, thus increasing the asymmetry of information even further. In the developing countries, this was often done with the assistance of the World Bank, whom these companies were actively lobbying.

Moreover, their business model appears to follow two separate tracks. On the one hand, these public service TNCs want to take as little risk as possible, while obtaining the longest possible term contracts. Therefore, they are not primarily interested in privatization (i.e. in the buying of formerly public operators), but rather in what they call public–private partnerships (PPPs). As highlighted elsewhere in this book, they seek to manage infrastructures, which continue to be owned by the public authorities, whether local, regional or national. In doing so, the risks associated with these infrastructures will remain with the public authorities, while the profits from operating the infrastructures come to the TNCs.

On the other hand, these TNCs seek guaranteed income or funding. Here the strategy somehow differs between industrialized and developing countries. In developing countries, public service TNCs help national governments to obtain loans from the World Bank, which are then used for rehabilitating the infrastructures. These are the same infrastructures that the public service TNCs then manage. In industrialized countries, however, the strategy is quite different: here they lobby for stricter standards (e.g. water standards), which will force the public authorities to engage in some form of financing partnership with the public service TNCs. More concretely, the public services TNCs in the industrialized countries offer financing in exchange for long-term contracts.

This strategy and business model seems to have worked well until recently. Indeed, the various practices of public service TNCs have come under serious scrutiny and criticism, first by non-governmental organizations (NGOs), but later also by governments. Practices of corruption, overpricing, renegotiation of tariffs, etc., have led public authorities and citizens to become quite suspicious of public service TNCs, making them lose some of the concessions (e.g. in Manila, Jakarta, Mozambique and Brazil). In other cases, these TNCs have taken too much risk, for example by expanding into the multimedia sector in the case of Vivendi Universal. In any case, Vivendi and Suez have recently had to be substantially restructured, and for all of the public service TNCs, business will almost certainly become more difficult in the near future primarily because public authorities are increasingly learning how to deal with them (through, for example, tougher negotiation of contracts and stricter supervision). Furthermore, as a result of growing suspicion from political authorities, and due to the growing competencies of public authorities when it comes to regulating TNCs, it is not at all clear whether their competitive advantage in terms of information asymmetry will continue to be sustainable in the future.

Pros and cons

Nevertheless, not all is negative with public service TNCs. In fact, they bring many assets to the table. The three most important ones are as follows:

1 Public service TNCs generally offer high professionalism and quality. This is because they can reap the benefits of the latest technologies when it comes to public service provision (e.g. water and electricity), but also because they have significant managerial experience.
2 Public service TNCs also are efficient and, therefore, sometimes less expensive than traditional public service operators. However, these efficiency gains are generally offset by the dividends, which must be paid to the shareholders.
3 Finally, public service TNCs offer a certain stability. Indeed, because of their size and connections, they are often capable of leveraging funds beyond what public, especially local, authorities are capable of doing. On the other hand, powerful public service TNCs can walk away from their obligations without much legal consequences, leaving customers without any provision.

On the negative side, one must mention the fact that the model of public–private partnerships practised by the public service TNCs breeds, by its very nature, corruption. Indeed, public service TNCs seek long-term contracts and are thus willing to put up some money in order to obtain these contracts. This phenomenon is, of course, not limited to European public service TNCs, but applies to all companies who live off government contracts or concessions, and therefore basically acquire monopolies over a certain time period. Furthermore, the asymmetry of information and subsequent power leads to attempts to 'instrumentalize' the public authorities for business purposes, meaning that a powerful public service TNC is able – because of better information – to negotiate favourable contracts. Finally, efficiency gains genrally occur due to lay-offs – thus, the opposition of unions to public service TNCs, in particular, and to privatization and liberalization, in general.

HOW GATS (GENERAL AGREEMENT ON TRADE IN SERVICES) JEOPARDIZES ESSENTIAL SERVICES

Nancy Alexander and Timothy Kessler[4]

There are six ways in which the General Agreement on Trade in Services (GATS) of the World Trade Organization (WTO) jeopardizes the universal provision of essential services. Not only are healthcare, education and water services affected, but democratic processes, as well.

Introduction

Until GATS was devised (1 January 1995), the rules of the trading system pertained to trade in goods, not services. Whereas *tariffs* are the principal barriers to trade in goods, *domestic laws and regulations* are the barriers to trade in services.

The scope of GATS is breathtaking. It applies to any measure (e.g. law or regulation) taken by government at any level, from central to local, which affects specified services. At present, GATS is one of several agreements being negotiated in the current (2000–2005) round of WTO negotiations. The purpose of GATS is to progressively liberalize trade in 160 service sectors, such as financial, sales, legal, telecommunications, accountancy and construction services, as well as essential services, including healthcare, education, water and electricity.

Proponents of GATS argue that the agreement will promote economic growth by enhancing competition and efficiency. They stress that the sectors subject to the GATS rules will attract foreign direct investment (FDI), three-fifths of which now goes toward services (about 80 per cent of FDI comes from multinational companies located in North America, Europe and Japan). However, the United Nations Conference on Trade and Development (UNCTAD, 2000) declares that 'There is no empirical evidence to link any significant increase in FDI flows to developing countries with the conclusion of GATS.' GATS supporters also claim that developing countries will benefit from GATS provisions that liberalize temporary immigration of 'natural persons' who perform jobs in service sectors. However, such benefits will not materialize without consent from industrialized countries, none of which have yet made significant commitments.

Liberalization of services poses serious dangers for policy autonomy and development, as well as the quality and access of services, especially for the poor. Some of the risks are described here.

Exclusion for public services

WTO leaders dismiss, and even ridicule, claims that GATS will lead to the privatization of government services. They point to a provision stating that services are excluded from GATS jurisdiction if they are *'supplied in the exercise of governmental authority'*. Yet, services meet this criterion only when 'supplied neither on a commercial basis, nor in competition with one or more service suppliers'. This is rarely the case. Proponents also cite the preamble of GATS, which recognizes the 'right to regulate'. However, this language is non-binding. Actual GATS provisions make it clear that regulations are allowed only as long as they are consistent with the agreement. This judgement will be made not by governments, but by appointed WTO dispute settlement panellists. Finally, despite WTO assurance that 'we're not after your public services', many countries have already made extensive commitments to liberalize hospital, medical and dental services, health insurance and higher education under GATS. Moreover, the European Union (EU) has requested that 72 countries liberalize their water distribution systems. Thus, assurances that the agreement protects government services have already been proven false.

Irreversibility

Where GATS has jurisdiction over a service, it 'locks in' sectors as they are liberalized, thereby making liberalization practically irreversible. While reversing commitments is technically permitted, governments can only do so by negotiating 'compensation' for all affected partners – a prohibitively costly undertaking. Indeed, the WTO states that 'because unbinding is difficult, [government] commitments [to a sector] are virtually guaranteed'.[5] This means that if subsequent events reveal serious negative social or economic effects, it may be too late to take corrective action.

Development impact

Historically, governments have insisted that foreign investors take steps that ensure benefits to local economies, such as establishing joint ventures with domestic partners; equity ceilings on foreign capital; performance requirements in areas such as technology transfer and public service provision; and the employment or training of local staff. Furthermore, governments have sometimes used human rights, labour or environmental standards as criteria for entry by a foreign company. Under GATS, governments could be barred from employing such means to promote local development.

In addition, if performance requirements (or other conditions on investment) are waived for one foreign investor, they must be waived for all investors under the *most favoured nation* (MFN) rule, which requires governments to treat service providers from all other member countries in the same manner.

GATS rules could adversely affect local interests in two ways. First, under the *national treatment* rule, foreign corporations must be treated at least as favourably as domestic companies, which may prevent governments from promoting local service businesses. Under this rule, governments that subsidize the provision of essential services (as most do) may be compelled to subsidize provision by multinational corporations, as well. Second, under the *market access* rule, foreign service providers must be granted virtually unrestricted entry into the sector. They can set up as many operations as they want, which may undercut environmental and social goals. For instance, the environment may be degraded if too many tourism operators exploit a delicate ecosystem.

Constraining state autonomy

Under proposed rules on 'domestic regulations', member countries might have to prove to trade dispute tribunals that their regulations (e.g. technical standards, licensing and qualifications) are 'not more burdensome than necessary'. In other words, burdensome regulations will be deemed 'trade restrictive'. One expert says that healthcare licensing requirements that restrict healthcare fees for poor patients may be viewed as trade restrictive since it impedes profit-making and could repel foreign investors.[6] If implemented, rules on domestic regulations could have a 'chilling effect' on the passage and enforcement of environmental, labour and public health regulations (see Box 13). The EU proposes that when a WTO member brings a claim to the dispute panel body against another government, that panel could apply a 'necessity test' to regulations under challenge. The WTO said that the purpose of a necessity test is to 'balance … two potentially conflicting priorities: promoting trade expansion versus protecting the regulatory rights of governments'.

The WTO has global, binding enforcement powers that have profound political implications for the sovereignty of nations. The WTO's dispute settlement mechanism functions as a judiciary that hears complaints and establishes binding judgements. *When it finds a government in violation of its rules, a tribunal can compel a member nation to strike down its own laws and enact WTO-compliant rules.* Its power to enforce economic sanctions may cause governments to back away from implementing even potentially non-compliant regulation, regardless of its social or economic utility. As well, the history of WTO rulings in trade disputes shows a marked bias towards interpreting the balance between regulation and trade expansion to the benefit of business.

Undermining transparency and democracy

Byzantine negotiation processes are used to achieve a progressively higher level of liberalization. Each of the WTO's 147 members can make *requests* to other governments for liberalization of specific sectors; in response to these requests, member governments make *offers* to liberalize selected sectors. These negotiations occur in *secret, bilateral* meetings where the weakest countries are often pitted against the strongest. Moreover, the US and European trade negotiators make their requests based on pressure from corporate service lobbies seeking expanded markets, not development goals.

Box 13 The California Senate speaks out

Writing to Robert Zoellick, US Trade Representative (28 March 2003), the California State Senate stated:

The proposed rules on 'domestic regulation' could allow foreign corporations and governments to challenge a wide range of California healthcare regulations as 'more burdensome than necessary'. This could include nurse-to-patient staffing ratios, professional licensing standards and laws against discrimination by licensed insurance companies on the basis of genetic characteristics. Service rules could also have devastating impacts on the environment by restricting the ability of governments to limit permits for oil drilling, land use and waste incineration. Drinking water standards, pesticide application standards, renewable energy laws and toxic waste laws could also be challenged under domestic regulation, as well as national treatment or market access provisions.

These implications are very troubling and strike at the heart of our ability to regulate in the public interest. Recently leaked negotiating documents from the European Union (EU) reveal that the EU not only seeks market access to our service sectors, but explicitly requests future limits on state and local regulatory authority. These documents request that the US open up a number of public services to trade by multinational corporations, including drinking water, electricity, and postal and sanitation services. In addition, they request the limitation of state oversight of insurance, the extension of small business loans to foreign companies and the limitation of approximately 44 specifically identified state laws.

... in spite of the magnitude of these requests, neither state nor local law-makers nor the public have been granted access to these documents.

Frequently, governments fail to disclose draft or final copies of requests and offers, which effectively excludes the public and many elected officials at state and local levels from participation in decision-making. The EU's requests were leaked to the public, revealing their request for liberalization of water distribution systems.

Imposing liberalization

GATS architecture is often said to be 'development friendly'. Technically speaking, it is true that each WTO member can choose which sectors to liberalize and what limitations to put on the liberalization process. It is also true that certain GATS articles (Articles IV and XIX, p2) are intended to accommodate the needs of developing countries. However, in reality, developing countries are often subject to unyielding pressure to liberalize.

Donors and creditors, such as the International Monetary Fund (IMF) and the World Bank, are increasingly promoting sector liberalization and privatization. The IMF often exerts pressure by choking off subsidies for public services (Nellis, 2003). In many instances, the donor and creditor communities agree to starve public sector services of external support (Dubash et al, 2002). The World Bank and the regional development banks have adopted private-sector development (PSD) strategies that introduce a third generation of structural adjustment programmes (SAPs) to promote liberalization of investment regimes and the privatization of basic services.

In each service sector, the donor and creditor communities, often led by the World Bank, promote competition for provision at commercial rates. If governments fail to comply, they could lose critical financing, trade credits and debt relief. Donor and creditor communities are laying the foundation for subjecting each service sector to GATS disciplines. Sometimes industrialized countries exert direct pressure on developing countries, as when the EU stipulated that unless developing countries liberalize their banking and insurance markets, the EU will not enlarge market access for developing countries' agricultural, textile and clothing products (UNDP et al, 2003).

Conclusion

GATS expands the rights and protections of corporate investors. By expanding the reach of global institutions with legally binding authority over national policy decisions, transnational corporations seek to replace the complex role of the state with a single goal: pursuit of profit. The European Commission acknowledged that GATS is 'first and foremost an instrument for the benefit of business, and not only for business in general, but for individual service companies wishing to export services or to invest and operate abroad'. The main organizations representing these firms include the European Service Network and the US Coalition of Service Industries, a 67-member lobby organization whose top 12 members had combined revenues of about US$700 billion in 2000.[7]

Developing countries need services, particularly to meet the Millennium Development Goals (MDGs), such as reducing the number of people living in poverty by half by the year 2015. Reaching these goals involves massive scaling-up of healthcare, education and water services. However, the MDGs should not be a pretext for privatizing essential services, especially if the privatization occurs without the consent of citizens and their elected officials.

What can be done?

WTO member governments must be persuaded to take – 'carve out' – essential services from the negotiations. State or provincial and local governments should be clearly exempted from the jurisdiction of GATS.

Governments must make the negotiating process transparent. Part of that effort will require even-handed analyses of the impact of liberalization in different sectors, particularly social and sovereignty impact assessments of the application of GATS rules.

Public service commitments made under GATS must not be irreversible. Governments should insist on safeguards that enable them to measure negative

Box 14 The General Agreement on Trade in Services (GATS)

The General Agreement on Trade in Services (GATS) is a multilateral agreement, forming part of the World Trade Organization's (WTO's) legal framework that establishes principles and rules for trade in services. The stated purpose of GATS is the expansion and progressive liberalization of such trade in services as a means of promoting economic growth and development. The agreement's scope is very broad: it applies to all service sectors, including public services. Although GATS exempts services that are 'provided in the exercise of government authority', the definition of 'government authority' requires that the service must be provided on neither a commercial nor a competitive basis. Because most public services exhibit one of both of these characteristics, they could become subject to GATS disciplines. Trade in services is defined as the supply of a service, under four distinct 'modes':

1 *Cross-border supply*: services supplied from one country to another (including by way of mail, email, and telephone).
2 *Consumption abroad*: consumers travelling to another country to use a service (such as tourists).
3 *Commercial presence*: foreign suppliers establishing commercial presence in a member's territory, such as by setting up an agency or subsidiary Branco.
4 *Presence of natural persons*: individuals travelling to another country to provide a service.

WTO members must ensure that any domestic measure that affects any of these four modes of supply, including regulations adopted by federal, state and local government, are consistent with GATS rules. These rules include general as well as specific obligations. General obligations apply to all WTO members and all service sectors, and include:

* *most favoured nation treatment* (MFN), which requires that the services or service suppliers of one trading partner are not favoured over another; and
* *transparency*, which requires that members publish their domestic laws and regulations that affect trade in services.

Other *specific* obligations apply only when governments enter into specific commitments for specific service sectors and modes of supply:

* *National treatment* requires governments to treat foreign services and service suppliers no less favourably than domestic services and service suppliers. Under such disciplines, treatment that modifies the conditions of competition in favour of domestic providers, even as an unintended consequence of promoting social goals, will be considered less favourable and discriminatory.
* *Market access* restricts governments from placing limits on, *inter alia*, the number of service suppliers or employees in a sector, value of transactions, the types of legal entities or the participation of foreign capital.

Box 14 CONTINUED

Other rules are currently under negotiation. Of particular importance are *domestic regulation* rules, which could introduce a 'necessity test' for regulations such as professional qualification, technical standards and licensing. Under the GATS framework, a member could bring a dispute (in order to protect its investors and service providers) complaining that another member's regulations are 'more trade restrictive than necessary', or are otherwise not 'reasonable, objective and impartial'. WTO panels or the appellate body could rule that offending regulations be repealed or redesigned. Other GATS rules still under negotiation apply to subsidies and government procurement.

Source: adapted from Carnegie Council and Friedrich Ebert Foundation (2003); see also www.wto.org

social impacts from liberalization, specify a 'trigger level' for applying safeguards, and respond with regulatory and subsidy actions that may not be WTO consistent.

PRIVATIZATION AND DEVELOPMENT

Andreas Obser

Introduction

The rolling-back of state ownership in the economy through privatization gathered considerable pace in the world (see Figure 57). Privatization of state-owned enterprises (the terms state-owned enterprises and public enterprises are often used interchangeably) has become an important phenomenon. This process of privatization is having an impact on economies across the globe, most notably by giving market mechanisms a greater influence over resource allocation. Over the past couple of decades, privatization has featured prominently on the agenda of reforms, particularly in developing countries. Their share in global privatization revenues rose from 17 per cent in 1990 to 22 per cent in 1996 (*The Economist*, 1997).

During the 1980s and the 1990s, a wave of privatizations swept the developing world. Privatization is now so widespread that it is hard to find countries not using the approach. North Korea, Cuba and, perhaps, Myanmar make up the shrunken universe of the resistant. Counting the transition, post-communist states, well over 100,000 medium and large enterprises have been privatized in one form or another. Divesture has touched every sector, from companies producing tradable goods, through infrastructure firms, and, more recently, to units providing social services, such as health and education (World Bank, 2002a). Including the many firms partially or fully privatized in the transition economies, the number of firms undergoing ownership change now

Billion US$

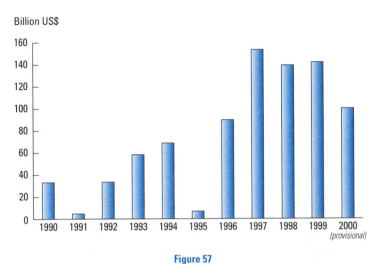

Figure 57

Sales revenues from privatization worldwide. The process of privatization peaked in the late 1990s, though the cumulative stock of privatized enterprises continued to increase.
Source: Mahboobi (2002).

well exceeds 100,000; and the total value of assets transferred has been very large, particularly in Latin America, East Asia and the transition region, though much less so in South Asia, the Middle East and sub-Saharan Africa. Despite the massive shift to private ownership, a surprising amount of firms and assets remain in the hands of the state – particularly in China and Vietnam, but also in India, and in the transition countries where the large and high-value infrastructure firms have yet to be sold (Birdsall and Nellis, 2002, p3).

As an illustration of the relevance of privatization policy, Figure 58 shows the change in public enterprises' share in gross domestic product (GDP) between 1980 and 1997, for all the economies in the world, grouped by income level according the World Bank classification. Even though the change does not only respond to privatization strategies, it is strongly linked to it, as explained below. It reflects a major revision of the role of the public sector as owner of productive assets in the economy (Sheshinski and López-Calva, 1999).

Privatization in developing countries has often been part of an adjustment agreement with the World Bank. The motives of privatization have primarily been that the private sector works more efficiently than the public sector and, as a result, – from an economic point of view – there should be benefits from privatizing public sectors where there is no natural monopoly (Nellis and Kikeri, 1989; Kragh et al, 2000). Nancy Birdsall and John Nellis (2002, p1) argue that privatization has not been a popular reform and the record on privatization has been mixed. Economic assessments of the effects of privatization on economic welfare and growth in developing and transitional economies have generally been positive. But evidence of political chicanery and corruption in Russia and Malaysia, of fiscal mismanagement in Brazil, of

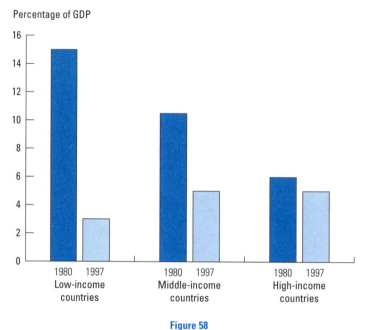

Percentage of GDP

Figure 58
Public enterprises' activity as a percentage of GDP. Privatization has been predominantly a phenomenon affecting the low-income countries.
Source: Sheshinski and López-Calva (1999); estimations based on World Development Indicators.

escalating prices in Argentina, and of lost jobs in a great many countries have sullied its reputation even among proponents of the liberalizing reforms of the last two decades. Nobel laureate Joseph Stiglitz thus campaigns for slower and more deliberate privatization (Stiglitz, 2002), and critics of the larger liberalizing agenda known as the Washington Consensus conclude that privatization should be entirely opposed. Most of the contemporary discussion on privatization focuses on whether and to what extent privatization is or is not efficient and welfare enhancing. Birdsall and Nellis argue that it is important to examine the distributional effects of privatization.

Objectives, methods and initiatives

The World Bank is the leading institution in the preparation and support of privatization programmes, providing advice and loans to cover costs associated with privatization, and also providing investment loans to help restructure privatized enterprises. The World Bank also supports in the post-privatization phase by assisting governments to set up the facilitating and regulatory framework for the privatized sectors, by assisting the enterprise sector to adjust to the new situation, and by assisting the financial sector to deal with the new private enterprise. Many bilateral donors have supported the privatization processes in developing countries, as well (Kragh et al, 2000). Traditional foreign aid has often been directed to public infrastructure and utilities in order to prepare them for privatization. Donors have also contributed to cover expenditure and clear debt in the privatization processes. Debt-for-equity swaps have been facilitated by donor funds, and sometimes donors have provided funds to finance the privatization. Bilateral donors have also supported government directly in the privatization process, helping to create an optimal environment for privatization and assisting with technical assistance, policy advice and capital.

From the 1960s through the 1980s, the World Bank lent and credited member governments throughout the world very large sums for the purpose of creating and financing, and then strengthening and reforming, public enterprises. The World Bank's magic formula behind its support of member governments has been based on the hope that in addition to providing basic needed services in an efficient and cost-effective manner, 'public enterprises would assist the development of "strategic sectors", gain access to commercial credit that would be denied to small private businesses, fill "entrepreneurial gaps", empower numerically large but economically weak segments of the population, maintain employment levels, and raise the level of savings and investments' (Nellis and Shirley, 1991).

The main reform objectives have been to make public enterprises more efficient and effective providers of goods and services, and to reduce subsidies from the national budget. Instruments are:

- financing of restructuring;
- reduction of surplus workers;
- clarification of enterprise objectives and relations with governments via performance contracts;
- strengthening management and improving management incentives; and
- substituting *ex-post* for *ex-ante* government controls (Berg, 2000).

The structural adjustment programmes have been used as an instrument to encourage governments in developing countries to pursue active divesture and public-sector reform programmes. Among developing economies, those countries most dependent upon World Bank loans were the most active in privatizing state-owned enterprises (Ernst, 1998). Privatization is one of the key elements in structural adjustment programmes that embrace free trade, financial liberalization and deregulation and a reduction of state involvement in the economy. The prominence given to privatization in the adjustment programmes implemented by many developing countries is based on the perceived superiority of the private sector in providing goods and services that were earlier deemed to be the exclusive preserve of the public sector (Adam et al, 1992). Several arguments are cited in support of this perception. Perhaps the most ostensible economic rationale is the consideration of allocative efficiency. It is argued that the public sector tends to use resources less efficiently than the private sector. Furthermore, technological developments have made it possible to create competition in markets that were traditionally considered to be natural monopolies. The basis for public provision of many goods and services in order to avoid monopolistic inefficiencies has thus been eroded (Islam and Monsalve, 2002).

Whether these and other arguments are sufficient grounds to justify the generalized turn towards privatization merits further examination. A key question is whether a country's welfare is likely to improve after a change in ownership. In turn, this will depend upon a host of conditions that vary from country to country. Limiting the debate to that of improved resource allocation, it is apparent that the implicit economic structures, which underpin successful privatization, such as credible and efficient regulatory regimes and reasonably functioning capital markets, are all too often absent in developing countries. There are also important distributional and strategic considerations that impinge upon a country's welfare. Any analysis of the benefits of privatization must take these considerations into account. Thus, in some situations, reforming the public sector may be more welfare enhancing than divestiture. Changes in ownership will not, in and of themselves, lead to improvements in efficiency. Furthermore, since privatization has often gone hand in hand with sweeping structural reforms, any credible empirical analysis must distinguish the efficiency-enhancing effects of privatization from those of other reforms. Such analyses are fraught with difficult attribution problems that are often not adequately addressed in the literature (Islam and Monsalve, 2002).

Lessons learned

The strength with which privatization is pursued in the developing world belies both the controversy that, at times, attends its implementation and the contested nature of its impact. International experience shows that privatization policy engenders particular controversy:

- if public assets are sold for markedly less than their true value or, alternatively, when purchase-of-service contracts are awarded without due care or due process;
- when foreign capital or foreign corporations are allowed to become dominant participants; and
- where the application of privatization policy to a particular domain lacks legitimacy, either because the economic case is weak, or because it has failed to win key stakeholder support (Ernst, 1998).

Limited outcomes

Results of about two decades of reforming public enterprises and shrinking the size of the public enterprise sector are, by almost all accounts, slender (Berg, 2000). Elliott Berg reviews several assessments on aid in the field of public-sector management and public enterprise reform as one of its primary targets. Among others, a study of the International Monetary Fund (IMF) on the experience of 19 countries under its Enhanced Structural Adjustment Facility (ESAF) is referred to. The study concludes that only a few countries –

Bolivia, the Gambia, Guyana, Senegal, Sri Lanka and Togo – made significant inroads into the problem of public enterprise reform (Schadler et al, 1993). Similarly, the World Bank report entitled *Bureaucrats in Business: The Economics and Politics of Government Ownership* provides striking general evidence of the limited progress in public enterprise reform, at least until the early 1990s (World Bank, 1995).

An intensive evaluation of adjustment lending in sub-Saharan Africa by the World Bank, in 1994, comes to the general assessment that despite some encouraging stories, there is little evidence of successful public enterprise reform (World Bank, 1994). The report notes that financial control of public enterprises remains rudimentary. Even strategic enterprises are rarely audited by independent accountants. In only 4 of 29 countries (Zimbabwe, Malawi, the Gambia and Burundi) were many firms audited annually, and there was a long delay in publishing any accounts at all. Accounting for external funds on-lent to the public enterprises is unsystematic, as is tracking repayments and arrears.

Another international analysis, with a different regional focus, comes to quite similar results. Based on the evaluation of project completion reports of the World Bank, the analysis concludes that implementation of public enterprise reform programmes was satisfactory in only 5 countries (Argentina, Chile, Peru, the Gambia and the Philippines) and weak in 20 countries (Datta-Mitra, 1997). The privatization record in Africa is of special interest because donor interventions have been particularly intensive there. According to another World Bank study, 2600 transactions have occurred by the end of 1996, which is a reduction of one third in the number of public enterprises (White and Bhatia, 1998). But three-quarters of the countries in the region have done very little divesting, and the economic weight of successful privatization is limited. As of 1996, privatization activity was concentrated in ten countries and effective in fewer. Of the ten main privatizers, only Zambia, Ghana, Mozambique and Benin earn good grades as effective in process and results.

In 1995, the Operations Evaluation Department (OED) of the World Bank conducted a review of the International Development Agency's (IDA's) assistance to privatization. It found a very mixed record of performance across countries and sectors. Performance tended to be worse in low-income countries where pre-conditions for successful privatization were not met. These pre-conditions were stable macro-economic conditions, broad ownership among stakeholders (not just the government), policies conducive to competition, an existing robust private sector, and administrative capacities to implement the programme. For the lower-income countries, intermediate solutions – such as management contracts, leases or partial privatization – were seen as attractive alternatives for large enterprises such as public utilities. Reforms that introduce hard budget constraints, options for bankruptcy, increased competition and improved governance lay the ground for successful privatization at a later time (Précis–OED, 1995). Some of the major lessons are that privatization has worked better with:

- political commitment to the privatization process;
- administrative capacity to implement the programme;
- macro-economic conditions, policies and regulations that encourage economic competition; and
- a private sector that can take advantage of market opportunities.

Not surprisingly, higher-income countries with strong government commitment, robust private sectors, and greater administrative capacity have had more success with privatization. In low-income economies, results have been disappointing at times.

Since the 1995 report was prepared, the World Bank's assessments of privatization projects show that although most supported privatization efforts by the IDA have improved results at the firm level, macro-economic and distributional results have been mixed. Problems with the methods and sequencing of privatization and weak institutions are partly to blame. As the report had warned, where legal and regulatory institutions are weak, privatization has not improved (and has sometimes worsened) equity and has done little for short-run productivity. Trying to reform state enterprises rather than divest them has not been any more successful. Privatization in transition countries where corporate and overall governance are poor has been especially problematic (World Bank, 2001a).

Critical impact

On technical accounts privatization is frequently classified as a success. At the same time, it remains widely and increasingly unpopular, largely because of the perception that it is fundamentally unfair, both in conception and execution (Birdsall and Nellis, 2002). A common perception is that privatization has enriched the few at the expense of many, and that benefits to new private owners are large and immediate, while benefits to consumers and citizens are smaller and uncertain, sometimes never emerging at all. Birdsall and Nellis (2002) review the respective literature and conclude that most privatization programmes appear to have worsened the distribution of assets and income, at least in the short run. According to the data analysed, this is more evident in transition economies than in Latin America, and less clear for utilities such as electricity and telecommunications, where the poor have tended to benefit from much greater access, than for the banks, oil companies and other natural resource producers.

At the heart of much of the criticism is a perception that privatization has been unfair – hurting the poor, the disenfranchised and, in some cases, beleaguered workers, and benefiting the already rich, powerful and privileged. Privatization is seen as throwing large numbers of people out of work or forcing them to accept jobs with lower pay, less security and fewer benefits; as raising the prices of goods and services sold; as providing opportunities for the enrichment of the agile and corrupt; and generally making the rich richer and the poor poorer. The complaint is that, even if privatization contributes to improved efficiency and financial performance (and some contest this as well), it has a negative effect on the distribution of wealth, income and political power. The negative perception is widespread and growing: 63 per cent of people surveyed in the spring of 2001 in 17 countries of Latin America disagreed or strongly disagreed with the statement: 'The privatization of state companies has been beneficial.' The extent of disagreement was much greater than in 2000 (57 per cent) or 1998 (43 per cent). Over 60 per cent of Sri Lankans interviewed in 2000 opposed the privatization of the remaining state-owned firms. It would not be hard to find other expressions of popular dissatisfaction with privatization, of a similar magnitude, from the transition countries, in general, and Russia, in particular (Birdsall and Nellis, 2002, p2).

It is further elaborated that some of the popular and critical perceptions and assertions are quite accurate – there can be little doubt that mistakes have been made and promises not kept – but a good number are not. An argument can be made that the concrete outcomes of privatization have, in many cases, been better than people think, or that privatization may not be the actual cause of the real difficulties that they perceive. What matters is the actual distributional effect of privatization because inequality itself matters, in at least three ways:

1 Most societies possess and exercise some implicit limits on their tolerance for inequality, independent of its effects on growth and efficiency.
2 There is mounting evidence that inequality can and does hinder growth, particularly in developing economies where institutions and markets are weak.
3 It is increasingly evident that inequality can perpetuate itself by affecting the nature and pace of economic policy and by locking in unproductive political arrangements.

The research of Birdsall and Nellis (2002) shows that the distributional outcomes depend, to a great extent, upon the efficiency and productivity results produced by privatization, shifts in interpretation of the overall economic consequences of privatization, as well as shifts in the assessment of the distributional impact. It is referred to as a third, long-recognized gap in the analysis (i.e. the extent to which changes over time in income distribution are associated with privatization, or are produced by other reforms and policies that take place contemporaneously) (Birdsall and Nellis, 2002, p25f).

Conclusions

Privatization efforts have taken place across all economic sectors and developing countries. It is often part of a larger economic reform programme, which makes it difficult to identify and measure the overall effects of privatization. While output and employment effects are difficult to quantify, efficiency gains have been reported at company level. It is therefore difficult to draw general conclusions about the outcome of these efforts and their effect on the development of the countries concerned. However, in general terms the outcome has been more successful in Asia compared to Africa because of greater economic flexibility and, generally, more favourable business conditions, including the availability of investment capital. Likewise, the commercially most attractive sectors such as telecommunication are easier to privatize than other sectors, such as water and sanitation (van de Walle, 1989; Kragh et al, 2000). The best data available on privatization is based on the experience and analyses of privatization processes in Eastern Europe. There, the results show that privatization creates higher efficiency and larger growth rates, but, adversely, creates unemployment and poverty (Gillis et al, 1996; Kragh et al, 2000).

Fundamental issues of development, such as institutional development and governance, require long-term strategies and sustained efforts. A long-term perspective is especially important in dealing with the structural dimensions of development. Privatization in transition economies – besides civil service reform and deregulation of the financial sector – is pinpointed among recent failures to take the long view (Stiglitz, 1998b). Privatization increases inequality without contributing growth if the appropriate regulatory framework and environment for private-sector development are missing. In transition economies the rush to mass privatization, without establishing the underpinnings of capitalism, led to corrupt sales, asset stripping, lack of restructuring, insider-dominated transactions, and failure to induce domestic and foreign investment. The more ambitious the reform, the more time and resources that are needed to prepare the way (Hanna, 2002).

Controversy continues about the effects of privatization, especially in countries or sectors where complementary reforms are not in place. Here competition is still limited, and regulatory and supervisory capacity is nascent. Birdsall and Nellis (2002, p13) argue that the evidence generally shows that privatization has been among the more successful of the liberalizing reforms, in the sense that privatization, in more cases than not, has yielded good returns to new private owners, has freed the state from what was often a heavy administrative and unproductive financial burden, has provided governments in place with a one-time fiscal boost, and has helped to sustain a larger process of market-enhancing economic reforms.

Hence, the question is not about *if* privatization and private-sector development should occur, but about *how* it can be done in an optimal way: how to increase private savings and attract investments through external assistance; how to reach social goals through enterprise growth; how to avoid market distortions by supporting enterprises; and how to regulate and dialogue the business sector (Nellis and Kikeri, 2002; Kikeri and Nellis, 2004). Assets formerly held (in theory) for the public at large are now held by a small number of owners. Jobs are usually lost. Prices often go up; aggressive collection of fees hits the poor and middle class. And, often, sales revenue is eaten up by the rising cost of public debt. Yet, reversing privatization would hurt the world's poor. Privatization usually improves the operating and financial performance of a business, increases the financial resources available to governments, and leads to expansion of utility coverage – all of which still make privatization a pretty good deal for the poor. How should governments minimize equity losses while securing efficiency gains? There are lessons to apply: deal with regulation before, not after, the sale; concentrate on the

Box 15 The World Bank and Privatization

Katharina Hay

The Bretton Woods system, including the International Monetary Fund (IMF) and the World Bank, was established in 1944. Its goals are to help the poorest countries in the world, to support economic and social progress, to improve living standards and to eliminate the worst forms of poverty.

Today, the World Bank is the most important source of financial aid (as opposed to investment) for developing countries. It provides nearly US$18 billion in loans annually to more than 100 client countries. The World Bank offers financial services, policy advice and technical assistance to the governments of creditworthy low- and middle-income countries (World Bank Group, 2004a).

The World Bank consists of two institutions, the International Bank for Reconstruction and Development (IBRD) and the International Development Association (IDA). The World Bank Group includes three more affiliated organizations: the International Finance Corporation (IFC), the Multilateral Investment Guarantee Agency (MIGA) and the International Centre for Settlement of Investment Disputes (ICSID). The Group has 184 member countries. It is directed by a Board of Governors composed of one representative from each member country. In both the World Bank and the IMF, the United States is the largest contributor and has the most weighted voting power (Center for Strategic and International Studies, 2002). By a long-standing, informal agreement, the president of the World Bank, who is selected by the Bank's Board of Executive Directors, is an American, while the director of the IMF from Europe (The World Bank Group, 2004a).

During the 1960s and 1970s, when state-led development and import substitution policies were pursued, the focus of the World Bank was on the provision of classic 'development aid' rather than the promotion of private investment (World Bank, 2002b). Following the Bank's reorganization of 1987, private-sector development (PSD) became a programme of special emphasis. With the collapse of the Bretton Woods system and the Soviet bloc, the field of activities of the World Bank broadened. A massive campaign was started to establish free-enterprise systems and to shift from centrally planned to market economies. As a result, the importance of the IFC as the main institution for direct assistance to private firms increased.

The IFC was established in 1956. As a legally and financially independent institution in the World Bank Group, its purpose is to grant loans to private organizations for projects in the developing world. The IFC supports private-sector investment, helps companies to acquire additional financing in international markets, and provides technical advice and assistance (IFC, 2003). The IFC is the largest public source of financial investment for private-sector projects in developing countries.

quality, not just the quantity, of new owners; use the proceeds in ways that are socially astute and financially sound. John Nellis's and Sunita Kikeri's (2002) important bottom line is: privatize – but do it right.

BOX 16 THE WORLD BANK'S PRIVATIZATION POLICIES

Katharina Hay

After 1993, private-sector development' (PSD) became a general principle. Private-sector development divisions and departments were created throughout the Bank (World Bank, 2002b).

During the last 15 years, the World Bank has been assisting privatization in more than 80 countries. More than 8500 state-owned enterprises (SOEs) have been privatized, transferring close to US$1 trillion in assets from government-controlled enterprises into private hands (Dyck, 2001). In the past, the International Finance Corporation (IFC) has provided advisory services in the water, power and telecommunications sectors. Prominent recent transactions include Cameroon's electricity utility (SONEL – Société Nationale d'Electricité de Cameroun), Mauritania telecom (Mauritel), Panama's power sector (IRHE – Instituto de Recursos Hidráulicos y de Electrificación), Bucharest water (RGAB – Regia Generala de Apa Bucuresti), Uganda Telecom (UTL), Manila Metropolitan Waterworks and Sewerage System (MWSS), and Gabon's water and electricity utility (SEEG – Société d'Energie et d'Eau du Gabon). But the IFC has also been active in airlines, ports, national parks, health and irrigation.

Supporting the process of economic restructuring is now one of the main activities of the World Bank. For the World Bank, a 'vital private sector' is essential for success in the development of a country (World Bank Group, 2004b).

Some of these privatization activities of the World Bank were criticized by non-governmental organizations (NGOs) and even by the World Bank's own economists. From the critics' point of view, there is growing reason to believe that private firms have significant weaknesses, especially in providing services to the poor. In the eyes of many NGOs, the privatization process did not reach its goals. Privatization sometimes brings better services; but transparency is lost in many cases and corruption is on the rise. Furthermore, there is growing evidence that private investment (e.g. in water systems) is smaller than expected. The World Bank economist Nemat Safik grants: 'we were too optimistic concerning the willingness to invest in these countries ... despite far-reaching reforms, many countries do not find investors' (Hoering, 2003).

Another World Bank economist, John Nellis, states that in 'some institutionally weak transition economies, ownership change has, so far, not delivered on its promise. In far too many privatization transactions, in far too many transition countries, mass and rapid privatization has turned over mediocre assets to large numbers of people who have neither the skills nor the financial resources to run them well' (Nellis, 1999, ppix, 16). So, the World Bank seems to be aware of the problems associated with private projects in less developed areas (see also Kessides, 2004). While for NGO activists these problems are serious enough to justify discontinuing privatization initiatives, Nellis and other economists at the World Bank argue that overall the privatization processes have proven their worth. As they put it: 'the admission of error should not be overdone. The fact remains that when it can be carried out correctly, privatization is the right course of action' (Nellis, 1999, p28).

PRIVATIZATION AND CORRUPTION

Frédéric Boehm, Juanita Olaya and Jaime Polanco

Introduction

Corruption is commonly defined as the misuse of entrusted power for private gains and involves a broad range of different types, among them bribery, favouritism, fraud, embezzlement and extortion.[8] It can range from 'petty corruption' to cases of 'grand corruption', involving higher amounts and high-placed officials or politicians. It is now widely accepted that corruption is highly damaging to a country's economic, social and democratic institutions.

In this section, we point out the risks of corruption associated with privatization.[9] It is not our task to explore or to answer the question of whether privatization is superior to public ownership and operation. We will first discuss the view that privatization can reduce corruption. Next, we will analyse the opportunities for corruption during privatization: from decision making and process preparation, to tender and bidding, contract implementation and, when necessary, issues of further regulation.

Privatization to reduce corruption?

It is sometimes argued that privatization will reduce the opportunities for high-level corruption because it reduces the amount of resources under the control of politicians (Savas, 2000, p223; Torres, 2000, p145). Indeed, misuse of state-owned enterprises (SOEs) by politicians has been identified as one of the major causes of inefficiency. This is why it is usually presumed that politicians shun privatization for fear of losing convenient privileges and powers. However, politicians can use their influence to obtain benefits in the process of privatization, as well.[10] As Stiglitz (2002) points out:

> ... *government officials have realized that privatization meant that they no longer needed to be limited to annual profit skimming. By selling a government enterprise at below market price, they could get a significant chunk of the asset value for themselves, rather than leaving it for subsequent office holders.*

The question remains whether privatization could reduce this type of high-level corruption in the long run. Corruption as a result of privatization may be limited in its long-term effects, which can be seen as preferable to the continued misuse of SOEs. However, this is an open question because cronyism does not disappear with the advent of private operators.[11] For example, as Finger and Allouche (2002, p15) argue, liberalization and privatization in the water sector will increase the role of the state, rather than decrease it. Hence, where corrupt political interference is in place, privatization alone will not solve the problem if, afterwards, the same administration is responsible for regulation.

Another hope in overcoming corruption, especially on lower levels, is the introduction of competition. Clarke and Xu (2002, pp4, 6) argue that, on the one hand, by becoming a residual claimant of the profits, private firms will face stronger incentives than the state to prevent losses through corruption in order to survive in the market. In competitive markets, consumers can switch to another firm when faced with corruption, so competition will drive dishonest ones out of business. On the other hand, the authors argue that privatization could reduce small-scale corruption by removing capacity restrictions and waiting lists, and thus avoid the need to pay 'speed money' for better and faster service provision. The trouble is that in the case of natural monopolies, such as water supply through a single pipe system, competition is hardly conceivable. Much will thus depend upon contract specification, regulation and control. Finally, it has to be kept in mind that firms will try to avoid competition in the first place, and one way for a firm to end up with market power is to undermine the privatization process through corruption.

Opportunities and risks for corruption in privatizations

Any privatization requires a political will to privatize. This is susceptible to influence from the various interests involved in such a decision, including the public official. Influence can be exerted legally and fairly, but can also manipulate with bribes or favours by those expecting benefits from privatization. Pressure to privatize may come from multinationals seeking new markets, especially in developing countries. Firms can use the weaknesses of governmental institutions to favour their particular interests and count on their own capacity to override or buy regulation for their own benefit. Multinationals can further exercise pressure through political connections to home governments. International financial institutions such as the World Bank or the International Monetary Fund (IMF) may bias the decision-making process, deliberately or not. It is obvious that to tie financial aid to privatization could prevent alternative reforms from being considered seriously. Lastly, the scale of financial aid creates considerable room for corruption. These risks, which are related to the way in which the decision-making process may be influenced, may entail embezzlement by politicians or public officials who face conflicts of interests, or who are willing to extract political or economic benefits directly from the deal.

In kleptocracies such as Mobuto's in Zaire or Suharto's in Indonesia, privatization may be designed in order to maximize possible bribes. Rose-Ackerman (1999, p117) notes that kleptocrats will be particularly eager to privatize monopolies, enabling them to extract benefits from firms or to directly participate in the deal – in person or through family or clan members. 'White elephants' – projects that are simply not needed – can result. The decision to privatize can be then, in itself, corrupt.

Once the decision to privatize is taken, corruption can also arise during the preparation of the tender. The ways in which the tender requirements are specified, and the design of the project and the process itself, can create room for corruption. Complex details, bid-time management or unnecessary quality requirements can hide the pre-selection of one bidder or the exclusion of any other (i.e. ear-marked projects) under apparently transparent processes. Furthermore, the valuation of the assets to be privatized can be subject to corruption in many ways, as Rose-Ackerman (1999, pp35ff) points out, favouring bidders, politicians or decision-makers. Information about the real value of assets can be marketable, or the final privatization price may be strategically underestimated or overestimated in order to justify privatization and to discourage some competitors, enabling the firm with inside information to win the contract at low cost. The riskier the project appears in the first place, the better the bargaining position of the firm concerning the contract negotiation. It appears straightforward to assume that the higher the remaining monopoly power after privatization is, the higher the incentive for corrupt behaviour will be.

The subtle management of time also creates room for corruption. Savas (2000, p223) counts a speedy process as a guard against corruption; but speed can restrict competition by enabling only the participation of firms that were already well prepared in advance – for example, firms benefiting from insider information. Furthermore, according to Hawley (2000, p18), corruption arises because 'the inflexible and hasty deadlines set by the IMF and World Bank' often leave no time to establish an adequate framework to regulate the privatization process. Manzetti (1999, p327) points out that the 'need to act quickly' may only serve as an excuse for covering illegal practices. Time constraints may also restrict the response capacity of interested firms, as well as opportunities for civil society to articulate views and monitor the process. Finally, Rose-Ackerman (1999, p86) warns about pushing privatization when the government does not have 'the capacity to provide effective oversight of public contracts. Otherwise the result will simply be the creation of new sources of private gain at the expense of the general public.'

Once the privatization is decided and the project designed, the government needs to call for a tender, receive and evaluate the bids, and, finally, decide to award the contract. Again, politicians or public officials could, as noted by Rose-Ackerman (1999, p75), 'unduly favour the businesses in which they have a personal interest'. At this stage, a firm could also fall back on corruption in order to influence the award and win. For this purpose, two forms of collusion can arise during the tender and the bidding process. First, a firm competing for a contract can pay a bribe or confer some other favour in order to win the award. For example, favours may, as Bardhan (1997, p1321) notes, consist in providing real or fake jobs (e.g. as consultants, to politicians or public officials). Officials responsible for the tender could accept bribes from a firm that wants to be included in the list of candidates, or to exclude other firms. A firm could also pay to influence the tender conditions or to gain insider information about requirements that would lead to an advantage in the bidding process. Even fraudulent practices may arise, when a firm provides false information in order to win the contract. This firm may also need to bribe the tender official to prevent further investigations. Second, firms which are supposed to be competing against each other could either fix prices, or aim at dividing the national or international market between them. This strategy may involve bribing the tender official in order to install and stabilize such a cartel and to prevent investigations. Signs of both forms of collusion are, for example, non-competitive bids, a small number of contractors, or bids that are very close to the estimates provided by the government. Lack of transparency and unnecessary confidentiality can protect these types of collusion.

Occasionally, the bidding process is itself privatized, following the idea that some specialized private firms have more experience and know-how in handling auctions. This should not be used to reduce the standards of accountability that would be required from a public agency, and to legalize payments that otherwise would have been labelled as corrupt. Moreover, the use of private firms, such as consultancies, could be a way of obfuscating corrupt transactions by interposing a third actor between politicians or public officials and the private bidders.

After the formerly state-owned enterprise or contract has been awarded to a firm, corruption may also take place during contract implementation. Rose-Ackerman (1999, p19) notes that after a competitive bidding process without corruption, a firm could, nevertheless, be induced to pay bribes to politicians or public officials in order to increase its gains *ex post*. For example, a firm may pay bribes in order to obtain a positive business climate or 'friendly' regulation. Bribes may also be paid in order to enable price increases or a reduction of the quality provided afterwards through changes in the contract, buying 'blind' contract supervision or through changes in the regulatory regime. Because it tries to change the conditions upon which the contract was originally awarded, this form of corruption undermines the rationale and legitimacy of the competitive bidding process, as a whole.

Conclusion

Rose-Ackerman (1999, p42) writes that privatization is both an anti-corruption policy and an opportunity for corruption. While privatization may reduce some problems of low-level ('petty') corruption after the reform, it may, however, involve increased risks of 'grand corruption' throughout the privatization process. If those risks are not taken into account, corruption can undermine the stated aims of privatization.

To minimize the risks, transparency is of crucial importance at all stages of the process, from the start of discussions on whether to privatize or not. The discussion should be open and allow for the participation of all stakeholders and civil society. Although this may be time consuming and involves transaction costs, it will provide both transparency and deeper understanding of the sector to be privatized, and will help in the formulating of appropriate regulations, including anti-corruption measures. This process will further break the 'information monopoly' of politicians and officials, and enhance community involvement – thereby giving credibility and sustainability to the political process and its outcomes. If privatization is to go ahead, then it is important to accompany the process with transparency-enhancing measures, such as the integrity pacts developed by Transparency International (2002), monitoring schemes, and access-to-information guarantees that ensure accountability by all parties involved. Furthermore, post-privatization regulatory schemes need to provide for transparent means that facilitate accountability and strengthen government's credibility.

Privatization, despite its shortcomings and problems, will remain a major reform policy instrument worldwide – a strong reason to introduce transparency and accountability to these privatization and regulation processes.

EMPLOYMENT IMPACTS OF PRIVATIZATION

Rolph van der Hoeven and Hella Hoppe

Employment: One of the most pressing concerns

Roughly one third of the world's labour force, or about 1 billion people, are seeking a job. This number includes 160 million unemployed, 300 million underemployed and about 530 million workers who are unable to earn enough money to keep their families above the poverty line, the so-called 'working poor'. The figures are valid for 2000 (ILO, 2001); but the situation has rather become worse. Until the end of 2003, the total number of unemployed reached a new peak of 186 million (ILO, 2004). Two developments are especially noteworthy in this context. First, women and youth are particularly hit by the employment crisis. Second, many unemployed were pushed into informal work due to eroding, even completely lacking, social security coverage in many countries (ILO, 2003).

It is a widespread apprehension that many lay-offs are directly connected to the globalization of the world economy. People not only fear that globalization leads to increasing unemployment, but also to a race to the bottom concerning wages and labour standards and to a loss of national policy autonomy (Lee, 1996, p486).

Of course, there has always been the expectation, or at least the hope, that freer markets and globalization lead to increased growth and employment, which might more than outweigh job losses caused by intensified competition. However, growth figures from the last four decades, which can safely be called the decades of trade liberalization, show diminishing, not increasing, growth rates (World Commission,[12] 2004, p36)!

Unemployment and insufficient wages have been a major social policy challenge for a long time, but in the age of globalization it has become one of the most pressing concerns.

Specific impacts from privatization?

In the context of this book, we are particularly interested in the employment effects of privatization. Privatization is meant to increase economic efficiency. That, however, typically means a reduction of the labour force. In developing and transitional countries, the state used to be the biggest employer and was

World GDP per capita growth as percentage

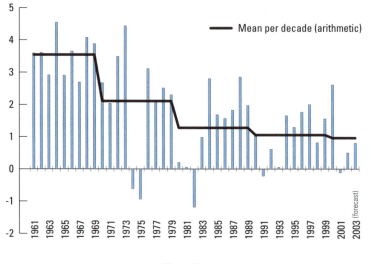

Figure 59
The historical reality about global growth rates: Contrary to widespread belief, decades of liberalization and privatization have brought about dimishing, not increasing growth rates.
Source: World Commission (2004, p36).

seen as economically very inefficient. Structural reforms, often superimposed by the International Monetary Fund (IMF), as well as economic transformation programmes, were introduced to remedy that inefficiency (Van der Hoeven and Sziraczki, 1997). Such reforms and programmes shifted the steering responsibility from the state to the market, with a view to inducing a stronger sense of cost efficiency.

Economic reforms were not designed to increase employment. Rather, they were meant even to sacrifice jobs under the expectation that increased efficiency would spur growth and, eventually, employment. Another objective was to curb inflation and to rebalance public budgets, both important factors for a healthy economic development.

A recent survey of 308 privatized firms (Chong and López-de-Silanes, 2002) shows that privatization has led to the loss of jobs in 78 per cent of the cases and no change or job gains in only 22 per cent. As one would expect, positive employment development occurred only in typical growth sectors, such as the telecom sector.[13] In some cases, counted under the favourable 22 per cent, job losses from privatization were only prevented by explicit job-guarantee contracts, which, however, will eventually expire.

Moreover, there are significant changes in payment and in the quality of jobs. Manager salaries typically rise while ordinary work gains lower wages and social benefits. Birdsall and Nellis (2003, p1626) offer some evidence that privatization leads to longer working time and a reduction in fringe benefits and security of tenure.

What is perhaps more disquieting is the fact that privatization tends to have specifically negative impacts on women. In most countries, the public sector is the largest absolute employer of women and is at the forefront of equal gender opportunities. Furthermore, the gender wage differentials are typically much smaller in the public sector than in private business. Downsizing the public sector can therefore be expected to deteriorate gender equity (Young and Hoppe, 2003).

Another gender effect from privatization has been observed relating to the de-subsidization of everyday services. If water, public transport and other public services become more expensive, it is typically women in the lower strata of society who lack the purchasing power to afford non-subsidized services. As a consequence, they are spending much more time on survival and reproduction activities (ILO, 1999b; Young and Hoppe, 2003).

If privatization is meant to increase economic efficiency, it must be allowed also to ask what is *meant* by efficiency. If social, livelihood and equity losses are monetarized or are counted as economic losses, privatization may actually fail to increase the overall efficiency (see ILO, 1999a).

Scanty evidence

A general problem for us lies in the lack of sound statistical data. To be sure, it is not at all easy to assess the employment effects of privatization in a fair and balanced manner. Early in the process, one would *expect* job losses. And one should expect that in classical sectors such as railways or power distribution, no new jobs would be created after privatization so that the net employment effect would be negative. According to economic theory, however, that is not to be deplored, but to be welcomed because it should set loose capacities for modernization and the creation of jobs in new sectors. But it will always remain difficult to prove that the creation of modern jobs belongs to the effects of privatization. And those losing their traditional jobs without a remote chance of winning a new job will deplore the structural change anyway.

An interesting, if inconclusive, study was done by Paukert (1997) for the Czech Republic. She found that during the first four years after the 1990 revolution, 1 million new jobs were created in small private enterprises; but job losses from the former state enterprises were considerably higher. The total number of jobs in the country decreased by some 10 to 12 per cent. Nevertheless, the official unemployment rate did *not* increase. She explains this surprising fact by a decline of labour supply due to early retirement, by an increase of the informal or 'black' economy and by migration, mostly to Western Europe (Paukert, 1997, p161).

Another case study carried out by the International Labour Organization (ILO) deals with the privatization processes in manufacturing in China and five selected countries of the former Soviet Union, Armenia, Georgia, the Kyrgyz Republic, Russia and the Ukraine (Evans-Clock and Samorodov, 2000). The study argues on the basis of surveys from about 2200 manufacturers with a total employment of more than 1.5 million. Results showed that, on average, there was a total job loss of 10 per cent, with 3 per cent in China and 15 per cent in the Kyrgyz Republic due to the privatization process. However, many companies were still overstaffed. Statistics reveal that a higher share of privatized companies than of state enterprises had surplus workers. Due to such underemployment, to work-place practices such as unpaid leave, to reduced work schedules and to lacking wage payments, poverty grew. The situation even worsens as enterprises cut back benefits and social services. Whereas in Russia, Armenia and the Ukraine women's job losses were equal to their employment share, in Georgia and Kyrgyz Republic women accounted for two-thirds of all job losses in comparison to 50 per cent of employment. Women were also more discriminated against – for example, in the form of hiring or unpaid maternity leave (Evans-Clock and Samorodov, 2000).

In South Korea, in contrast, different case studies show that privatization caused hardly any job losses. One reason is that privatized enterprises stayed part of the public sector or were defined as institutions that serve the public sector's interests (Park, 1997, p44). Other reasons frequently are guarantees of employment and job protection in the privatized enterprises (Van der Hoeven and Sziraczki, 1997, p9).

The important question is whether privatization will contribute to an overall economic climate, which will allow stronger economic growth and employment absorption in the long run also for those who have lost out in the initial phase. Cross-country studies report different outcomes. Furthermore, most of these country studies mix developed, transition and developing country cases, which makes such studies less relevant for policy advice to developing countries. To our knowledge, three studies deal mainly with cross-country analysis in relation to developing countries. Plane (1997) concludes on the basis of a sample of 35 developing countries that reform increased economic growth from 0.8 per cent to 1.5 per cent between sub-periods 1984–1988 and 1988–1992. Barnett (2000) argues on the basis of 12 developing countries and 6 transition countries that privatization of 1 per cent of gross domestic product (GDP) resulted in an increase in real growth of between 0.4 per cent and 0.5 per cent during the period afterwards. These results are contested by Cook and Uchida (2003), who argue that the variables used in these two studies to characterize privatization, in effect, reflect more general reform measures. Trying to isolate privatization from other economic reform measures, they find a robust negative partial correlation between privatization and economic growth in developing countries.

The situation is somewhat different for Organisation for Economic Co-operation and Development (OECD) countries. Privatization has not yet been a major trend in the industrialized countries (see Obser, in this volume). But the situation is likely to change in the context of the General Agreement on Trade in Services (GATS). The liberalization of public services will, in many cases, lead to their privatization. As in OECD countries, some 65 per cent of all jobs are in the service sector, and many of the more attractive service jobs are in the public sectors, privatization is bound to have major impacts, some of them surely negative. As in developing and transitional countries, the publicly owned enterprises have offered relatively fair conditions to women. This situation may not survive privatization (see German Bundestag, 2002a).

WOMEN'S RIGHTS UNDER PRIVATIZATION: THE EXAMPLE OF BULGARIA, POLAND, RUSSIA AND THE UKRAINE[14]

Anne Zollner

Political freedom, democratic rule and economic opportunity were all dreams that Soviet and East European citizens felt within their grasp at the end of the Soviet empire. People believed that reforms would strengthen the economy and, thus, their personal circumstances.

Twelve years later, some have benefited from the transition; but others have suffered a drop in living standards and quality of life, growing unemployment, reduced social benefits and rising inequality. Women, in particular, have not achieved free-market prosperity. While the transition from a command to a market economy has generally increased freedom and choice, it has also increased structural gender inequality by giving free reign to pre-existing prejudices, while simultaneously creating new opportunities for employment discrimination. The process of privatization has contributed to labour-force gender stratification.

In order to study this phenomenon, Women, Law and Development International[15] and its local partners (the Bulgarian Gender Research Foundation, the Women's Rights Centre in Poland, the Institute of Urban Economics and Femina in Russia, and the Kharkiv Centre for Women's Studies in the Ukraine) undertook an extensive research effort between 1998 and 1999 to investigate and document the impact of privatization on women's labour and economic rights.

Regional context for privatization and employment discrimination

While the transition to a free market was intended to lift the circumstances of all citizens, the legacy of socialism left men in a better position to take advantage of economic opportunities than women. Women were disproportionately disadvantaged by policies of transition such as privatization, reduction of social supports, price liberalization, currency devaluation, high interest rates and reforms in public-sector spending. By eliminating jobs and social benefits, these policies tended to increase women's responsibilities and the time burden on household tasks, such as food preparation, domestic work, and child and family heathcare. At the same time, they decreased women's access to opportunities and control over economic resources.[16]

Privatization is generally beneficial to men in terms of resources, opportunity and mobility (as they are most often in a position to acquire equipment, production processes, majority shares and credit); it is often detrimental to women's economic opportunities and status as marginal workers who are more likely to face unemployment and discrimination.

Like globalization, privatization's success is measured by production output; labour market flexibility; a high concentration of private ownership; reduced regulation and cost to firms; and efficiency rather than economic opportunities for the public, fair labour practices, and equal or relative distribution of share ownership. While privatization did not cause sex discrimination in the work place, it contributed to an environment and produced conditions where pre-existing gender biases are unleashed; simultaneously, government structures are rendered powerless to protect women's economic rights.

Broad research project

For the purposes of this section, privatization is defined broadly to include not just the selling of state-owned enterprises to private interests and private-sector development, but also the accompanying changes in employment-related laws and policies (including the reduction of social supports), law enforcement and institutions, and public beliefs regarding privatization and the law (such as the attitude that labour law does not apply and cannot be expected to be enforced in the private sector).

The main hypothesis of the research was that privatization has disproportionate negative consequences for women despite equal rights to participate in the process granted to women and men by law. Four questions were posited to understand how the process of privatization affects women in the formal sector:

- How do business, social and labour laws, and/or their lack of enforcement, encourage and/or discourage the use of female labour?
- How does the process through which enterprises privatize or incorporate[17] affect the use of female labour? What are the trends regarding enterprise characteristics and use of female labour?
- How do employers' preferences and attitudes towards female workers affect labour policy formation and the use of female labour?
- What are women's perceptions and experiences in the process of privatization?

To answer these questions, both qualitative and quantitative methods were employed, including:

- analysis of labour, social, privatization and gender laws, and interviews with judges, lawyers and in-house counsel about the application of those laws;
- secondary analysis of existing gender-based economic data and surveys of 927 business enterprises in order to determine their practices;[18]
- in-depth interviews with 120 managers to assess their attitudes and practices towards the use of female labour; and
- discussions within 61 focus groups with more than 500 employed and unemployed women in order to uncover real-life work-place experiences and women's awareness of their own rights.

Summary of principal findings

Gender is one of the basic parameters along which socio-economic processes evolve. As the private sector is increasingly emphasized, women's economic position and status have both declined. The following findings are results of an increasingly rigid division of power between women and men.

Discrimination in discharge and unemployment

The decreased demand for labour and resulting unemployment from state inefficiency and privatization is disproportionately borne by women. Newly created private enterprises found that the supply of skilled women far exceeded demand. Governments also abdicated their responsibilities to enforce laws that protect women's employment rights, which allowed enterprises to discharge women with impunity.

Unemployment has a female face in both the public and private sector. In the Ukraine, for example, between 1994 and 1998, fully 80 per cent of 'downsized' employees were women and only 20 per cent were men. Similarly, among the firms surveyed in Russia, 25 per cent reported that future lay-offs would be 'only women' and 23 per cent said 'mainly women', while only 5 per cent of firms said they planned to dismiss 'only men' and 4 per cent said 'mainly men'.

The way in which privatization proceeded in the region further contributed to the numbers of female unemployed through the phenomenon of hidden unemployment. This is the systematic under-recording of unemployment, also known as labour hoarding, in industry branches with high redundancy levels (often industries such as textiles where women dominate). In the Ukraine, it is estimated that hidden unemployment is 40 per cent of all unemployment. Labour hoarding occurs because it is less expensive for managers of enterprises to retain redundant workers at small or no wages, rather than the three-month severance pay required of them. This is a phenomenon that primarily affects women, keeping them bound to an enterprise that may or may not pay them and will probably result in unemployment.

One reason that managers lay off women is that they perceive them to be costlier and less reliable employees because women are expected, by their cultures, to put family responsibilities before work responsibilities and are usually entitled to maternity leave. In all four of the countries, pregnant women were often dismissed, in blatant disregard of the law. Due to the decreased demand for labour and the state's inability to provide daycare and other benefits, women's labour is being shifted from the productive sphere to the reproductive sphere. By leaving the workforce, women open positions for men (an interesting trend to note is the recent male domination of sectors that were formerly female, such as banking, accounting and communications, with a corresponding increase in pay). By returning to the home sphere, women take care of domestic responsibilities that the state formerly provided. If this trend continues unchecked, women will increasingly come to be identified in their roles as domestic caretakers rather than citizens and workers, thus further economically and politically disenfranchising them.

National statistical data also reveals a clear trend towards the long-term unemployment and economic marginalization of women. In Bulgaria, women made up just a little over half of the long-term unemployed in 1993; by 1996, two-thirds of the long-term unemployed were women. In Poland, women's long-term unemployment is consistently a quarter longer than that of men's.

Throughout the countries studied, women's role in the economy is shifting from full participation in the labour force to entrenched unemployment and underemployment. But it is important to note that women who leave formal employment do not disappear. They move into the informal sector as market vendors, sex workers and subsistence farmers – educated professionals eking out livelihoods in whatever ways they can without benefits or contracts. For example, small-scale retail, wholesaling and shuttle trading have become popular survival instruments for women in Russia. Particularly widespread is the employment of women as 'dummy proprietors': women who sell goods in kiosks for private owners, who own neither the goods nor stalls but are forced to pay the penalties and fines for tax and sales violations.

Discrimination in hiring

Increased competition over fewer positions has meant that despite higher education and more transferable skills, women face explicit discrimination in hiring. Employers and unemployment bureaus tend to view men as main breadwinners and tend to give them preference for available positions. This discrimination is a result of the increased autonomy and cost effectiveness required of new enterprises. Employers openly admit that they are hesitant to hire women because of the perceived costs of women's labour instability or because they think the costs of benefits generate higher costs for the company. In all four countries, women are routinely asked improper, personal questions in job interviews – questions never asked of men – and rejected for employment because of family responsibilities or childbearing plans. And when they are hired, women are more often than not offered lower salaries for the same work as men in order to compensate for real or hypothetical increases in the cost of female labour.

For example, in Russia, although female job-seekers tend to have more education than their male counterparts, surveyed employers conceded that they expect their future hires to be at least 40 per cent men and only 21 per cent women. Often women face age discrimination, as well – young women are passed over because of children or the possibility of children, and women over 40 are considered obsolete. In fact, employers do not even attempt to hide their preference for hiring men. Classified ads normally state the gender (and age) of desired applicants, and those ads overwhelmingly specify 'M' for man.

Laws in all of these countries purport to defend gender equality in the work place; but they do not apply to the hiring process:[19] women have no legal recourse if they are denied a job because of sex discrimination.

Discrimination in pay

In all four nations, women have been concentrated in less well-paid sectors of the economy and in the less well-paid positions within firms. Both factors contribute to an overall lower rate of pay, which has been exacerbated by the transition. For example, in Russia the ratio of women's to men's pay ranges from 65 per cent in civil engineering (where women are 42 per cent of the workforce) to 82–90 per cent in clothing and footwear production (where women are 70 per cent of the workforce). Similarly, in Poland, women earn less than men in both the state sector (88 per cent of men's wages and 80 per cent of men's monthly salary) and in the private sector (85 per cent of men's wages and 82 per cent of men's monthly salary). Indeed, women's hourly wage rates fell relative to men in both state and private sectors between 1994 and 1998.

Like men, women tend to earn more when they are employed in the private sector. For women, however, this is offset by the instability of the private sector where they do not necessarily receive benefits and where they might agree to a wage and then might be paid less or nothing at all. Focus group quotes from all of the countries demonstrated an attitude by managers that women tended to be less legally informed and disinclined to create conflict over violations.

Reductions in social supports

Privatization has led to significant reductions in employment and social benefits. When such benefits are scaled back, women are affected the most. These social benefits had been largely constructed to support women's workforce participation with the traditional gender expectation that women would have primary responsibility for the family. As a result of reduced benefits, women are unable to fulfil their expected obligations to family and/or are forced to leave the labour market when they cannot afford private daycare. Despite laws requiring such employment benefits, private businesses routinely do not provide them and employees do not recognize that the private sector has the same obligations to workers as the state does.

Women's responsibility for family, and the health and care of children and elderly family members, makes these social support reductions particularly deleterious for them. Less availability of healthcare forces women to forego their own health, work and education in order to take greater care of family members at home. In the Ukraine, Russia and Bulgaria, decent medical care is financially inaccessible for the majority of the population, so women will likely bear the brunt of care-taking responsibilities. In poor or resource-stricken environments, caring for dependents, especially sick dependents, can take a high proportion of a household's available (or willing) labour power.

Discrimination in pensions and retirement

Privatization has had a demonstrable negative effect for women because of the changing state pension systems. As part of the state's effort to reduce its financial obligations to the citizenry, pension systems have been restructured.

Women's pensions never matched those of men; but now with a calculation system based on earnings rather than years worked, women's pensions have significantly fallen. Former legislation designed to subsidize retirement for lower-earning workers, such as women, has been swept away in the post-communist era, and maternity leave and childcare leave no longer count towards pension earnings. These changes have resulted in an institutionalized system of discrimination against women and, in turn, resulted in massive poverty for older women. Without hope of employment and with pensions not being enough to live on, older women sweep streets and common areas in their apartment buildings, make handicrafts and food to sell on the street, and the most desperate lay out blankets at the market and sell personal articles from their homes.

In Poland, women's pensions used to be 79 per cent of men's. Today, the post-communist system will provide a pension for a woman that is only 62 per cent of a man's, even if they have earned the same salary, because of a lower retirement age (not mandatory, but treated as such by employers) and childcare leave. In Russia, a woman with the equivalent education and wage dynamics of a man is likely to receive 70 per cent of her male counterpart's pension. One standard childcare leave will lower that woman's pension savings to 63–71 per cent of a man's. Taking three childcare leaves lowers a woman's pension saving further, to 50–58 per cent of a man's (Baskakov and Baskakov, 1997). Because of Baskakov and Baskakov's research on the gender aspects of pension reform in Russia, the issue was placed on the reform agenda and proposals have been put forward attempt to level the difference between men's and women's pensions.

Sexual harassment

One dimension of female work experience that is often mentioned in the research phase is sexual harassment. Sexual harassment in the work place is rampant in the region. If they can find work, recent college graduates generally get their first jobs in the service sector as secretaries, shop assistants, waitresses and clerical staff. It is in this predominantly private sector, with a high concentration of young women, that sexual harassment rates are growing rapidly. Women are particularly vulnerable in these small firm settings where on-the-job practices escape legal oversight. Male managers wield power to elicit sexual favours from women who desperately need to keep their jobs.

In a recent Polish study of small-scale enterprises, over a quarter of women admitted being the victims of harassment – and it is suspected that even this group under-reported the problem. And in Nabrezhnie Chelnie, Russia, nearly every interviewed woman reported cases of sexual requirements imposed by potential employers during search for work.

The newly emerging private sector lends itself to more abuses of women by virtue of the fact that labour regulations are rarely enforced on these firms, and the avenues women formerly had to fight or remedy such violations are less accessible and effective. In fact, few in government are concerned or care about this problem. Culturally, sexual harassment is viewed as trivial unless it is extremely violent. There is a lack of understanding and sensitivity to how men's power and women's lack of power in the work environment can lead to situations where women are left unable to assert their rights. This dynamic robs women of their basic physical integrity. The vast majority of lawyers and judges have not handled any sexual harassment cases. By virtue of their economic vulnerability, women are unlikely to pursue legal recourse out of fear of losing their work, an unresponsive legal system, and their lack of a language or terminology to discuss the problem. Without legal consequences or public opposition to sexual harassment, it is likely to persist.

Adverse impact of non-contractual labour

In order to avoid unemployment, women are often forced to work in the private sector without formal contracts. These non-contractual positions tend to be not only below women's educational qualifications, but also in substandard work conditions. Without contracts, women are not eligible for unemployment benefits and basic social guarantees, and they run the risk of non-payment. Decreased governmental oversight has increased these illegal job practices by allowing firms to practise non-contractual labour on a regular basis and without consequence.

Research in Bulgaria, for example, revealed dramatic violations of job safety regulations and common practices of making women work without a contract and then cheating them out of their pay. Non-contractual labour and contractual violations are most likely to occur among small enterprises in textiles, food and services, which are female-dominated employment spheres. This phenomenon results in the further economic marginalization of women by reinforcing the message that their labour is less valuable, confining them to low-skill jobs, as well as contributing to their increased stress and declining physical health.

Discrimination of women as shareholders

By involving the public in the privatization process through the distribution of shares, the state hoped to commit the population to the economic transformation process. But the flawed and manipulated implementation of mass privatization failed to achieve this goal. Women were more vulnerable to the violations of this process by virtue of their tenuous position – for example, having to sell their shares or vouchers out of a desperate need for money. As shareholders, women generally are kept uninformed about company decisions, rules and policies, making it impossible for them to participate as co-owners of privatized businesses.

Furthermore, there is a common management practice of accumulating the majority of shares in an enterprise by withholding salaries, essentially forcing workers to cheaply sell their shares for cash. Women are especially vulnerable to such practices because of their lack of alternative sources of income and their tenuous position in the labour market. A case study in Nabrezhnie Chelnie, Russia, demonstrated how women in a large truck-manufacturing enterprise who questioned these kinds of illegal practices were fired without cause. These kinds of rights violations have become common practice

Conclusion

Due to both structural and cultural factors, Bulgarian, Polish, Russian and Ukrainian women faced increasing discriminatory practices during privatization. The research indicates that women were far more likely than men to lose employment, face discrimination in hiring and pay, and by virtue of their more desperate employment status be subject to violations of labour regulations, such as non-contractual work, sexual harassment and unpaid social insurance.

The original research questions sought to answer four questions regarding laws and policies, employer practices and attitudes, and workers' perceptions and experiences in the privatization process. While laws in the region, including the laws that govern privatization, provide for equality between men and women, they are simply ignored and most female workers do not have access or the means to get them enforced. In the process of privatization, women have been treated as a secondary labour force and certain types of privatization (i.e. manager–worker buy-outs) and industries (i.e. textiles, food processing and services) result in blatant rights violations of women workers. Moreover, the process of privatization excluded women by virtue of their lack of access to the resources and credit needed to be owners, and their rights as shareholders were easily violated by their lack of power. Employers state that they treat women and men equally; but their own identified practices reveal otherwise in terms of dismissals and hiring. Women have suffered the costs of privatization in a different and more substantial way than men; at the same time, men have enjoyed the benefits of economic change to a much larger extent than women.

ENVIRONMENTAL IMPACTS OF PRIVATIZATION

Ernst Ulrich von Weizsäcker

To Magda Lovei and Bradford Gentry of the World Bank, it is all fairly simple: privatization is good for the environment (Lovei and Gentry, 2002). The authors present examples in their report of a dirty state handing responsibilities over to international private investors and operators who finally introduce clean technologies, make efficient use of natural resources and, ultimately, clear the mess left over from earlier times. The main concern of these World Bank authors is that the state authorities agree on a fair deal with their private partners regarding the terms of such transactions.

Nobody would disagree with the World Bank's assessment if the universe of cases pertained only to the formerly state-centred East European economies. They have, indeed, been notorious for creating unbelievable environmental pollution and for wasting natural resources in a profligate manner, resulting, in part, from Lenin's strange idea that the free supply of electricity, heat, water and bread were essential for societal well-being. This is not to say that privatization (e.g. in Russia) has *always* improved environmental performance.

The World Bank study is a lot weaker with regard to examples from Latin American and Asia. Some of its statements seem dubious, such as the assertion that privatization provides an opportunity to make strategic decisions 'with long-term economic, social, and environmental benefits' (Lovei and Gentry, 2002, p2). As a rule, the state has a *more* long-term perspective than the private sector, as long as the state has not been deprived of its capacity to govern and to set long-term standards.

It seems necessary to take a closer and less biased look at the mutual relations between privatization and the environment.

Owners of natural resources do not want to destroy them

Historically, and without any direct relation to modern World Bank times, it is fair to say that private ownership can offer a healthy condition for nature protection and resource conservation. It is in the interest of the proprietor to safeguard the value and productivity of his property. Feudal game reserves in geographically stable situations are a point in case. They were meant to maintain a self-sustaining population of game. Geographically changing situations, on the other hand, were often accompanied by disastrous 'rape, ruin and run' practices for which the near extinction of the North American buffalo was perhaps the most conspicuous example.

But this attitude of conservation is not restricted to private proprietors. Furthermore, *public* ownership of common property has traditionally been conservation oriented. Members of the community had open access to the *commons* but were not allowed to overexploit. The 'tragedy of the commons' according to Garrett Hardin (1968) is the situation where the state or the community can no longer protect its commons against intruders or even trespassing community members. This is the typical situation for the *international* commons which lack a reliable state authority to set rules and to police compliance with the rules.

A tragic example is ocean fishery. Ocean fish stocks remained healthy so long as fishing techniques did not allow overexploitation. Upon the advent, during the 1970s, of high-efficiency fishing equipment, the fish stock began to decline. Coastal states were the first to worry and, putting the blame on intruders, began fighting for a generous geographic extension of their exclusive fishing zones. The legitimation was to re-establish and monitor a regime of sustainable fishing within that zone. Unfortunately, most coastal states – with a few notable exceptions such as the Norwegian/Russian regime for the shared fish stock of the Norwegian Sea – have almost done the opposite and have either themselves overexploited 'their' fish stock or given fishing licences to international companies far beyond sustainable levels. But the situation is even worse in the open oceans, which lack an identifiable proprietor and certainly lack a strong regime of sustainable harvesting.

Privatization can have unexpected positive effects on the environment. When speaking about the former communist countries, the usual topic is heavy industry and classical pollution. However, *farmland* privatization in the former Soviet block has rather consistently led to environmental improvements. Here, the causal chain was hardly predicted by anybody. The main reason for improvements has been the introduction under market conditions of realistic (i.e. non-subsidized) prices for fertilizers and pesticides. Farmland privatization has also increased the number of smallholder farms showing a propensity for good environmental stewardship.

New forms of negligence

The World Bank experience with positive environmental effects of privatization is surely only one side of the coin. On the other side we see a shift from local public (or private) ownership to shareholder-owned international companies. These companies have no built-in incentive to protect local natural resources as long as there are more resources available somewhere else. Under the conditions of global competition, profit maximization actually encourages non-sustainable methods of resource exploitation. This is especially true for extractive industries.

A striking example involves logging concessions awarded to private timber companies with explicit permission to clearcut timber located on public lands. Reforestation typically remains at the discretion of the logging firms and is applied only if there is sufficient assurance that the same company will be awarded the same concessions a generation of trees later – not exactly something shareholders tend to trust in. On the other hand, it would be incorrect to blame unsustainable logging on the private sector alone. Often the state as proprietor is the culprit. States in urgent need of cash find selling logging concessions extremely convenient. A depressing fact is that public officials responsible for forest management often fall for bribery, which is surely an indicator of non-sustainable practice.

An entirely different field where privatization causes environmental concerns is international trade in seeds. Seed companies live from selling seeds to farmers on a regular basis and have no interest in traditional farmers' rights to use part of the harvest to propagate the next generation of seedlings. Seed companies are interested in the development of large and standardized consumer markets, which tend to force farmers to supply standardized produce as opposed to more varied outputs. Thus, commercial markets tend to reduce agricultural biodiversity and to make farmers depend upon the reliable supply of standard seeds, often involving genetically engineered crops. Small wonder, then, that subsistence farmers in developing countries are in the vanguard of the fight against international patent laws for seeds under the World Trade Organization's (WTO's) Agreement on Trade-related Aspects of Intellectual Property Rights (TRIPS). It is reasonable to assume that local seeds are better adapted to and more sustainable in the local environment than internationally standardized crops.

The case of water

In the case of water, it is hard to find conclusive evidence of beneficial or adverse environmental effects of privatization, although there tends to be a positive correlation in industrialized countries between public ownership and environmental care. Germany and The Netherlands have long restricted water privatization and have maintained the highest standards of drinking water quality in the European Union (EU), while France, with its two private water giants, is notorious for not fulfilling the EU drinking water directive because nobody wants to bear the costs of replacing old-fashioned leaded water pipes. A general expectation is that private owners are less likely to value uses of water that cannot be marketed or are hard to market, such as the ecological roles of wetlands or mangrove forests.

In some EU countries, the municipal waterworks that operate under state laws have entered into contracts with farmers in their catchment areas, compensating them for reducing the use of agrochemicals in order to protect freshwater resources. In developing countries, we tend to see a *positive* correlation between privatization of water and the environment. Some of the examples in this book and the quoted World Bank study (Lovei and Gentry, 2002) indicate that public ownership of waterworks is often associated with a depressing lack of finance to maintain, modernize and expand drinking water supply and sewage systems. Privatization can remedy the financial situation to the benefit of public health and the urban environment, provided, of course, that strict regulations are in place that also ensure affordable access for the poor.

The case of energy

In the electricity markets, *liberalization* has had mostly negative environmental effects. To be sure, liberalization is not identical to privatization. But liberalization does not make sense without mutually competing private suppliers.

Liberalization of the power markets became the order of the day in the US around 1990. It essentially put an end to the earlier concept of least cost planning (LCP). LCP was an ingenious idea implemented in California and other US states under the conditions of area monopolies for electricity. It made construction permits for new power plants depend upon evidence that no lower-cost solution was available to meet the demand. As a result, power suppliers were forced to engage in energy efficiency programmes as long as these programmes were more cost effective than new power plants. LCP has spurred energy efficiency in many US states and in some other countries, including Denmark, Germany and Thailand. As energy efficiency is surely the best answer to energy-related environmental problems, the end of LCP came as a blow to the environment. Liberalization typically moved energy prices downwards and thus invited more wasteful use of the scarce resource. Liberalization, oddly, also led to under-investment in power generation and, ultimately, to corresponding blackouts.

Privatization, globalization and politics

Privatization has been associated historically with globalization. Many critics of *privatization* have *globalization* in their minds when expressing their concerns. Globalization has had both positive and negative effects on the environment. In some cases, it helped worldwide penetration of environmental technologies, partly because multinational corporations typically find it inconvenient for reasons of internal management and staff mobility – or, indeed, immoral under corporate social responsibility (CSR) principles – to apply lower environmental standards abroad than at home. But there are also many examples of multinationals investing in or moving operations to less developed countries because this enables them to cut costs by setting lower environmental standards.

Negative effects accrue from increased transport intensity of production, from an increase in the use of throw-away products and from sharper global cost competition. Cost competition tends to reduce firms' and countries' room to manoeuvre regarding costly measures of environmental protection.

Political parties that are more closely aligned with private business seem to show a tendency to reduce or water down environmental standards and commitments. Most significantly, the Republican party in the US has shown open distrust of the Environmental Protection Agency since 1981 and has generally – with the notable exception of the ozone treaty – blocked rather than promoted international environmental agreements. In this, the US typically finds its allies in Australia, Japan and some European countries with 'conservative' governments. The usual argument is that the relevant measures of environmental protection will prove too 'costly' for their private sectors.

DOES PRIVATIZATION PROVIDE THE RIGHT CHOICE OF CHOICE? OBSERVATIONS FROM THE UK

Roger Levett

Expanding consumer choice has been one of the main motivations for privatization. Faced with poor or absent public services, the idea of opening them up to creative and enterprising private operators and letting the users decide who is offering the best deal seems obvious and attractive. As many of the examples in this book show, choice between competing alternatives can help to drive dramatic service improvements.

The UK has embraced and applied this idea through liberalization and privatization more thoroughly than any other country. In 2004, the two main political parties are still competing to offer yet more choice, especially in services such as education and health, which are still largely state provided. Both wish to diversify provision by opening these up to more involvement of the private and non-profit sectors, although both avoid calling this 'privatization' because of the unpopularity which the results of previous privatizations have given the term.

However, there are signs of a backlash against 'choice' as a guiding principle of public service management (see, for example, Levett et al, 2003). This section offers an overview of some of the arguments now being raised, using examples from the gamut of UK privatization and deregulation. If they are valid, they undermine one of the most persuasive and confidently assumed justifications for privatization.

Anxiety and discontentment

It is generally assumed that any increase in individual choice must be an improvement because some people can now choose products or services which suit them better, while people who do not exercise the new choices are no worse off. American psychologist Barry Schwartz argues that beyond a certain point, further increase in choice does not make people happier; instead, the opposite occurs (see Schwartz, 2003). This is how his argument goes. If you believe that the perfect choice is available, and what you have chosen is less than perfect, it must be your own fault for having chosen poorly. This will make you feel more anxious and pressurized as you choose. After you have chosen, and inevitably discover shortcomings, the promise that the perfect one is still 'out there' makes you resent the imperfections, spoiling whatever pleasure you might take in its good qualities. Dissatisfaction leads you to choose again … starting another cycle of anxious choice, followed by inevitable disappointment. Marketing and advertising, of course, play on this, seeking to create dissatisfaction with last year's offering by explaining how this year's is even better, so that even if you think you made the right choice last year, you should choose again now.

Schwartz contrasts 'maximizers' – people who always seek the best, and are restless, critical and discontent – with 'satisficers', a term he has coined for people who know when what they have is good enough, and relax and enjoy their good fortune rather than obsessively seeking the last – possibly unobtainable – step to perfection.

Satisficers – people who appreciate what they have – will be more comfortable customers for public services than maximizers, who tend to be unreasonably demanding and ungrateful, and are prone to complain, criticize and demand compensation for even trivial shortcomings. The offer of choice may turn satisficers into maximizers. More demanding and critical 'customers' may help drive up standards, but even if services do improve, maximizers will still not be satisfied. Schwartz's theory may therefore help to explain a puzzle that frustrates ministers promoting a 'choice culture': on 'objective' measures, many public services are getting much better, yet the users remain critical and dissatisfied.

Of course, this is all a matter of degree. Schwartz's argument does not mean that people are happiest in a planned economy with no choice. Denial of choice was one of the main reasons the Soviet economies failed. Choice, at some level, is the way we show politicians, bureaucrats and companies what we want, and make them deliver it. Choosing is freedom in action. The point is, rather, that individual consumer choice is not the only kind of choice, and that endless increases in it cannot be assumed to make people happier.

Choice requires information and understanding

Consumer choice depends on people having sufficient information and understanding to choose intelligently. This is the trivial experience every tourist makes in front of exuberant food or carpet markets in exotic countries.

Liberalization of personal financial services has pushed many people into a very exotic country. It was intended to allow people to choose the pension, mortgage or investments precisely suited to their requirements. In practice, however, few have had sufficient understanding to make a rational choice that matches their needs. Moreover, there have been a series of scandals where customers were deliberately sold financial services products that were clearly unsuited to their needs, sometimes disastrously so, often because intermediaries could make more commission from them. Some of the worst cases were eventually compensated, and regulation was tightened to prevent recurrence. But a much larger number of customers are left with a nagging feeling that they were sold what suited the salesperson or the company, not what was best for them.

Can people choose what they really want?

When stock markets fell after 2000, it became clear that the apparently vast range of choice of financial services offered did not include what many people *really* wanted: certainty of future financial security regardless of the performance of stock markets. The experience in countries such as France and Germany shows that state pension systems cannot provide perfect certainty either under the conditions of an ageing society. But severe losses in some companies, which had been confidently recommended by advisers as prudent and 'safe', brought a dismaying realization that even with the best expert advice customers could not reliably choose even the degree of risk they would take.

Where choice does not make sense

'Shopping around' for the best 'deal' is simply not the way people want to approach certain services. Sick people do not want to leaf through alternative brochures in the way they might choose a holiday: they simply want their doctor to arrange for them to get the medically appropriate treatment promptly *and* competently *and* as locally as possible, given the level of specialist expertise needed. Most people will only wish to choose a different hospital if the nearest one offering the relevant treatment is poor or has a longer waiting time; so the exercise of such choice should be seen not as a valuable extension of freedom but as a sign that the local hospital was below an acceptable standard. The desirable response in such a situation must surely be to improve such a hospital so that patients have no need to try to avoid it. It is not clear how diverting management resources into administering choice, or leaving bad hospitals underused or used by those patients too desperate to wait for better ones, can help achieve this. Schooling is another example. The UK government is energetically promoting diversity – for example, by offering extra funding to schools to develop specialist strengths and encouraging non-public sector bodies, such as businesses and faith groups, to set up schools with distinctive characteristics. The government assumes that parents approach schooling for their children in the same way that they go out for a meal: the more different restaurants they can choose between, the more likely they are to enjoy their meal. But the analogy is misleading. Most parents want very similar things from a school: an orderly *and* friendly atmosphere; support for academic work *and* cultural *and* sporting pursuits; excellence nurtured *and* different levels of aptitude provided for. These are not alternatives, so having to choose *between* them is a restriction, not a liberation. Most families also hope that a school will be able to cater for whatever aptitudes, interests and needs each child may develop over several years without having to move to a different school. Most families would prefer to be able to send siblings to the same school, even if they have different interests, and for the school to be close to home in order to minimize the time, effort and cost of travel.

All these preferences could best be met by non-specialized neighbourhood schools if they were well enough resourced and managed to provide a range of subjects and activities, all to a high standard. Having to choose between schools with different specialisms (and, by implication, relative weaknesses in other areas), which cannot all be near where all their students live, would make these preferences harder to achieve, not easier. As with healthcare, a desire to exercise choice is often a sign of deficiencies in current service provision, rather than an added benefit.

The effects of choice on social systems

Schools illustrate a further problem: in complex social systems, choices can have perverse knock-on effects. In parts of England where there is already some degree of 'parental choice' for schools, this actually means that the more popular schools can choose which pupils to take. Naturally, they tend to choose more able, promising and unproblematic children, who tend to keep a school performing well, while the problem children are concentrated in the less desirable schools, which makes it harder for them to improve their academic results or behaviour standards, however hard the teachers work. Choice thus tends to entrench and perpetuate inequality. It also creates a huge buzz of movement every school day, with lucky and unlucky children passing each other on their way to schools in each other's neighbourhoods.

Transport offers another example. Every time someone chooses to make a journey by car instead of bus, the bus operator loses a bit of ticket income, while experiencing more traffic that will delay the bus. This will tend, at the margin, to make the bus service poorer, encouraging more people to choose to drive instead of using the bus, further reducing ticket income and further adding to congestion, and so on. We have a *positive feedback loop*, where a change has further consequences that amplify the original change. Over time, the cumulative loss of income will force the bus operator to cut back on services. This will, of course, encourage more people to shift from bus to car –

another turn of the loop. Faced with this shift, shops and other amenities that need to be attractive and within easy reach of their customers will place more importance on having a location with good road access and parking. These locations tend to be further out of town centres, and less accessible by bus. This encourages people to make more journeys by car. Faced with loss of amenities and worsening traffic, people will tend to move out of town if they can – and then drive more because suburbs and rural areas cannot support good bus services. And so on.

The example of deteriorating public transport shows how perfectly sensible and rational individual choices can cumulatively lead to a situation that nobody chose or wanted: more traffic, longer and more stressful journeys, urban decline and a life getting worse in absolute, not only relative, terms for anyone who cannot opt to drive. The market is not always Adam Smith's 'invisible hand', allocating resources optimally through the pure impersonal interaction of demand and supply. It can, instead, be an 'invisible elbow' (a phrase borrowed from Michael Jacobs[20]) shoving us all into a corner that no one wants to be in.

Interventions such as subsidies for public transport, restrictions on driving or parking and spatial planning can resist the problems. Central London's congestion charge, introduced in 2003, is an exciting example. Such interventions restrict and constrain choice, and thus improve the overall situation for most. The English cities that have had the most success in resisting the vicious circle described above are mostly 'special' places, such as Oxford or York, which have the least need to compete with others.

Benefits of monopoly

One of the main arguments for choice is that it breaks monopoly. However, two UK transport examples show the disadvantages of taking this too far. Gatwick Airport to central London is one of the few rail services where competition was introduced within one route. The justification was that many business travellers would be willing to pay a higher fare for a fast direct service to London, while many others would prefer to pay less and take slightly longer over the journey on ordinary local trains. Tickets are not transferable. The flaw in the argument is that the journey time reduction of the premium 'Gatwick Express' is often less than the extra time spent waiting for the next express train instead of getting an ordinary train. Competition, therefore, requires bemused travellers to try to work out which train will actually get them to London faster – and to risk both paying more *and* taking longer. It is hard to avoid the conclusion that the train service between A and B is a natural monopoly, and attempting to introduce choice is silly when most users just want to be able to get on the next train to their destination.

The second example is deregulation and the introduction of competition within local bus services, which was intended to drive up standards by giving passengers choice. As elementary market theory would predict, this resulted in extra operators putting buses onto busy, profitable routes until the passengers were spread so thinly they were only just breaking even. In some towns, there were complaints that the resulting concentration of buses was causing congestion, increased journey times and – because many operators bought up older buses – air pollution. Because these services were only breaking even, there was no longer any monopoly profit to cross-subsidize less popular routes. These were therefore cut back unless local authorities were willing to subsidize them. The result was a surfeit of choice of quarter-full buses on the busy routes; but many people were deprived of the choice to travel by bus at all, despite higher public subsidies. Bus usage declined everywhere in England except London, where services were franchised instead, and usage steadily grew. The results of unregulated competition were so dire that there has been little protest as a few big operators have driven out competition and re-established near monopolies in many places, and the government is considering re-regulating services. The franchise model, where the proceeds of selling rights to profitable routes can cross-subsidize unprofitable ones, would seem an obvious way forward.

Transaction costs

As several of the examples show, choice often imposes significant and unwelcome transaction costs. Service providers must divert resources into winning and keeping customers; customers have no choice but to keep choosing. Customers who do not keep studying the market for mobile phone packages, savings accounts and gas and electricity supplies risk being left on poor or expensive tariffs, thus subsidizing the newer tariffs and special deals which suppliers create to win new customers. The large number of customers moving between suppliers is quoted as evidence that people really do want choice, but it might just as likely indicate pointless 'churning' created artificially by the difference between every supplier's standard terms and special offers to new customers. The cost of competitive marketing, and of opening and closing accounts, ultimately falls to the customers.

In 2004, the replacement of the previous monopoly telephone enquiries service with a competitive market was almost universally greeted with derision and weariness. Any potential benefits derived from unleashing the full creativity of entrepreneurial innovators on the business of looking up telephone numbers were not felt to be worth the trouble of working out which of six alternative suppliers offered the best combination of fixed and time-dependent fees, extra numbers, recommendations for services (of questionable objectivity) and basic competence and reliability (which several of the new entrants conspicuously lacked).

Equity

In several of the examples, choice tends to deepen inequity and social exclusion. People with lower educational attainments are least able to make informed judgements about, for example, the best pension, investment or even phone or gas tariff, and are most likely to be sold a bad deal and left subsidizing smarter customers. People who cannot afford or cannot drive a car are excluded from amenities that have moved to locations only easily accessible by car; but social groups with the least access to cars experience the most car-related pollution and disturbance. Children with less academic promise and more personal problems are concentrated in the schools nobody wants to go to, and the concentration of problems reduces the time the teachers can give any of them. Confident, successful people make choice work for them; the less successful, articulate and adept at working the system finish up with what is left.

Conclusions

None of this is to deny that making public services more responsive to their users' wishes and preferences has led to many important and, arguably, long overdue improvements. But the examples show that 'more choice' cannot be a panacea. Choice and competition cannot be assumed to deliver what people really want, either individually or collectively. Competition can reduce the efficiency and effectiveness of service delivery. Choice can deepen inequity and impose unchosen transaction costs on customers and service providers, which must ultimately be paid for in the form of higher charges or lower service levels. The existence of alternative providers, and people churning between them, is not in itself evidence that people are better off, or that they really wanted the choice. Nor is economic growth in so far as it is made up of competitive bidding and marketing, churning between essentially similar suppliers, and more travel to distant providers.

So, when privatization or liberalization are claimed to increase choice, this should be the beginning of policy debate, not the end. What kind of choice, for example, is involved? Who benefits and who loses? What are the broader consequences for society? This section suggests that the choices that have been provided by privatization and liberalization in the UK have too often been spurious, unwanted, too difficult or impossible for most people to exercise, or self-defeating in their broader effects.

PART IV

Governance of Privatization

INITIAL REMARKS

Oran R. Young

We turn now to the issue of how to respond to the limits to privatization and the need to rebalance the private and public spheres. We have no simple and singular cure for the wide range of concerns identified in previous sections of this book. Just as the problems of privatization involve a number of distinct patterns or syndromes, efforts to respond to these problems require a toolkit, including a range of distinct strategies. Taken together, these strategies can provide an effective means of meeting the overall challenge of governance arising from the limits to privatization.

In this part, we introduce and evaluate a range of specific approaches to governance that are available to address the limits to privatization in specific situations. Sometimes, it is appropriate to turn to (re)regulation. But the emphasis here should be on new forms of regulation that are designed to avoid the pitfalls (e.g. the loss of efficiency, the outright capture of regulatory agencies) characteristic of traditional forms of regulation. In other cases, there is considerable scope for private governance in such forms as the adoption of non-mandatory responses to major environmental problems (e.g. climate change) or the establishment of voluntary codes of conduct through such arrangements as the Forest Stewardship Council (FSC) and the Marine Stewardship Council. There is much to be said, as well, for initiatives that enhance roles for civil society and stress the importance of transparency, the exchange of information and the strengthening of ethical standards. New approaches to financing a variety of public goods are coming into focus, as well. Just as the limits to privatization involve a number of distinct patterns, efforts to meet the resultant challenge of governance should include a range of appropriate strategies. In all cases, however, we are convinced that democracy in the sense of a reliance on participatory processes, coupled with a commitment to basic rights, must be part of the mix not only to maximize the effectiveness of individual strategies, but also to ensure that all relevant stakeholders accept them as legitimate. As Raimund Bleischwitz puts it in his chapter ('"Co-evolution" between State Regulation and the Private Sector'), markets may need more regulation, but we could benefit from seeking a more cooperative or 'co-evolutionary' kind of regulation, involving feedbacks between the state, the private sector and civil society.

Regulation

Matthias Finger

This chapter presents the issue of regulation, using the network industries –
postal services, telecommunications, energy, water, broadcasting and transport
– as examples. Liberalization and privatization first took place in these
industries, and, subsequently, regulation has been developed both to control
the evolution of the industries and to ensure public policy objectives. However,
as this section will show, regulation (as it is being developed in the network
industries) can easily be extended to other sectors, such as health or education.

The chapter begins with a brief description of the structure of the network
industries prior to liberalization, as well as an outline of the very nature and
consequences of liberalization on the network industries. It then places the
issue of regulation within a larger public policy framework, because regulation
– even purely economic regulation – can ultimately only be justified on public
policy grounds. Thirdly, it draws out the five main regulatory functions in the
network industries, which will serve as a checklist for what needs to be
regulated in a liberalized environment. It then addresses institutional set-ups
for regulation. Finally, it extrapolates from the regulation of the network
industries to the regulation of other liberalized sectors, such as health, security
and higher education.

LIBERALIZATION OF THE NETWORK INDUSTRIES AND THE NEED FOR RE-REGULATION

Historically, the network industries – telecommunications, postal services,
public transport, air transport, electricity, gas, water distribution and
broadcasting – were generally nationally organized. They were often integrated
within the same enterprise; but even where this was not the case, the
professional nature of these industries ensured that all concerned actors
collaborated, nationally as well as internationally. Economically, these

industries operated under what is called a 'cost+ regime', thus primarily paying attention to the technical aspects and only secondarily to financial and/or customer considerations. These industries generally had public service objectives. These were not secured by regulation, but by means of public ownership (see Sichel and Alexander, 1996; Henry, 2001).

Thus, the state had combined two functions: providing the services and ensuring public policy objectives. Because the state was also the owner of the operational activities, a distinct regulatory function was not seen as necessary.

Liberalization questions all of these features of network industries. Liberalization combines *unbundling* – a primarily technical endeavour – and *competition*, for which unbundling is a pre-requisite. To a lesser extent, *privatization* of the operators is also relevant. Formerly integrated industries are becoming fragmented and the different actors within the industry who previously cooperated are now increasingly competing. Liberalization thus attacks both the administrative and the professional logics.

However, in most network industries, only some segments can be liberalized, while others remain monopolistic for both technical and economic reasons (e.g. railway infrastructure and air traffic control). This *'imperfect' liberalization of the network industries* leads to the need to maintain some functions previously assumed by the industry but 'lost' because of liberalization – for example, ensuring the integrity of the infrastructure systems and the continuous learning of the sector. There needs to be some means of guaranteeing that would-be competitors can obtain a fair allocation of any limited resources that may be essential to deliver the service, such as railway track space or broadcasting bandwidth. Finally, in the age of liberalization, public service objectives can no longer be assumed to be safeguarded through state ownership, and therefore must be enforced by some external entity. Thus, after liberalization (and, ideally, parallel to it), the network industries must be re-regulated in order to ensure their proper functioning for the benefit of both citizens and customers. Figure 60 summarizes the above arguments with the example of railways.

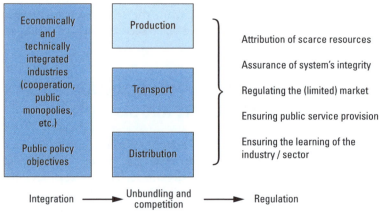

Figure 60
Liberalization of the network industries and the need for re-regulation.

REGULATION WITHIN A PUBLIC POLICY FRAMEWORK

Liberalization may necessitate regulation of the network industries, as just argued; but regulation must be rooted in public policy objectives. This section demonstrates how regulation must be conceptualized as public policy, or rather as a *combination of several public policies*, and that its implementation must change as a result of network industry liberalization (see Francis, 1993).

All liberal states have regulations for fair competition, the prevention of cartels and the functioning of markets more generally. Ideally, these would simply be extended to the newly liberalized sectors. But liberalization of network industries generally leads to setting up sectoral-specific regulations and regulators. This often leads to conflicts with the established competition regulator, as is discussed later. Moreover, in formerly monopolistic network industries, markets and competition first need to be created, leading to calls for 'asymmetric' regulation that treats the incumbent less advantageously than new entrants. The imperfect nature of the 'market' in the network industries makes competition regulation complicated because of the dangers of distortion. This also means that in the network industries, competition regulation can never be entirely separated from technical regulatory activities, thus raising the question of whether competition regulation and technical regulation (see below) should be integrated within the same institution.

States also have policies on *public service* objectives. Historically, public enterprises 'internalized' these, notably in economic, regional and social development (e.g. employment), but also in security. In the age of liberalization, however, ownership can no longer implement such policies, since public service obligations can handicap the historical operator vis-à-vis competitors and/or can distort the market. Public service objectives thus also need to be regulated, and are quite sector specific, so regulation is generally sectoral in nature. Furthermore, liberalization calls for a new form of public service objective: consumer protection. One aspect of this is in the European Commission's term *'universal service'*, meaning the same treatment of all consumers across a given territory. However, citizens are not only consumers and many historical public policy objectives, such as employment and regional development, were never geared towards consumers. These *'services in the general interest'* (as the European Commission calls them) must also be regulated in a liberalized environment, generally through traditional public policy means (e.g. subsidies and incentives). Use of scarce resources, such as water, airwaves and airspace, was generally assimilated to public service objectives. But in the age of liberalization, this must also be regulated since access to *scarce resources* can no longer be the privilege of the historical operator, but must be fairly distributed

States also have sector policies (e.g. for energy, transport or communications). These were generally developed and applied with or through the historical operator, and affected the infrastructure system's development, integrity and functioning; yet most of these policies remained internal to the public operator. Under liberalization, such sectoral policies must become much more explicit, and the responsibility for the sectors' development and integrity falls back – once the industry is unbundled – to the public authorities, who then must turn to *'sector' regulation* or invent other means of implementing these policies.

All these three different public policy objectives – competition, public service and the integrity and development of public service systems – were traditionally implemented by a combination of public ownership and administrative oversight. In the age of liberalization, this mode of implementing public policy objectives is no longer appropriate, and must increasingly occur via some sort of regulation. In the network industries, at least, regulation is not a transitory phenomenon, but rather a new and more appropriate way of implementing public policies. This transition from public policy implementation by means of ownership to public policy implementation by means of regulation is a process of profound institutional change, and is difficult and politically controversial. The issue is not just how to implement substantive public policies differently, but is also an issue of politico-administrative institutional change, raising the question of distributing power differently among actors. This makes the transition from public enterprises to sector regulation and regulators politically controversial. The emergence of sector regulation is thus part and parcel of the privatization process.

THE FIVE MAIN OBJECTIVES OF REGULATION IN THE NETWORK INDUSTRIES

The previous section argued that, in a liberalized environment, responsibility for ensuring public policy objectives falls back from the operators to the political authorities (see Newbury, 2000). Let us summarize here the five main public policy objectives which regulation in the network industries should safeguard:

1 Liberalization means competition. The most important regulatory function to be provided in a liberalized environment is, thus, to *regulate competition*, including stimulating it if it does not emerge spontaneously. Where competition in the market is not possible – for example, because a service is a natural monopoly, such as a water distribution grid – competition regulation should instead seek to create competition *for* the market – for example, by awarding a franchise to operate the grid for a fixed period through a competitive bidding process. Thus, competition regulation does apply to all network industries, as well as to all liberalized sectors.

2 Liberalization requires unbundling, and unbundling means fragmentation. Consequently, a second, most important, function of regulation is to *ensure the system's integrity*. This matters most where coherence of the network is a pre-condition for the provision of the public service – for example, in railways (coherence between infrastructure and train operations), gas and electricity (coherence between production, transport and distribution), and

water. Regulation here must ensure that the different components are well articulated (e.g. that competing trains can access the rail infrastructure, but without overloading it).

3 Political authorities must also ensure that the system evolves and learns from experience. Once different segments of an infrastructure system are unbundled, the actors start to behave strategically (i.e. furthering their own commercial interests rather than those of the system). Regulation must therefore also *ensure that the system adapts to changing demands and technology*. Telecommunications services must keep up with technological advances; the electricity system must ensure security of supply. This challenging regulatory function requires substantial capacity and competence in the regulator.

4 The regulator must ensure that both *'services in the general interest' (for citizens) and 'universal services' (for consumers) continue to be provided*, as operators no longer have an interest to provide such services by themselves, given that these public services are, in general, less lucrative than commercial services. This is especially the case in the access of the poor to basic services. Using the example of water services, Südhoff shows that a poverty-oriented regulation policy is possible through binding guidelines on price, supply and competition (see the following snapshot, 'Example: Water privatization working for the poor'). But there is essentially a need for reliable and strong public authorities.

5 Finally, there is the function of *regulating access to, and the use of, the scarce (public) resource*. Such scarce resources do not exist in all sectors, and regulation here is thus limited to specific sectors, such as the water sector (water as a scarce resource), the air transport sector (regulation of scarce airspace), and the telecommunications and audiovisual sector (regulation of spectrum).

As mentioned earlier, not all of these five regulatory functions are necessarily taken on by the regulator. However, in all infrastructure sectors, there is a need to regulate competition and the provision of public services. In some of the sectors, there is also a need to regulate the system's integrity as well as the system's learning – namely, in the railways, the gas and the electricity systems. It is currently controversial whether this regulatory function also applies to the telecommunications and the postal sectors. Finally, the function of regulating the scarce resource must be fulfilled in the water, air transport, audiovisual and telecommunications sectors.

INSTITUTIONAL AND ORGANIZATIONAL ASPECTS OF REGULATION

The emergence of regulation and regulators is not just a matter of ensuring public policy functions; it is also about new institutional arrangements among politico-administrative actors. This section discusses the main institutional and organizational issues raised by the emergence of sector-specific regulation, highlights the newly emerging institutional arrangements, and defines the four main criteria against which emerging regulation must be judged.

Implementing public policy by means of regulation requires new institutions, the so-called *regulators*. This process raises questions of inter-organizational relationships, control and power:

1 There is first the *tension between sector-specific regulators and competition regulators*. Liberalization of network industries, sector by sector, leads to setting up sectoral regulators, each in charge of sector-specific regulatory functions, such as the distribution of scarce resources and system integrity and learning, as well as public service provision. But on competition regulation there is generally an inbuilt conflict between the sectoral regulator and the already existing competition regulator, particularly because technical and public service regulatory functions have implications on competition. There is, so far, no institutional solution for this tension, although different regulatory frameworks have different impacts on the regulatory process and outcomes. In some countries, there are still other organizations involved in regulation. For example, in Germany, the judiciary plays a significant role in *ex-post* regulation.

2 There is, secondly, the issue of the *independence of the regulator*. Sector (and even more so, competition) regulators must be independent of the operators whom they are supposed to regulate. Institutions promoting independent regulators, such as the European Commission and the World Bank, argue that regulators should also be at 'arm's length' from government. In this author's view, the intellectually solid argument for this is that one of the regulated operators remains owned by the state. This issue of independence has a bearing on the questions of who nominates the members of the regulatory bodies; how long they serve; who the regulator reports to (the government, the parliament or a special commission?); who oversees the regulator (parliament, the judiciary or still another body?); and power (see next point).

3 A regulator can be very independent, yet have little power. It is therefore important to consider the *powers of the regulator*. Can the regulator make and enforce decisions on its own, or merely make recommendations? Can the regulator investigate on its own initiative or only act upon complaints? Can the regulator intervene in advance, or only after rules have been broken? Does the regulator have to consult with other bodies (e.g. price surveillance) before acting? The regulator's financial resources and autonomy (what is its budget and who pays it: government, consumers, operators or a combination?), and the size and competencies of its staff also affect the pressure that the regulator can exert and the results that it can achieve (see list below for 'regulatory pressure').

4 Finally, there is the issue of the *level of regulation*. Regulatory bodies have generally been set up nationally. But in Europe, some regulatory functions are being shifted to the European Commission, either because the rules of

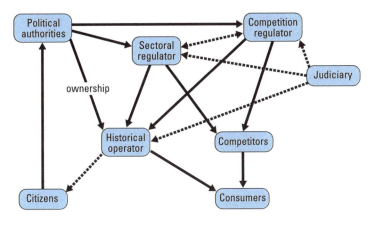

Figure 61
Ideal regulatory institutional framework. Dotted lines indicate secondary influence.

national regulation are being defined there or because the commission is explicitly taking on regulatory functions – for example, the European Safety Agency in air traffic control. Especially in federalist countries, some regulatory functions are being devolved to, for instance, the German *Länder* or Swiss cantons (e.g. electricity and public transport regulation).

These four dimensions – relevant organizations, independence, power and level – allow variety between regulatory institutions in different countries. Regulatory institutions are closely related to the history and political tradition of a country (i.e. Anglo-Saxon tradition, German tradition, Scandinavian tradition and Latin tradition), and the state system (centralized or federal). Nevertheless, there is a strong pressure towards converging regulatory institutions, driven (in the developing countries) by the World Bank and (in Europe) by the European Commission, as well as by the nature of the different sectors. Figure 61 describes the main *actors* of the institutionalized regulatory framework in a given country, as well as the ideal relationships between these actors.

This institutional framework of regulation and regulators can be judged against four more *criteria*: comprehensiveness, coherence, regulatory pressure and performance:

1 This chapter has highlighted three regulatory functions (competition, public service and technical operations) and five objectives (competition, scarce resources, universal service, systems integrity and system learning). '*Comprehensiveness*' asks whether a regulatory regime covers all of these.
2 '*Coherence*' asks whether all of the relevant actors in a given regulatory regime work towards the same public policy objectives in an efficient way (i.e. without redundancy, duplication or conflict of interest). Are the regulatory functions logically and coherently distributed?

3 *'Regulatory pressure'* refers to the regulator's pressure exerted upon the operators. It basically measures the degree to which the operators do (or do not) feel pressured by the regulators.

4 Finally, *'performance'* of an institutional regulatory framework is the most important, but also the most difficult, to measure. It seeks to determine whether (or the extent to which) the institutional regulatory framework and the relevant actors actually involved do contribute to the achievement of the defined public policy objectives.

GENERALIZING REGULATION

This chapter has discussed regulatory functions and institutions within the network industries. How far can similar regulatory functions and institutions be applied to other sectors that are also currently being liberalized?

The view taken here is that regulation must also be considered as a possible answer in all other sectors. Liberalization and privatization in health, education or security raise issues of competition (sometimes *for* the market rather than *in* the market – for example, in security), as well as issues of public service. Regulation is an appropriate means of ensuring both competition and public service provision in a liberalized and privatized environment. Where sectors have network characteristics, for example health, there would also be a need to regulate the integrity and learning of public service systems. But scarce resource regulation is probably only needed in the water, broadcasting, telecommunications and the air and rail transport sectors.

EXAMPLE: WATER PRIVATIZATION WORKING FOR THE POOR – FIRST DOS AND DON'TS OF REGULATION

Ralf Südhoff

In general, involving private companies in the water supply of developing countries has three objectives: to increase the efficiency of supply, to relieve public budgets and to improve access to water. Privatization has had a very variable record in improving access, especially for the poor. But the decades-long practice of purely public supply in many countries also contributed to the current situation that more than 1 billion people are acutely short of water (Franceys, 2001). Hence, it is important to understand both negative and positive privatization experiences and to ask when and how privatization can work for the poor.

Here, the decisive point is regulation. The results of regulation depend upon the institutional framework, as well as upon specific rules and tools to benefit the poorest – the latter being the focus of this snapshot. Is it, for example, possible to identify the rules and tools of regulation policies that can make private water supply a success for the poor, and if so, how do they work?

The nature of regulation depends upon the type of privatization. We use franchise as an example since this requires the most extensive regulation. To make private water supply work for the poor, regulation is needed in three core areas: *supply*, *price* and *competition*. A range of successful balancing acts must be performed in these areas: between the need for enforcement and the desire for the greatest possible flexibility from the company; between social progress and profitability; and between the desire for simple, transparent and un-bureaucratic guidelines and the existence of complex aims and target groups.

The experiences of the last few years indicate that regulators have been quite successful with socially oriented guidelines when they have been written into the franchise agreement in a binding manner and relate mainly to the *output* (targets) of privatization, but where investors have been granted as much flexibility as possible with regard to the *input* (means) with which they intend to achieve these targets.

Supply

A regulator can promote poverty-oriented expansion through measures such as guidelines, subsidies and incentives. To be effective, guidelines must be fixed clearly, explicitly and with adequate priority in the tender and the franchise agreement. Many tenders focus on the investors' lowest price offer and only define expansion targets in the second stage. In many cases, this has resulted in the franchise being won by investors with unrealistically low price suggestions, who then sought renegotiation since; allegedly, they could not obtain sufficient returns on their investment with the original tariff schedule.

In contrast, in Chile, for example, the regulator successfully practised the principle of *negative franchise*: the tender is won by the bidder who requires the lowest subsidy for the desired expansion in water connections for poor households. In El Alto, Bolivia, the bidders even had to commit themselves to an expansion of water connections without subsidies and to accept the priority of poverty-oriented water supply for the tender. In addition, the World Bank has developed the tool of *output-based aid* (OBA). Here, subsidies are only given to private companies when expansion targets have been met or previously defined needy sections of society have been supplied. OBA is said to have achieved encouraging results in Paraguay. However, to date, OBA schemes are rarely implemented and experience with the principle is very limited (Marin, 2002). In any case, OBA should be managed with care so that indigenous (or financially weak) suppliers still have a chance of winning a contract. This is a challenge since, for instance, OBA schemes usually require that bidders postpone their return on investment until performance targets are reached.

Overall, such detailed guidelines for the expansion of connections (output) have produced positive results for poorer customers when they were clearly measurable and easy to check. Here, *absolute guidelines* are usually more successful than percentile or soft factors: for instance, an operator's commitment to a certain number of new connections in an area can be established in the contractual agreement. On the other hand, it is often not easy to discern whether 55 per cent, 60 per cent or 65 per cent of a population have access to water. For example, in Côte d'Ivoire, about 70 per cent of the people without water access live in illegal settlements and lack legal property titles (a major legal problem for both private or public suppliers). This problem can best be circumvented by means of simple guidelines, such as those that designate a target number of new connections, while soft rules, such as those that require new connections wherever they 'did not incur substantial additional expenditure compared to existing connections' are easily 'subject to debate' (Komives, 1999; Komives and Stalker-Prokopy, 2000).

Subsidy policies also have proven quite successful as a means of expanding networks to the poorest. In particular, *cross-subsidization* of the connection costs is widespread. In its simplest form, this means that uniform connection costs are charged, which subsidizes more expensive (and poorer) marginal areas at the expense of the lower-cost (but more affluent) central areas. Further subsidy is possible, for example, where existing consumers subsidize new connections with a regular charge (as, for example, in Côte d'Ivoire and Argentina). This is often appropriate for social reasons, as well as for reasons of fairness, since before privatization the primarily affluent consumers frequently did not bear a realistic cost of their connections. For both options, policy-makers need to clarify how operators should reach the needy target group in the simplest and most effective manner (see 'Prices' below).

Nevertheless, connection costs can still be too high for the poorest households. This can even be the case where costs are fixed by the regulator and instalment payments are made. For example, in Buenos Aires, customers could pay off the connection cost of US$240 for drinking water and sewage over a full five years, with no interest. But even the remaining payment of US$4 a month was a serious hurdle for the poorest households. This demonstrates how important *micro-credit programmes* can be in the water market, as offered in some countries.

Moreover, many case studies have shown how useful it is if investors were not too rigidly bound by technical and qualitative standards (input). For example, the '*condominial systems*' have often proven to be a successful means of making drinking water connections affordable. The principle was first used in Brazil and is based on a mixture of simpler technical standards (thinner pipes, overground pipe-laying and possible community connections) and the labour contributed by consumers. The cost of new connections is thus reduced by 20 to 90 per cent. Swiss technical assistance in developing countries also combined the tool with comprehensive participatory elements. This approach was only thoroughly successful in some cases (Finger, 2001; Finger and Allouche, 2002). However, thanks to condominial systems, numerous Brazilian suburbs could afford drinking water connections and many cities adopted the approach. For example, in El Alto, Bolivia, it cut connection costs by 30 per cent and an additional 10,000 households were connected to the water system.

Thus, skilful regulation can set out water connection prices in compliance with the goal of supplying the poor. However, this does not yet answer the question of socially acceptable water tariffs.

Prices

The objectives of cost-covering and social compatibility conflict when formulating water prices. In order to reconcile them, regulators have often used a mixture of sliding-scale prices, personal allowances and direct subsidies.

Direct subsidies given to every impoverished family are considered as the 'first best practice', in this respect. In Chile and parts of Colombia, assistance is given in this way. However, the cost is high and basic welfare state structures are usually required, but rarely exist in developing countries.

For this reason, sliding-scale prices in the form of *increasing block tariffs* have partly proven their worth. This is also a form of cross-subsidization among the consumers: when the consumption of poor private households is frugal, they pay the lowest amount. Large consumers (commercial consumers and industrial operations) pay the highest rate. Charges increase as the amount of water consumed increases.

The lowest *social tariff* is often a fixed-rate basic charge for the first 10 or 15 cubic metres of water. Some providers even guarantee a free *minimum personal water allowance* (e.g. South Africa). The average consumption of poor households is often estimated at approximately 6 to 8 cubic metres. For example, in impoverished El Alto, consumption is approximately 8 cubic metres; but in neighbouring La Paz, it is 24 cubic metres. The social tariff therefore makes the water bill of poor households affordable and, at the same time, all consumers have an economic incentive to save water.

Nevertheless, the principle of sliding-scale prices based on volume has its vagaries. For example, the often-charged basic fee for the first 10 cubic metres of water has proven problematic. First, this subsidy is not targeted since the millionaire in his villa also pays a subsidized tariff for this quantity (or even nothing, in the case of the minimum personal water allowance). Second, thanks to the basic rate, the subsidy mostly benefits the middle class. In Manila, the poorest households use only, for example, 6 cubic metres of water, but pay the full basic fee corresponding to 10 cubic metres – hence, their water rate (based on the price of each cubic metre) is almost doubled. On the other hand, the middle-class family that consumes 10 or 11 cubic metres will receive the full benefit of the subsidy. Moreover, in some countries schemes did not reduce the price per volume for users of shared connections. As a result, these usually poor families pay a higher price for less service as total consumption is above the social tariff volume.

Regional subsidies are thus being applied as an alternative to subsidy by volume. For example, in Dakar, Buenos Aires or Manila, prices are lower in poorer areas and higher in more affluent ones. The attraction of this alternative is its simple, non-bureaucratic applicability. It is also impossible to avoid a degree of inexactness here due to partial intermixing of sections of society;

however, especially in urban areas – usually the target of private investors – regional classification can often be carried out, which is then relatively effective for the subsidization of both water tariffs and connection charges. In the meantime, some experts recommend using combinations of regional and consumption criteria.

However, in the long term, such *social tariffs* can upset the desired balance of social orientation and economic viability (PPIAF, 2001a, b; GTZ, 2003): if the social tariff, as it is quite common, is less than the cost of service, poor customers will constitute loss-making business for the operator. This has two serious consequences: first, it leaves the operator high and dry with regard to further investment, particularly when regulation is successful and the investor supplies an ever-greater number of poor households with connections. Second, it robs the operator of all incentive to win impoverished customers on his own – profit-driven – initiative. Here, a measure comes into play that may be of decisive importance for long-term poverty-oriented water supply: the best way of supplying the poor is one that is profitable, thereby ensuring companies have an economic incentive to do so.

But increasing all tariffs to a profitable level – as some World Bank experts recommend – is no solution for the poor (Nickson, 2001; Thompson, 2001). Instead, good results depend upon schemes that involve regulatory agencies. For example, in Côte d'Ivoire, Chile and, to some extent, Senegal, private suppliers charge poor customers only a non-cost-covering tariff for water or a new connection. However, where the provider receives a reward for every new poor customer reached, provision to the poor can become highly profitable. Moreover, strains on public budgets can be avoided when this policy is financed by other means. For example, in Côte d'Ivoire, wealthier customers pay higher prices than poorer customers as in many other places. However, in this case, it is crucial that a part of the higher prices is not paid directly to the supplier but contributes as a special fee to a fund which is supervised by the regulatory agency. The agency uses the money for rewarding the investor when he has improved service to the poor and for subsidizing their supply.

Moreover, higher profits from poor customers can place the state in a position to demand higher licence fees from the investor, which, in turn, can be used for such conditional subsidies (these licence fees can be substantial sums; for example, Suez in La Paz pays up to US$3 million per year to the state). Of course, this also demands institutional capacity and an efficient, independent agency. Where this is available, such *subsidized real prices* are one option for harmonizing profit orientation and the needs of the poor.

Competition

Nevertheless, there will always be cases and areas where it is unprofitable for private investors to expand water connections, at least in the short term. Here, the question of competition comes into play, which is a difficult one since the water sector's infrastructure demands, in principle, a 'natural monopoly'. However, where a provider has the exclusive right to provide all customers in a specified area, such exclusivity can block improvements in water supply and services. This is especially the case where unrealistically high standards coexist with exclusivity rights. For example, in Jakarta and in Gabon, investors gained such total exclusivity. In El Alto, the investor even had the right and the duty to close off other water sources such as standpipes and stop users from extracting groundwater. These are consequences of rigid input guidelines given to the investor by the state. Exclusivity may only make sense where investors themselves offer water at social tariffs. However, since they never do this from one day to the other in the whole supply area, a *conditional exclusivity* – the right to exclusivity only when access requirements have been fully met – is more acceptable.

A greater degree of flexibility for the investor can, at the same time, be guaranteed and reconciled with social targets if the investor can work together with other suppliers in areas that are still unexploited. In Côte d'Ivoire, Manila and many other cities, the private operator can also fulfil his supply obligations by selling water from a central point. For example, good results have been seen with *water kiosks* (e.g. in Burkina Faso), community groups or small co-operative neighbourhood networks. Here, poorer residents do not have an individual connection but, nevertheless, have regular access to drinking water. If this is successful, there is a good balance between economic incentives (increased water sales with basically protected exclusivity) and social progress (rapid supply of marginal areas). However, experience with private resellers using tanks or hand carts has shown that this practice does not always meet poverty-oriented targets. Water purchased from free traders often costs three to four times more than what the franchisees charge. A simplified form of regulation must therefore also be applied to these traders, whether by means of trading licences or price guidelines. Without regulation, customers may not benefit any more than they do when buying from peddlers who often charge ten times the normal price for water.

Conclusion

The business focus of the Global Players in the water market has recently shifted away from developing countries. For this reason, it is hard to predict to what extent multinational companies will invest in these regions in the near future. However, previous experience demonstrates that when foreign or domestic private companies are investing, regulatory agencies have many tools and options to make private companies offer a water supply that serves the poor people (by setting a good framework of incentives, regulations etc. as this section has shown).

If these agencies are independent and competent, privatization, profits and efficiency goals can exist in harmony with a poverty-oriented water policy and equity goals.

As illustrated above, privatization can work for the poor in urban areas if it is set out in advance in the concession contract, with polished guidelines of supply, price and competition, which should focus on output targets. However, these guidelines must be carefully adjusted to local circumstances, and the best way to establish a poverty-oriented water supply must be checked measure by measure since the details can vary from location to location.

For this reason, water sector experts have already developed 'poverty-oriented checklists' for regulating agencies (see PPIAF, 2001a, b). As these regulation requirements are both very complex and crucial, many developing countries will need assistance in building up institutional capacity. Therefore, development cooperation in the water sector should focus on the advice and accompaniment of poverty-oriented regulation policies. Building up institutional capacity in this respect will be crucial even for countries that may prefer to transform their inefficient public suppliers into viable state-owned companies. Making these efficient and sustainable in social and financial respects will demand substantial regulation policies, too.

EXAMPLE: ACCOUNTABILITY INSTEAD OF PRIVATIZATION – THE PARANA (BRAZIL) SCHOOL PERFORMANCE REPORT CARDS

Alcyone Vasconcelos and Simon Schwartzman

In Brazil, most basic education[1] is provided through state and municipal education authorities. The education census of 2001 listed 2.3 million teaching posts.[2] The state education authorities are the biggest public employers of the country.

Traditionally, school teachers are civil servants, school principals are nominated according to political or other personal criteria, students are allocated to schools according to their place of residence, and school life is dominated by central curricula; but student assessment is left to teachers. The teachers are mostly unionized and often go on strike for better salaries and exert considerable influence on education authorities. School principals and education authorities are notoriously overloaded, with complex administrative chores and political struggles for money. All in all, the system cannot be considered very cost efficient. During the last several years, the Brazilian national government started to implement student assessment, including participation in the Organisation for Economic Co-operation and Development's (OECD's) Programme for International Student Assessment (PISA) (OECD, 2001). Not surprisingly, Brazil comes out with the worst outcomes, not far from Mexico and Chile, and well below Cuba and European and Asian countries. In these assessments, private schools show much better results than public ones. In large part, this is because they recruit students from wealthier backgrounds and are free to expel under-performing and trouble-making students. More importantly, their principals are involved in devising course content, take care of the schools' achievement levels, are free to hire and fire their teachers, and make decisions on financial, pedagogical and administrative matters (Oliveira and Schwartzman, 2002).

Is privatization, then, the solution for the education problems of Brazil? In Latin America, the only large-scale privatization of education took place in Chile during the military government, and the results are questionable (Gauri, 1998). In Brazil, wholesale privatization is politically out of question; but many think that public education should take quality control and modern curriculum content more seriously, far beyond existing bureaucratic routine.

In the state of Parana (9.5 million inhabitants), in the southern region of Brazil, a policy of this kind was implemented during 1999–2002. Its main feature was the development of school report cards, to be delivered to school principals, teachers, and parents. The *Parana school report cards* (PSRC) focus on the performance of individual schools, not individual students. They allow comparisons of school averages with state and regional (municipality) averages. On a case-by-case basis, the PSRC also allow comparisons between schools. They are simple, concise (four pages) and are designed to be understood by specialized (teachers), as well as non-specialized (parents) members of school communities. They present valid, stable and reliable information, both objective (statistics) and subjective (opinions), covering selected dimensions of school performance: student learning, school structure and parents' opinions.

Six sets of information are covered: student achievement (results from statewide testing of fourth and eighth graders); student flow (promotion, retention, and dropout rates from the annual national school census); school characteristics (teachers' full-time equivalent and percentage with higher education; pupil enrolment and average class size); students socio-economical background and impressions about schooling life (from questionnaires attached to the statewide tests); principals' style (self-statements); and parents' opinions about the school's organization. The parent survey, also introduced in 2001, represented the first effort to track parental opinions and perceptions on key elements of the school environment, including their own involvement. It triggered a process through which parents increased their awareness about their role as educators, citizens and consumers of education services – for their children. Producing the annual report cards was a large, though relatively simple, operation. Both existing and newly collected data were necessary. Large databanks were integrated. Inputs were collected from parents, teachers and administrators. In the end, 1.3 million annual report cards (about one per student) were distributed.

The state education ministry supported the dissemination of the cards, with particular attention given to teaching target audiences how to read, interpret and use the information provided by school report cards. Nevertheless, use of the novel evaluation system is still unsatisfactory and is not being used to its full potential. Ultimately, the ministry hopes that teachers, school directors and parents will collaborate in generating solutions towards better schools, using school report cards as primary information sources for establishing empirical baselines, implementing improvements and, subsequently, monitoring progress. The assumption is that the systematic supply of useful information to communities about the effectiveness and quality of their schools will enhance the engagement of parents, both as educators and as watchdogs of schools and of the government. Such engagement breeds empowerment of parents to demand results from schools and the government, which, in turn, calls for active interaction between associations of parents and the state. The school report cards are envisaged as empirical, reliable and simple bases for this desirable interaction. The transparency of the school report cards is expected to increase the government's accountability – without any change of property and without other problematic effects of privatization.

It is too early to assess the impact of the PSRC initiative on school performances. But it has already helped to create, among parents, a growing sense of local ownership and responsibility – for example, by organizing ten regional associations. These associations attempt to agree on a common agenda of actions, including specific demands on government officials. School report cards are not solutions themselves, but seem to serve as an instrument of *increasing transparency and accountability* in a sector plagued by inefficiencies and, sometimes, cronyism. They are tools for management by results and they encourage the increased participation of parents.[3]

Privatization and Municipal Democracy

Nele Schneidereit and Ernst Ulrich von Weizsäcker[1]

Alexis de Tocqueville (1835), in his pivotal study of democracy in America, saw the municipalities as the 'school of democracy'. Citizens' capacity for democratic participation in their local communities is, indeed, at the roots of a functioning democratic society. In our days, however, we observe a dangerous process of an erosion of that capacity, caused, in part, by globalization and privatization.

'Globalization' has three effects on communal participation. One is the global spreading throughout all cultures of the world of mass fabricated, cheap goods that tend to suppress and supplant locally adapted goods. A second is that global standards of administrative techniques and cultural habits intrude within all villages and towns of the world. This works as a disadvantage to traditional people, who are accustomed to contributing their wisdom to local communities. In a way, it is a problem as old as civilization itself that the older generation finds it difficult to adapt to the new generation's habits and preferences. But this time, cultural change has occurred everywhere and at once – a shock in many parts of the world.

The third aspect of globalization, the topic of this chapter, is the worldwide spreading of neo-liberal ideas associated with deregulation and the 'lean state'. After the end of the Cold War, such concepts were strongly supported by the sudden dominance of the world capital markets, which induced cut-throat cost competition among global firms. States were weakened (see Figure 42 in this book) and stumbled into 'harmful tax competition' (the Organisation for Economic Co-operation and Development's, or OECD's, own term!) against each other. The public revenue base eroded in many parts of the world. Municipalities were particularly hit in the process and often had to turn to brutal or desperate austerity measures of cutting public services.

Privatization is, in part, an *unwanted* consequence of that new fiscal situation. Municipalities, in particular, experienced an exceptional fiscal

Figure 62
The classical pattern of a mutual relation between citizens and their municipalities.

emergency that forced them to sell public assets to private investors just to balance their annual budgets. But privatization also resulted from a *voluntary* 'lean state' policy of neo-conservative parties that were successful in municipal elections.

There is a need, then, to reflect on the new relations between citizens and the municipalities in which they live. What are the new duties and opportunities of municipalities and how can citizens meaningfully participate under the conditions of globalization and privatization?

Municipalities traditionally have enjoyed considerable political influence in the democratic state. They are typically entrusted with applying and enforcing laws adopted at the national levels. In many countries, they can pass their own laws, manage urban planning and development, and run schools and other public services. They also have well-organized paths of influence for legislation and policies at the provincial and national levels.

In simplified terms (see Figure 62), we can consider the classical relation between municipalities and their citizens as bipolar.

Privatization has introduced a new dimension into this simple picture. Some see it as enrichment per se because of manifold experiences with incompetent, corrupt or otherwise unsatisfactory local authorities. However, in typical Central European cities, the experience is rather of the opposite kind. Local authorities traditionally had a very good standing with their citizens, showed a remarkably competent performance with the provision of public services and served very well, in de Tocqueville's sense, as the schools of democracy. Hence, in this part of the world, globalization and privatization are typically experienced as a threat to the harmonious life of cities.

Negative aspects of privatization on the democratic life of cities include the following:

- The provision of public services has traditionally formed the core of trust in municipal authorities and, thus, their political credibility. Municipalities which transfer public services to private enterprise risk losing an important element of contact with their citizens. Furthermore, the function of local authorities may become less clear to their citizens, possibly leading to an increased perception of local government as superfluous and 'bureaucratic'. This can result in political apathy and disengagement of citizens, in general, not just at municipal level.
- Through the process of privatization, citizens are confronted with two partially conflicting systems of values – namely, social cohesion and economic efficiency. The classical relation between municipalities and their

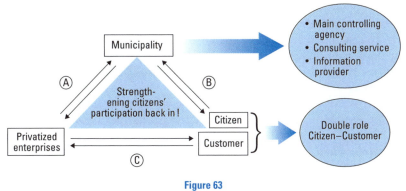

Figure 63
Triangular structure of relations at municipal level caused by privatization.

citizens as depicted in Figure 62 can be assumed to be dominated by cohesion considerations, while the private service supplier must be guided primarily by economic efficiency and shareholder value.

Hence, privatization may threaten elements of democratic governance even if it is successful in economic terms.

Where are the perspectives and opportunities, then, for democracy and citizens' participation in the modern era of widespread privatization of 'public' services? We relate our thoughts to concepts of an 'enabling state' put forward by authors such as Gapski and Hollmann (2000) and Bogumil (2000). Moreover, we support the idea of a politically active *consumer* of public services, even if they are supplied by private operators or owners (Wohlfahrt and Zühlke, 1999). Municipalities should develop the capacity to initiate and sustain partnerships for service delivery that also target the weak (Plummer, 2002).

For a better understanding of the new set of relations, we propose a *triangular* structure with three types of relations: *A* for relations between the city and the private firm, *B* for the familiar relation and *C* for the relations between the firm and the citizens in their double capacity as customers and as citizens (see Figure 63).

The idea of an enabling state is to encourage citizens to actively participate in the shaping of public life. Today, this involves encouraging citizens' participation in their double role as part of the municipality (relation *B* in Figure 63) and as politically active consumers (relation *C* in Figure 63). However, consumer influence in relation *C* is effective only if citizens possess an exit option, meaning that they have a genuine choice to move to a significantly different private supplier, or a continuing public provider, or simply not to use the service in question.

If customers play an active role in relation to the private suppliers of public services, this may give local authorities a stronger political mandate, although its exercise may be restricted by, for example, central government requirements for tendering or limits on local authority powers.

The idea of an educated and politically active consumer is by no means new: the question of how to reconcile the 'bourgeois' (private interest) and the *'citoyen'* (public interest) roles of the citizen have been debated for centuries. In our days, this challenge means to stimulate peoples' interest not only in clean water but also in the contractual agreements between the city and the water suppliers.

Three steps, in particular, may help to reactivate democracy at the municipal level. All three can be derived from the Aalborg Charter (1994):

1 *Transparency and information*: to create a transparent and comprehensible set of responsibilities at the municipal level, thereby developing a new profile of the city as an information provider. People particularly need advance explanations of the 'why and how' of privatization measures (relation A in Figure 63); of consumer rights with regard to the intended operator or owner of the utility (relation C in Figure 63), and of their future political rights in relation to the respective service (relation B in Figure 63).
2 *Empowerment and participation*: to build civic capacity and to supply people with political expertise and increase their political awareness so that they can understand, fulfil and benefit from their role as citizens; and to provide opportunities for civil society participation.
3 *Governance*: despite outsourcing and the delegation of responsibilities, the municipality must remain in charge of ultimate quality control. Preferably the right should be reserved to terminate the contract with the private operator.

Opportunities do exist to encourage citizens to adopt a meaningful participatory role. At least under the privileged conditions of good 'old Europe', consumers are reasonably well informed about global affairs, about global firms that are active in the city, and about their rights towards suppliers and the state. Ulrich Beck, the German sociologist, emphasizes that the *'bourgeois'* (the consumer) has long arrived in the globalized world, while the *'citoyen'* (the political animal) needs to speed up in order not to be left behind and blackmailed by globalization (see, for example, Beck, 1998, 2000).

The perspective – idealistic, perhaps, under the prevailing conditions of globalization – could be that active citizens of their respective municipalities demand and help to promote globally powerful alliances among local authorities and with other political actors, including civil society. The ultimate aim, then, is 'social equity as the basis for international stability' (Savir, 2004). This is an agenda often referred to as 'glocalization' – the interplay of global opportunities and local interests and the call for a more pronounced role of local actors in addressing global challenges on a human scale (CERFE, 2003). In some states this agenda would require a constitutional strengthening of municipalities. But that is certainly desirable from the point of view of democracy. The municipality is, after all, the public place where people most directly experience the necessity for non-economic values and where they can be empowered to influence politics.

Financing Global Public Goods: Challenges

Inge Kaul[1]

INTRODUCTION

Why do we address global public goods in a book about the limits to privatization? Three reasons come to mind.

First, at the international level, nation states tend to behave like private actors in the pursuit of their national self-interest, which, seen from a global perspective, is particular and private. Such self-interested behaviour is likely to increase, the more economic openness, liberalization and marketization place countries and governments into a situation of intense global cost competition (see also 'Post-war history: The ups and downs of the public sector' in Part III). Thus, the provision of global public goods, such as international financial stability, communicable disease control, or sustainable management of the global natural commons, is likely to suffer from two sets of pressures: from added policy emphasis on using markets, and from increased rivalry among states.

Second, while public goods provision comes under pressure nationally and internationally, there is, however, also a growing realization that the success or failure of privatization depends upon an adequate supply of these goods. Efficient markets require institutional embedding, and this means that they require such public goods as a rule-based system for trade, finance or transport in order to enhance predictability, reduce risks and lower transaction costs. As markets integrate, many of these public goods become interlocked, assuming the character of border-transgressing, global public goods.

Third, despite the growing recognition of the importance of global public goods, there has been limited change in terms of putting in place policy instruments to enhance their provision. Tools and mechanisms for the joint, cooperative financing of these goods are especially lacking. In most instances, governments resort to using existing development assistance (i.e. aid) resources. However, this often leads to the wrong actors being targeted and ineffective means being used. For example, aid to the poorest countries can usually do very little about stemming the risk of global warming. Some new financing arrangements have emerged. Yet, they have generally happened ad hoc, often in response to urgent challenges, such as the outbreak of a potentially global health epidemic or an international financial crisis.

This chapter is intended to contribute to a more systematic understanding of global public goods financing. It examines some of the new financing arrangements in order to understand where change is headed and how it could be furthered. The main policy messages emerging from the discussion are:

- The bulk of global public goods financing has to occur at the national level, based on public finance policies that discourage negative cross-border spillovers and encourage positive ones.
- Global public goods come in different forms, with different underlying incentive structures. Therefore, each good needs a tailor-made financing strategy.
- Improved international democracy is key to making the complementary international dimension of global public goods financing work because internationally, too, the principle of 'no taxation without representation' holds. Actors want to have a fair say about which global public goods to provide, how much of them, and at what net-benefit/cost to whom.

INTRODUCING PUBLIC GOODS AND GLOBAL PUBLIC GOODS

Economic development and, ultimately, people's well-being depend upon two main types of goods: private goods and public goods.[2] Private goods are goods with excludable benefits: individuals can appropriate them and prevent others from enjoying the good. Public goods, by contrast, are in the public domain, available for all to consume or affecting all. Examples are the natural commons, such as the moonlight or the high seas. It is virtually impossible to stop others from enjoying these goods. More or less the same, however, also applies to human-made public goods, such as a judiciary system. Public goods that have non-rival properties, such as scientific knowledge, especially lend themselves to being public in consumption because one person's consumption of the good does not reduce its availability for others.

Transnational, global or regional public goods are those goods whose benefits are public (as opposed to private) and cut across several countries (in the case of regional public goods) or countries in several regions, as well as several generations (in the case of global public goods). The benefits – and costs – of public goods can be different in reach. Some may just have a local span (e.g. a street sign). Others, such as judiciary systems, can be of national reach. Yet others may be of transnational, regional or global scope. An example of a regional public good could be the control of river blindness, since this disease is endemic only in certain parts of Africa; and an example of a global public good would be the moonlight. Yet, whether local or global in reach, public goods matter to people primarily as ingredients of their well-being. And just as people have varying preferences for private goods, their preferences for public goods, including global public goods, vary. For example, fostering international financial stability would have higher priority for those participating in capital markets than for those eking out an existence on one dollar a day.

Varying preferences for public goods are particularly significant because public goods are often not only public in consumption, but also public in production (i.e. dependent upon cooperative efforts).

Thus, *from the consumption side*, global public goods are public goods whose benefits and costs span across national borders and regions, even generations. *From the production side*, global public goods typically are public goods that cannot be adequately produced through domestic policy action alone, but require international cooperation, even if this cooperation only consists of national-level policy adjustments to discourage or encourage cross-border spillovers. As the following discussion shows, both the consumption and the production characteristics of global public goods have important implications for their financing.

DIFFERENT GLOBAL PUBLIC GOODS: DIFFERENT FINANCING PURPOSES AND TOOLS

It is clear that paying for global public goods may require action at the national, as well as the international, level. Taxes, subsidies and other fiscal measures, including non-financial instruments such as regulation, must ensure that all concerned actors allocate appropriate resources to these goods. In some instances, achieving an appropriate allocation may entail increasing the level of both public and private spending on the good. In other instances, it may mean decreasing current resource allocations. In yet other cases, the best option may be to increase (or decrease) the costs of certain actions so that actors, at a given expenditure level, consume or produce less (or more) of a particular good.

Clearly, given the differing nature of public goods (global and otherwise), notably the differences in their production paths, there exists no single formula for financing them. Financing arrangements have to be goods specific.

Nevertheless, when examining some of the financing measures for global public goods that have emerged, the following main sets of measures can be distinguished.

National-level financing arrangements to discourage negative and encourage positive cross-border spillovers

Many countries have adopted policy instruments to prevent *negative externalities* from spilling across national borders and adversely affecting other countries. Examples are national carbon or energy taxes. Other examples are improvements in human rights conditions that ease international flows of asylum seekers, or strengthening banking supervision that may help to prevent financial crises and potential international contagion effects.

The main motive for such measures may be to improve the national public domain, not the global public good. As pointed out earlier, national public goods are important ingredients of global public goods. Where national public goods are adequately provided, there is often no need for special corrective international-level interventions.

Similarly, national-level policy measures can foster the production of *positive cross-border spillovers*. For example, national support for scientific research may benefit researchers worldwide. Negative cross-border spillovers often receive considerable policy attention; but positive spillovers are often just quietly enjoyed by the global public, free of charge. However, the unilateral provision of a global public good, such as pharmaceutical knowledge, is not necessarily appreciated.

There is little data on national and international-level spending on global public goods. It seems that national-level spending – expenditure on reducing negative spillovers or encouraging positive ones – constitutes the bulk of global public goods financing. Even when only considering public financing, the ratio of national-level financing to international-level financing, according to some estimates, ranges between 200:1 and 400:1. Of course, private financing also happens nationally. Moreover, as states are withdrawing from the direct provision of public goods, focusing their role on creating incentives for private actors and employing such methods as marketization (e.g. user fees for state-provided services), private spending is likely to be a growing part of the total spending on these goods.

Sharing the operating costs of common international-level facilities

International institutions for state and non-state actors to come together and negotiate international cooperation issues are themselves global public goods: without such facilities, international cooperation and the provision of other global public goods would suffer. It is perhaps also for this reason that the few binding financial commitments which the international community has so far agreed primarily concern nation states' contributions to the regular budget of international organizations, such as the United Nations, its specialized agencies and the Bretton Woods institutions.

In most instances, the cost-sharing formula applied follows the 'ability to pay' principle, sometimes modified by other criteria, such as the country's volume of civil aviation traffic, postal mail or telecommunication.

Resourcing international-level financial intermediaries

International-level financial intermediaries are created for several purposes, including the following.

Supporting 'weak-link' providers

Some national providers have a weak ability to pay for public goods. It may be globally beneficial for stronger providers to assist weaker ones. For example, civil aviation safety calls for vigilance and proper screening processes at all airports.

Providing compensation for the provision of global public services

Where actors (primarily countries) make efforts, aimed at, for example, carbon sequestration or biodiversity conservation, beyond what they would do solely for national self-interest, global funds (e.g. the Global Environment Facility, or GEF, can reimburse the extra costs since these efforts benefit the world as a whole).

Offering pooled incentives to 'best-shot' providers

Where the national motivation is strong, individual governments may provide incentives for actors to contribute to a particular global public good (e.g. the fight against a global communicable disease, such as tuberculosis). But often it would be more efficient for countries to pool resources internationally in order to encourage a technological pioneer (or 'best-shot actor') to provide the good. Such encouragement could, for example, take the form of guarantees to buy a certain quantity of the good in order to allow the provider to recoup related research and development costs.

Valuing scarce global public goods

An important group of global public goods are the natural commons that are non-excludable (i.e. in the global public domain), but have rival consumption properties and are, therefore, at risk of being overused and becoming depleted. Ostrom (1990) speaks of 'common-pool resources'. Some of the afore-mentioned national measures (e.g. national carbon taxes), as well as some of the international-level financing arrangements, such as the incremental cost payments of the GEF, could help to avert these risks. Yet, additional measures to support such purposes include the assignment of user allowances, such as fishing quotas or greenhouse gas emission permits. If these allowances are made tradable or 'leasable', actors with excess permits can exchange them against payment of a price with actors who desire additional allowances.

Levying user fees for global services

Some UN agencies and organizations help in providing a global public good. In the case of the World Intellectual Property Organization (WIPO), for example, it is patent protection and global knowledge management. However, at the same time, the services of WIPO generate important private benefits for the patent holders, who are therefore willing to pay a patent registration fee. The revenue generated from these fees constitutes a major part of WIPO's income.

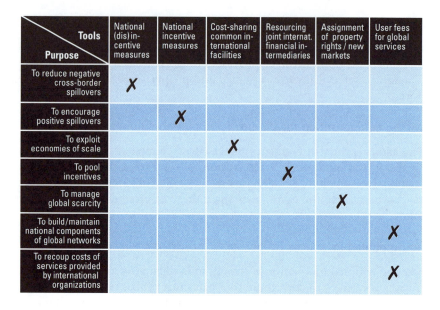

Tools / Purpose	National (dis)incentive measures	National incentive measures	Cost-sharing common international facilities	Resourcing joint internat. financial intermediaries	Assignment of property rights / new markets	User fees for global services
To reduce negative cross-border spillovers	X					
To encourage positive spillovers		X				
To exploit economies of scale			X			
To pool incentives				X		
To manage global scarcity					X	
To build/maintain national components of global networks						X
To recoup costs of services provided by international organizations						X

Figure 64
Purposes and tools for financing global public goods.

For similar reasons, it is possible for the International Treaty on Plant Genetic Resources for Food and Agriculture (which constitutes and regulates a sort of global gene pool) to charge the users of the gene pool, and to use these charges to pay for the preservation (and to the providers) of the genetic resources (many providers are farmers in developing countries).

The global systems of civil aviation or postal services would not be possible without all countries contributing – through state or private provision – components of harmonized national infrastructure. These benefits justify a variety of user charges.

These are three selected examples of *private*-sector fees for *public* goods. It can be expected that the system of having private-sector beneficiaries of public goods pay for their use will become much more normal. The reason is, in part, that many states, not only in developing countries, face great difficulties in balancing their budgets and see hardly any room for manoeuvre to finance additional global activities.

Figure 64 presents the above list of financing arrangements for global public goods in summary form. It shows that different goods and financing purposes call for different financing tools.

TOWARDS A SYSTEMATIC APPROACH TO THE FINANCING OF GLOBAL PUBLIC GOODS

The financing of global public goods calls for a number of important policy reforms. Yet, given that some of the required changes already exist in a nascent form or on a pilot basis, the desirable further steps might be quite 'doable'. Approaching the issue of global public goods financing in a more explicit, as well as a more coherent and integrated, manner is, perhaps, the most critical step – always keeping in mind that in today's world of individual (and often competitive) nation states, international cooperation has to make economic sense for all if it is, as it must, to happen voluntarily. The possible reform steps include:

- Recognizing the dual agenda of international cooperation financing with regard to the 'aid + global public goods' agenda in order to avoid the frequent confusion between the two modalities, which appears detrimental to both.
- Formulating a theory of global public goods financing with a view to refurbishing the toolkit of policy-makers with tested and reliable instruments.
- Tapping new financing sources for global public good purposes (e.g. to replace, as necessary, the current official development aid, or ODA, resources). An obvious source would be the budget of the concerned national government agency. Thus, environment ministries could, for example, support not only the national building blocks of 'their' global public goods, but also the international cooperation components that might be required. Moreover, as mentioned above, an international system of user fees for global public goods and for the services of international organizations should be developed.
- Acquiring better information, notably on whether action to reduce a global public 'bad' is a good investment compared to private goods or other public goods. Without better information, many global public goods will only be addressed when under-provision reaches crisis level. Figure 65 provides a rough preliminary assessment of the cost of current under-provision of selected global public goods and the costs of possible corrective action. Even with major scientific and normative caveats, Figure 65 seems to indicate that corrective action can be much less costly than inaction.
- Improving participation in international negotiations – in line with the principle of fiscal equivalence.[3] This may require enhanced participation by various national constituencies that may, at present, not feel fully represented by their country's international negotiating team. And it would require giving full voice to all governmental teams, notably those from developing countries. Inasmuch as the private sector is meant to shoulder some of the cost of global public goods, adequate private-sector participation should also be secured. Such enhanced participation of the various stakeholder groups in the decision-making on global public goods would allow for fairer and fuller competition between private and public concerns.

Yet, for participation to be able to contribute to more balanced development, it must be based on informed decision-making, notably on knowledge about the nature of various global public goods, the financing options available, and

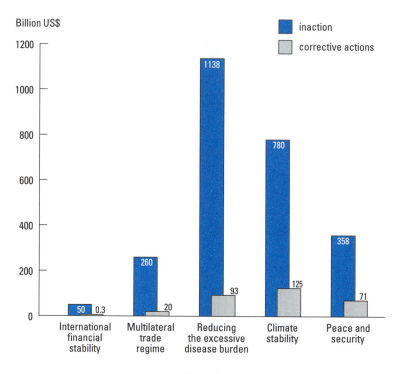

Figure 65

Rough estimates of annual costs of inaction and corrective actions for provision problems of selected global public goods. Further substantiations of the estimates are presented by Kaul et al (2003, p159).

the distribution of the costs and benefits that action or inaction entail. Figure 65 and the challenges of financing global public goods make the case for global governance very compelling.

EXAMPLE: PRIVATE FUNDING OF INFRASTRUCTURE IN DEVELOPING COUNTRIES

Peter Wolff

Infrastructure: Essential for poverty reduction

Infrastructure plays a critical role in supporting both economic growth and in improving social service delivery to the poor. With the proclamation of the United Nations Millennium Development Goals (MDG) in 1999, clear targets have been set for reducing absolute poverty as well as – among other goals – the proportion of people without sustainable access to adequate quantities of affordable and safe water until 2015. These goals will only be met when basic infrastructural services – roads, transport, communications, energy, water supply and sanitation – are provided to the poor. The inequality of access to basic services – linked to infrastructure provision – is what many regard as the basic challenge of development (World Bank, 2003b).

There are tremendous unmet needs for infrastructure investment and for improvements in service delivery in developing countries. A recent study on infrastructure demand roughly estimates that the annual investment and maintenance needs in infrastructure for developing countries over the period of 2005–2010 could amount to – at a minimum – US$465 billion per annum or on average 5.5 per cent of each country's gross domestic product (GDP), and up to 6.9 per cent of the GDP of the poorest countries (Fay and Yepes, 2003). *The Report of the World Panel on Financing Water Infrastructure* estimates that annual investment in water services for developing countries will have to be increased from US$75 billion in 2001 to US$180 billion in 2002–2025, if the 2015 targets are to be met and sustained (Camdessus, 2003). *Recurring* expenditure on administrative overheads, operations, maintenance, routine repairs and periodic replacements have to be added, as shortfalls in these items lead to the need for higher investment in the future.

It is clear, however, that increases in spending alone cannot solve the problem of services failing to reach the poor. Public spending on infrastructure is typically enjoyed by the non-poor. Despite high public spending for water and electricity, in many developing countries the poorest fifth of the population rarely has access to these services. Typically, subsidized public services are handed out as political patronage with poor people rarely the beneficiaries. Therefore, the question of how service providers – public or private – can be encouraged to serve the poor by using adequate arrangements for pricing, subsidies and delivery mechanisms, and how to hold them accountable for the quality of their services, is crucial. Only with more effective use of resources, in terms of reaching the poorest, can the argument for additional resources become persuasive.

Private provision of infrastructure: Boom and bust

The 1990s marked a rapidly rising involvement of the private sector in providing and financing infrastructure. As many public utilities found themselves unable to meet increasing demand and extend services to the poor, governments, facing severe budget constraints, resorted to the private sector for help. Developing countries saw investment of nearly US$755 billion in nearly 2500 infrastructure projects over the period of 1990 to 2001. The nature and scope of private involvement varied, from simple management contracts through to the outright sale of existing assets. There was a rush to certain sectors and regions, ranging from independent power plants in Indonesia and Thailand, to toll roads in Mexico and power distribution companies in Brazil. Although investments were concentrated in a few countries, mainly in Latin America and East Asia, by 2001 over 132 developing countries had undertaken private infrastructure projects in one or more sectors, with the bulk of this in the power and telecommunications sector (Harris, 2003, p6).

In the wake of the East Asian financial crisis, investment flows began to decline after 1997. The macro-economic crises in Brazil and Argentina added to a widespread pessimism of private investors with regard to infrastructure investments in emerging markets and developing countries. Many projects have been cancelled or renegotiated. The number of new private infrastructure projects declined dramatically and public sentiment, particularly in Latin America, has turned against the private provision of infrastructure, in general.

What are the reasons for this rapid decline of interest in private infrastructure projects after governments in many developing countries had moved away from the traditional model of public provision of infrastructure services?

- Governments and investors had clearly underestimated the risks and challenges inherent in infrastructure projects, particularly with regard to the pricing of services. Governments in developing countries have a long tradition of holding prices below their economic cost, the difference to be covered by the public budget. At the beginning of the 1990s, revenues for electricity and water in developing countries recovered, on average, as little as 60 per cent and 30 per cent of costs, respectively. Bringing in the private sector required price increases that were politically not sustainable in many cases.
- Large currency devaluations, triggered by the economic crises in Asia and Latin America, rendered many projects unfeasible since the prices for services, as well as for capital cost, had in most cases been determined on the basis of foreign currencies. These problems were compounded by falling demand for infrastructure services as real incomes contracted following large exchange rate devaluations. The currency mismatch – income in local currency and outlays in foreign currency – turned out to be a major risk of externally funded infrastructure projects.
- Some of the large multinational corporations which were aggressively pursuing infrastructure projects in emerging markets and developing countries, such as Enron and AES in the power sector, and Vivendi and Suez in the water sector, were experiencing project failures, high long-term liabilities from these investments and dramatic falls in their stock prices. On the background of increasing difficulties in their home markets, they had to retreat from emerging market risks. Thus, some of the leading investors of the 1990s are not on the market any more. Large sums have been lost in infrastructure projects in Indonesia and Argentina, to be covered only partly by export credit insurance agencies. New market entrants, as well as financing institutions, are hesitant, therefore, to take in new developing country risks.

What are the lessons learned from this *boom-and-bust* scenario of the past ten years? First, governments must address the question of how infrastructure services are paid for, since public funds will not be available to subsidize these services across the board. Second, where services to the poor are concerned, governments have to integrate targeted subsidies when developing private participation schemes. Third, regulatory frameworks have to be developed that are both credible to investors and viewed as legitimate by consumers. Finally, financing issues, particularly those related to handling exchange rate risks, will remain difficult but have to be addressed.

Pricing

Going forward, governments will have to explicitly recognize that only consumers and taxpayers pay for infrastructure services. Unless tax revenues can provide sufficient levels of subsidies, revenues from user fees will have to rise through price increases and improved efficiency and consistency in revenue collection, including an end to any indulgences to favoured clients. In the traditional model of public provision with controlled prices, it cannot be assumed that groups who are not provided with adequate services yet will be served better in the future.

Serving poor customers

Increasing prices towards cost-covering levels on the one hand and pursuing social objectives on the other hand can be reconciled only by effectively targeting subsidies to poor customers. In the past, subsidies often failed to reach the poor, in part because they were not linked to results. Where governments are concerned that the private sector may not invest in expanding networks to thinly populated areas, schemes can be designed where performance risk is in the private sector, and subsidies are only paid when services are delivered. This output-based approach can be combined with competitive bidding, where providers bid for the minimum subsidy required to provide a specific service in targeted rural areas or to targeted poor customers.

Contracts for the private provision of services can be combined with the obligation to expand services, backed by financial penalties for non-compliance. Private providers should be free to choose low-cost technical solutions for their services. This strictly output-based approach helps to avoid over-engineered solutions imported from industrialized countries and encourages low-cost solutions for poor customers – provided the outputs are appropriately defined. Governments may need disinterested advice – for example from appropriate technology non-governmental organizations (NGOs) – in order to resist pressures from potential bidders to set unnecessarily elaborate technical standards.

Regulation

About 200 regulatory agencies have been created in developing countries over the last decade. Experiences are mixed, and there are different options for tariff regulation (e.g. price cap, cost of service and rate of return), with different degrees of incentives for greater efficiency and for the distribution of risks between providers, consumers and governments. Experience has shown that due to changing circumstances, there is a need for periodic renegotiations of contracts. This can lead to opportunistic behaviour by private providers, trying to shift risks to consumers or taxpayers. Renegotiation should only be allowed when external circumstances, not under the control of the providers, have changed. Regulation is, indeed, an appropriate answer to many of the problems stemming from privatization. However, there is one problem for which regulation is not actually an answer – namely, the problem of security of supply. Indeed, if operators decide to walk away from the contract or concession, there is generally little the regulator can do about it.

Financing

The financing of infrastructure projects through loans denominated in foreign currency has proven to be the Achilles heel of many projects. During the private infrastructure boom of the 1990s, there was too much emphasis on multinational corporations as the key players in infrastructure provision and foreign loans as the major instrument for financing new investments. Generally, the specific risk structure of infrastructure projects (high long-term investments; returns in local currency; politically sensitive pricing) makes financing in foreign currency a dangerous option.

Long-term local financing is better. However, this type of financing is rarely available in developing countries as local capital markets are severely underdeveloped, consisting mainly of short-term money and credit instruments. There has been some recent increase in the use of local currency bonds for infrastructure financing. Chile, Mexico, Brazil, Peru and Bolivia in Latin America and Malaysia, Thailand and South Korea in Asia are countries which have seen substantial use of domestic currency markets and pension funds to fund infrastructure.

Taking into account the large investment needs stated above, it would be tempting to expect substantial additional amounts of capital to be raised on an international level (e.g. official development assistance, global funds, foreign direct investment and private loans). However, the experience of the 1990s has shown that it would be an illusion to believe that international corporations and international capital could solve the problem of increasing the quantity and quality of infrastructure service provision in developing countries in a sustainable way. All of these funding sources will have to play a role, and there will be new initiatives to mobilize private funds through the use of complementary public financing instruments, such as guarantees. The major role, however, has to be played by the domestic private sector as a service provider and the domestic capital market as a source of finance.

Outlook

What are the perspectives for reviving private financing and private provision in infrastructure (both essential if the developmental goals are to be achieved)?

Box 17 Grameen Shakti: An alternative approach to financing energy in rural Bangladesh

Noara Kebir, Daniel Philipp, Jürgen Scheffran and Martin Stürmer

In 1996, Grameen Shakti emerged as a subsidiary of the internationally recognized Grameen Bank, an organization that has achieved success in providing micro-credit to the poor. From this beginning, Grameen Shakti has grown into a source of rural electrification featuring the use of renewable energy, combined with small-scale loans. Grameen Shakti is a non-profit enterprise that operates independently, financing itself through its own income.

Grameen Shakti sells solar home systems based on solar cells for domestic power supply through an independent network of more than 100 branches. The product consists of the technical system, micro-financing, on-the-spot installation, customer training, and a three-year maintenance warranty. The standard model is a 50-watt system that costs approximately €400. With a term that typically lasts three years, the monthly payments amount to about €10, with a down payment ranging from €60 to €100. The down payment is comparable to the cost of a rechargeable battery, and the monthly instalments to the average costs of using kerosene, candles and recharging and transporting their batteries. So the customers gain a long-term benefit; after paying the last instalment and becoming owners of their systems, they start to save money.

As of June 2004, almost 25,000 systems had been sold. The success of this initiative is based on several factors: the high demand in rural areas for alternative sources of electricity; the availability of micro-financing; and the complete range of services provided. Grameen Shakti enables its customers to become independent of central, state-controlled sources of power and to avoid depending upon commitments or promises from the government.

Grameen Shakti shows how decentralized private actors – including non-profit enterprises – can succeed in providing energy infrastructure. In contrast to government agencies, private suppliers must provide products adapted to local needs. Careful market research within the micro-energy sector has revealed the potential for private business and has played a key role in opening the market to consumers at lower levels of the social hierarchy.

Worldwide, 2 billion people are without a secure source of power due to insufficient financial resources, lack of government provision or both. The example of Grameen Shakti shows that the private sector offers a means of filling this need, at least partially. Local governments and international agencies could take steps to facilitate the replication of this model of micro-financed renewable energy systems. To this end, there is a need for local market research to channel private efforts in order to supply power to poorer people located in areas that lack a power grid. This can be done by revealing such opportunities and clarifying the conditions needed to make such initiatives work.

Source: Kebir, N. and Philipp, D. (2004) 'MicroEnergy Project: Ländliche Elektrifizierung auf der Basis von erneuerbaren Energien in Kombination mit Mikrofinanzierung'. Berlin: Peoples Globalization Edition.

For service provision to be sustainable, the basic principle will have to be full cost recovery, at least of the current cost, including maintenance and replacement, on the level of the service provider. Cost recovery, in many cases, will entail a degree of subsidization for specific groups or regions. When this principle is generally accepted, the question of private or public ownership becomes secondary. Appropriate solutions, therefore, depend upon the circumstances in each sector and country (e.g. regulatory capacity, capacities of public and private providers, etc.). In many cases, governments will opt for continued public ownership and responsibility for investment finance, with operations and service provision privately financed and managed.

Particularly at the sub-central level, governments have to create an enabling environment for the private sector in order to participate in the delivery of infrastructure services. There is a large scope, (e.g. in the water sector) to develop a domestic water industry if services are contracted out by the public sector.

The sub-central level of government has the greatest potential to raise the quantity and quality of infrastructure services. Where provision is inadequate, sub-central bodies can best identify local solutions, organize their implementation and manage distribution, including local participation throughout. As financing is the greatest bottleneck on the sub-central level, access to – mainly domestic – long-term capital markets for sub-sovereign bodies is key. New lending and guarantee instruments, focusing on domestic currency financing, and on the sub-central level, are urgently to be developed if the ambitious development goals are to be met.

Escaping Pernicious Dualism: Civil Society between the State and the Firm

Teodor Shanin and Ernst Ulrich von Weizsäcker

One of the most powerful tools of applied mathematics is binarity. Messages in computers can be reduced to sheer endless rows of binary digits (i.e. of *yes* or *no* or *black* or *white* decisions). Binarity has been so successful in our computerized civilization that black and white thinking seems to have become the normal mode of thinking. Caricature aside, reality is full of shades of grey. Regarding the topic of this book, reality is mostly state as well as private sector. In a simplified model, we can associate each economic activity some place on a continuum between state and private sector. Public–private partnership (PPP) is the rule, not the exception, for activities touching public interests and requiring good and cost-efficient management.

Regional railways that are operated by private firms, but with public subsidies for services that cannot be made profitable, are a point in case. In some instances, the public interest needs no subsidies but entrepreneurial imagination, as was the case with the famous Grameen Bank in Bangladesh created by Muhammad Yunus, which is successfully operating with mostly female customers who were completely ignored as customers by the private banking sector. In the case of small-scale European savings banks, municipal governments offer a backstop guarantee for services to small and local enterprises even in rural districts – services that are outside the scope for international commercial banks. Will this system survive the black-and-white mentality of the European Competition Commissioner and the Basle 2 accord on credit rules for banks?

The continuum between private and public is still *one dimensional* and, therefore, deficient with respect to the full and rich reality of healthy societies. Privatization is also deficient if it is nothing else than private-sector *economic* efficiency encroaching on state *economies*. Civilization is more than high or low economic efficiency.

Let us try to identify functions and institutions that escape binarity and the purely economic universe. We find a fascinating universe of institutions already in existence that are not structured by governments' plans or by shareholders' profit thinking. Many of the institutions we are talking about are non-governmental, not-for-profit organizations, mostly charities. Their *raison d'être* is neither profit-making, nor typical state functions. They typically draw on voluntary labour of people joining in a common interest, such as ethical convictions, ecological objectives or urgent tasks popping up at local, national or global levels.

A fine example in the UK is the National Trust. It 'was founded in 1895 to preserve places of historic interest or natural beauty permanently for the nation to enjoy'.[1] Its members elect its governing bodies. It collects considerable resources through tax-deductible gifts and wills, membership subscriptions and entrance fees for visits to its properties. Over time, the National Trust has become one of the country's largest landowners. Although it does not seek profits, the National Trust is run highly efficiently in terms of financial management

Thousands of charities and other civil society organizations (CSOs) exist worldwide. They all have philanthropic, cultural or ecological goals, which the profit-seeking private sector cannot systematically pursue and which the state has either no money or no mandate to take care of. Acknowledging the necessary functions both of the state and the private sector, and yet seeing the huge scope of charities, we speak of a *triangular relation*. The expression is meant to indicate the impossibility of finding liveable solutions under the restriction to the one-dimensional, mostly economic, continuum between the state and the private sector.

Although there are certain parallels, we do not include in our notion of the third sector the 'informal economy', which is still the prevalent reality in the poorest parts of the world. The informal sector also enjoys a remarkable degree of independence from the state and from the formal economy. But it is the explicit and widely agreed objective of governments in developing countries to overcome the misery associated with the informal sector.

The third sector of charities and CSOs can play a strategic role in our days.[2] As has been argued in 'Post-war history: The ups and downs of the public sector' in Part III of this book, the last 20 or 25 years of history have resulted in a situation of a highly weakened nation state. We see scope for CSOs graduating as a third player next to nation states and the private sector in the search for a balanced world. International CSOs exert pressure on states, as well as on private companies, to respect human rights and the natural environment. They are gaining influence at international conferences and in the media. They have begun to be instrumental in shaping global governance. They can sometimes mobilize consumers' purchasing power behind them, which to private firms is perhaps the most important factor influencing commercial success.

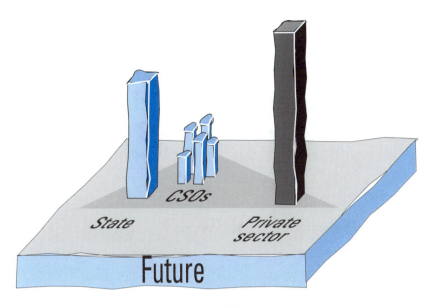

Figure 66
A third pillar, civil society, is emerging, giving hope for a rebalancing of powers between public and private interests.

Figure 42 in Part III characterized the new weakness of the nation state under the conditions of global financial markets and the prevailing doctrine of privatization. The considerations above can induce us to view CSOs as part of a remedy, not with regard to old-fashioned roles of nation states, but in relation to public interests that, in the past, were represented or defended by the state against private profit pressures. Figure 66 depicts CSOs as a third pillar serving as an independent power and helping to maintain the balance between public and private interests.

Private Governance: Private Rules for Privatization?

Marianne Beisheim

Regulatory institutions of *national* welfare states designed to prevent or compensate negative market effects are being undermined by processes of globalization and deregulation (see Part III). *Global* regulatory regimes have yet to be established or are often ineffective, and there is good reason to believe their improvement or implementation will be long in coming. Effective control of privatization has been notably absent. In this context, new modes of governance based on self-regulation by non-governmental actors deserve exploration.

THE IDEA: PRIVATE FORMS OF GOVERNANCE

There has been much talk of diverse forms of industry self-regulation, civil regulation, soft law or private market governance as opposed to hierarchically structured, top-down regulatory controls. Such forms of private governance or private regimes[1] include voluntary agreements, codes of conduct and multi-stakeholder[2] initiatives. All of these intend to set or implement minimum standards for business. This is especially important in cases where law-making and enforcement by national governments or intergovernmental agreements is not in sight.

Business representatives see self-regulation or voluntary initiatives as the *better alternative* to state or international regulation. Critics rate them as a *second-best substitute* – if not 'window-dressing' by big corporations. This chapter argues that private governance is best viewed as *complementary* to global or state governance, as a special type of regulation that does not rely on hierarchical coercion but on persuasion and horizontal cooperation. The focus is on 'partnership' – though not all partners have the same rights, responsibilities, abilities, resources or legitimacy.[3] The key difference is that those formerly subject to regulation would now be their own regulators. Some call this process a transformation in, or shifting pattern of, 'authority' (Cutler, 2003; Haufler, 2003). Forms of private governance are supposed to fulfil the legislative, administrative, regulatory and conflict-resolving role of classical public law. Haufler (2001) speaks of a growing 'public role' for the private sector.

Its ability to fulfil this role is, however, disputed. *Compliance* is clearly necessary for effective governance. How can this best be achieved? Instead of legally binding rules and punitive enforcement, private governance relies on informal negotiations in which rules are drafted by the private actors themselves. For example, a multinational corporation could draft and adopt policies (e.g. a code of conduct) that regulate its own behaviour in economic, social and/or environmental affairs. If these are regarded as legitimate, and if there is 'ownership', actors are expected to apply their own regulatory norms more readily than if imposed from outside and, thus, achieve greater compliance. Of course, this is meaningful only if the relevant standards are not negotiated down to the 'lowest common denominator', are transparent and have clearly defined targets and quantifiable objectives that can be controlled.

Motivations identified in the literature for business (and trade unions or non-governmental organizations – NGOs) to be part of such a private initiative include intrinsic, moral motivation; social learning; an understanding of good corporate citizenship (see 'Example: The corporate social responsibility navigator' later in this chapter); avoidance of external threats about reputation from anti-corporate advocacy campaigns by NGOs or the media; or an aim to forestall other, more disadvantageous, regulatory initiatives. Literature also claims that these factors are decisive for the success of any such initiatives.[4]

PRIVATE GOVERNANCE AND PRIVATIZATION

Few codes of conduct have been drafted with an explicit focus on the issue of *privatization*. Examples – from local, highly specialized initiatives to a global voluntary 'compact', all fairly new and not yet well developed – include the following:

- Public Services International (PSI) is the international trade union federation representing public-sector trade unions in 135 countries. The PSI executive committee approved a Water Code of Conduct.[5] The code addresses such issues as public service obligations, democratic regulation, environmental standards and fair labour practices on the basis of several key international labour conventions. One of the underlying goals of the code is to ensure a level playing field of competition among water companies seeking investment.
- Private schools in Nepal teach about 30 per cent of students' population and employ around 150,000 people. The rapid commercialization of these elite

private schools, following privatization of education, has been turning government schools into schools of last resort for those unable to pay exorbitant private fees. The Private and Boarding Schools' Organization of Nepal (PABSON) has been put under intense societal pressure to reduce tuition fees. PABSON has created its own 11-point code of conduct (including commitments to reduce exorbitant fees) and announced that it will take legal action against member schools if they fail to comply.[6] But student organizations have charged that PABSON is not imposing its own decision, claiming that many private schools have raised their fees instead of reducing them. Meanwhile, the government has formed a committee and a task force to recommend a ceiling for the fees charged by private schools.[7]

- In Australia, in the lead-up to privatization of the telecommunications industry, attempts have been made within the industry to develop policy on privacy protection. In operation for less than a year by 2004, the Telecommunications Privacy Committee, established by the Australian Telecommunications Authority (AUSTEL), has too short a record for its effectiveness to be judged.[8]
- Statoil, a Norwegian-based state multinational corporation (scheduled for partial privatization) and the 20 million-member International Federation of Chemical, Energy, Mine and General Workers' Unions (ICEM) signed a 'framework labour agreement', which not only guarantees respect for their labour rights and for their health and safety on the job, but also holds their employer to a commitment to promote human rights, environmental and labour standards in their respective communities. The agreement is specifically patterned on the guiding principles of the Global Compact initiative launched by UN Secretary-General Kofi Annan. The Global Compact brings together multinational businesses, global labour and civil society organizations to seek ways of ameliorating the negative effects of globalization and privatization. While critics of the Global Compact are concerned about a 'corporate-dominated UN' (Paine, 2000), Statoil Vice-President Geir Westgaard states that the stakeholder dialogue aspects of the Global Compact – which encourages representatives of civil society, labour and business not just to set standards but also to meet face to face to work out solutions to common problems – are particularly valuable to business.[9]
- Transparency International (TI) proposes a code of conduct to address the problem of corruption (see 'Privatization and corruption' in the 'Special Issues' chapter of Part III). TI states that 'trends in government privatization and corporatization give fresh impetus to the development of standards which regulate the relationship between government and private enterprise, especially in relation to the engagement of former ministers and public officials'.[10] Recently, TI was successful in adding a tenth principle to the Global Compact, addressing the fight against corruption.
- Corporate governance is increasingly being regulated by transnational private authorities (e.g. the self-regulation of accountancy and auditing through the International Accounting Standards Board and its International

Financial Reporting Standard (IFRS), and also through national codes such as the US Generally Accepted Accounting Principles (GAAP).

• The trend towards private governance is also an enormous business opportunity for consultants or certifying agents. In Malaysia, for example, VFM Corporate Services Sdn Bhd – a private consultancy firm – formulated a Code of Ethics for Company Directors to enhance the standard of corporate governance and corporate behaviour.[11] In their advertisements, they claim that 'experiences have shown the need to formulate standards of corporate behaviour to create an ethical corporate climate'.

PROS AND CONS – AND FIRST LESSONS LEARNED

Self-regulation is promoted as a more flexible alternative to regulation by public authorities (MacGregor et al, 2000, pp12–13). Moreover, other attributed benefits include the capacity to utilize up-to-date stakeholder expertise, a speedy responsiveness to changing conditions and a lower level of bureaucracy. Industry bodies advocate industry self-regulation on the grounds that it is as effective as external regulation, yet cheaper.

So far it is difficult to judge whether initiatives of the kind mentioned are succeeding. But the potential pitfalls are obvious, such as orientation to private rather than public interest, lack of transparency and opportunities for abuse (e.g. to block legislation). Forms of private governance and soft law may be easier to achieve, but also easier to circumvent or evade. Learning, fairness, social responsibility and a high degree of trust are therefore considered important features of the partnership approach to regulation. But what do we do when non-compliance is detected? There is often a lack of enforcement instruments; persuasion, training or withdrawing selective benefits may not be enough.

Critics argue for a more power-based approach to these networked forms of governance. Civil-society NGOs should act as 'watchdogs' and as countervailing powers to multinational corporations. Negotiated multi-stakeholder agreements with independent monitoring and verification systems should take the place of single-handed voluntary initiatives, together with an independent, confidential and accessible complaints mechanism. And, of course, there must also be penalties for non-compliance. A minimum requirement should be the publication of outcomes and reports of monitoring processes. This, then, could be a basis for 'blaming and shaming' – either by the industry bodies themselves or by other actors, such as NGOs or unions.

Private governance of such kind will be contested and exposed to politicization by a broad range of actors. Internal conflict and oppositional agendas are unavoidable. Conflicts will arise between multinational corporations, trade unions and environmental or human rights NGOs over core labour standards or environmental protection. But this debate is compatible with the idea of 'participatory governance' (see Box 18). There is not only an efficiency gap, but also a participatory gap in today's governance

Box 18 Participatory governance

Participation of stakeholders in the process of decision-making (in contrast to more passive forms of participation) is the core element of new forms of 'participatory governance'. The basic idea is to involve both ordinary people affected by specific problems and officials in the field, and to apply their specific knowledge, intelligence and interest to the formulation of solutions. The ultimate goal is to enhance the responsiveness and effectiveness of governance, while at the same time making it fairer, more deliberative and more accountable.

Several studies (see box source) have investigated projects based, at least partly, on a participatory approach. Examples include the participatory budget in Porto Alegre; the school decentralization councils and community policing councils in Chicago; stakeholder councils in environmental protection and habitat management; and community-managed water supply and sanitation services. These studies produced the following conclusions:

- Participatory governance helps to base policies on better information, and thus could, indeed, enhance responsiveness, effectiveness and efficiency.
- Giving community members a voice in the nature of community services and training them to manage and maintain the services produces better outcomes. Services were better sustained when communities participated in establishing the services, not just by contributing opinions and information, but also by exercising influence and control over project implementation, and having a say in management decisions.
- If people are involved in the planning of an endeavour, they are also more likely to care about its implementation and its evaluation. Policy-makers, administrators and those affected by the policies involved tend to be more committed when local ownership is promoted.
- However, empowerment and capacity-building (including resources such as time and money) that facilitate a 'voice' for the poor are necessary for making participatory governance a reality.

The latter, in particular, often proves to be a problem: in many developing countries, large numbers of the poor are not listed in registers as they live in illegal settlements and/or are frequently on the move. They are difficult to contact or interview; hence, it is difficult to judge the provision of goods and services, as well as individual and community financial situations and needs. Assessment of conditions in urban ghettos where traditional bonds are no longer in place is even more difficult.

Where community need has been successfully identified, some programmes specifically integrate participatory elements to support the poor. For example, the consumer-focused and poverty-sensitive programme 'condominial water' establishes shared management of piped sewerage systems: a group of householders undertakes to manage a network of sewers using a single connection to a secondary network managed by the utility organization. This shared management model allows a substantial reduction in cost through increased participation. Moreover, this type of improved programme of governance has resulted in beneficial features, such as help desks, hotlines, appellate bodies, stakeholder meetings and participatory assessments.

Sources: Grote and Gbikpi (2002); Fung and Wright (2003); Jimenez (2004); Osmani (2000); Schneider (1999); WSP (2001); WSP et al (2003).

(Reinicke and Deng, 2000): increasing numbers of interested individuals and organizations are finding that they have a decreasing impact on public policy outcomes, which could lead to a disillusionment of constituents and a credibility crisis. Multi-stakeholder codes and the partnership approach, in general, would entail lively and transparent debates about further liberalization, and/or deregulation or re-regulation of markets. Expanded dialogue of this nature could increase public engagement and corporate credibility.

PRIVATE GOVERNANCE AND THE NEED FOR LEGITIMACY

The delegation of regulatory tasks to private actors is accompanied by new concerns about the social responsibility and the legitimacy of private governance. Like other forms of governance, private governance faces challenges over accountability or democratic participation. Transnational bodies may also fail due to capture and coordination dilemmas (Mattli, 2003, pp224ff) and private forms of governance are again dependent upon national political authorities for their effectiveness (Haufler, 2003). Moreover, there is also unease with 'too many cooks in the regulatory kitchen' (MacGregor et al, 2000, p228). There is already an array of different voluntary initiatives, making evaluation difficult.

Private governance is not 'better' than public governance but complementary, and the two should not be played against each other. One could even say that public governance is a necessary condition for any private governance – without legislative framework, private initiatives would be at a loss and a large degree of failure of any voluntary approach would likely result. Teubner (2000) asks for a new 'constitution' for private regimes. While forms of private governance such as those above may be part of a 'tool box' to manage privatization, there is a need to set general 'rules of the game'. For example, the Global Reporting Initiative (GRI) is a multi-stakeholder process and independent institution whose mission is to develop and disseminate globally applicable Sustainability Reporting Guidelines. The GRI guidelines are for voluntary use by companies for reporting on the economic, environmental and social dimensions of their activities, products and services. Other institutions to guide the 'governance of private governance' could be precepts for democratic participation of all relevant stakeholders and for independent monitoring of implementation, as well as the development of obligatory safeguards for securing the basic rights of all members of society and for protecting the environment.

The main questions remain: can voluntary regulation be effective? What are the conditions for successful private law regimes governing privatization and public goods? Future research should focus on these questions. When is private governance likely to work and when would we be ill advised to rely on this method of controlling behaviour. We also should learn more about measures that we can take to enhance the prospects for success.

EXAMPLE: THE 'CSR NAVIGATOR'[12]

Björn Stigson and Margaret Flaherty

Most pertinent to our discussion here is corporate social responsibility (CSR), or strategies by which companies can provide a lead in working toward social change. The World Business Council for Sustainable Development's (WBCSD's)[13] CSR navigator is a guide for companies on their journey towards implementing CSR. This navigator is both a tool and a conceptual approach and should be applied in light of each company's assessment of their own particular situation. It indicates direction and demands vision, but does not dictate the speed of progress. It is flexible enough to respond to individual company challenges and dilemmas. The navigator emphasizes that the vigour with which a particular company pursues its vision on CSR is specific to that company's individual location – its geography, industrial sector, etc. – and should be tailored to what works best for the company. The WBCSD navigator consists of distinct reference points, which can be used along a company's CSR journey.

It might seem that Western sensitivities over labour standards, human rights, religious and political freedom and environmental impacts are luxuries that many Asian businesses cannot yet afford. Why should the industrialized West impose their version of these ideas, when they have pursued capitalist expansion unfettered for more than a century? Asian businesses engaged in the day-to-day struggle to be competitive may see the scrutiny of their practices as unwarranted. What is more, in many areas of Asia the role of enterprises has long had a social objective, particularly in the era of state communism. Furthermore, bonds of family and friendship have traditionally played a more important role in the East than in the West, where the separation of ownership and control and the impact of mobility have weakened such ties.

In today's markets, however, concerns are no longer localized. The trend toward socially responsible investment has reached a stage in Europe and the US where it is affecting the way in which companies work, and these companies are already operating in Asia. Smart business leaders throughout Asia will see the competitive advantage in anticipating the demands for greater accountability and socially responsible practices. In the WBCSD's stakeholder dialogues worldwide, we discovered that while the understanding of what CSR meant differed from place to place, the constant theme was that companies should engage with and listen to communities in order to strengthen their licence to operate.

Determine your 'magnetic north'

Companies should determine and articulate their CSR direction – their CSR 'magnetic north', so to speak – at the start of their journey. Repeatedly, our global consultations have reinforced this simple message. Though the terminology might be different – people variously referred to values, ethics, religion, tribal custom or codes of conduct – the overriding message is clear: determine and articulate your company's vision and values – your corporate magnetic north. Tell people what you stand for and what you are prepared to be judged on. If you fail to do this, other people will tell you what you should do. Determining a company's magnetic north is neither easy, nor straightforward. However, it is essential if the company is to address the complex and expanding business/social agenda emerging in the new millennium. So the message is: start now. Involve your best people throughout your organization. Demonstrate top-level involvement and commitment. If you don't, your company will fall behind, and any attempt to embark on the CSR journey will be longer and harder.

Build in the strategic business case

Integrating social responsibility within an overall company strategy demonstrates your company's readiness to ensure that social concerns are an integral part of your business strategy. A holistic approach to the challenges we face in our companies is usually the most productive, and CSR can be managed most effectively if woven into the philosophical and operational fabric of the company.

Approach CSR as you would any investment: look for positive returns or reduction of risk. Seek buy-in from managers, supervisors and employees. Work with them, provide support and encourage them to recognize the good business sense of a CSR strategy.

The intrinsically pragmatic approach to business in Asia means that companies that embrace globalization will generally accept the discipline imposed by exposure to international capitalism and the need to conform to global best practice.

Focus on individuals

Overall, CSR reaches out to the collective entity of stakeholders: shareholders, employees, communities, non-governmental organizations (NGOs), consumers, partners, etc. But to be truly effective, CSR needs to take account of the implications for individuals. Determine ways for the individual citizen, consumer, employee and manager to contribute to corporate social responsibility, as well as the means for determining individual accountability.

The primary direction of globalization is toward liberalism, a fundamental premise of which is individualism. Indeed, the increasing wealth of Asians may itself lead to a shift in cultural values away from collectivism and toward individualism. As we shall see, companies that recognize the power of the small entrepreneur are already capitalizing upon this trend. This vital level of business activity is also being boosted by micro-credit programmes (see Box 19).

BOX 19 DEUTSCHE BANK MICRO-CREDIT DEVELOPMENT FUND

From the rural villages of Asia to urban centres of the US, small loans to emerging entrepreneurs create opportunities for self-employment and dignified lifestyles for millions. With micro-credit, loans are given to those who need it most – the poor at the grassroots level. Without micro-credit, such loans would not be possible since these people are unable to meet the requirements of traditional banking practices, which call for collateral or previous credit experience.

Micro-credit institutions are proving to be a revolutionary force in enabling families to rise from poverty through the creation of opportunities for self-employment. Furthermore, in the context of group borrowing structures, recipients of micro-credit are proving to be good credit risks. Micro-credit institutions lending to the poor typically achieve repayment rates exceeding 97 per cent, with such loans currently reaching nearly 23 million borrowers, with the industry growing rapidly.

Micro-finance has established itself in recent years as one of the most effective weapons in the fight against poverty. By providing unsecured micro-loans of typically US$100 to the world's poorest, institutions such as the Grameen Bank in Bangladesh have enabled literally millions to rise above the poverty line. Moreover, such institutions operate profitably and often have repayment rates higher than commercial banks. For the past few years, the Deutsche Bank Micro-credit Development Fund has been working to assist such institutions by providing capital and technical support.

A loan from the Deutsche Bank Microcredit Fund of US$75,000 was made to the Society for Helping and Awakening Rural Poor through Education (SHARE), who serve very poor skilled and unskilled rural female entrepreneurs in India. This loan, at 10:1 leverage, realizes a US$750,000 increase in lending capacity over the average 11.5-month term (equivalent to US$780,000 per annum), for a total impact of US$3,900,000 over the five-year Deutsche Bank Micro-credit Fund loan term.

With loans from SHARE, Hafiza Bee, her husband and their six children are experiencing new-found hope. Hafiza's relationship with SHARE began in 1988 when she organized four other women to become the first group in their village to participate in the SHARE loan programme. With her first loan of US$80 (4000 rupees), Hafiza purchased a buffalo. Sales of 3 litres of milk a day gave her a sense of achievement as she repaid the loan and also had funds to cover household expenditures. With the additional income, the family could begin to save a portion of the earnings from her father's tailoring business. Additional loan proceeds have resulted in expanded family enterprises, including new sewing machines for her sons, who are now tailors in the family business. Hafiza began to expand her own hand-stitching and embroidery business, which resulted in her appointment as a teacher of a government stitching centre in her village and provided her with a regular monthly salary.

Determine your legacy: Foster competence and capacity

Instil an ethic of education and learning, and institute processes to foster it: this is how you focus on long-term sustainability. Strive to leave as small an industrial footprint as can reasonably be expected, but as large a local contribution and sustainable livelihood legacy as you can. It is no longer enough to provide a salary and pay taxes. People want to learn how to build a better future. With Asia's burgeoning populations, this attention to fostering sustainable livelihoods will be a long-term business imperative.

Box 20 Unilever: Entrepreneurs in Indonesia

In Indonesia, 90 per cent of all business are small or medium sized and are responsible for generating over half of the country's income. They are a major engine for growth in the local economy, so the Indonesian government is keen to find new ways of encouraging more entrepreneurs to start businesses.

Unilever Indonesia works with over 2000 small and medium-sized suppliers and distributors; therefore, it is an appropriate partner to work with the country's Department of Trade and Industry and others to create more first generation small business start-ups.

A series of pilot projects, begun in 2000, has been highly successful, not only for the economy but also for Unilever Indonesia. One scheme has involved training unemployed youths to become entrepreneurs selling Unilever products, while another has created a new distribution channel for the company to reach small shops and kiosks in rural areas. Unilever Indonesia is now establishing a business incubator to provide training and business advice for entrepreneurs.

Source: Global challenges local actions (Unilever ESR overview)

Put employees first: Assets, agents and ambassadors

In the quest to enhance shareholder value, be prepared to say that your employees are the number one consideration among a range of other stakeholders. This does not imply that other stakeholders are not important; but CSR includes decisions about setting priorities, facing dilemmas and making trade-offs. Community groups, regulators, NGOs and employees are all vital when addressing CSR. However, based on our global consultations, employees and employee relations matter most when addressing CSR. Transform your workforce into active agents for change. Convince them that socially responsible business practices are central to a company's continued success. Encourage diversity, initiative and the open exchange of ideas, rather than conformism and narrow thinking. Provide the skills training to make jobs more portable. Survival in Asia's growing knowledge-based economies depends upon this and, collectively, your employees can be the greatest driver for promoting good CSR practice.

Know your neighbour: Community and culture

Understand and define who and what your community is and assess its implications for your operations. Invest in identifying what makes communities different or similar. Explore how local culture, language and religions complement or conflict with management approaches. Show respect for differences as well as similarities.

Debate and dialogue: Establish a system and process

Focus on the process for systematic and transparent dialogue. Use this to understand the impact of your company on people's lives. This is best done early with an attitude of constructive engagement. Inaction means losing contact and becoming out of touch with those who matter. As we have seen, the constant theme in our stakeholder dialogues was the call for greater interaction and consideration of stakeholders' views.

Pursue smart partnerships

Who would argue with establishing partnerships? For many companies this has become almost routine. Strategic collaborations with clear objectives are an essential component for any company looking to address corporate social issues, and we encourage companies to foster such relationships. However, recognizing partnerships for the sake of publicity undermines credibility and dilutes the effect of valuable collaborations. Partnerships that provide cover for inaction or have dubious objectives will sap peoples' energy and waste time and money. Involve your employees, consult stakeholders and look for win–win situations.

Remember reputation matters

Reputation is a key business asset and should be carefully protected. That is part of the business case for investing in CSR, which provides the framework in which a company does, and is seen to be doing, the right thing for reasons other than immediate financial returns. Transparency and credibility will build a strong reputation over time and generate loyalty that can be relied upon in times of crisis.

Be a good guest, but let your story be heard

Your company is a guest in various communities and should behave accordingly. Show respect and consideration for your hosts. At the same time, find the appropriate way to communicate with them openly about your contributions to society. That open relationship will also be an asset if problems arise.

Measure and account for what you do

Take a positive and proactive attitude to measuring and reporting progress. Whatever method your company selects, the important thing is to be prepared

Box 21 adidas-Salomon: Supply-chain management

Using an external supply chain has allowed adidas-Salomon to keep its costs down and remain competitive. However, the company's supply chain is long and complex, relying on about 570 factories around the world. In Asia alone, its suppliers operate in 18 different countries. Moreover, its cost-saving use of external suppliers is not without risks: in particular, the company has less control over work-place conditions at its suppliers' factories than it would have at company-owned sites.

Outsourcing supply should not mean outsourcing moral responsibility. Recognizing this, and having regard to the risks and responsibilities associated with managing a global supply chain, adidas-Salomon has designed and implemented a comprehensive supply-chain management strategy.

This strategy is to source the company's supplies from the cheapest acceptable sources, rather than from the cheapest possible. The company has its own so-called 'standards of engagement' (SOE) and the level of acceptability is based on the values of the company itself. Contractors, subcontractors, suppliers and others are therefore expected to conduct themselves in line with adidas-Salomon's SOE.

Before a relationship is formed with any new supplier, an internal audit is carried out to ensure that working conditions in that supplier meet adidas-Salomon's SOE criteria. All business partners sign an agreement committing themselves to comply with the SOE and to take responsibility for their sub-contractors' performance on work-place conditions. The monitoring process is continuous as suppliers are audited at least once a year, and more often if serious problems are detected.

to meet demands for measurement and accountability. Signals indicate that these demands will increase in the years ahead. If you are not properly equipped to manage this challenge, your credibility and reputation will suffer.

One of the ways to approach this challenge is to align a company's principles with a code of practice. Internal accountability will make the transition to better practice easier, however.

Box 21 provides an example of the way in which one of the realities of modern business – the outsourcing of operations to cheaper labour markets – can be monitored to protect against reputation-damaging revelations.

Handle information, knowledge and technology with care

The results of the technology revolution and the implications of our knowledge-based economy are only just beginning to be apparent; but they are bringing profound change on a global scale. Communications technology offers great potential for inclusion and education, and new ways for companies to communicate their philosophies and accomplishments. But the frontiers of new technology also pose challenges: they can exclude and are open to exploitation, and careful thought is needed to safeguard against this.

Going forward

We would like to conclude by summarizing the developments that companies will need to watch closely as they move towards a more sustainable, socially responsible era of business.

There will be a need for increased attention and sensitivity to the concerns of suppliers and customers, especially as the latter become more informed. The questions of human rights and the tolerance of religion in the work place will continue to gain momentum and visibility as issues of fundamental importance.

Public antipathy to corporations that, for example, use child labour or attempt to foist genetically modified produce on unsuspecting consumers will lead to a rise in the use of product labels which guarantee the absence of such practices.

We will see ever-closer scrutiny by stakeholders and the media of business practices, accountability, transparency, the treatment of employees and customers, ingredients, marketing, advertising and sourcing. The levels of board/CEO compensation will also be watched carefully, and to avoid reputation-damaging criticism, should be kept commensurate with a company's performance. Companies that can bear such scrutiny with relatively unblemished reputations will benefit from positive media coverage and publicity. The adherence to codes of practice and external standards is one route to this goal – those provided by the United Nation's Global Compact, the Global Reporting Initiative, the Global Sullivan Principles of Social Responsibility or the Social Accountability 8000 standard (SA8000).

The key challenge for business in contributing to a sustainable future will not be how corporations are managed. It will, instead, be how we address the expectation that business should play a larger role in building well-functioning societies. A successful future awaits companies that can link existing decision processes with input from society in a meaningful way. Business cannot and should not replace governments. But it is also impossible to provide goods and services in a sustainable way in non-functioning societies.

Business cannot succeed in societies that fail.

'Co-evolution' between State Regulation and the Private Sector[1]

Raimund Bleischwitz

The general argument of this chapter is that proper public governance enables proactive changes of private actors' behaviour. Such governance involves interaction between public and private actors, both in policy formulation and implementation. This interactive governance goes well beyond the traditional idea of governments 'setting the frame'. The 'co-evolution'[2] between private and public rule-making is particularly advisable in two fields:

1 privatization and private-sector management of classical 'public' services (i.e. the topic of this book); and
2 the international domain, where public governance is weak and where corporate social responsibility (CSR) has emerged; the voluntary 'type II' commitments made at the World Summit for Sustainable Development (WSSD) in Johannesburg, 2002, are good illustrations of co-evolution.

MARKET FAILURES *AND* GOVERNMENT FAILURES

Markets are known for being dynamic and powerful, but imperfect, especially with regard to public goods. Stiglitz (2000), among others, has well analysed the economics of the public sector. The question is where learning from failures works best. Is it mostly endogenous learning by market participants or is it, rather, external influence by the state? In the provision of *public goods*, state ruling is indispensable. But contrary to widespread belief, even the public goods' attributes of non-rivalry in use and open access can go along with market opportunities for private firms – and those attributes may change (Nelson, 2002). Harbours and lighthouses, Adam Smith's classical examples of necessary state functions, have become accessible to private provision due to technological improvements and better pricing possibilities.

In simplified models, citizens enjoying public goods are usually taken as one aggregated unit. In reality, however, they benefit from public goods in innumerable ways. Needs and preferences are often heterogeneous and change over time. This diversity and temporal variability blurs the assumption of a fixed borderline between private and public goods. The European Union (EU) terminology of 'universal services' and 'services in the general interest', as well as notions such as 'the commons' – which is equivalent to 'common-pool resources', according to Ostrom et al (2002) – and 'club goods' are indications of the blurry borderline.

Let us now look at two types of market failures that are relevant for privatization. One of the best-known market failures is the creation of 'external' damages accruing not to the producer or the consumer, but to third parties, including future generations. Efforts to 'internalize' and thereby (partially) avoid externalities typically require negotiations between the affected parties. However, for practical and sometimes also political reasons, not all affected parties may participate. Future generations are not available by definition, and the available negotiators are always inclined to serve their respective voters or clients first. Vulnerable and less well-organized groups are in danger of being overlooked. Participation is clearly a crucial issue in internalization strategies, as well as in the privatization of goods and services that are susceptible to the occurrence, under market conditions, of negative externalities.

The concept of *adaptation deficits* refers to the speed at which markets and firms adapt to new circumstances arising from new legislation and other factors. Evolutionary economics realistically assumes that markets are not rigid but evolve step by step (Pelikan and Wegner, 2003; Witt, 2003) and tend to be shaped by pioneers and early imitators. Consumers, too, are relevant in this process because their specific demands often are vague to begin with and co-evolve with market development. Incremental corporate change, consumer behaviour and stakeholder involvement become driving forces that are at least as important as the forward-looking entrepreneur or any 'breakthrough' technology, although the incremental process is less visible. Allowing for gradual learning and adaptation is also a plausible postulate for privatization.

Looking at market failures, in general, the conclusion is that to function properly, markets need participation and learning among and beyond market actors. If their efficiency is to be maintained and improved, *markets need guidance and rules for stimulating participation and learning*. Such guidance and rules can be provided by appropriate governance structures. The findings of famous economists such as Douglass C. North (1990), Mancur Olson (1996) and Joseph Stiglitz (1998a) support this conclusion, which also fits in with the theories of New Institutional Economics (Ahrens, 2002; www.isnie.org) and the German *Ordnungspolitik*. Beyond general statements, however, it seems that the real challenge is to stimulate continuous participation and learning processes, rather than undertake heroic efforts of setting an everlasting frame. This interactive and dynamic concept is fully in line with the appreciation of 'third' actors, mostly from civil society (see 'Escaping Pernicious Dualism: Civil Society between the State and the Firm').

Recent theories of government failures have yielded similar findings (Majone, 1998; Buchanan and Musgrave, 1999; Stiglitz, 2000; Dror, 2001). Government failures, such as the self-interest of politicians and bureaucracies, over-taxation and exposure to vested interest groups, put the development of both markets and society at risk by slowing down the dynamics of progress, causing high regulatory costs ('deadweight losses'), or by crowding out voluntary action and other non-paid civil activities.

Not surprisingly, our initial considerations confirm that bad government produces bad market outcomes, while good government can improve market outcomes. Government failures are, of course, no reason to give up on regulatory policies, but a challenge for improvement. Two government functions, in particular, remain crucially important:

1 to guarantee certain legal and structural conditions; and
2 to monitor and counteract major market failures that cause severe negative impacts on society.

Market and government failures call for a governance structure that actively involves corporate and societal actors. Such involvement is not only necessary in terms of making the voices of interest groups and affected groups heard. It is also essential in terms of *knowledge creation*. Seen from this angle, the continuous and evolutionary process of rule-making becomes more decentralized and – by and large – more democratized compared with purely state-driven law-making.

GUIDANCE AND RULES AS CO-EVOLUTION

Our notion of co-evolution starts from the proposition that markets and governments alike have a positive role to play in societies' development, not a negative one. These positive roles can be seen where markets provide goods and foster new technologies, and where the state guarantees the conditions for an amenable life of its citizens and for healthy business development. Both markets and the state rely upon the people in their respective roles as consumers and as citizens, or as *'bourgeois'* and *'citoyens'*, according to Beck (2000). Co-evolution refers to these respective roles. A market economy relies on a wide array of both market-based and political institutions that perform stabilizing, regulatory and legitimizing functions. Governance takes place in multiple arenas, partly within and partly outside the scope of the state. It involves polycentric steering institutions (Young, 1999; Héritier, 2002), with a strong emphasis on subsidiarity – which happens to be one of the core guiding principles of the EU.

In such perspective, the traditional dichotomy between market and state, or between *laissez-faire* and intervention, loses some of its importance. Market and state serve complementary functions that keep the system running. A well-performing market economy is a mixed composition of state and markets.

Rodrik (2000) has proposed the following list of basic types of market-supporting institutions: property rights; macro-economic stabilization (including public investments); social insurance (including social security systems); regulatory institutions; and conflict management. The last of these refers to the need to arrive at decisions by society as a whole and presupposes democratic participation. According to Rodrik's econometric analysis (2000), participatory politics and democracy also enhance *economic* stability – understood in terms of resilience (i.e. the ability to adapt and co-evolve).

NEW MODELS OF THE FIRM

How does the notion of profit-oriented firms fit into such a governance structure? Would profit-maximizing firms not try to escape responsibility and act as free riders? This may often be the case. But there are also business opportunities in new markets for common goods, chiefly for two reasons. First, there is a widespread willingness to pay for the provision of goods and services associated with common goods, such as clean water. Second, firms can gain competitive advantages by superior market knowledge; in the modern world, this can include familiarity with the changing aspirations of post-materialist international clients.

On the first point, other examples besides the provision of drinking water are the provision of renewable energies and energy efficiency to replace carbon and nuclear energies, or the organization of car-sharing with a view to saving mobility costs for their customers and, at the same time, saving public costs for parking space. Yet other firms engage in value-chain management in order to keep costs at a minimum throughout the entire production chain, while maintaining high social and environmental standards – 'selling' this asset to certain clients. In Swiss and Dutch supermarkets, the *Havelaer* brand is successful and advertises social equity correctness in the supply chain. Huge commercial successes of this kind may be the exceptions so far, but help to create a new model of firms that avoids free riding (see, for example, Gabel and Sinclair-Desgagné, 1998; van Dijken et al, 1999; Porter and van der Linde, 2000).

On the second point, you can see firms advancing new goods and participating with stakeholders in the evolution of new markets in order to gain learning advantages and have shorter adaptation times. Some transnational companies (TNCs), including chemical giant BASF and the oil companies British Petroleum (BP) and Shell, have started to learn from failures made during their 'dirty times'. These companies now create new markets (solar energy, hydrogen and new materials) that relieve environmental pressure and act, in part, as knowledge-based firms, combining the value-adding activities of manufacturing and services. They also communicate intensively with stakeholders from various societal groups.

What the giants can do is, perhaps, more easily doable for small firms. They often have more flexibility to act as knowledge-based firms and innovators.

Of course, there is an intense debate going on about the phenomenon of 'Green-washing', which is often associated with such communication strategies and with participation in clubs such as the Global Compact or the World Business Council for Sustainable Development (WBCSD) that publicly adhere to ethical or ecological principles. Our point, here, is that even firms that honestly adhere to noble principles can commercially benefit from them, at least through improved customer relations and staff motivation – and (possibly) in terms of market share, reputation and risk avoidance.

MARKETS FOR COMMON GOODS?

Technological change has a definite bearing on market evolution (Langlois and Robertson, 1995; Freeman, 1998). Discoveries can set the course for cleaner and more resource-efficient production and products. As mentioned above, technological change can thereby shift the borderline from public goods administration towards private-sector activity and make privatization compatible with the care for the commons. Markets for common goods involve a multitude of actors. Of some common goods, consumers have only a vague notion and a very limited willingness to pay. Their awareness and, if possible, engagement need to be awakened (Loasby, 2001). Public policy instruments such as tax preferences for proactive choices, or else charges and fees on the use of scarce resources, can help. So can advertising and factual information from both the public and private sectors. A coordinated co-evolution, again, seems like the swiftest way towards the desired change of technologies and, indeed, of the mindset. Management practices are also bound to change in the process and can lead to 'ethical' improvements in the supply chain.

The case of eco-efficiency (von Weizsäcker et al, 1997; Bleischwitz, 2003; Bleischwitz and Hennicke, 2004) seems to demonstrate that a market evolution for certain common goods is actually taking place. Climate protection has moved up on the public agenda. Correspondingly, goods and services offering the same quality at less climate impact have gained ground. Furthermore, the acceptance has grown for policy measures that penalize the wasteful use of energy. Germany has experienced a reduction of petrol consumption in four consecutive years since 1999 – without reduced mobility. The reason is said to be a mixture of climate concerns, rising crude oil prices, Green taxes, and the automobile industry's ability to provide more fuel-efficient cars. In a similar manner, markets for renewable energies soared as a reaction, in part, to public policy measures and to consumer demand. The relevant industry swiftly responded.

RESPONSIVE REGULATION

Governance of common goods means applying different policy measures, ranging from moral suasion up to strictest command-and-control approaches

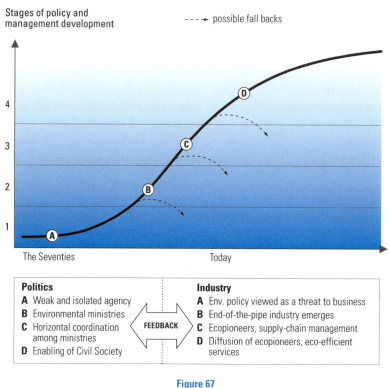

Stages of policy and
management development

- - - → possible fall backs

The Seventies   Today

Politics		Industry
A Weak and isolated agency		**A** Env. policy viewed as a threat to business
B Environmental ministries	**FEEDBACK**	**B** End-of-the-pipe industry emerges
C Horizontal coordination among ministries		**C** Ecopioneers, supply-chain management
D Enabling of Civil Society		**D** Diffusion of ecopioneers, eco-efficient services

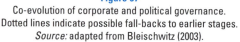

Figure 67
Co-evolution of corporate and political governance.
Dotted lines indicate possible fall-backs to earlier stages.
Source: adapted from Bleischwitz (2003).

(prohibiting free riding and phasing out hazardous substances or dangerous practices). Dietz et al (2003, p1910) have discussed strategies for meeting requirements of 'adaptive' governance of the commons. For long-term tasks such as climate protection, the toolkit itself should be subject to learning and change. For this, the notion of *responsive regulation* (Ayres and Braithwaite, 1992) is useful. It involves the kind of co-evolution that we have proposed before in order to deal with uncertainties and knowledge deficits in a manner that honours and benefits from the creativity of the human race.

Responsive regulation is by far more flexible than the law alone. Responsive regulation tends to bring heterogeneous actors together, often on ad hoc challenges without precedent. The ideal is to establish win–win coalitions, with no specify action determined in advance. A good example is the European 'EnergyPlus' activity, where different organizations with some support of the European Commission have created a network for the dissemination of energy-efficient household appliances.

Figure 67 illustrates this view, again using environmental issues as a subject. It depicts the development from immediate problem-solving to the emergence of innovative, adaptive and preventive approaches. The figure suggests that participatory and administrative processes play an increasingly important role both in governments and the private sector. The importance of adaptive flexibility increases with the degree of uncertainty and change. For governance aiming at long-term change with varied innovation, adaptive flexibility is, therefore, at least as relevant as an *ex-ante* framework. This is also why continuous empirical research on real actors' behaviour is so important.

What does that mean for privatization? Literature on governance of political and corporate actors may be helpful for a next generation type of privatization. The observations outlined above may allow some preliminary conclusions:

- Privatization should not interrupt, but rather enhance the communication between state actors and private operators.
- Privatization should enhance civil society's influence on the operations in question.
- Privatization should encourage 'responsive regulation', rather than build on rigid regulation.
- When technological developments newly allow appropriate private-sector management, such opportunities should be explored.
- The transition from resource-intensive to knowledge-based services should be promoted and not hindered by the privatization process.

PART V

Conclusion

Lessons Learned from Privatization

Ernst Ulrich von Weizsäcker, Oran R. Young,
Matthias Finger and Marianne Beisheim

EVALUATION: LIMITS TO PRIVATIZATION

So far, this book has provided an overview of privatization as one of the major trends of our time, with a range of evidence regarding the consequences of privatization in different sectors and parts of the world. Let us now offer some more systematic conclusions.

Privatization produces positive results under some conditions, negative consequences under others. Our goal is to identify the determinants of success and failure, rather than to argue ideologically for or against privatization.

Our cases fall into three broad groups:

1 *Success stories* featuring improved economic performance, better services and an orderly, transparent and largely democratic process of privatization. These include the privatization of state industries in former communist countries, telecommunication in the majority of the Organisation for Economic Co-operation and Development (OECD) countries, and postal services, railways, airlines, utilities and water supplies in a number of countries around the world. These have been widely publicized in the mainstream literature (e.g. Savas, 2000), so not many are included here.
2 *Mixed results*, where the principle may have been good but implementation caused significant negative consequences. For example, the bidding process may have been badly organized or the contract was weak and allowed for unfavourable renegotiation, affecting poorer segments of society.
3 *Outright failures*. In many cases, costs exceed benefits. This can be the case if benefits fall far short of expectations. Or the state monopoly may be replaced by a private monopoly that is even less susceptible to customer

control than the public utility, and that gets away with indecent pricing. In some cases, fraud and corruption are also involved in the process of privatization. Moreover, we find cases of 'involuntary' privatization regretted by those who felt coerced to proceed, and leading to unsatisfactory results due to a lack of participation on the part of relevant stakeholders. We also observe *systematic failures* that result from neglect of the value of the relevant public goods. These cases crop up in areas in which privatization is destroying the commons and where the state should remain fully responsible. Examples include the privatization of traditional knowledge (e.g. patents on neem tree chemicals) or the area of general security. This category also includes the privatization of certain types of infrastructure, assuming that it could be profitable when, in fact, it is not.

We cannot offer a simple recipe for avoiding the problems of privatization or curing them once they arise. We do feel justified, however, in drawing cautious conclusions about some *patterns* that surface regularly.

In the next two sections, we discuss, first, some positive patterns and then some negative ones. We do not claim that our analysis is exhaustive, and our sample of cases is not, strictly speaking, representative. But our examination of the evidence highlights some prominent and important features to be considered when reflecting on privatization.

Finally, we add some observations on arrangements that do not fit clearly into either the private sector or the public sector. It turns out that this middle ground is substantial; human ingenuity has produced a wide array of hybrid arrangements at different times and in different places. But do these arrangements, taken together, offer hope for escaping the need to balance the private and the public? The answer to this question is much the same as the answer to our basic question about the limits to privatization. Some hybrid arrangements work well. But hybridization is not a panacea; it offers no easy escape from confronting the core issues of this book.

THE BRIGHT SIDE: POINTERS TO BENEFICIAL PRIVATIZATION

Privatization can produce positive results under the right circumstances. Our analysis highlights the following benefits.

Increased investments. Privatization can attract investment to the development of infrastructure. In many countries, the public sector has not been in a position to finance necessary investments in water and sanitation, telecommunications and transportation systems. In the areas of telecommunications and transportation, there are numerous examples of successful privatization and of public–private partnerships in such forms as build-operate-transfer (BOT) schemes. Relatively few are included in this book because they are already well documented.

Better quality of services. In the case of telecommunications, the quality of services has improved dramatically after privatization, although it remains unclear what proportion of that effect has to do with private ownership and how much stems from technological progress. Quality improvement was usually a main reason for privatizing water and sanitation. In the postal sector, to take another case, public services have been lamentable in a number of countries, and privatization has helped to restore the quality of services for the customer, albeit often at a higher price. Even so, positive results in terms of improving quality of services are often accompanied by equity problems.

Saving taxpayers' money. It is widely assumed that privatization increases economic efficiency. An educated guess, based on figures regarding staff employed, is that efficiency typically increases twofold (Shelley, 1998). The main reason for this is that privatization usually removes earlier restrictions on staff redundancies. Of course, it is grossly simplified to assume that the remaining staff can do the same job. Moreover, redundancies usually cause persisting unemployment, with highly undesirable social side effects. There are a few sectors (notably telecommunications and air transport), on the other hand, in which employment actually increased after privatization and liberalization because the markets expanded.

Innovation and capacity-building. Regardless of the potential for market expansion, operators exposed to competition tend to be more innovative and creative than public operators. Due to their exposure to international competition, private actors typically have a strong incentive to turn to the most modern technologies available. This drive to innovate may turn out to be the most convincing argument for privatization, not least because it also involves capacity-building – improving skills and knowledge in the broadest sense in order to make use of modern technologies and to improve competitiveness. Therefore, proponents of privatization say that 'private ownership should generally be preferred to public ownership when the incentives to innovate and to control costs must be strong' (Shleifer, 1998, p147). Still, it is important not to overdo this argument. There are cases, such as the ascent of high technology in Japan, where the state acted to stimulate aggressive and commercially successful innovation. And cut-throat competition in the global markets of today has forced many firms to substantially reduce their research and development budgets in order to survive.

Re-regulation. The success stories have one thing in common: a strong state capable of defining and, when necessary, policing the rules of the game. As privatization has often been preceded by deregulation and liberalization of markets, it has frequently proven necessary to reintroduce regulations in order to protect consumers and prevent severe damage to the environment. In developing countries, regulations are also important in connection to the pursuit of equity and social access. Südhoff has given some advice on guidelines for good practice in Part IV (see 'Example: Water privatization working for the poor – first dos and don'ts of regulation'). Nevertheless, a recent World Bank policy research report on privatization states that 'creating regulatory institutions that render decisions legitimate to citizens and credible to investors has proven to be the most vexing problem of every infrastructure reform programme' (Kessides, 2004, pp16ff).

To all of these factors, we add the caveat that gains may be attributable as much to increased competition as to privatization per se. This implies that competition is an important factor for the success of the private provision of services.

THE DARK SIDE: SIGNS OF HARMFUL PRIVATIZATION

Yet, privatization clearly has its dark side, and certain patterns show up repeatedly in cases involving undesirable outcomes. The following conditions are commonly associated with unsatisfactory results (see also Carnegie Council/Friedrich Ebert Foundation, 2003).

Inadequate rules governing investments. Public authorities – not only in developing countries – often lack the political power and the experience needed to deal effectively with powerful international corporations. In many cases, governments are unable or unwilling to secure legal certainty and administrative continuity, and lack adequately formulated rules that guide the operations of private investors. Governments, under public pressure, often define unrealistic targets regarding matters of performance and prices that drive private investors away.

Insufficient competition and private monopolies. Supporters of privatization often claim that it will lead to more competition, which will increase efficiency. But some cases of privatization – especially those accompanied by deregulation – lead to the concentration of power in the hands of a few suppliers and, ultimately, to the negative consequences associated with conditions of monopoly or quasi-monopoly. Consider the transfer of municipal power plants into private hands and the elimination of rules prohibiting or restricting branch banking as cases in point. This allows suppliers to capture a disproportionate share of the market, leaving consumers with few options in securing the goods and services that they need. Moreover, corporations tend to raise prices once a dominant market position is established. Hence, before privatization, competition policies and anti-trust laws should be put in place.

An obvious problem with privatizing infrastructure occurs when there are 'natural monopolies'. When the service in question is a single water system or electrical grid, competition remains an illusion. Even bidding itself is typically non-competitive. In the water sector, for example, a small number of international companies dominate the market and can act like a cartel to obtain long-term exclusive contracts.

'Cherry-picking' and marginalization of the poor. Public utilities can provide services to all as a matter of public policy. But it is often commercially rational for private companies, especially in developing countries, to cherry-pick or, in other words, to serve the well-to-do rather than the poor in order to limit their supply of services to the better-off urban areas. Rich people generally find cost-covering prices acceptable, while the poor cannot afford to pay. Privatization can divide societies into 'haves' and 'have nots', with large differences in the access to, or quality of, the services (e.g. education, police protection, and clean drinking water, electricity and recreation facilities) available to the two groups. In many cases, after privatization the poor have to spend a much higher proportion of their income to satisfy such 'basic needs'.

Using the example of water access, Südhoff (see 'Example: Water privatization working for the poor – first dos and don'ts of regulation' in Part IV) demonstrates how a poverty-oriented regulatory policy may avoid 'cherry-picking' and may even improve the access of the poor to public goods. Concession contracts should include binding guidelines on supply, price and competition. The *World Development Report 2004* (World Bank, 2003b) discusses some more innovative examples of how to increase poor clients' choices and participation in service delivery. The latest World Bank policy research report on privatization revisits privatization's effects on distributional equity and calls for regulatory safeguards, including safety nets and tariff-rebalancing schemes (Kessides, 2004, pp16, 23ff). Pricing policies should 'strike a balance between economic efficiency and social equity', and new ways must be explored to increase poor people's access to services.

Termination of cross-subsidies. Public authorities have a long tradition of using 'cross-subsidies' in providing services. European cities, for instance, have routinely subsidized their public transport systems by using income from profitable electricity networks or waterworks. State telephone services have provided subsidies for postal systems. Profitable state-owned companies were often used to subsidize services involving health, education and welfare. Privatization has stopped such cross-subsidies. This often leaves the government to provide services to the poor with insufficient resources or to subsidize firms to provide affordably priced services. But this begs the question: why use scarce government resources to sponsor private profits? On the other hand, that may still be the cheapest solution if the state is unable to provide the necessary services on its own.

Deficient contracts: Shifting risks and externalizing costs. Contrary to naive expectations, privatization is seldom a one-time event that commits companies to strict standards of performance. Most cases deal with evolving relationships that change with events and circumstances and that often undergo constant renegotiation. In this process, governments – and citizens – often find themselves at a great disadvantage. They usually lack information that the experienced international companies possess. Companies often use political connections, pressure or bribery to secure regulatory decisions to their liking.

In extreme cases, they can threaten to terminate supply contracts altogether, a strategy that is tantamount to blackmail.

Privatization is meant to shift certain risks from governments to firms. In practice, it often works the other way around. Many contracts include a guaranteed rate of return. Companies entering uncertain economic environments routinely demand protection from fluctuations in currency and local demand. In the energy sector, power-purchasing agreements typically ask *public* utilities to buy electricity from *private* suppliers at fixed prices calculated in hard currency, regardless of changes in the exchange rate or in the level of demand. Such contracts have driven huge public utilities to the brink of collapse and, in some cases, over the edge. The World Bank actually supports such asymmetric contracts in order to encourage private companies to invest in public services.

Even in advanced economies, the transfer of risks is often illusory. Politically, governments cannot afford to allow companies supplying essential public services to collapse. In many cases, there are irresistible pressures to bail out private providers, even when their problems are self-inflicted.

Contracts seldom force private operators to take external costs into account. Such costs range from the local impacts of toxic wastes to global warming, and from the degradation of earlier public services (e.g. high-quality public transportation) to the erosion of local cultures. In the absence of effective rules of the game, private companies are free to pull up stakes and move on when conditions in a particular location become unfavourable or to find ways of diverting the harmful side effects to distant locations through measures such as the use of tall smokestacks.

Fraudulent practices and corruption. In some cases, the critical divide is not between public and private provision, but rather between law-abiding and transparent business practices, on the one hand, and tax-evading and even criminal activities, on the other. Here, the state and law-abiding companies have a common interest in orderly and transparent business practices. Whenever privatization and relentless cost-cutting following privatization lead to incentives to move operations into illicit work, losses from a growing shadow economy can easily outweigh any gains from increased efficiency.

Privatization and deregulation can create conditions that allow corporations to engage in a variety of fraudulent practices. As the recent energy crisis in California makes clear, this can happen in advanced industrial societies that normally operate on the basis of respect for principles of democracy and good governance. In California, regulatory reform divided the production and distribution of electricity between separate companies and capped the prices that distributors could charge consumers without capping the prices that suppliers could charge distributors. The result was a golden opportunity for producers to manipulate the system to their own advantage. As the story of Enron shows, fraud can occur all the way up to the top of the corporate world. In developing countries and countries in transition, opportunities for fraud are greatly magnified. The exploitative actions of a small number of 'oligarchs' in the Russian Federation, who amassed huge fortunes during and after the wave of privatization of the 1990s, constitute a striking case in point.

Corruption flourishes under conditions of privatization, although state monopolies can also be open to bribery. In the case of privatization, the vulnerability to corruption seems to be highest in the *process* of bidding and decision-making on the sale or leasing of state property. The experiences collected in this volume do not provide any conclusion on whether state or private ownership is more vulnerable and under which specific conditions. But both phenomena are widespread.

Generally, cost efficiency is improved through redundancies without sensitive employee adjustment plans – generating the negative social side effects mentioned above. Fair and sensitive adjustment plans for redundant employees could help (see Savas, 2000, p311). All too often, in order to save money, private providers hire unskilled workers and fail to train them. In the case of private prisons, schools or private police forces, this has tremendous negative effects for the quality of services.

The fox in the hen house. Privatization and deregulation can create situations in which the activities of former regulators are captured by those whose actions they were intended to supervise. For example, privatization of air traffic control can allow airlines to acquire substantial holdings in the air traffic control industry, leading to increased dangers of competitive advantage of one company, as well as safety concerns.

Costly competition. Counter-intuitively, competition can result in higher prices for customers. In the case of compulsory fire insurance for private homes in Germany, the fees of the state-run insurance monopoly were lower than those of the new, competitive private insurers, even with the state using part of its income from fees to subsidize fire brigades and preventive measures. Private insurers, by contrast, distribute part of their income to shareholders and allocate some to advertising campaigns designed to win customers from their competitors.

Weakened democracy and reduced participation. Historically, democracy at the local level has focused on decisions regarding the use of public (municipal) property. People tend to be well informed about who runs the local utilities and whether they have done a good job. There is a sense of 'common ownership' among members of the electorate with regard to waterworks, power stations, public parks and public transport. The public sector is part of a broader public domain that is the realm of citizenship: a set of practices embodying values such as equity or accountability (see Marquand, 2004). In developing countries, public services are perceived as part of a process of democratic 'nation-building'. After privatization, state supervision of the performance of privately owned utilities is rather abstract and may not be conducive to high levels of democratic participation. Hence, we ask whether privatization may have the effect of discouraging democratic participation and even of alienation from government.

This concern grows stronger when the private owner is a multinational corporation, whose decision-making processes are impenetrable to the local population. Our cases involving privatization of municipal water supplies exemplify this pattern. The typical pattern features the creation of a private utility to supply water, and the subsequent takeover of that supplier by a multinational corporation, which soon proceeds to raise prices beyond the means of many local residents and, in some cases, ultimately to pull out again on the grounds that supplying water to the affected community is not profitable. The community is left high and dry with little capacity to supply water to itself in the aftermath of a breach of promise on the part of the distant supplier.

Public goods. Public goods are what we all need or cherish and what we traditionally have expected the state to supply. Of course, it is possible for the state to subcontract the provision of public goods to private operators and to pay for them when they cannot be produced at a profit. When the state cannot afford to pay an appropriate price, it is tempting for the state to introduce rules allowing a contractor to collect fees from beneficiaries of the services. This invariably raises severe equity problems. The supply of military and police services provides a good example. If human security, one of the most central public goods, becomes dependent upon the ability of recipients to pay, the very notion of a democratic state ('one person, one vote') is called into question. Things get worse if the private police or military forces succumb to the temptation to exercise power outside their mandate and get involved in embezzlement or other criminal activities. In 'failed states', private police forces may be better than nothing. But it should be a primary goal for society to re-establish the public authority and not to let 'markets' determine who gets the benefits of security and protection.

Another lesson about the supply of public goods emerges from the case of railway privatization. The results have differed dramatically in the UK in contrast to Japan. In the UK, the privatization of rail tracks produced outcomes so lamentable that the government finally had to re-nationalize them. Japan applied much more caution in the first place. It kept the infrastructure in public hands and even paid subsidies to private coach operators for maintaining services to remote places. The system worked to the full satisfaction of customers. Thus, well-maintained rail tracks can be seen as public goods and the supply of service to thinly populated areas as a non-profitable 'public' task.

Our preliminary conclusion is that certain types of public goods and associated infrastructure will not be suitable for privatization so long as the state is unable (as in many developing countries) or unwilling (as in the UK in the early 1990s) to pay for the corresponding services.

Weak position of indebted states. Public indebtedness has emerged in recent times as a major driver of privatization. Global competition for ever-lower levels of taxation has reduced the financial capacity of states worldwide. In this situation, the temptation is strong for budget ministers to deal with their yearly struggles to balance budgets by selling off what is left of valuable state assets. And it is also tempting to give the 'public good' of a balanced budget priority over the public good of social fairness in access to education, water, energy, mobility, security and other vital services. Our book reports only a few of the many known cases where privatization took place not to achieve greater efficiency or better results, but simply to produce income to balance public budgets.

The privatization of telecommunications, electricity and air traffic control in Lebanon with unsatisfactory results illustrates this syndrome (Abla, 2003). The Latin American cases involving the privatization of telecommunications services show good results in Mexico, poor results in Argentina, and good results as a consequence of avoiding privatization in Uruguay. In Mexico and Uruguay, the state maintained a strong position. In Argentina, the state was weak, and private operators were allowed to establish regional monopolies. This experience suggests the need for a strong state that sets the rules for private business and monitors compliance with the rules.

The situation is particularly worrisome in developing countries that suffer from the highest ratio of foreign debt to gross domestic product (GDP). As Sheshinski and López-Calva (1999) have shown, the dynamics of privatization are strongest in developing countries anyway. The authority of the state tends to be weak in these countries. These countries might need technical and financial assistance to strengthen their regulatory capacity and to set up appropriate bodies. It has been suggested, for example, to set up learning and networking initiatives in order to enhance the transfer of skills and exchanges of experience, or to prepare model clauses so that future contracts can avoid the pitfalls of past ones (UNDP, 2003, p121). Otherwise, the result, all too often, is a weak negotiating position on the part of the state, followed by weak supervision by the state. Rumours to the effect that the international financial institutions (IFIs) are demanding an acceptance of more privatization on the part of indebted developing countries are disquieting in this context. On the other side, investors may hesitate because of weak enabling environments (e.g. slow processes and lack of information), uncertainty and security concerns (e.g. lack of political stability and ownership protection).

A THIRD WAY?

Drawing a sharp distinction between the private and the public makes life easy for the analyst. It has provided a convenient structure for much of the discussion in this book. But as Shanin and von Weizsäcker observe in Part IV (see 'Escaping Pernicious Dualism: Civil Society between the State and the Firm'), it is dangerous to focus exclusively on binary relationships. There are many hybrid arrangements that do not belong unambiguously either to the public sector or to the private sector. We may face not a simple 'either–or' choice between public and private, but a variety of options in institutional forms and modes of ownership, control and finance (see also Starr, 1987). There are historical precedents for this: think about the Dutch East India Company founded in 1602 or the Russian-American Fur Company founded in 1799. Or consider the Charter of Pennsylvania (1681) that granted ownership of a large territory to a single individual, but with the expectation that he would use it to establish a colony governed as a part of the British Empire.

Today, we have public corporations (e.g. the Tennessee Valley Authority, or TVA, in the US); mixed public/private corporations (e.g. Intelsat); social service provision by non-governmental organizations (e.g. primary schools run by the Bangladesh Rural Advancement Committee); complex leasing arrangements that allow private actors to use public lands on a long-term basis (e.g. grazing lands in a number of countries); and arrangements under which governments build infrastructure to be used by private interests (e.g. roads providing access to timber on public lands, dams used in generating electricity and controlling floods).

What lessons do these hybrids offer for the concerns of this book? It seems clear that there are good hybrids and bad hybrids, just as there are good and bad forms of privatization. Some cases have mixed results. The Russian-American Fur Company, for instance, produced marketable products and revenue for the czar, but at a staggering cost in terms of the lives of Native peoples in Alaska. The Tennessee Valley Authority is often described as a success; it carried out a regional development plan beyond the capacity of private actors and at a time (the 1930s) when such actions were desperately needed. But the TVA has a poor record on environmental impacts; some even doubt its usefulness in producing hydroelectricity under current conditions. Our point is not to condemn these hybrid arrangements. Although there is no basis for assuming that they constitute a third way that can provide a general solution to the problem of balancing the private and the public, we still find them promising and suggest the value of devoting more research to such institutional arrangements.

CONCLUSION: BEWARE OF EXTREMES!

We return, finally, to our starting point. We hope readers of this book will be convinced by our primary message: beware of extremes!

Privatization is not an end in itself. Privatization should be treated as a means of increasing efficiency and not as a way of reducing or undermining the role of the state. Privatization may be the best option in some cases; but reforming the public sector, instead, may be the better choice in other cases. We advocate a healthy awareness of the limits to privatization, rather than unconditional approval or rejection. To achieve the best of both worlds, we need strong private enterprises and capable public agencies working together as partners. The lessons learned can in caricature brevity be summarized as:

- Develop good governance, strong regulations and regulatory institutions.
- Do not privatize what the public sector can still do.
- Never privatize for ideological reasons.
- Secure democratic control over regulatory institutions, and enable the state to reverse privatization in cases of severe failure.
- Develop the third sector between the state and the private sector: foundations, charities, civil society.

Before taking a decision on whether and how to privatize, all involved should consider the context and specific local factors relevant to the case at hand. Experience shows the importance of involvement by relevant stakeholders at early stages of the process. All initiatives involving privatization should be accompanied by strong and sophisticated procedures for anticipating the kinds of problems identified in this book, and for intervening promptly and effectively to deal with them.

We conclude with a checklist for public actors embarking on privatization (see Box 22), and a list of some of the key issues with good and bad examples

BOX 22 A PRIVATIZATION CHECKLIST

Public actors are responsible to society as a whole and should insist on this mandate when negotiating with their private-sector partners. To this end they should:

- Maintain or set up a reliable *regulatory framework* that defines the objectives or targets to be met by the private operators.
- Ensure fair and meaningful *competition*, securing a competitive, transparent and accountable bidding process.
- Monitor and control the *performance* in a way that convinces the citizens or the respective state, province or municipality.
- Impose *penalties* if necessary.
- Involve *civil society* and make use of local knowledge.
- Look at *external costs* and try to create an incentive structure that induces private operators to avoid externalities.
- Protect the *weak* and deal with (transitional) social costs.
- Apply '*cross-subsidies*' if that is the best way of maintaining unprofitable, but essential, elements of public service that are necessary on social equity grounds.
- Protect *public goods/the commons* – for example, by preventing incentive structures that invite private actors to overuse, let alone destroy, public goods.
- Prevent natural monopolies from turning into commercial *monopolies*.
- Secure a sufficient financial basis to pay private operators for necessary services (such as access to water, education, energy, communication and transport) whenever customers are not in a position to pay cost-covering prices. This implies that states should join hands in fending off 'harmful international tax competition'!

Issues	Positive examples	Negative examples
Competition	Telecommunications, Mexico	Fire insurance, Germany
Process of privatization / regulation	Water services, Tanzania (Kiliwater)	Water services, Grenoble, France
Improved quality of services	Railways, Japan	Railways, UK
Investments in infrastructure	Water services, Tanzania (Kiliwater)	Energy, California
Efficiency and cost effectiveness	Water services, El Alto, Bolivia	Healthcare, US
Public goods	Copper Refinery, Bulgaria	Neem tree, India
Distributive consequences and social equity	Water services, Tanzania (Kiliwater)	Healthcare, Chile
Employment	Postal services, The Netherlands	Zambia copper mines
Local economy	Private forests, Germany	Municipal electricity suppliers
Corruption	Not applicable	Water services, Grenoble, France
Gender		Many cases in Eastern Europe
Participation	Water services, Tanzania (Kiliwater)	Water services, El Alto, Bolivia

Figure 68
Guiding questions and examples.

(see Figure 68). We hope these, and the whole book, will help to ensure that privatization delivers its real and important potential benefits, while avoiding its equally real and important potential harms.

About the Editors and Authors[*]

Professor Dr Ernst Ulrich von Weizsäcker is chairman of the Environment Committee as well as SPD-spokesman for sustainable development at the German Bundestag, Berlin, and member of the Club of Rome. He was born in 1939, is a member of parliament (SPD) for Stuttgart since 1998 and former chairman of the Bundestag Study Commission on Globalization (1999–2002). Trained in physics and biology, he served as a professor of biology at the University of Essen, as president of the University of Kassel and as director at the United Nations Centre for Science and Technology for Development. He was formerly director of the Institute for European Environmental Policy (1984–1991) and founding president of the Wuppertal Institute for Climate, Environment and Energy (1991–2000). Ernst Ulrich von Weizsäcker is author of several books, among them *Factor Four: Doubling Wealth, Halving Resource Use* (Earthscan, London, 1997, with A. B. and L. H. Lovins) and *Earth Politics* (Zed Books, London, 1994).
www.ernst.weizsaecker.de, *ernst.weizsaecker@bundestag.de*

Professor Dr Oran R. Young is a professor in the Donald Bren School of Environmental Science and Management, University of California, at Santa Barbara, US. He served for six years as the founding chair of the Committee on the Human Dimensions of Global Change of the US National Academy of Sciences and is now chair of the Scientific Steering Committee of the international project on the Institutional Dimensions of Global Environmental Change (IDGEC) under the auspices of the International Human Dimensions Programme on Global Environmental Change. He also co-chairs the Scientific Steering Committee of the Global Carbon Project under the auspices of the Earth System Science Partnership. Dr Young served for six years as vice-president of the International Arctic Science Committee and is currently chair of the Board of Governors of the University of the Arctic. Dr Young's scientific work encompasses basic research, focusing on collective choice and social institutions, and applied research, dealing with issues pertaining to international environmental governance and to the Arctic as an international region. Oran R. Young is the author or co-author of over 20 books and numerous scholarly articles. Among his recent books are: *The Institutional*

---

[*] The opinions and conclusions expressed in the book are entirely those of the editors and authors and do not necessarily represent the views of their affiliated institutions.

Dimensions of Environmental Change (MIT Press, Cambridge, MA, 2002); *Governance in World Affairs* (Cornell University Press, Ithaca, 1999); *Creating Regimes: Arctic Accords and International Governance* (Cornell University Press, Ithaca, 1998); *International Governance: Protecting the Environment in a Stateless Society* (Cornell University Press, 1994); and *International Cooperation: Building Regimes for Natural Resources and the Environment* (Cornell University Press, Ithaca, 1989).
young@bren.ucsb.edu

Professor Dr Matthias Finger is chair and professor of Management of Network Industries at the College of Management, Swiss Federal Institute of Technology (EPFL), as well as dean of the School of Continuing Education, EPFL, Lausanne, Switzerland. He focuses on the liberalization of the main network industries' sectors – postal services, telecommunications, energy, public transport, water and air transport – on the changes undergone by the historical operators in these sectors, and on issues of regulation and public service. He is particularly interested in the implications of the new information and communication technologies on issues of governance, innovation, regulation and risks. He has written numerous articles and books on this subject and consults with public enterprises, as well as with public administrations and political authorities in Switzerland and internationally. Previously, he was a professor at Syracuse University, New York (1989–1991), at Columbia University, New York (1992–1994), and at the Swiss Graduate School of Public Administration (1995–2002). His most recent book is entitled: *Water Privatisation: Transnational Corporations and the Re-regulation of the Global Water Industry* (SPON Press, London, 2002).
matthias.finger@epfl.ch

Nancy Alexander is the founder and director of the Citizens' Network on Essential Services (CNES), US.
ncalexander@igc.org

Dr Marianne Beisheim is assistant professor at the Free University Berlin, Institute for Political Science, and a research associate in the office of Dr Ernst Ulrich von Weizsäcker, Deutscher Bundestag, Germany.
marianne.beisheim@gmx.de

Dr Roland Benedikter is a member of the scientific staff of the Institute for the History of Ideas and Research on Democracy, Innsbruck, Austria, and of the Laboratorio Freudiano, Scuola Superiore di Psicoanalisi,

Milan, Italy.
rolandbenedikter@yahoo.de

Dörte Bernhardt is with Germanwatch, Berlin, Germany.
bernhardt@germanwatch.org

Professor Dr Joachim Betz works for the Institute of Comparative Overseas Studies, Hamburg, Germany.
betz@duei.de

Black Sea University Foundation, contact person: Professor Mircea Malitza, Romania.
www.bsufonline.org,
m_malita@rnc.ro

Professor Dr Raimund Bleischwitz is co-director of the Research Group of Material Flows and Resource Management, Wuppertal Institute, Germany, and Toyota chair for Industry and Sustainability, College of Europe, Brussels, Belgium. *raimund.bleischwitz@wupperinst.org* and *rbleischwitz@coleurop.be*

Dr Zsolt Boda is with the Hungarian Academy of Sciences, Political Sciences Institute, and the Budapest University of Economic Sciences and Public Administration. *boda@mtapti.hu*

Frédéric Boehm is a doctoral student at the Berlin University of Technology, Germany. *frederic_boehm@yahoo.fr*

Jochen Boekhoff works for the Deutscher Bundestag, Berlin, Germany. *jochen@boekhoff-berlin.de*

Ruth Brand is a doctoral student at the Free University, Berlin, Germany. *ruthbrand@gmx.de*

Aziz Choudry is an activist and writer with GATT Watchdog, Aotearoa, New Zealand. *notoapec@clear.net.nz*

Fabian Fechner is a student at Tübingen University, Germany. *fabianfechnerat@hotmail.com*

Professor Felix R. FitzRoy works for the Centre for Research into Industry, Enterprise, Finance and the Firm (CRIEFF), University of St Andrews, UK. *frf@st-andrews.ac.uk*

Margaret Flaherty is director of Capacity Building, Financial Sector and Corporate Social Responsibility, World Business Council for Sustainable Development (WBCSD), Geneva, Switzerland. *flaherty@wbcsd.org*

Nessie R. Golakai works for the Consumers International Region Office for Africa, Harare, Zimbabwe. *ngolakai@ci-roaf.co.zw*

Maria Gordon is a freelance editor and office manager with the Program on Governance for Sustainable Development, University of California, Santa Barbara. *mcgordon1@cox.net*

Tim Gürtler is a student at Tübingen University, Germany. *tim.guertler@web.de*

Professor Dr Michael von Hauff lectures at the University of Kaiserslautern, Germany. *hauff-stuttgart@gmx.de*

Katharina Hay is a student at the University of Stuttgart, Germany. *katharinahay@web.de*

Dr Ernst Hillebrand is with the Friedrich Ebert Foundation, Chile. *ehillebrand@fes.cl*

Dr Rolph van der Hoeven is manager of the World Commission on the Social Dimension of Globalization, International Labour Organization (ILO), Geneva, Switzerland. *hoeven@ilo.org*

Dr Hella Hoppe is a scholar of the Fulbright New Century Scholars Program, 2004/2005, and a visiting Researcher at the Friedrich Ebert Foundation, New York Office.
hella_hoppe@gmx.net

Diwata Olalia Hunziker is a freelance researcher in Switzerland.
diwata.hunziker@bluewin.ch

Alexander Juras is deputy executive director of the Regional Environmental Centre for Central and Eastern Europe, Budapest, Hungary.
ajuras@rec.org

Dr Inge Kaul is director of the United Nations Development Programme's (UNDP's) Office of Development Studies, New York.
inge.kaul@undp.org

Noara Kebir is a member of the Managing Board of MicroEnergy International, Berlin, Germany.
noara.kebir@microenergy-international.com

Dr Tim Kessler is a research director with the Citizens' Network on Essential Services (CNES), US.
tkessler@coditel.net

Beate Klein is an assistant in the office of Dr Ernst Ulrich von Weizsäcker, Deutscher Bundestag, Berlin, Germany.
ernst.weizsaecker@bundestag.de

Raffaela Kluge formerly worked for the Development Department of the Salzburg Festival, Austria, and is now responsible for marketing and communication at Haus der Kunst, München, Germany.
raffaela@klugeconcepts.com

Roger Levett is a partner in Levett-Therivel Sustainability Consultants, UK.
roger@levett-therivel.fsnet.co.uk

Brighton Lubansa is a bilingual analyst for Millennium Care, Toronto, Canada.
blubansa@yahoo.com

Tobias Luppe is a policy adviser for Access Campaign Ärzte ohne Grenzen/Médecins sans Frontières (MSF), Berlin, Germany.
tobias.luppe@berlin.msf.org

Professor Dr Verdiana G. Masanja lectures at the University of Dar es Salaam, Tanzania.
vmasanja@maths.udsm.ac.tz

Brenda Mofya is a Quaker International Affairs representative for Southern Africa, Harare, Zimbabwe.
brenda@ecoweb.co.zw

Tonia Sophie Müller is a student at Tübingen University, Germany.
tsophie.mueller@gmx.de

Dr Andreas Obser is with the Department of International Politics, Economics and Social Science Faculty, University of Potsdam, Germany.
aobser@t-online.de

Juanita Olaya is public contracting programme manager with Transparency International.
jolaya@transparency.org

Daniel Philipp is a member of the Managing Board of MicroEnergy International, Berlin, Germany
daniel.philipp@microenergy-international.com

Jaime Polanco is a student at Universidad Externado de Colombia, and MPM (Master of Public Management), University of Potsdam, Germany.
pacande2@yahoo.com

Akira Proske is a student and intern at the Wuppertal Institute for Climate, Environment and Energy, Germany.
akisebpro@gmx.net

Geneviève Reday-Mulvey is a social economist and head of the Four Pillars research programme (research on social security, pensions and employment), International Association for the Study of Insurance Economics, The Geneva Association, Switzerland.
genevieve_reday@genevaassociation.org

Dr Dušan Reljić is a senior researcher with the German Institute for International and Security Affairs (SWP), Berlin, Germany (until 2003, he was with the European Institute of the Media).
dusan.reljic@swp-berlin.org

Olaf Rotthaus is an assistant in the office of Klaus Kirschner, Deutscher Bundestag, Berlin, Germany.
klaus.kirschner@bundestag.de

Dr Jürgen Scheffran moved in August 2004 from the Potsdam Institute for Climate Impact Research in Germany to the University of Illinois at Urbana-Champaign in the US where he works as a senior research scientist with ACDIS.
scheffra@uiuc.edu

Todd Schenk is project officer with the Regional Environmental Center for Central and Eastern Europe, Budapest, Hungary.
todd@rec.org

Professor Dr Jorge A. Schiavon is director with Oficina de Vinculación y Desarrollo (OVD), and profesor-investigador, División de Estudios Internacionales (DEI), Centro de Investigación y Docencia Económicas (CIDE), México.
jorge.schiavon@cide.edu

Nele Schneidereit is a doctoral student at the Free University Berlin, Germany.
nschneidereit@web.de

Professor Dr Simon Schwartzman is with the Instituto de Estudos do Trabalho e Sociedade (IETS), Brazil.
simon@iets.inf.br

Kai Senf is an assistant in the office of Fritz Schösser, Deutscher Bundestag, Berlin, Germany.
fritz.schoesser@bundestag.de

Professor Dr Teodor Shanin lectures at the University of Manchester and is rector of the Moscow School of Social and Economic Sciences.
shanin@msses.ru

Dr Vandana Shiva is director of the Research Foundation for Science, Technology and Ecology, New Delhi, and bearer of the Alternative Nobel Prize.
vshiva@giasdl01.vsnl.net.in

Dr Sabine Speiser is with Interculture Management, Frankfurt, Germany.
speiser@interculture-management.de

Simon Stähler is a student at Tübingen University, Germany.
sstaehler@gmx.de

Björn Stigson is president of the World Business Council for Sustainable Development (WBCSD), Geneva.
info@wbcsd.org

Martin Stürmer is a student with the Institut d'Etudes Politiques de Paris and Free University Berlin, Germany.
mastuermer@gmx.de

Ralf Südhoff is a research assistant at the Deutscher Bundestag, Berlin, Germany.
ralf_suedhoff@hotmail.com

Max Thümmel is a student at the University of Cologne, Germany.
max.thuemmel@web.de

Thomas Thümmel is a student at the Leibniz Kolleg Tübingen, Germany.
thomas.thuemmel@gmx.net

Professor Dr Thomas von Ungern-Sternberg lectures at the Ecole des HEC, University of Lausanne, Switzerland.
thomas.vonungern-sternberg@hec.unil.ch

Professor Dr Alcyone Vasconcelos is an international consultant with the World Bank and a former state minister of education in Brazil.
alcyone.v@terra.com.br

Martin Weidauer is a research associate and doctoral student at the University of Kassel, Germany.
martin.weidauer@baustadt.de

Dr Peter Wolff is a senior researcher at the German Development Institute (GDI), Bonn, Germany.
peter.wolff@die-gdi.de

Dr Anne Zollner is international labor rights officer for the Bureau of International Labor Affairs at the US Department of Labor (until 2003, she was privatization project director at Women, Law and Development International – WLDI).
annezollner@starpower.net

John Züchner is a student at the Free University Berlin, Germany.
john.zuechner@gmx.de

Notes

INTRODUCTION

1   For futher reading, see von Hayek (1944), Friedman (1962) and Coase (1974).

PRIVATIZATION IN MANY SECTORS: CASE STUDIES AND SNAPSHOTS

Water

1   Further information on this section can be found at www.france-asso.com/ades/dossiers/eau/index.html, www.seaus.org, http://eausecours.free.fr, www.suez.com and www.ondeo.com and www.ville-grenoble.fr.
2   Suez is a French multi-utility group (approximately €39.6 billion revenues in 2003). Its water division is named Ondeo (approximately €5.9 billion revenues in 2003 and about 91 million inhabitants supplied with drinking water and 49 million inhabitants with sanitation services). At the beginning of the events in Grenoble, Suez was known as Lyonnaise des Eaux, later as Dumez-Lyonnaise des Eaux, and then Suez-Lyonnaise des Eaux. For ease, the name Suez is used throughout this text.
     The world leader in water services is the French company Vivendi Water (now Veolia Water), with approximately €13.3 billion revenues and about 110 million people supplied with water services in 2003.
3   The population of Grenoble and its surrounding region was about 415,000 in 2003.
4   The then CEO of Suez, Jérôme Monod, was heard by the court only as a witness. Today, he is the closest adviser to the French President Jacques Chirac (www.elysee.fr/pres/coll.htm).
5   The exact figure was 1009 billion French francs (in 1989 terms). For further information, see Chambre Régionale des Comptes Rhône-Alpes (1995).
6   For the conversion of Philippine pesos, the rate of 1 Philippine peso = US$0.01815 (equivalent to €0.01635) has been used (September 2003).
7   Ramos, Fidel Valdez (1928–) was president of the Philippines from 1992 to 1998.
8   87 to 147 Philippine pesos.
9   For further information on this section, see Bakker (2004), Finger and Allouche (2002) and the Thames Water website: www.thames-water.com.

10 It must be noted that many Western countries have also privatized many of these essential services in the belief that private enterprises are more efficient and often more effective.

11 Both companies later went through name changes or transferred ownership internally; by 2003, these shareholders were known respectively as Vivendi Environment and Berlinwasser Holding AG.

12 The specific details of the privatization agreement are not public for commercial confidentiality reasons. This is to the chagrin of many who feel that the citizens of Budapest, indirectly the FCSM's largest shareholders, have a right to full knowledge of the arrangement.

13 The fact that the EBRD will sell a portion of its 30 per cent stake in the SPC to the other shareholders at a pre-agreed price and moment (both covered by commercial confidentiality), while also providing regulatory and risk 'carve-out' protection to them, does little to challenge the notion that EBRD involvement provides little more than a sweetening of the deal to the private firms.

14 Translated and adapted from Unternehmensinstitut (2003, pp 19–20).

Metals and Cement

1   This was recognized early on, even before the more pronounced shifts out of communist rule took place, by many both within and outside of the region. Environmental non-governmental organizations (ENGOs) were, in fact, often players in the political changes and among the strongest in civil society during the early days of democracy.

2   A great deal of literature exists on the tragic Baia Mare and Borsa mining accidents, both of which leaked dangerous contaminants into the Tisza River basin in Romania during early 2000. These accidents created a great deal of controversy over liability, foreign investment and transboundary watercourse management.

3   Voucher privatization is an approach in which vouchers are distributed free or at a nominal cost to eligible citizens to be used to bid for shares or assets being privatized. It is an effective way of rapidly (and somewhat more equitably than usual) privatizing, while encouraging the development of capital markets.

4   Because the Bulgarian state was in urgent need of money, a parallel contract was signed with the World Bank. The Bank financed a 'soft loan' for US$16 million of the US$25 million necessary for remediation, with the other US$9 million financed by the Bulgarian National Trust Ecofund (interview). Incidentally, this was the first time that the World Bank entered into such a deal.

5   See www.um.be/comrel/en/pirdop/index.htm.

6   See the 'community relations' section of the Umicore website: www.um.be/comrel/en/pirdop/index.htm.

Other Resources

1   All of the documentation data in the database was collected and compiled by the Council of Scientific and Industrial Research (CSIR) of India and were provided to the World Intellectual Property Organization (WIPO) with a request to make the data available online. The database is now available at www.ipdl.wipo.int/en/guest/tkdl/search-bool.html.

2   BBC News Online (2002).

3   International collaborative efforts to systematically collect, conserve and share traditional rice varieties and wild rice species existed since 1962. Constructed in 1977 – and significantly renovated and upgraded in 1994 – the International Rice Genebank (IRG) has facilities for storing rice seeds. More than 100 countries have donated germplasm to the Genebank (www.irri.org/GRC/irg/biodiv-genebank.htm).

4   According to IRRI, the National Seed Storage Laboratory, part of the US Department of Agriculture, holds a backup copy of the entire International Rice Germplasm Collection under 'black box' conditions, solely to restore IRRI's Genetic Resources Collection in the event of some catastrophe. It was not supposed to distribute, use or monitor the viability of the collection in any way (www.irri.org/GRC/GRChome/link.htm).

5   The Green Revolution is a process of technological development of agricultural techniques that spread throughout the world from the 1960s onwards. Its goal was to increase the efficiency of agricultural processes so that the productivity of crops was increased and could help developing countries to face their growing populations' needs. The two main categories of innovation are the breeding of new plant varieties and the development of new agricultural teechniques such as irrigation and the use of chemical fertilizers.

6   For a complete list of all signature states to the Convention on Biological Diversity (CBD), see www.biodiv.org/world/parties.asp.

7   The regulation was made by the Madrid Agreement for the Repression of False or Deceptive Indications of Source on Goods in 1981. Germany, for example, joined the agreement in 1935 while other states such as the US and the former USSR never ratified it. This is why they continue using terms such as 'Champagne' and similar wordings for products not originating from the French region. Under EU regulation, the problem was first treated in Council Regulation (EEC) No 2333/92 of 13 July 1992, which laid down general rules for the description and presentation of sparkling wines and aerated sparkling wines.

8   Geographical indications of all products are covered by TRIPS Article 22, which defines a standard level of protection. This states that geographical indications have to be protected in order to avoid misleading the public and to prevent unfair competition. Article 23 provides a higher or enhanced level of protection for geographical indications for wines and spirits. They have to be protected even if misuse would not cause the public to be misled.

9   See www.capise.org/eng/documents/troyan_horse.pdf.

10   Conservation International website: www.conservation.org.

11   See www.capise.org/eng/documents/troyan_horse.pdf.

12   Orin Langelle, personal communication, 24 September 2003.

13   Human Rights Centre Bartoleme de las Casas statement, 23 January 2004, at www.chiapas.mediosindependientes.org/display.php3?article_id=107110.

14   Rainforest Action Network website: www.ran.org.

Energy

1   The utilities won their ability to create holding company structures in a 1987 decision by the Republican-dominated California Public Utilities Commission. It allowed holding companies to protect their profitable arms from sharing profits with ratepayers.

Telecommunication and Postal Services

1   See www.tpgpost.nl.

Transportation

1   British Rail is one of the best-investigated cases of privatization. It is evident that this snapshot's condensed presentation cannot cover all facts and analyses. For further reading, refer to the references cited in the text.
2   The data refers to the period between 1991 and 1997 and stems from a private Argentine institute.

Insurance

1   Council Directive 92/49/EEC of 18 June 1992.
2   This snapshot is a brief summary of the results of a more in-depth analysis of the German market published in von Ungern-Sternberg (2004). The robustness of our conclusions is strengthened by the fact that they are based on the study of the property insurance market in five countries: the UK, Spain, France, Germany and Switzerland.
3   See von Ungern-Sternberg (2004).
4   The best way to obtain the appropriate level of a positive externality is to internalize the benefits.

Health

1   See www.internationalreports.net/theamericas/chile/2002/presidentlagos.html.
2   Zambia is divided into nine provinces, namely: Northen, Luapula, Copperbelt, Eastern, Central, Western, North-Western, Southern and Lusaka.
3   The majority of the estimated 1.2 million are adults aged between 15 and 49.

Education

1   An ironic expression for a group of highly trained economists, disciples of Milton Friedman at the University of Chicago, who were swarming out to Latin America, starting with Chile, since the late 1970s.
2   This snapshot covers the situation until the end of 2003.
3   The PRONADE model has been used as a model for decentralization at the beginning of 2003, but had to be withdrawn for political reasons.
4   Seventy-five per cent of PRONADE schools with Maya children have at least one bilingual teacher, a number which is not even reached in the 'normal' public schools.
5   In 1964, Tanganyika and Zanzibar united to form Tanzania.

Pensions

1   Labelled after section 401(k) of the Internal Revenue Code, which defines this sort of defined contribution plan.
2   '... financed through a payroll tax of 12.4 per cent split evenly between employer and employee' (Hinz, 2000).
3   'PBGC is a federal corporation created by the Employee Retirement Income Security Act of 1974' (PBGC, 2003).

Police and Security

1 For a series of pro-privatization evaluation studies, see CCA (2004) and NCPA (1995). However, it is difficult to compare the cost efficiency of private and public operated prisons because public prisons often rely on other government agencies to provide services (accounting, data processing, legal, etc.), and private prisons depend upon government services (such as healthcare), to a variable extent.
2 Median time in prison per Bureau of Justice statistics (www.ojp.usdoj.gov/bjs/prisons.htm).

PRIVATIZATION IN CONTEXT

The General Context

1 I wish to thank Martin Stürmer for manifold suggestions and assistance.
2 Fukuyama actually coined his term 'the end of history' in an article as early as 1989 under the impression of the blood shed on Tiananmen Square, the Russian Perestroika and the revolution in Central and Eastern Europe. For Fukuyama, this showed the triumph of Western liberal democracy, while communism was losing legitimacy. He picked up this term in his 1992 book.
3 Stern (1990) gives a good overview of the expansion of the communist world, but also of its inner conflicts.
4 The Group of 77 was established on 15 June 1964 by 77 developing countries signatories to the Joint Declaration of the Seventy-Seven Countries issued at the end of the first session of UNCTAD in Geneva. Membership has since increased to 132 countries.
5 For an introduction to contemporary perspectives on collective action problems, see Hardin (1982).
6 Many blue-ribbon commissions and panels have suggested numerous reforms in the UN System. For a prominent example see Commission on Global Governance (1995).
7 The International Criminal Court opened its doors on 1 July 2002. But its effectiveness will remain limited unless and until the United States decides to join.
8 While consideration of interactions among these three broad sectors has a long history, the phrase 'three pillars' is attributable to Ernst von Weizsäcker.
9 Most democratic systems have specific procedures (e.g. a bill of rights) to prevent the majority from trampling on the basic rights of minorities.
10 As Richard Cooper says, IMF votes 'are weighted according to a formula ... that is designed to reflect roughly both the importance of each country in the world economy and the importance of world trade for each economy' (Cooper, 1987, p244). But this hardly precludes the occurrence of a democracy deficit in the operation of the IMF.

The Regional Context

1 Of course, after the joining of Russia, G7 has now evolved into G8. But as we will address privatization in Russia in the section on Eastern and Central Europe, we will continue to use the term G7 here.

Special Issues

1 The terms 'privatization' and 'private provision' are used here interchangeably to connote variants of provision by firms or non-profit organizations, including so-called 'public–private partnerships'. Private provision refers to control over management, allocation or pricing or assets, but not necessarily ownership.
2 For evidence of efforts by multilateral development banks to pressure borrowing countries to privatize essential services, see Dubash et al (2002); Woodroffe and Joyner (2000); Bijlmakers and Lindner (2003); Bayliss and Hall (2001); MacCuish (2003); Kessler and Alexander (2003).
3 J. F. Talbot (2002) 'Is the water business really a business?', CEO of Saur International, World Bank Water and Sanitation Lecture Series, 13 February 2002, www.worldbank.org/wbi/B-SPAN/docs/SAUR.pdf.
4 Reprint of Nancy Alexander and Timothy Kessler (2003) 'How GATS jeopardizes essential services, *Social Development Review*, September, vol 7, no 2 (Citizen's Network on Essential Services)
5 WTO (2002) *Trading into the Future*, online guide to the WTO Agreements, 1999, quoted in Sinclair and Grieshaber-Otto (2002), p34.
6 See Gould (2002); this paper cites the judgement of Professor David Luff at a World Bank/OECD Conference in March 2002, p13.
7 See www.corpwatch.org and www.polarisinstitute.org.
8 For a good overview on the topic of corruption, see Andvig et al (2000), Lambsdorff (2001), Bardhan (1997) and the information available at Transparency International's website: www.transparency.org.
9 See also Boehm and Polanco (2003).
10 The case study on Grenoble is an illustration of this danger (see 'A "Waterl'eau" in Grenoble, France' in Part II).
11 For an extended argumentation of this question, see Boehm and Polanco (2003, p12f).
12 Ernst von Weizsäcker, co-editor of this book, was a member of the World Commission on the Social Dimension of Globalization.
13 As the comparative study of the telecom sectors in Mexico, Uruguay and Argentina seems to show (see 'Telecommunications in Mexico, Uruguay and Argentina: A tale of contrasts' in Part II), growth, modernization and the creation of new jobs do not truly depend upon privatization. Hence, it can be concluded that, as a rule, privatization upfront means the shedding of labour.
14 The views expressed here are solely those of the author and may not necessarily reflect the official positions or opinions of the US Department of Labor.

At the July 1998 Research Design Meeting in Warsaw it was determined that both qualitative and quantitative methods would be used to research legal structures and the labour situation of women. This unique triangulation of various methods gives the most accurate and balanced data to develop a comprehensive understanding of women's labour experiences in the transition. First, the legal component consisted of research on existing laws, as well as on the structure and culture of the laws. Secondary materials, interviews with in-house counsels, and case studies were used to understand how privatization and labour laws encourage or discourage the use of female labour. In addition, focus groups explored whether women know their rights and how to enforce them. Second, the intersection between enterprise characteristics and women's work was investigated through a national survey to explore whether there is a relationship between certain enterprise traits and the negative treatment of female labour. For example, preliminary evidence in Poland suggested that worker–manager buy-outs are more likely than other types of ownership structures to result in disproportionate female lay-offs. Third, to assess employers' attitudes toward female labour, in-depth interviews were conducted with enterprise managers on their perceptions and preferences for their workforce members. Finally, to explore how privatization impacts people on a day-to-day basis, focus groups were conducted with employed and unemployed women to hear about personal experiences in the privatization process. The anecdotal evidence provided by the qualitative methods, such as one-on-one interviews and focus groups, complements the rigorous, categorical evidence given by quantitative surveys. By drawing on these various points of view, this section aims to provide a comprehensive portrait of women in the privatization process.

15 See www.wld.org.

16 This is less true of Poland where economic recovery has been more successful and a better social safety net was constructed to contend with the deleterious consequences of the transition.

17 In other words, gain corporation status by following procedures as prescribed by law and that invest the enterprise with the right to enter into contracts, buy and sell property and other rights granted to individuals.

18 In each country, a stratified sample was formed on the basis of parameters related to privatization, such as ownership structure, number of employees and sector of the economy. The survey was conducted in the capital city and between 5 to 14 other cities in each of the countries. While the sample may not be scientifically representative, it covers a broad range of industries and regions and provides a reliable massif for exploring privatization and the status of women.

19 With accession to the European Union (EU), Poland and Bulgaria will have to harmonize laws such as this in order to be consistent with the rest of the EU.

20 General Secretary of the Fabian Society and adviser to the UK Chancellor of the Exchequer, Gordon Brown.

GOVERNANCE OF PRIVATIZATION

Regulation

1 Primary and secondary schools, corresponding to OECD's ISCED-97 levels 1 to 3.

2 The same teacher can hold more than one teaching post.

3 The entire 2001 and 2002 editions of the *Parana School Report Cards* are available in Portuguese from www.pr.gov.br/cie/boletim/boletim.html. To learn more about the PSRC, write to alcyone.v@terra.com.br or simon@schwartzman.org.br.

Privatization and Municipal Democracy

1 The authors gratefully acknowledge input, feedback and editing by Maria Gordon, Marianne Beisheim, Tim Gürtler and Katharina Hay.

Financing Global Public Goods: Challenges

1 The views expressed here are the author's and do not necessarily reflect those of the organization with which she is affiliated.

2   The term 'good' is used here to denote entities (such as bread), services (such as the control of communicable diseases) or conditions (such as international financial stability). Thus, the term 'good' is value neutral.

3   This principle calls for matching the jurisdiction of those taking decisions on providing a public good, with the range of those affected. For example, local public goods should be decided locally, national public goods should be decided nationally, and, by implication, global public goods in fora where all concerned parts of the global public can be heard and fairly represented.

Escaping Pernicious Dualism

1   See www.nationaltrust.org.uk/main/nationaltrust/facts.html.
2   See Anheier (2004), Florini (2000), Weiss and Gordenker (1996) and Zimmer et al (2004).

Private Governance: Private Rules for Privatization?

1   Private regimes are broadly defined as institutions 'in which states do not participate in formulating the principles, norms, rules or procedures which govern the regime members' behavior' (Haufler, 1993, p100).

2   The 'multi-stakeholder' model of governance states that all those affected by, or with a stake in, the decisions of (public or private) authorities in any domain have the right to a voice in the governance of those matters; this may include employees, unions, suppliers, NGOs, local communities, the general public, or possibly even nature.

3   Of course, in democracies, only governments make laws and this monopoly must not be removed. Governance by private actors does not include the making of laws, only the setting of rules without the force of law – and this, indeed, is surely an inherent weakness of this kind of governance as sanctions and penalties can only come from stakeholders, even if the harm done is to society as a whole.

4   Other important factors are commodity characteristics or consumer responsiveness. For further reading see Bortolotti and Fiorentini (1999), Shelton (2000) and Witte et al (2003). Many unpublished papers on the issue may be found on the internet, as, for example, Pattberg (2004).

5   See www.psiru.org/educ/Resources/Res30.htm.
6   See www.nepalnews.com.np/contents/englishdaily/ktmpost/2003/jan/jan15/index1.htm.
7   See www.nepalnews.com.np/contents/englishweekly/spotlight/2004/may/may21/national7.htm.
8   See www.austlii.edu.au/au/other/privacy/smart/57.html.
9   Cited according to www.un.org/News/dh/latest/gcompct.
10   See www.transparency.org/working_papers/carney/3c-codes.html.
11   See www.jaring.my/cch/vfm/vf03001.htm.
12   Björn Stigson is president of the World Business Council for Sustainable Development (WBCSD); Margaret Flaherty is director of the WBCSD's Capacity Building and Financial Sector Projects. This snapshot summarizes some of the main findings of the WBCSD regarding corporate social responsibility. While the editors of this book find the ideas expressed in the snapshot generally attractive, the 'voice' heard is that of Stigson and Flaherty speaking on behalf of the WBCSD.

13 The World Business Council for Sustainable Development (WBCSD) is a coalition of 170 international companies united by a shared commitment to sustainable development via the three pillars of economic growth, ecological balance and social progress. Member companies are drawn from more than 35 countries and 20 major industrial sectors. The WBCSD's activities reflect the belief that the pursuit of sustainable development is good for business and business is good for sustainable development. See www.wbcsd.ch.

'Co-evolution' between State Regulation and the Private Sector

1 A more elaborate and scientifically rigorous version of this chapter has been published in Bleischwitz (2004).
2 Co-evolution is a term from evolutionary biology signifying that two species each give mutual stimuli for further evolution of the other. Typically, co-evolution can only be proven to have taken place in the past, while it remains unpredictable for the future. It is surely too early to speak of past co-evolution between the regulatory state and the private sector. We use the term, rather, as a postulate than as a proven fact.

List of Acronyms and Abbreviations

AA	Aerolineas Argentinas
AAC	Anglo American Corporation
ABC	American Broadcasting Corporation
ACLU	American Civil Liberties Union
ADB	African Development Bank
ADB	Asian Development Bank
AHC-MMS	Mining Municipal Services (Zambia)
AIDS	acquired immune deficiency syndrome
AISA	Aguas del Illimani S.A. (French-Bolivian-Argentine consortium)
ANC	African National Congress
AOL	America On-Line
AT&T	American Telephone and Telegraph Company
AUSTEL	Australian Telecommunications Authority
BMS	Bristol-Myers Squibb
BOAC	British Overseas Airways Corporation
BOT	build-operate-transfer
BOOT	build-own-operate-transfer
BP	British Petroleum
BRISCOs	British Rail infrastructure service companies
BT	British Telecom
BTO	build-transfer-operate
CAPISE	Centro de Analisis Politico e Investigaciones Sociales y Economicas (Mexico)
CBD	Convention on Biological Diversity
CCK	Communications Commission of Kenya
CD	compact disk
Cdn	Canadian
CEE	Central and Eastern Europe
CEO	chief executive officer
CI	Conservation International
CIEPAC	Centro de Investigaciones Económicas y Políticas de Acción Comunitaria (Mexico)
CMI	compulsory monopoly institution (Germany)
CN	Canadian National Railways
CNBC	Cable National Broadcasting Corporation
CO_2	carbon dioxide
COE	Council of Europe

COEDUCAs	education committees (*comités educativos*) (Guatemala)
COGESE	Compagnie de Gestion des Eaux du Sud-Est (France)
CSIR	Council of Scientific and Industrial Research (India)
CSO	civil society organization
CSR	corporate social responsibility
CTI	Comprehensive Technologies, Inc
DAWASA	Dar es Salaam Water and Sewerage Authority
DB	defined benefit
DC	defined contribution
DEG	Deutsche Investitions- und Entwicklungsgesellschaft mbH
€	euros (European Union monetary currency)
EA	East Africa
EACs	community schools (*escuelas de autogestión comunitaria*) (Guatemala)
EBRD	European Bank for Reconstruction and Development
EC	European Community
EDF	Electricité de France
EDM-SA	La Société Energie du Mali
EEC	European Economic Community
EIA	environmental impact assessment
EKTM-I	East Kilimanjaro Trunk Main
ENEL	Ente Nazionale per l'Energia Elettrica (Italy)
ENGO	environmental non-governmental organization
ENI	Ente Nazionale Idrocarburi (Italy)
EO	South African Executive Outcomes
EOSAT	Earth Observing Satellite Corporation
EPA	extraordinary price adjustment
ESAF	Enhanced Structural Adjustment Facility (of the World Bank)
ESR	Education for Self-reliance (Tanzania)
EU	European Union
FCC	Federal Communications Commission (US)
FCSM	Fóvárosi Csatornázási Múvek Részvénytársaság (Budapest's municipal sewer works)
FDI	foreign direct investment
FONASA	Fondo Nacional de Salud (Chile)
FSC	Forest Stewardship Council
G7	group of seven leading industrialized nations (Canada, France, Germany, Italy, Japan, UK, US)
G77	The Group of 77 (non-aligned countries)
GAAP	Generally Accepted Accounting Principles
GATS	General Agreement on Trade in Services (WTO)
GATT	General Agreement on Tariffs and Trade
GDP	gross domestic product
GDR	Democratic Republic of Germany
GE	General Electric
GEF	Global Environment Facility
GMO	genetically modified organism
GNP	gross national product
GRI	Global Reporting Initiative
GTE	General Telephone and Electronics Corporation (now part of Verizon) (US)

GTZ	Deutsche Gesellschaft für Technische Zusammenarbeit (German agency for international cooperation on sustainable development)
ha	hectares
HÁLÓZAT	Foundation for Customers in Budapest and for People with Outstanding Charges
HDR	*Human Development Report*
HMO	health maintenance organization (US)
ICEM	International Federation of Chemical, Energy, Mine and General Workers' Unions
IDA	International Development Agency
IFC	International Finance Corporation (World Bank Group)
IFI	international financial institution
IFOAM	International Federation of Organic Agriculture Movements
IFRS	International Financial Reporting Standard
ILO	International Labour Organization
IMF	International Monetary Fund
IPO	initial public offering
IRG	International Rice Genebank
IRRI	International Rice Research Institute (the Philippines)
IRS-1A	Indian Remote Sensing
ISAPREs	Instituciones de Salud Previsional (Chile)
ISEs	educational services (*instituciones de servicios educativos*) (Guatemala)
ISI	import substitution industrialization
ISS	International Space Station
IT	information technology
JFTC	Japan Fair Trade Commission
JNR	Japanese National Railways
JNRSC	JNR Settlement Corporation
JR	Japan Railway
JRCC	Japan Railway Construction Public Corporation
JTSPC	Japan Tobacco and Salt Public Corporation
KCM	Konkola and Nchanga Mines (Zambia)
KDD	Kokusai Densin Denwa Corporation
km	kilometre
l/cd	litres per capita per day
LCP	least cost planning
LED	light emitting diode
LME	London Metal Exchange
m	metres
MCO	managed care organization (US)
MDB	multilateral development bank
MDG	Millennium Development Goal
MFN	most favoured nation
MMD	Movement for Multiparty Democracy (Zambia)
MNC	multinational corporation
MPT	Ministry of Post and Telecommunications (Japan)
MSF	Management Stabilization Fund (Japan)
MSF	Médecins sans Frontières
MSNBC	Microsoft–National Broadcasting Corporation
MTS	Manitoba Telephone Systems
MWCI	Manila Water Company Inc

MWSI	Maynilad Water Services International
MWSS	Metropolitan Waterworks and Sewerage System (Manila)
NAC	National Airways Corporation
NAFTA	North American Free Trade Agreement
NBC	National Broadcasting Corporation
NCCM	Nchanga Consolidated Copper Mines (Zambia)
NEAP	Near Earth Asteroid Prospector
NGO	non-governmental organization
NIEO	New International Economic Order
NSTI	Nyegezi Social Training Institute (Tanzania)
NTT	Nippon Telegraph and Telephone Corporation
NZ	New Zealand
OBA	output-based aid
ODA	official development aid
OECD	Organisation for Economic Co-operation and Development
OED	Operations Evaluation Department (of the World Bank)
OFWAT	Office of Water (UK)
OPEC	Organization of Petroleum Exporting Countries
OPER	Operation Performance Evaluation Review
OST	Outer Space Treaty
PABSON	Private and Boarding Schools' Organization of Nepal
PARC	Provisional Commission for Administrative Reform (Japan)
PBGC	Pension Benefit Guaranty Corporation (US)
PCK	Postal Corporation of Kenya
PDD-23	Presidential Decision Directive
PDS	Partei des Demokratischen Sozialismus (Germany)
PG&E	Pacific Gas & Electric (US)
PMC	private military company
PPA	power purchasing agreement
PPP	public–private partnership
PRONADE	Programa Nacional de Autogestión para el Desarrollo Educativo (Guatemala)
PSD	private-sector development
PSI	Public Services International
PSRC	Parana school report cards (Brazil)
PTT	post and telecommunications
3R	reduction, reuse and recycling
R&D	research and development
RAFI	Rural Advancement Foundation International
RCCEs	rapid climate change events
RCM	Roan Consolidated Mines (Zambia)
ROSCO	rolling stock company
RST	Roan Selection Trust
RTC	Royal Technical College (Nairobi)
RTO	rehabilitate-transfer-operate
RWE	*formerly known as* Rheinisch-Westfälische Elektrizitätswerk AG (German Power Supplier)
SA8000	Social Accountability 8000
SAMAPA	Servicio Autonomo Municipal de Agua Potable y Alcantarillado (municipal water company, La Paz, Bolivia)

SAP	structural adjustment programme
SEC	Securities and Exchange Commission (US)
SEG	Société des Eaux de Grenoble
SERMENA	Servicio Medico Nacional de Empleados (Chile)
SGEA	Société Grenobloise de l'Eau et de l'Assainissement
SHARE	Society for Helping and Awakening Rural Poor through Education
SHC	Shinkansen Holding Corporation
SI	Sandline International (South Africa)
SI	sum insured
SNS	Servicio Nacional de Salud (Chile)
SOE	standards of engagement
SOE	state-owned enterprise
SPC	special purpose corporation
SPD	Sozialdemokratische Partei Deutschlands (Germany)
TEAL	Tasman Empire Airways Limited
TI	Transparency International
TNC	transnational corporation
TOC	train operating company
TPG	Dutch Postal Service
TRIMS	Trade-related Investment Measures
TRIPS	Agreement on Trade-related Aspects of Intellectual Property Rights
TVA	Tennessee Valley Authority (US)
UCLAS	University College of Lands and Architectural Studies (Tanzania)
UDSM	University of Dar es Salaam
UK	United Kingdom
UMPC	Union Miniere Pirdop Copper (Bulgaria)
UNCTAD	United Nations Conference on Trade and Development
UNDP	United Nations Development Programme
UNEP	United Nations Environment Programme
UNESCO	United Nations Educational, Scientific and Cultural Organization
UNIP	United National Independence Party (Zambia)
UPE	universal primary education
US	United States
USAID	United States Agency for International Development
UTH	University Teaching Hospital (Zambia)
UTL	Uganda Telecom
WBCSD	World Business Council for Sustainable Development
WHO	World Health Organization
WIPO	World Intellectual Property Organization
WSSD	World Summit for Sustainable Development (Johannesburg)
WTO	World Trade Organization
ZCCM	Zambia Consolidated Copper Mines
ZESCO	Zambia Electricity Supply Company

References

Aalborg Charter (1994) *Aalborg Charter of European Cities and Towns towards Sustainability*, www.iclei.org/ICLEI/la21.htm

AARP (American Association of Retired Persons) (2003) *The Policy Book*. Washington, DC: AARP

Abla, Z. (2003) 'Confronting the fiscal crisis through privatization'. In: Social Watch (ed) *Social Watch Report 2003: The Poor and the Market*. Montevideo, Uruguay: The Third World Institute–Social Watch

ACLU (American Civil Liberties Union) (1997) 'Cashing in on black prisoners', http://archive.aclu.org/news/w093097a.html

Adam, C., Cavendish, W. and Mistry, P. S. (1992) *Adjusting Privatization: Case Studies from Developing Countries*. London: James Currey

Afrol (2003) 'More public funds for Tanzanian water supplier', *afrol News*, 28 May, www.afrol.com

Ahrens, J. (2002) *Governance and Economic Development: A Comparative Institutional Approach*. Cheltenham and Northampton: Edward Elgar

Air New Zealand (2004) *Air New Zealand: History*. Air New Zealand Ltd

Akande, W. (2002) 'Water privatization in Africa', www.YellowTimes.org Alternative News and Views, Thursday, 6 June

Alley, R. B. (2000) *The Two-Mile Time Machine: Ice Cores, Abrupt Climate Change, and Our Future*. Princeton: Princeton University Press

Amuzegar, J. (1999) *Managing the Oil Wealth: OPEC's Windfalls and Pitfalls*. London and New York: Tauris

Andvig, J. C., Fjeldstad, O.-H., Amundsen, I., Sissner, T. and Soreide, T. (2000) *Research on Corruption: A Policy Oriented Survey*. Report commissioned by NORAD, collaborative work between Chr. Michelsen Institute and NUPI, CMI, Bergen, wwwuser.gwdg.de/~uwvw/ downloads/contribution07_andvig.pdf

Anheier, H. K. (ed) (2004) *Civil Society: Measurement and Policy Dialogue*. London: Earthscan

Arevalo-Correa, C. (2000) 'El Alto Pilot Project: the microcredit component'. Washington, DC: Programa de Agua y Saneamiento, PNUD–World Bank

Arteaga, A. M. (2003) 'The brutal rationale of privatization'. In: Social Watch (ed) *Social Watch Report 2003: The Poor and the Market*. Montevideo, Uruguay: The Third World Institute–Social Watch

Associated Press (2001) 'Davis seeks long-term energy contracts to resolve crisis', *North County Times*, 10 January, www.nctimes.com

Associated Press (2002) 'Regulators, PG&E creditors OK deal', 22 August

Augustus, T. (1997) 'Pakistan power needs and environment', *TED Case Studies*, Vol. 7, No. 1, www.american.edu/TED/pakpower.htm

Avrillier, R. (1996) 'ADES, Eau de Grenoble: autopsie d'un 'Waterl'Eau'! Grenoble'. Unpublished manuscript

Ayres, I. and Braithwaite, J. (1992) *Responsive Regulation: Transcending the Deregulation Debate*. Oxford: Oxford University Press

Bagdikian, B. H. (2000) *The Media Monopoly*, sixth edition. Boston: Beacon Press, ppxx–xxi

Baijal, P. (2002) 'Privatisation: compulsions and options for economic reform', *Economic and Political Weekly*, 12 October

Baker, P. (2001) 'Tito plans to promote space tourism', *Washington Post*, 9 May, A26

Bakker, K. (2004) *An Uncooperative Commodity: Privatizing Water in England and Wales*. Oxford: Oxford University Press

Bardhan, P. (1997) 'Corruption and development: a review of issues', *Journal of Economic Literature*, Vol. 35, No. 3, September, pp1320–1346

Barnett, S. (2000) 'Evidence on the fiscal and macroeconomic impact of privatization', IMF Working paper, July. Washington, DC: International Monetary Fund

Barrientos, A. and Lloyd-Sherlock, P. (2000) 'Reforming health insurance in Argentina and Chile', *Health Policy and Planning*, Vol. 15, No. 4, pp417–423, Oxford University Press

Baskakov, V. N. and Baskakov, M. E. (1997) *On Pensions for Men and Women*. Moscow: MFF

Bayliss, K. (2001) *Water Privatisation in Africa: Lessons from Three Case Studies*. Report of the Public Services International Research Unit, University of Greenwich, UK, May

Bayliss, K. (2002) 'Water privatisation in sub-Saharan Africa: progress, problems and policy implications'. Paper presented at Development Studies Association Annual Conference, University of Greenwich, November, pp12–13

Bayliss, K. and Hall, D. (2001) 'A PSIRU response to the World Bank's Private Sector Development Strategy', Public Services International Research Unit, October

BBC News Online (2002) 'Patent to protect ancient knowledge', 19 February, http://news.bbc.co.uk/1/hi/in_depth/sci_tech/2002/boston_2002/1828438.stm

BDWS (Bundesverband Deutscher Wach- und Sicherheitsunternehmen e. V.) (2003) 'Aktuell vom 07.11.2001: Bundeskabinett beschließt neuen Rechtsrahmen für privates Sicherheitsgewerbe', BDWS, www.bdws.de/3.aktuellarchiv04.htm (accessed 30 April 2003)

Beck, U. (1998) 'Weltbürger aller Länder, vereinigt euch! Demokratie jenseits des Nationalstaates: Europa muß den Anfang machen. Thesen für ein kosmopolitisches Manifest', *DIE ZEIT*, Archiv 30, www.zeit.de/archiv/1998/30/199830.t_kosmo_.xml

Beck, U. (2000) *What is Globalization?* Cambridge, UK: Polity Press.

Bellinghausen, H. (2002) 'US, world and transnational agencies want to clear indigenous out of Montes Azules', *La Jornada*, 25 March, 2002

Benson, J. (1998) *Property rights in Space*, International Astronautical Federation's 41st International Colloquium on the Law of Outer Space, 29 September, www.spacedev.com/media/papers/98-09-29_IISL-98-IISL.1.05.html (accessed 14 November 2001)

Berg, E. J. (ed) (2000) *Aid and Failed Reforms: The Case of Public Sector Management. Foreign Aid and Development. Lessons Learnt and Directions for the Future*. London: Routledge

Bernhardt, H. (1996) 'Kurzstatement aus der Sicht eines Polizeipraktikers'. In: R. Weiss and M. Plate (eds) *Privatisierung von polizeilichen Aufgaben*, pp57-62

Beste, H. (1996) 'DFG-Projekt Wahrnehmung von Sicherheits- und Ordnungsfunktionen im öffentlichen Raum durch private Sicherheitsdienste'. In: R. Weiss and M. Plate (eds) *Privatisierung von polizeilichen Aufgaben*, pp111–117

Bhagwati, J. N. (ed) (1977) *The New International Economic Order: The North-South Debate*. Cambridge, MA: MIT Press

Bigler, R. (2002) 'Stock market slump bleeding traditional pension funds; unions can expect battles over pension costs at the bargaining table', *LRA Online*, 17 October, www.laborresearch.org/page_src.php?id=238&src=bigler (accessed April 2004)

Bijlmakers, L. and Lindner. M. (2003) *The World Bank's Private Sector Development Strategy: Key Issues and Risks*. Amsterdam: WEMOS

Birdsall, N. and Nellis, J. (2002) *Winners and Losers: Assessing the Distributional Impact of Privatization*. Washington, DC: Center for Global Development

Birdsall, N. and Nellis, J. (2003) 'Winners and losers: assessing the distributional impact of privatization'. *World Development*, Vol. 31, No. 10 (October), pp1617–1633

Bleischwitz, R. (2003) 'Governance of eco-efficiency in Japan: an institutional approach', *Internationales Asienforum/International Asian Quarterly*, Vol. 34, No. 1–2, pp107–126

Bleischwitz, R. (2004) 'Governance of sustainable development: co-evolution of political and corporate strategies', *International Journal of Sustainable Development*, Vol. 7, No. 1, pp27–43

Bleischwitz, R. and Hennicke, P. (eds) (2004) *Eco-Efficiency, Regulation and Sustainable Business: Towards a Governance Structure for Sustainable Development*. Cheltenham and Northampton: Edward Elgar

Boehm, F. and Polanco, J. (2003) *Corruption and Privatisation of Infrastructure in Developing Countries*. Transparency International's Integrity Pacts and Public Contracting Programme, Working Paper No. 1, www.transparency.org/integrity_pact/resources/working_papers/wk1_boehm_polanco.html

Bogumil, J. (2000) 'Staatsaufgaben im Wandel', In *Der Staat*. Ideengeschichtliche Grundlagen, Wandel der Aufgaben, Stellung des Bürgers, hg. v. Uwe Andersen e.a. (Politische Bildung 2000, Jahrgang 34, Bd. 3.), pp28–40

Bortolotti, B. and Fiorentini, G. (1999) *Organized Interests and Self-regulation: An Economic Approach*. Oxford: Oxford University Press

Botelho, A. and Addis, C. (1997) 'Privatization of telecommunications in Mexico'. In: R. Van der Hoeven and G. Sziraczki (eds) (1997) *Lessons from Privatization*. Geneva: International Labour Organization, pp71ff

Böttger, C. (2002) 'Das Insolvenzverfahren der Railtrack', *Internationales Verkehrswesen*, Vol. 6, pp274–277

Bradshaw, B. (2001) 'Lessons from a railway privatization experiment', *Japan Railway & Transport Review*, No. 29, pp4–11, www.jrtr.net/jrtr29/pdf/f04_bra.pdf (accessed 17 May 2003)

Braham, L. (2001) 'Special report: how to retire', *BusinessWeek online*, 30 July, www.businessweek.com:/print/magazine/content/01_31/b3743608.htm?mz (accessed May 2003)

Bruno, M. and Sachs, J. D. (1985) *Economics of Worldwide Stagflation*. Cambridge, MA: Harvard University Press

Buchanan, J. M. and Musgrave, R. A. (1999) *Public Finance and Public Choice: Two Contrasting Visions of the State*. Cambridge; London: MIT Press

Bull, H. (1977) *The Anarchical Society: A Study of Order in World Politics*. New York: Columbia University Press

Business Line (2001) 'Basmati battle won, not lost', 22 August, www.hvk.org/articles/0801/129.html

Bussoletti, E. (2000) 'Environment impact'. In: A. Pompidou (ed) *The Ethics of Space Policy*. Paris: UNESCO World Commission on the Ethics of Scientific Knowledge and Technology (COMEST) and European Space Agency (ESA), June, p46

Butzlaff, M. E., Kurz, G. K., Käufer, K. (1998) 'Managed Care im Brennpunkt', *Das Gesundheitswesen*, Vol. 60, pp279–281

Calcott, P. and Walls, M. (2000) 'Can downstream waste disposal policies encourage upstream "design for environment"', *American Economic Review*, Vol. 90, No. 2, pp233–237

California Independent System Operator (2001) Data sheet, www.caiso.com/docs/2001/03/22/2001032214552322811.pdf (accessed 14 September 2004)

California Public Utility Commission (2002) 'Historical information on electric markets', www.cpuc.ca.gov/static/industry/electric/electric+markets/historical+information/index.htm (accessed 14 September 2004)

Camdessus, M. (2003) *Financing Water for All*. Report of the World Panel on Financing Water Infrastructure, Chaired by Michel Camdessus

Campaign for Press and Broadcasting Freedom (2001) 'Response to Consultation on Media Ownership Rules by DCMS and DTI', November. Campaign for Press and Broadcasting Freedom, http://keywords.dsvr.co.uk/freepress/body.phtml?id=156&category=policies&finds=0&string=&strand=

Cap Gemini Ernst & Young (ed) (2002) 'Versandhandel mit Arzneimitteln in den USA: ein Modell für Deutschland?' Berlin: Cap Gemini Ernst Young, www.de.capgemini.com/servlet/PB/menu/1001426/index.html (accessed 15 November 2004)

Carnegie Council on Ethics and International Affairs and Friedrich Ebert Foundation (2003) *Privatization and GATS: A Threat to Development?* New York: Carnegie Council on Ethics and International Affairs and Friedrich Ebert Foundation

Carter, T. S. (1997) 'The failure of environmental regulation in New York: the role of co-optation, corruption and a cooperative enforcement approach', *Crime Law and Social Change*, Vol. 26, No. 1, pp27–52

CCA (Corrections Corporation of America) (2004) 'The corrections industry', www.correctionscorp.com/researchfindings.html

Center for Strategic and International Studies (2002) 'The IMF and the World Bank', Centre for Strategic and International Studies, www.globalization101.org/issue/imfworldbank/5.asp (accessed June 2004)

CERFE (2003) *Glocalization: Research study and Policy Recommendations*. Rome: CERFE in cooperation with the Glocal Forum and the Think Tank on Glocalization, May, www.glocalforum.org/New_Glocal_Website/downloads/ttank/full.pdf

Chambre Régionale des Comptes Rhône-Alpes (1995) 'Observations définitives de la gestion des services de l'eau et de assainement de la commune de Grenoble (Isère)', 24 November, pp25–26, http://eausecours.free.fr/juris/chambre/crc24111995.html (accessed 11 November 2003)

Chong, A. and López-de-Silanes, F. (2002) 'Privatization and labor force restructuring around the world', World Bank Policy Research Working Paper No. 2884, September

Chong, A. and López-de-Silanes, F. (2003) *The Truth about Privatization in Latin America*. IADB Research Network Working Paper No. R486

Choudry, A. (2003) 'Conservation International: privatizing nature, plundering biodiversity', *Seedling*, October, www.grain.org/seedling/?type=36

CIEPAC (1999) 'Genetically modified organisms: implications for Mexico and Chiapas', *Chiapas al Dia,* No. 175, 18 September, www.ciepac.org/bulletins/ingles/Ing175.html

Clark, G. and Sohn, L. B. (1958) *World Peace through World Law*. Cambridge: Harvard University Press

Clarke, G. and Xu, L. (2002) *Ownership, Competition, and Corruption: Bribe Takers versus Bribe Payers*. Washington, DC: World Bank

cms-info (Chiltern Magazine Services) (2003) 'KDDI Corporation: a downloadable web report', www.biz-lib.com/ZPB2230.html

Coase, R. (1974) 'The lighthouse in economics', *Journal of Law and Economics*, Vol. 17(2), pp357–376

Cohausz, D. (2001) 'Endstation Pflegeheim', *Handelsblatt*, 14 August, p10

Commission on Global Governance (1995) *Our Global Neighborhood: The Report of the Commission on Global Governance*. Oxford: Oxford University Press

Consumer Reports (1996) 'How good is your plan?' *Consumer Reports*. August, 246–250

Contra Costa Times (2004) '$84 million PG&E pay on the way', 3 January

Cook, P. and Uchida, Y. (2003) 'Privatization and economic growth in developing countries', *The Journal of Development Studies*, Vol. 39, No. 6 (August), pp121–154

Cooper, L. A. (2003) 'Encouraging space exploration through a new application of space property rights', *Space Policy*, Vol. 19, Issue 2, May, pp111–118

Cooper, R. N. (1987) *The International Monetary System: Essays in World Economics*. Cambridge: MIT Press

Corral, B. and Hall, D. (2001) *FDI Linkages and Infrastructure: Some Problem Cases in Water And Energy*. London: Public Services International Research Unit

Crespo, C. and Laurie, N. (2002) 'An examination of the changing contexts for developing pro-poor water initiatives via concessions', Final report SSR Project R7895. Newcastle: Newcastle University (UK)/CESU San Simon University (Bolivia)

Cronkite, W. (2000) 'Walter Cronkite on the media – and The Media Channel', Media Channel.org, 3 February, www.mediachannel.org/originals/cronkite.shtml

CRS (Congressional Research Service) (2002) *The Enron Bankruptcy and Employer Stock in Retirement Plans*. Washington, DC: CRS

Culp, R. F. (1997/1998) 'Privatization of prisons: the public policy debate', www.geocities.com/CapitolHill/Lobby/6465/topic.html

Cutler, C. A. (2003) *Private Power and Global Authority: Transnational Merchant Law in the Global Political Economy*. Cambridge: Cambridge University Press

Dahl, R. A. (1989) *Democracy and Its Critics*. New Haven: Yale University Press

The Daily News of Los Angeles (2001) 'State power woes grow', 20 January

Datta-Mitra, J. (1997) *Fiscal Management in Adjustment Lending*. Washington, DC: OED, World Bank

David, L. (2001) 'Beyond Tito: space travelers wanted', *SpaceNews*, 1 May

DB AG (Deutsche Bahn Aktiengesellschaft) (ed) (2003) *Daten und Fakten 2000–2003*. Berlin: DB AG

de Soto, H. (2000) *The Mystery of Capital: Why Capitalism Triumphs in the West and Fails Everywhere Else*. New York: Basic Books

de Tocqueville, A. (1835; republished in 2004) *Democracy in America*. New York: Library of America

Departamento de Informática de PRONADE (2003) www.mineduc.gob.gt/administracion/dependencias/Centrales/pronade/pronade_anexo.htm#cobertura_pronade

Deppe, H.-U. (1993) 'Gesundheitspolitik in Europa und den USA', *Arbeit und Sozialpolitik*, Vol. 47, pp41–46

Devraj, R. (2001) '"Basmati" patent win not final, say food security experts', Third World Network, www.twnside.org.sg/title/basmati.htm

Dietz, T., Ostrom, E. and Stern, P. (2003) 'The struggle to govern the commons', *Science*, Vol. 302, 12 December, pp1907–1911

Dror, Y. (2001) *The Capacity to Govern*. A Report to the Club of Rome. London and Portland, Oregon: Frank Cass

Drugs for Neglected Diseases Working Group (ed) (2001) *Fatal Imbalance: The Crisis in Research and Development for Drugs for Neglected Diseases*. Geneva: Médecins Sans Frontières Access to Essential Medicines Campaign and the Drugs for Neglected Diseases Working Group

Dubash, N. K., Bouille, D., Clark, A. et al (2002) *Power Politics: Equity and Environment in Electricity Reform*. Washington, DC: World Resources Institute

Dyck, A. (2001) 'Privatization and corporate governance: principles, evidence, and future challenges', *The World Bank Research Observer*, Vol. 16, No. 1, Spring, pp59–84

EBRD (European Bank for Reconstruction and Development) (1999) 'Budapest Waste Water Services privatisation', 23 April, www.ebrd.com/projects/psd/index.htm (accessed 26 May 2003)

EBRD (2003) 'Budapest Waste Water Services privatisation: summary of the Operation Performance Evaluation Review', July

ECIS (European Centre for Infrastructure Studies) (ed) (1996) *The State of European Infrastructure, 1996*. Rotterdam: ECIS

Economic Policy Institute (2003) 'Retirement security: facts at a glance'. Washington, DC: Economic Policy Institute, www.epinet.org/content.cfm/issueguides_retirement_facts (accessed April 2004)

The Economist (1997) 'Financial Indicators: Privatization', 22 March, p125

Econstats (2004) 'Stock markets: Dow Jones Industrial Average – 30 stocks, US monthly', www.econstats.com/eqty/eq_em2.csv (accessed 14 September 2004)

Ericson, E. (1996) 'Shuttlebucks', *Metro*, 23 May, www.metroactive.com/papers/metro/05.23.96/nasa-9621.html

Erklärung von Bern (1998) 'Fürstlicher Profit auf Kosten indischer Reisbauern', www.evb.ch/index.cfm?page_id=223&yy=1999

Ernst, J. (1998) 'Privatization'. In: J. M. Shafritz (ed) *International Encyclopedia of Public Policy and Administration*, Vol. 3, pp1741–1744, Boulder, CO: Westview Press

Esguerra, J. (2001) 'The corporate muddle of Manila's water concessions: how the world's biggest and most successful privatisation turned into a failure'. Manila: Institute for Popular Democracy

European Community (1998) 'Directive 98/44/EC of the European Parliament and of the Council of 6 July 1998 on the legal protection of biotechnological inventions', *Official Journal* L 213, 30 July 1998, pp0013-0021

European Patent Office (2004) *Espace Access*, DVD-Rom, Vol. 2004/1 (January), München

Evans-Clock, C. and Samorodov, A. (2000) 'The employment impact of privatization and enterprise restructuring in selected transition economies'. Interdepartmental Action Programme on Privatization, Restructuring and Economic Democracy – Working Paper IPPRED-16. Geneva: ILO

Families USA Foundation (1997) 'Comparing Medicare HMOs: do they keep their members?' Washington, DC: Families USA Foundation, December, www.familiesusa.org/site/PageServer?pagename=media_reports_mhmo1#planc (accessed 15 November 2004)

Faure, M. and Skogh, G. (2003) *The Economic Analysis of Environmental Policy and Law: An Introduction*. Cheltenham/Northampton: Edward Elgar

Fay, M. and Yepes, T. (2003) 'Investing in infrastructure: what is needed from 2000 to 2010?', World Bank Policy Research Working Paper 3102. Washington, D.C: World Bank

FCSM–Budapest Sewage Works Co Ltd (2003) *Business Report 2002*. Budapest: FCSM Rt

Fein, R. (1998a) 'Can HMOs be fixed?', *Dissent*, Vol. 45, No. 2, pp67–73. New York: Foundation for the Study of Independent Social Ideas

Fein, R. (1998b) 'The HMO revolution: how it happened, what it means', *Dissent*, Vol. 45, No. 1, pp29–36. New York: Foundation for the Study of Independent Social Ideas

Ferroni, M. and Mody, A. (eds) (2002) *International Public Goods: Incentives, Measurement, and Financing*. Dordecht: Kluwer

FIEL (Fundación de Investigaciones Económicas Latinoamericanas) (2002) 'Los servicios públicos en Argentina: balance de los 1990s', FIEL, http://24.232.76.6/server1/cursos/regul/fiel02/pres1.pdf (accessed 20 April 2004)

Finger, M. (2001) 'Angepasste Wasserprojekte: Schweizer Export-Schlager', *epd-Entwicklungspolitik*, No. 20/21/2001

Finger, M. and Allouche, J. (2002) *Water Privatisation: Trans-national Corporations and the Re-regulation of the Water Industry*. London and New York: Spon Press

Finnemore, M. (1996) *National Interests in International Society*. Ithaca: Cornell University Press

FitzRoy, F. R. and Smith, I. (1999) 'Season tickets and the demand for public transport', *Kyklos*, Vol. 52, pp219–238.

Florini, A. M. (ed) (2000) *The Third Force: The Rise of Transnational Civil Society*. Tokyo: Japan Centre for International Exchange

Foerster, S. R. and Macgraw, P. A. (2002) *Air New Zealand: The Recapitalization Decision*. Ivey School of Business, The University of Ontario

Foster, V. (2001) 'Water and Sanitation Program, Andean Region: economic and financial evaluation of El Alto Pilot Project'. Washington, DC: The World Bank Group

The Foundation for Taxpayer and Consumer Rights (2000) 'Factsheet: the history of the deregulation debacle', 8 December, www.consumerwatchdog.org

Franceys, R. (2001) 'Why should governments serve the poor?', *Id21 Research Highlight*, 12 June

Francis, J. (1993) *The Politics of Regulation: A Comparative Perspective*. London: Blackwell Publishers

Freeman, C. (1998) 'The economics of technical change'. In: D. Archibugie and J. Michie (eds) *Trade, Growth and Technical Change*. Cambridge: Cambridge University Press, pp16–54

Friedman, M. (1962) *Capitalism and Freedom*. Chicago: University of Chicago Press

Friedrich Naumann Foundation (ed) (2001) 'Newsletter Internationaler Politikdialog "Die amerikanische Gesundheitspolitik"'. Washington, DC: Friedrich Naumann Foundation, www.fnstusa.org/GesNews.pdf (accessed 15 November 2004)

Fujii, Y. (2001) (Japanese Book about a Japanese Lawyer). Tokyo: Kettei Publishers

Fukuyama, F. (1992) *The End of History*. New York: Free Press

Fung, A. and Wright, E. O. (eds) (2003) *Deepening Democracy: Institutional Innovations in Empowered Participatory Governance*. Real Utopias Project Series. London: Verso

Gabel, H. L. and Sinclair-Desgagné, B. (1998) 'The firm, its routines and the environment'. In: T. Tietenberg and H. Folmer (eds) *The International Yearbook of Environmental and Resource Economics 1998/1999*. Cheltenham/Northampton: Edward Elgar, pp89–118

Galiani, S. and Petrecolla, D. (2000) 'The Argentine privatization process and its aftermath: some preliminary conclusions'. In: M. H. Birch and J. Haar (eds) *The Impact of Privatization in the Americas*. Coral Gables, FL: University of Miami, North-South Center Press

GAO (United States General Accounting Office) (2001) *Private Pensions: Issues of Coverage and Increasing Contribution Limits for Defined Contribution Plans*. GAO-01-846. Washington, DC: GAO

GAO (2002a) *Key Issues To Consider Following the Enron Collapse*. GAO-02-480T, Washington, DC: GAO

GAO (2002b) *Retirement Income: Intergenerational Comparisons of Wealth and Future Income*. GAO-03-429. Washington, DC: GAO

Gapski, J. and Hollmann, R. (2000) 'Reform der Kommunalverwaltung. Mehr Bürgerorientierung durch aufgabenspezifische Leitbilder?' agis Info No. 10, June, pp5–8, www.agis.uni-hannover.de/agisinfo/info10/art02.pdf

Gauri, V. (1998) *School Choice in Chile: Two Decades of Educational Reform*. Pittsburgh, PA: University of Pittsburgh Press

German Bundestag (2002a) *Study Commission on Globalization of the World Economy: Challenges and Responses*. Summary of the final report, www.bundestag.de/parlament/kommissionen/archiv/welt/sb_glob_kurz_en.pdf (accessed 14 September 2004)

German Bundestag (ed) (2002b) *Schlussbericht der Enquete Kommission Globalisierung der Weltwirtschaft*. Opladen: Leske+Buderich

German Federal Statistics Office (2003) *Umweltstatistische Erhebungen. Abfallaufkommen*, www.destatis.de/basis/d/umw/umwtab1.php (accessed 10 September 2004)

Gerstberger, T. and Graack, C. (2003) 'Competition and deregulation in the Japanese telecommunications network industry', www.euroeiiw.de/telekom/db38.html

Gillis, M., Perkins, D. H., Roemer, M. and Snodgrass, D. R. (1996) *Economics of Development*. New York: W.W. Norton & Company

Gonzalez-Rossetti, A. and Chuaqui, T. (2000) *Enhancing the Political Feasibility of Health Reform: The Chile Case*. LACHSR, www.lachsr.org/documents/enhancingthepoliticalfeasibilityofhealthreformthechileancase-EN.pdf (accessed 8 November 2004)

Göpfert, C.-J. (1999) 'Private Hilfspolizisten haben sich bei Falschparkern nicht bewährt', *Frankfurter Rundschau*, 30 September

Gould, E. (2002) 'Draft TACD background paper on trade in services'. London: Trans Atlantic Consumer Dialogue (TACD), October

Grieco, J. M. (1990) *Cooperation among Nations: Europe, America, and Nontariff Barriers to Trade*. Ithaca: Cornell University Press

Grossman, K. (2001) 'Disgrace into Space', *The Ecologist*, March, http://home.earthlink.net/~envirovideo/karldisgrace.html (accessed 2 November 2001)

Grote, J. R. and Gbikpi, B. (eds) (2002) *Participatory Governance*. Opladen: Leske und Budrich

Gruber, L. (2000) *Ruling the World: Power Politics and the Rise of Supranational Institutions*. Princeton: Princeton University Press

GTZ (Gesellschaft für Technische Zusammenarbeit) (2003) *Privatsektorbeteiligungen im Wassersektor*. Bericht an das Bundesministerium für wirtschaftliche Zusammenarbeit und Entwicklung, Eschborn (non-public)

Gupta, N. (2002) 'Partial privatization and firm performance: evidence from India', William Davidson Working Paper 426, December

Gyohten, T. and Volcker, P. (1992) *Changing Fortunes: The World's Money and the Threat to American Leadership*. New York and Toronto: Times Books

Hall, D. and Lobina, E. (1999) *Water and Privatisation in Central and Eastern Europe*. Paper presented at a PSI conference on the water industry, Bulgaria, October 1999, and an OTV conference on the water industry, Essen, Germany, October 1999, www.psiru.org/reports/9909b-W-CEE.doc (accessed 28 May 2003)

Hall, D. and Lobina, E. (2001) 'Private to public: international lessons of water remunicipalization in Grenoble, France'. Paper presented at the AWRA conference, University of Dundee, 6–8 August, www.psiru.org/reports/2001-08-W-Grenoble.doc (accessed 7 May 2001)

Hanna, N. (2002) 'Promising Approaches to Development Challenges'. In: N. Hanna and R. Picciotto (eds) *Making Development Work: Development Learning in a World of Poverty and Wealth*. Washington, DC: World Bank, pp285–310

Hardin, G. (1968) 'The tragedy of the commons', *Science*, Vol. 162, December, pp1243–1248

Hardin, R. (1982) *Collective Action*. Baltimore: Johns Hopkins University Press

Harris, C. (2003) 'Private participation in infrastructure in developing countries: trends, impacts, and policy lessons'. Washington, DC: World Bank

Hass-Clau, C. and Environmental and Transport Planning (1998) *Rail Privatisation: Britain and Germany Compared*. London: Anglo-German Foundation for the Study of Industrial Society

Haufler, V. (1993) 'Crossing the Boundary between Public and Private. International Regimes and Non-State Actors'. In: V. Rittberger (ed) *Regime Theory and International Relations*. Oxford: Clarendon, pp94–111

Haufler, V. (2001) *A Public Role for the Private Sector: Industry Self-Regulation in a Global Economy*. Washington, DC: Carnegie Endowment for International Peace

Haufler, V. (2003) 'Globalization and industry self-regulation'. In: M. Kahler and D. A. Lake (eds) *Governance in a Global Economy: Political Authority in Transition*. Princeton: Princeton University Press, pp226–252

Hawley, S. (2000) 'Briefing 19: exporting corruption: privatisation, multinationals and bribery', *The Corner House,* Vol. 400, No. 19, www.icaap.org/iuicode?400.19

Hechinger, J. (2002) 'Once high-flying 401(k)s pale beside payouts from pensions', *Wall Street Journal,* 16 August, www.laborresearch.org/page_src.php?id=217&src=Hechinger (accessed April 2004)

Henriot, P. (2003) *The Challenge of Improving Zambia's Debt Contraction Process: A Review of the Special Jubilee-Zambia Research Report*. Lusaka, Zambia

Henry, C. (ed) (2001) *Regulation of Network Utilities: The European Experience*. Oxford: Oxford University Press

Héritier, A. (ed) (2002) *Common Goods: Reinventing European and International Governance*. London: Rowman & Littlefield Publishers

Hertz, N. (2002) *The Silent Takeover: Global Capitalism and the Death of Democracy*. London: Arrow Books

Himmelstein, D. U., Woolhandler, S., Hellander, I. and Wolfe, S. M. (1999) 'Quality of care in investor-owned vs not-for-profit HMOs', *JAMA,* 14 July, Vol. 281, No. 2, pp159–163

Hinz, R. (2000) 'Overview of the United States private pension system'. In: Organisation for Economic Co-operation and Development (OECD) *Private Pension Systems and Policy Issues*. Paris: OECD, pp23–40

Hitt, J. (2001) 'The next battlefield may be in outer space', *New York Times Magazine,* 5 August, www.nytimes.com

Hoering, U. (2003) 'Was nun, Weltbank? Oder: Lesson learned? Mehr Privatisierung und Großprojekte oder Förderung öffentlicher Unternehmen und dezentraler Lösungsansätze', *Global Issue Paper Water*. Berlin: Heinrich Böll Stiflung, www.boell.de/de/04_thema/2090.html (accessed 15 November 2004)

Holst, J. (2001a) *Krankenversicherung in Chile: Ein Modell für andere Länder?* Lage, Germany: Jacobs

Holst, J. (2001b) 'Private Krankenversicherer schreiben rote Zahlen'. In: *Chancen in Emerging Markets: Gesundheitswesen: Perspektiven für private Unternehmen*. S.139-144. Frankfurt am Main, Germany: FAZ-Institut

Hoover's online (2003) 'Nippon Telegraph and Telephone Corporation', www.hoovers.com/ntt/--ID__41780--/free-co-factsheet.xhtml

Hope, R. (2002) 'Accidents raise fears about Britain's fragmented railway', *Japan Railway & Transport Review* No. 33, pp32–40, www.jrtr.net/jrtr33/pdf/f32_hop.pdf (accessed 17 May 2003)

Hornig, F. (2003) 'Hinhalten und Zermürben', *Der Spiegel*, Vol. 25, pp92–93

Hsiao, W. (2000) 'What should macro-economists know about health care policy: a primer', *IMF Working Paper* WP/00/136, International Monetary Fund

Huber, F. (2000) *Wahrnehmung von Aufgaben im Bereich der Gefahrenabwehr durch das Sicherheits- und Bewachungsgewerbe. Eine rechtsvergleichende Untersuchung zu Deutschland und den USA*. Schriften zum öffentlichen Recht, Bd. 806. Berlin: Duncker & Humblot

IFC (International Finance Corporation) (2003) 'Basic facts about IFC', IFC, www.ifc.org/about (accessed June 2004)

IFOAM (International Federation of Organic Agriculture Movements) (2000a) '4-Patents: background paper on the neem patent challenge', www.gene.ch/genet/2000/May/msg00009.html

IFOAM (2000b) 'Press release: neem patent revoked!!!: Major victory against biopiracy', www.ifoam.org/press/ win_final_neu.html

ILO (International Labour Organization) (1999a) *Decent Work*. Report by the General for the International Labour Conference 87th Session, www.logos-net/ilo/150_base/en/publ/017_2.htm

ILO (1999b) *World Employment Report 1998–1999. Women and Training in the Global Economy*. Geneva: ILO

ILO (2001) *World Employment Report 2001*. Geneva: ILO

ILO (2003) *Global Employment Trends 2003*. Geneva: ILO

ILO (2004) *Global Employment Trends 2004*. Geneva: ILO

Imashiro, M. (1997) 'Changes in Japan's transport market and JNR privatization, Japanese railway history 12', *Japan Railway & Transport Review*, No. 13, pp50–53, www.jrtr.net/jrtr13/his_13.html (accessed 4 April 2003)

Inter-American Development Bank (ed) (2002) *Latin American Economic Policies*, Vol. 18

Internet Systems Consortium (2004) 'ISC Internet Domain Survey', www.isc.org/index.pl?/ops/ds/ (accessed 9 December 2004)

Irwin, T. (2003) 'Public money for private infrastructure: deciding when to offer guarantees, output-based subsidies and other fiscal supports', *World Bank Working Paper* No. 10. Washington, DC: World Bank

Islam, A. and Monsalve, C. (2002) *Privatization: A Panacea or a Palliative*. Bangkok: UN ESCAP

ISSER (Institute of Statistical, Social and Economic Research) (2002) 'The state of the Ghanaian economy in 2001'. Legon: University of Ghana, www.isser.org/sger2001overview.pdf

ITU (International Telecommunication Union) (2003) *World Telecommunication Indicators Database*, seventh edition. Geneva: ITU

Iwasaki, T. (1998) 'Struggle against the attempts to divide and "reorganize" the NTT with the aim of advancing into international telecommunications', *Rodo-Soken Journal* No. 24, July, www.yuiyuidori.net/soken/jour/j_24.html

Jack, W. (2000) 'Health insurance reform in four Latin American countries: theory and practise', *Policy Research Working Papers*, World Bank, www.eldis.org/static/DOC8206.htm (accessed 14 September 2004)

Jacobs, J. (1992) *Systems of Survival: A Dialogue on the Moral Foundations of Commerce and Politics*. New York: Random House

James, B. (2002) 'Doubts rise about guards-for-hire', *International Herald Tribune*, 10 January, www.iht.com/articles/44326.html (accessed 26 June 2003)

Jimenez, P. R. (2004) *Celebrating Participatory Governance in Nueva Vizcaya*. Manila: De La Salle University, Social Development Research Center

Johnston, N. (1998) 'The implications of the Basle Conventions for Developing Countries: the case of trade in non-ferrous metal-bearing waste', *Resources, Conservation and Recycling*, Vol. 23, pp1–28

Johnston, S. and Cordes, J. (2003) 'Public good or commercial opportunity? Case studies in remote sensing commercialisation', *Space Policy*, Vol. 19, Issue 1, February, pp23–31

Joshi, G. (2000) 'Overview of privatization in South Asia'. In: G. Joshi (ed) *Privatization in South Asia: Minimizing Negative Social Effects through Restructuring*. Geneva: International Labour Organization (ILO), pp1–8

Jost, T. S. (1998) 'Gesundheitsreform: Lehren aus den amerikanischen Erfahrungen', *Recht und Politik im Gesundheitswesen* (RPG), Vol. 4, No. 1/2, pp45–53

Kagan, R. (2003) *Of Paradise and Power*. New York: Knopf

Kahn, M. and Lynch, L. (2000) *California's Electricity Options and Challenges*. Report to Governor Gray Davis, California Public Utility Commission, 2 August

Kalotay, K. and Hunya, G. (2000) 'Privatization and FDI in Central and Eastern Europe', *Transnational Corporations*, Vol. 9, No. 1, April, pp39–66

Kangwa, J. (2001) *Mining and Society: Privatization and Social Management*. Kitwe, Zambia: African Institute of Corporate Citizenship

Kangwa, S. (2001) *Report on the Privatization of Zambia Consolidated Copper Mines*. Kitwe, Zambia: The Copperbelt University, www.iied.org/mmsd/mmsd_pdfs/SthAfrica_word_PPT/07_ThePrivatisationofZambiaConsolidatedCopperMines.doc

Kapur, D. and Ramamurti, R. (2002) 'Privatization in India: the imperatives and consequences of gradualism'. Center for Research on Economic Development and Policy Reform, Stanford University, Working Paper No. 142, July

Kaul, I. and Mendoza, R. U. (2003) 'Advancing the concept of public goods'. In: I. Kaul, P. Conceicao, K. Le Goulven and R. U. Mendoza (eds) *Providing Global Public Goods*. New York: Oxford University Press

Kaul, I., Conceicao, P., Le Goulven, K. and Mendoza, R. U. (eds) (2003) *Providing Global Public Goods: Managing Globalization*. New York: Oxford University Press (see, in particular, 'Financing global public goods', pp329–370)

Kaul, I., Grunberg, I. and Stern. M. A. (eds) (1999) *Global Public Goods: International Cooperation in the 21st Century*. New York: Oxford University Press

Kawamura, Y. (1996) 'NTT's split conditioned on consolidation-based taxation', *Accounting News in Japan*, 5 December, www2g.biglobe.ne.jp/~ykawamur/n961205.htm

KDDI homepage (2003) www.kddi.com/english/corporate/kddi/history/index.html

Keane, J. (2003) *Global Civil Society*. Cambridge: Cambridge University Press

Keeling, C. D. and Whorf, T. P. (2004) 'Atmospheric CO_2 records from sites in the SIO air sampling network'. In: *Trends: A Compendium of Data on Global Change*. Oak Ridge, Tenn.: Carbon Dioxide Information Analysis Center, US Department of Energy, http://cdiac.esd.ornl.gov/trends/co2/sio-mlo.htm (accessed 6 January 2004)

Kein Patent auf Leben! (2000) 'Biopiraterie: Stellungnahme zum Fall Neem', Kampagne 'Kein Patent auf Leben!', www.keinpatent.de

Kessides, I. N. (2004) *Reforming Infrastructure: Privatization, Regulation, and Competition*. Washington, DC and New York: World Bank and Oxford University Press

Kessler, T. and Alexander, N. (2003) 'Vanishing acts: how downsizing government contract out water and electricity services'. Paper prepared for the 707th Wilton Park (UK) conference on Private Foreign Investment and the Poorest Countries, 24–28 March, www.nsi-ins.ca/ensi/pdf/vanishing_acts.pdf

KfW (Kreditanstalt für Wiederaufbau) (2002) *Tansania: Ländliche Wasserversorgung Ost-Kilimanjaro* (Rural water supply in Eastern Kilimanjaro), Short project description, KfW, 16 January

Khor, M. (1995) 'Growing opposition to bio-piracy, life patents', *South–North Development Monitor*, www.sunsonline.org/trade/areas/intellec/10260095.htm

Kikeri, S. and Nellis, J. (2004) 'An Assessment of Privatization', *The World Bank Research Observer*, Vol. 19, No. 1, pp87–118

Klare, M. T. (1995) 'The global trade in light weapons and the international system in the post-Cold War era'. In: J. Boutwell, M. T. Klare and L. W. Reed (eds) *Lethal Commerce*. Cambridge, MA: Committee on International Security Studies of the American Academy of Arts and Sciences

Knight-John, M. (2002) 'Distributional impact of privatization: the Sri Lankan experience', Institute of Policy Studies, Colombo, December

Kobayashi, Y. (1997) 'Information technology in Japan: privatization and deregulation', Country assessment project for Management of Global Information Technology (MoGIT), American University, Washington, DC, 5 May, www.american.edu/initeb/yk8521a/privapage.htm

Koester, K. (1998) *Privatisierung von Staatsunternehmen in Japan: Entwicklung, Dynamik und Perspektiven der privatisierten Staatsbahn*. Baden-Baden: Nomos-Verl.-Ges

Komives, K. (1999) 'Designing pro-poor water and sewer concessions: early lessons from Bolivia'. *Policy Research Working Papers*. Washington, DC: The World Bank Group

Komives, K. and Brook Cowen, P. J. (1998) 'Expanding water and sanitation services to low-income households: the case of the La Paz–El Alto concession', *Private Sector Note* No. 178. Washington, DC: The World Bank Group

Komives, K. and Stalker-Prokopy, L. (2000) *Cost Recovery in Partnership: Results, Attitudes, Lessons and Strategies*. London: Business Partners for Development

Kovách, I. and Csite, A. (1999) 'A posztszocializmus vége. A magyarországi nagyvállalatok tulajdonosi szerkezete és hatékonysága 1997-ben', *Közgazdasági Szemle*, Vol. 46, No. 2, February, pp121–144

KPMG (2004) *KPMG Corporate Tax Rate Survey for 2004: Rates Still Falling*, www.kpmg.ca/en/news/documents/CorpTaxRateSurvey2004.pdf (accessed 14 September 2004)

Kragh, M. V., Mortensen, J. B., Schaumburg-Müller, H. and Slente, H. P. (eds) (2000) *Foreign Aid and Private Sector Development: Foreign Aid and Development. Lessons Learnt and Directions for the Future*. London: Routledge

Krasner, S. D. (ed) (1983) *International Regimes*. Ithaca: Cornell University Press

Lambsdorff, J. Graf (2001) *How Corruption in Government Affects Public Welfare: A Review of Theories*. Centre for Globalization and Europeanization of the Economy, Georg-August-Universität Göttingen, Discussion Paper 9

Langlois, R. N. and Robertson, P. L. (1995) *Firms, Markets, and Economic Change: A Dynamic Theory of Business Institutions*. London: Routledge

Lee, E. (1996) 'Globalization and employment: is anxiety justified?', *International Labour Review*, Vol. 135, No. 5, November, pp485–497

Legewie, J. (1997) 'Verkehrsentwicklung in Japan: Spezifische Probleme und Lösungsansätze', *Internationales Verkehrswesen*, Vol. 4, pp152–156

Legros, D., Ollivier, G., Gastellu-Etchegorry, M., Paquet, C., Burri, C., Jannin, J. and Büscher, P. (2002) 'Treatment of Human African Trypanosomiasis: present situation and need for research and development', *The Lancet*, Vol. 2, pp437–440

Leonhardt, D. (2003) 'House passes bill to loosen 401(k) rules', *New York Times Online*, 15 May, www.nytimes.com/gst/abstract.html?res=F60B14F6345B0C768 DDDAC0894DB404482 (accessed May 2003)

Levett, R., Christie, I., Jacobs, M. and Therivel, R. (2003) *A Better Choice of Choice*. London: Fabian Society

Link, H. (1997) 'Möglichkeiten und Grenzen der Privatisierung von Eisenbahnen: Ein Vergleich der Bahnreformen in Deutschland, Japan und Großbritannien'. In: K. König, and A. Benz (eds) *Privatisierung und staatliche Regulierung*. Baden-Baden: Nomos-Verlags-Gesellschaft

Link, H. (2003) 'Rail restructuring in Germany: eight years later', *Japan Railway & Transport Review*, No. 34, pp42–49, www.jrtr.net/jrtr34/pdf/f42_lin.pdf (accessed 23 June 2003)

Llanos, M. (2002) 'Über Gesetze und Dekrete: Eine Neuinterpretation der Beziehungen zwischen Präsident und Kongress im Argentinien der 90er Jahre'. In: P. Birle and S. Carreras (eds) *Argentinien nach zehn Jahren Menem: Wandel und Kontinuität*. Frankfurt/Main: Veruvert (Biblioteca Ibero-Americana)

Loasby, B. (2001) 'Cognition, imagination and institutions in demand creation', *Journal of Evolutionary Economics*, Vol. 11, pp.7–21

Lock, P. (2001) 'Sicherheit à la carte? Entstaatlichung, Gewaltmärkte und die Privatisierung des staatlichen Gewaltmonopols'. In T. Brühl, T. Debiel, B. Hamm, H. Hummel and J. Martens (eds) *Die Privatisierung der Weltpolitik*. Bonn: Dietz, pp200–229

Lora, E. (2001) 'Structural reforms in Latin America: what has been reformed and how to measure it', Research Department Working Paper W-466. Washington, DC, US: Inter-American Development Bank, Research Department

Lorenzi, R. (2002) 'Italian archeological treasures for sale?', Discovery News, *Discovery Channel*, 19 December, http://dsc.discovery.com/news/briefs/20021216/italy4sale_print.html

The Los Angeles Times (2004) 'Edition energy plan promised', 24 January

Lovei, M. and Gentry, B. S. (2002) 'The environmental implications of privatization: lessons for developing countries', World Bank Discussion Paper No. 426

Lynas, M. (1999) *Africa's Hidden Killers, October*, www.africawired.com/hiddenkiller.htm (accessed 5 June 2003)

MacCuish, D. (2003) *Water, Land and Labour: The Impact of Forced Privatization*. Ottawa, Canada: Halifax Initiative Coalition, www.servicesforall.org/html/Privatization/Water_Land_Labour.pdf

MacGregor, L., Prosser, T. and Villiers, C. (eds) (2000) *Regulation and Markets Beyond 2000*. Aldershot: Ashgate

Mahboobi, L. (2002) 'Recent privatisation trends in OECD countries. Long abstract', *OECD Financial Market Trends*, No. 82, www.oecd.org/dataoecd/29/11/1939087.pdf (accessed 12 September 2004)

Majone, G. (1998) 'From the positive to the regulatory state: causes and consequences of changes in the mode of governance', *Journal of Public Policy*, Vol. 17, Part 2, pp139–167

Mandel, R. (2000) 'The privatization of security', International Students Association, 41st Annual Convention, Los Angeles, US, 14–18 March, www.ciaonet.org/isa/mar01

Manzetti, L. (1999) *Privatization South American Style*. Oxford and New York: Oxford University Press

March, J. G. and Olson, J. P. (1998) 'The institutional dynamics of international political orders', *International Organization*, Vol. 52, pp729–757

Marek, T., Yamamoto, C. and Ruster, J. (2003) 'Policy and regulatory options for private participation', *Public Policy for the Private Sector*, No. 264, The World Bank Group

Marin, P. (2002) *Output Based Aid: Possible Applications for the Design of Water Concessions*. Washington, DC: World Bank, Private Sector Advisory Services

Marquand, D. (2004) *Decline of the Public: The Hollowing-out of Citizenship*. Cambridge: Polity Press

Masanja, V. G, Sumra, S. and Mutavangu, A. (2004, in press) 'Teachers' living and working conditions: a challenge for attaining quality education'. Working Paper of the Tanzania Teachers' Union and HakiElimu

Mathews, J. T. (1997) 'Power shift', *Foreign Affairs*, January/February, Vol. 76, No. 1, pp50–66

Mathieu, G. (2003) 'The reform of UK railways-privatization and its results', *Japan Railway & Transport Review* No. 34, pp16–31, www.jrtr.net/jrtr34/pdf/f16_mat.pdf (accessed 17 May 2003)

Mattli, W. (2003) 'Public and private governance in setting international standards'. In: M. Kahler and D. A. Lake (eds) *Governance in a Global Economy: Political Authority in Transition*. Princeton: Princeton University Press, pp199–225

Mayer, O. (1995) 'Als Fahrgast in Japan, Öffentlicher Verkehr im Land der aufgehenden Sonne', Part 1 in *Pro Bahn Zeitung*, Vol. 4, pp25–30; Part 2 (1995) in *Pro Bahn Zeitung*, Vol. 6, pp31–35

Mayewski, P. A. and White, F. (2002) *The Ice Chronicles: The Quest to Understand Global Climate Change*. Hanover, NH: University Press of New England

McChesney, R. (1999) *Rich Media, Poor Democracy, Communication Politics in Dubious Times*. Illinois: University of Illinois Press

McCully, P. (2002) 'Avoiding solutions, worsening problems: a critique of the World Bank's Water Resources Sector Strategy', International Rivers Network

Meacher, M. (2001) Keynote Speech delivered at International Conference on Freshwater, Bonn, Germany, 4 December

Melandri, G. (2003) 'Interrogazione parlamentare del 3 Marzo 2003 su avvenuto trasferimento di 36 beni culturali alla Carlyle Investment Group', www.dsonline.it

Michaelis, P. (2001) 'Staat oder Privat? Zu Wettbewerb und Privatisierung in der Abfallwirtschaft', *Zeitschrift für Angewandte Umweltforschung* (ZAU), H. 1–4, pp32–50

Ministry of Foreign Affairs of Japan (1999) 'Japan's approach to deregulation to the present', www.mofa.go.jp/j_info/japan/regulate/approach9904.html

Minogue, M. (2001) *Governance-based Analysis of Regulation*. Working Paper No. 3, Centre on Regulation and Competition, Institute for Development Policy and Management, University of Manchester, UK, http://idpm.man.ac.uk/crc/wpdl149/wp3.pdf

MNS (Malaysian Nature Society) (2001) 'May 2001 Newsletter. MNS position paper on solid wastes and incinerators', http://members.fortunecity.com/mnsperak/archives/2001-05/2001-may-09.html

Mofya, B. (2000) 'The human rights implications of Zambia's privatisation programme: a case study of Zambia Consolidated Copper Mines (ZCCM), Roan Antelope Mine, Luanshya Division'. Essay submitted to the University of Zambia Law School, Lusaka

Nambu, T. (1995) 'Competition and regulation of Japanese telecommunications industry', *International Comparison of Privatization and Deregulation: The Case in Japan*, ERI Discussion Paper Series, No. 62, August, www.esri.go.jp/en/archive/dis/abstract/dis62-e.html

National Sciences Foundation (1999) 'Federal R&D funding by budget function', National Sciences Foundation, www.nsf.gov/sbe/srs/nsf00303/pdf/nsf00303.pdf (accessed 14 September 2004)

National Trust EcoFund (2000) 'Pioneers in remediation of past environmental damages in Bulgaria', National Trust EcoFund, www.ecofund-bg.org/pioneri-eng.htm (accessed 26 May 2003)

NCPA (National Center for Policy Analysis) (1995) 'Private pensions succeed'. Dallas, TX: NCPA, www.ncpa.org/ba/ba191.html

Nellis, J. (1999) 'Time to rethink privatization in transition economies?' IFC Discussion Paper No. 38, ppix, 16, 28

Nellis, J. (2003) 'Privatization in Africa: What has happened? What is to be done?' Centre for Global Development, Working Paper Number 25, February

Nellis, J. and Kikeri, S. (1989) 'Public enterprise reform: privatization and the World Bank', *World Development*, Vol. 17, No. 5, pp659–672

Nellis, J. and Kikeri, S. (2002) *Winners and Losers from Privatization*. World Bank electronic 'Discussion Board'. Washington, DC: World Bank

Nellis, J. and Shirley, M. (1991) *Public Enterprise Reform: The Lessons of Experience (EDI Development Studies)*. Washington, DC: World Bank

Nelson, R. (2002) 'The problem of market bias in modern capitalist economies', *Industrial and Corporate Change*, Vol. 11, No. 2, pp207–244

New York Times (2003) 'The great blackout', 16 August

Newbury, D. (2000) *Privatization, Restructuring, and Regulation of Network Industries*. Cambridge, MA: MIT Press

Ngulube, T. J. and Mwanza, K. M. (1995) *The Health Reforms in Zambia a Summary of Baseline Findings: The Performance of Health Services in the Eastern Province*. Lusaka: The Centre for Health, Science and Social Research

Nickson, A. (1998) 'Organisational structure and performance in urban water supply: the case of the SAGUAPAC co-operative in Santa Cruz, Bolivia'. Working paper. Birmingham: School of Public Policy

Nickson, A. (2001) 'Tapping the market: can private enterprise supply water to the poor?', *Id21 Research Highlight*, 12 June

Nikolov, G. and Jordanov, P. (2003) Director of Legal Affairs and Manager of the Environmental Department, UMICORE's MDK Pirdop operation, personal interview, 9 July

North, D. C. (1990) *Institutions, Institutional Change and Economic Performance*. Cambridge: Cambridge University Press

NTT Group (Nippon Telegraph and Telephone Corporation) (2003) www.ntt.co.jp/index_e.html

Obergfell-Fuchs, J. (2000) *Möglichkeiten der Privatisierung von Aufgabenfeldern der Polizei mit Auswirkungen auf das Sicherheitsgefühl der Bevölkerung, Eine empirisch-kriminologische Analyse, Bundeskriminalamt*. Wiesbaden: BKA-Forschungsreihe, hrsg. v. BKA, Kriminalistisches Institut. Bd. 51

OECD (Organisation for Economic Co-operation and Development) (2001) *Knowledge and Skills for Life: First Results from PISA 2000: Education and Skills*. Paris: OECD Programme for International Student Assessment

OECD (2002) *Financial Market Trends*, No. 82, June

OECD (2004) *OECD Health Data 2004*. Paris: OECD

OED (Operations Evaluation Department) (2002) *Bolivia Water Management: A Tale of Three Cities*, Spring. Washington, DC: The World Bank Group, p222

Oliveira, J. B. A. and Schwartzman, S. (2002) 'A escola vista por dentro'. Belo Horizonte: Alfa Educativa Editora, www.schwartzman.org.br/simon/livrojb.htm

Olson, M., Jr (1965) *The Logic of Collective Action*. Cambridge, MA: Harvard University Press

Olson, M. (1996) 'Big bills left on the sidewalk: why some nations are rich, and others poor', *Journal of Economic Perspectives*, Vol. 10, No. 2, pp3–24

Onodera, R. (2003) 'Privatization of NTT: background and development', Paper presented at UNI APRO Workshop for Indian Telecom Unions, 14–15 February, http://apro.techno.net.au/apt446.htm

Osmani, S. R. (2000) 'Participatory governance, people's empowerment and poverty reduction', New York, UNDP, SEPED Conference Paper Series, Poverty Elimination Programme

Ostrom, E. (1990) *Governing the Commons: The Evolution of Institutions for Collective Action*. Cambridge: Cambridge University Press

Ostrom, E., Dietz, T., Dolsak, N., Stern, N., Stonick, S. and Weber, E. U. (eds) (2002) *The Drama of the Commons*. US National Committee on the Human Dimensions of Global Change. Washington, DC: National Academic Press

OTA (Office of Technology Assessment) (1984) 'Remote sensing and the private sector', Office of Technology Assessment, Congress of the United States, OTA-TM-ISC-20

Ottens, R. W., Olschok, H. and Landrock, S. (eds) (1999) *Recht und Organisation privater Sicherheitsdienste in Europa*. Stuttgart u.a.: Richard Boorberg Verlag

Pagnini, L. (2003a) 'Privatizing Italian culture'. Private manuscript. Associazione Limen – Beni culturali, www.limen.org, June

Pagnini, L. (2003b) 'Situation and future perspectives of privatization of Italian cultural heritage'. Private manuscript. Associazione Limen – Beni culturali, www.limen.org, August

Pagnini, L. (2003c) 'Scheda vendita Manifattura tabacchi Firenze'. Private manuscript. Associazione Limen – Beni culturali, www.limen.org, September

Paine, E. (2000) *The Road to the Global Compact: Corporate Power and the Battle over Global Public Policy at The United Nations*, www.globalpolicy.org/reform/papers/2000/road

Painter, D. S. (1999) *The Cold War: An International History*. London and New York: Routledge

Palieri, M. S. (2003) 'Ecco i tesori comprati dalla Carlyle', *L'Unità*, 5 March

Pardey, P. G., Alston, J. M., Christian, J. E. and Fan, S. (1996) 'Hidden harvest: US benefits from international research aid', *Food Policy Statement* No. 23, International Food Policy Research Institute, www.ifpri.org

Park, Y.-B. (1997) 'Privatization and employment in the Republic of Korea'. In: R. Van der Hoeven and G. Sziraczki (eds) *Lessons from Privatization: Labour Issues in Developing and Transitional Countries*. Geneva: ILO, pp1–45

Parson, E. A. (2003) *Protection of the Global Ozone Layer*. New York: Oxford University Press

Pattberg, P. (2004) 'The institutionalisation of private governance: conceptualising an emerging trend in global environmental politics', Global Governance Working Paper No. 9. Potsdam, Amsterdam, Berlin, Oldenburg: The Global Governance Project, www.glogov.org

Paukert, L. (1997) 'Privatization and employment in the Czech Republic'. In R. Van der Hoeven and G. Sziraczki (eds) *Lessons from Privatization: Labour Issues in Developing and Transitional Countries*. Geneva: ILO, pp145–163

PBGC (Pension Benefit Guaranty Corporation) (2003) 'About PBGC: our organization', www.pbgc.gov/about/organization.htm (accessed June 2004)

Pelikan, P. and Wegner, G. (eds) (2003) *The Evolutionary Analysis of Economic Policy*. Cheltenham and Northampton: Edward Elgar

Pereira, M. M. (2002) 'EU competition law, convergence, and the media industry'. Presentation at the Law Society of England and Wales, London, 23 April

Phiri, E. (2000) RAMCOZ Acting Head Public Relations and Administration, interview, 27 March, ('Mofya human rights implications of the sale of ZCCM: the case of Luanshya Mine')

PhRMA (Pharmaceutical Research and Manufacturers of America)(2004) 'Industry profile: focus on innovation. Washington, DC', PhRMA, www.phrma.org/publications/publications/2004-03-31.937.pdf (accessed 14 September 2004)

Plane, P. (1997) 'Privatization and economic growth: an empirical investigation from a sample of developing market economies', *Applied Economics*, Vol. 29, No. 2, February, pp161–178

Plummer, J. (2002) *Focusing Partnerships: A Sourcebook for Capacity Building in Public–Private Partnerships*. London: Earthscan

Pollitt, M. (1999) *A Survey of the Liberalisation of Public Enterprises in the UK Since 1979*. Cambridge: University of Cambridge Press

Porter, M. and van der Linde, C. (2000) 'Green and competitive: ending the stalemate'. In: E. F. M. Wubben (ed) *The Dynamics of the Eco-efficient Economy*. Cheltenham and Northampton: Edward Elgar, pp33–55

The Post (2003) 'Editorial', *The Post* Newspaper, Zambia, 24 January

Power Markets Week (2002) 'California gets some contracts redone, consumer groups mock savings claim', 29 April

PPIAF (2001a) *Pro-Poor Regulation: Challenges and Implications for Regulatory Design*. Washington, DC: PPIAF

PPIAF (2001b) *New Designs for Water and Sanitation Transactions: Making Private Sector Participation Work for the Poor*. Washington, DC: PPIAF

Prayas Energy Group (2002) 'The Bujagali Power Purchase Agreement: a study of techno-economic aspects', Commissioned by International Rivers Network

Précis–OED (Operations Evaluation Department) (1995) *Making Participation Work*. Washington, DC: World Bank

Public Citizen (2003) 'Water privatization fiascos: broken promises and social turmoil'. Special report. Washington, Oakland: Public Citizen, www.citizen.org/cmep (accessed 12 May 2003)

Public Citizen's Critical Mass Energy and Environment Program (2001) 'It's greed stupid! Debunking the ten myths of utility deregulation', January, www.citizen.org/cmep/energy_enviro_nuclear/electricity/deregulation/index.cfm?ID=5033&relatedpages=1&catID=114&secID=1026

Putnam, R. D. (2000): *Bowling Alone: The Collapse and Revival of American Community*. New York: Simon and Schuster

Queisser, M. and Vittas, D. (2000) 'The Swiss multi-pillar pension system: triumph of common sense?'. WPS2416. Washington, DC: World Bank

Queisser, M. and Whitehouse, E. (eds) (2003) 'Individual choice in social protection: the case of Swiss pensions'. OECD Working Papers (DELSA/WD/SEM(2003)11)

RAFI (Rural Advancement Foundation International) (1998a) 'Basmati rice patent: the (merchant) prince and the (Punjabi) paupers', www.etcgroup.org/article.asp?newsid=62

RAFI (1998b) 'RAFI launches postcard campaign to oppose basmati rice patent', www.etcgroup.org/article.asp?newsid=60

Rail Safety and Standards Board (2002) 'Annual Safety Performance Report 2001/02'. London: RSSB, www.rssb.co.uk/pdf/reports/Annual%20Safety%20Performance%20Report%202001-02.pdf (accessed 5 January 2005)

Ramamurti, R. (1997) 'Testing the limits of privatization: Argentine railroads', *World Development*, Vol. 25, No. 12, pp1973–1993

Raphael, D. (1998) 'The future of telecommunications: connectivity through alliances', Paper presented to NABE Silicon Valley Roundtable, California, 29 April, www.svrt.org/mtg/txt/summary/980429.txt

Reinicke, W. H. and Deng, F. M. (2000) *Critical Choices: The United Nations, Networks, and the Future of Global Governance*. Ottawa: International Development Research Centre

Research Foundation for Science, Technology and Ecology (2001) Press release: 'Ricetec loses in the basmati battle', www.makingindiagreen.org/pr35.htm

Rischard, J. F. (2002) *High Noon: Twenty Global Problems, Twenty Years to Solve Them*. New York: Basic Books

Rittberger, V. (ed) (1993) *Regime Theory and International Relations*. Oxford: Clarendon Press

Rodrik, D. (2000) 'Institutions for high-quality growth: what they are and how to acquire them', *Studies in Comparative International Development*, Fall 2000, Vol. 35, No. 3, pp3–31

Rose-Ackerman, S. (1999) *Corruption and Government: Causes, Consequences and Reform*. Cambridge: Cambridge University Press

Rosenau, J. N. and Czempiel, E.-O. (eds) (1992) *Governance without Government: Order and Change in World Politics*. Cambridge: Cambridge University Press

Rothstein, R. L. (1977) *The Weak in the World of the Strong: The Developing Countries in the International System*. New York: Columbia University Press

Rumsfeld, D. (2001) *Report of the Commission to Assess United States National Security Space Management and Organization*, January, www.defenselink.mil/pubs/space20010111.html

Saba, R. P. (2000) 'Regulatory policy in an unstable legal environment: the case of Argentina'. In: L. Manzetti (ed) *Regulatory Policy in Latin America: Post-privatization Realities*. Coral Gables, FL: University of Miami, North-South Center Press

Sala-i-Martin, X. (2002) 'The disturbing "rise" of global income inequality', National Bureau of Economic Research, Working Paper No. W8904

Salih, R. (2000) 'Privatization in Sri Lanka'. In: J. Gopal (ed) *Privatization in South Asia: Minimizing Negative Social Effects through Restructuring*. New Delhi: International Labour Organization

San Francisco Chronicle (2000a) 'Summer ushered in a power crisis that only promises to get worse', 29 December

San Francisco Chronicle (2000b) 'Genesis of State's energy fiasco: string of bad decisions on deregulation could end up costing consumers $40 billion', 31 December

San Francisco Chronicle (2003a) 'Consumers left out of energy refunds', 27 March

San Francisco Chronicle (2003b) 'PG&E execs awarded big bonuses: bankrupt utility says $17.5 million payouts needed to keep top talent', 11 April

San Francisco Chronicle (2003c) 'Power unit is bankrupt: PG&E plans to abandon National Energy Group', 9 July

San Francisco Chronicle (2003d) 'Panel lets utilities bill die: measure proposed system that existed before deregulation', 11 July

Sandler, T. (1998) 'Global and regional public goods: a prognosis for collective action', *Fiscal Studies*, Vol. 19, No. 3, pp221–247

Savas, E. S. (2000) *Privatization and Public-Private Partnerships*. New York and London: Chatham House Publishers and Seven Bridges Press

Savir, U. (2004) 'Glocalization: a new balance of power', *Development Outreach*, July, World Bank Institute, www1.worldbank.org/devoutreach/article.asp?id=226

Schadler, S., Rozwadowski, F., Tiwari, S. and Robinson, D. O. (1993) *Economic Adjustment in Low-Income Countries: Experience Under the Enhanced Structural Adjustment Facility*. Washington, DC: International Monetary Fund (IMF)

Scheffran, J. (2001) 'Peaceful and sustainable use of space: principles and criteria for evaluation'. In: W. Bender, R. Hagen, M. Kalinowski and J. Scheffran (eds) *Space Use and Ethics*. Münster: agenda, pp49–80

Schlosser, E. (1998) 'The prison-industrial complex', *The Atlantic Online*, www.theatlantic.com/issues/98dec/prisons.htm

Schneider, H. (1999) *Participatory Governance: The Missing Link for Poverty Reduction*. OECD Development Centre Policy Brief 17. Paris: OECD

Schröder, E.-J. (2001) 'Deutschland: Renaissance des Schienenpersonennahverkehrs', *Internationales Verkehrswesen*, Vol. 6, pp283–287

Schrogl, K. U. (2001) 'Space law and the principle of non-appropriation'. In: W. Bender, R. Hagen, M. Kalinowski and J. Scheffran (eds) *Space Use and Ethics*. Münster: agenda, pp251–255

Schuessler, J. F. (2001) 'Private sector involvement in the space program: some things to consider', Littleton, Co, May, www.bigelowaerospace.com/schuessler-pvt-sector.doc

Schwartz, B. (2003) *The Paradox of Choice*. New York: HarperCollins

Seeman, R. (1986) 'Telecommunications trade: NTT privatization', *The Japan Law Letter*, April, www.japanlaw.info/lawletter/april86/enz.htm

Settis, S. (2003a) *Italia S.P.A.*, Torino 2003

Settis, S. (2003b) 'La spada di Damocle sui beni culturali', *La Repubblica*, 11 July, www.osservatoriomonopoli.it/News/News_200703_Settis.htm

Sgarbi, V. (2003) 'Patrimonio svendesi, ma a pochi offerenti. Chi trae vantaggio dall'alienazione degli immobili pubblici?', *Bell'Italia*, No. 207, July, www.osservatoriomonopoli.it/News/News_200703_Settis.htm

Shah, A. (2003) 'Media conglomerates, mergers, concentration of ownership', *Global Issues.org*, 17 April, www.globalissues.org/HumanRights/Media/Corporations/Owners.asp

Sharma, D. (2001) 'Basmati patent: let us accept, India has lost the battle', 22 August, www.makingindiagreen.org/devinder2.htm

Shelley, T. (1998) *Reforming Public Enterprises – Case Studies: United Kingdom*. Paris: OECD

Shelton, D. (ed) (2000) *Commitment and Compliance: The Role of Non-Binding Norms in the International Legal System*. Oxford: Oxford University Press

Sheshinski, E. and López-Calva, L. F. (1999) *Privatization and Its Benefits: Theory and Evidence*. Cambridge, MA: Harvard Institute for International Development

Shichor, D. (1995) *Punishment for Profit: Private Prisons: Public Concerns*. Thousand Oaks: Sage

Shiva, V. (1997) *Biopiracy: The Plunder of Nature and Knowledge*: Cambridge, MA: South End Press

Shiva, V. (2000) 'The neem tree: a case history of biopiracy', Third World Network, www.twnside.org.sg/title/pir-ch.htm

Shiva, V. (2001) 'The basmati battle and its implications for biopiracy and TRIPS', 28 August, www.cb3rob.net/~merijn89/ARCH1/msg00376.html

Shleifer, A. (1998) 'State versus private ownership', *Journal of Economic Perspectives*, Vol. 12, No. 4, pp133–150

Sichel, W. and Alexander, D. (eds) (1996) *Networks, Infrastructure, and the New Task for Regulation*. Ann Arbor: University of Michigan Press

Simmons, B. A. and Martin, L. L. (2002) 'International organizations and institutions'. In: W. Carlsnaes, T. Risse and B. A. Simmons (eds) *Handbook of International Relations*. London: Sage Publications, pp192–211

Sina, R. (2003) 'Wie teuer muss Wasser sein? Privat organisiertes Wassermanagement in Ostafrika' (How costly does water have to be? Privately organized water management in Eastern Africa), WDR5 Morgenecho, 21 March

Sinclair, S. and Grieshaber-Otto, J. (2002) *Facing the Facts*. Canada: Canadian Centre for Policy Alternatives

Siniscalco, B. and Fantini, R. (2001) *Privatisation Around the World: New Evidence from Panel, Data Center for Economic Studies and Ifo Institute for Economic Research*, October 2001, www.papers.ssrn.com/abstract=288530

Sjoerdsma, A. G. (2000) 'Medical miracle frustrated: a wonder drug for sleeping sickness is not available in Africa', *Baltimore Sun*, 10 December

Smith, I. (2003) 'Britain's railways: five years after the completion of their privatization', *Japan Railway & Transport Review* No. 34, pp12–15, www.jrtr.net/jrtr34/pdf/f12_smi.pdf (accessed 17 May 2003)

Smith, L., Mottiar, S. and White, F. (2003) 'The Nelspruit water concession', Presented at the Commonwealth Finance Ministers Meeting on Provision of Basic Services, Bandar Seri Begawan, Negara Brunei Darussalam, 22–24 July

Smith, M. S. (1999) Testimony before the Subcommittee on Space and Aeronautics Committee on Science, US House of Representatives, 25 February

Social Watch (2003) *Social Watch Report 2003: The Poor and the Market*. Montevideo, Uruguay: The Third World Institute–Social Watch

Somlyódy, L. and Shanahan, P. (1998) *Municipal Wastewater Treatment in Central and Eastern Europe: Present Situation and Cost-Effective Development Strategies*. Washington, DC: World Bank

Sommer, J. H. and Gerber, D. S. (2001) 'Zukunft der sozialen Sicherheit in der Schweiz: Mehr Wettbewerb für die Altersvorsorge?', *Soziale Sicherheit*, April, pp199–204

Soros, G. (2002) *George Soros on Globalization*. New York: Public Affairs

Sousa-Poza, A. (2003) 'Low income, financial restrictions and coverage in the Swiss second and third pillars'. Discussion Paper No. 90, Universität St Gallen, June

SpaceDev (2002) 'Near Earth Asteroid Prospector Mission', 18 November, www.spacedev.com/

Srinivasan, T. N. (2003) 'Privatization, regulation and competition in South Asia', Mimeo., Yale University, Yale

SRU (Sachverständigenrat für Umweltfragen) (2002) *Umweltgutachten 2002: Für eine neue Vorreiterrolle*. Stuttgart

Starr, P. (1987) *The Limits of Privatization*. Washington, DC: Economic Policy Institute

Stern, G. (1990) *The Rise and Decline of International Communism*. Aldershot, Hants: Elgar

Stertkamp, W. (2000) 'Webfehler der Bahnreform', *Internationales Verkehrswesen*, Vol. 5, pp196–198

Stich A., Abel, P. and Krishna, S. (2002) 'Human African Trypanosomiasis', *British Medical Journal*, Vol. 325, pp203–206

Stiglitz, J. E. (1998a) 'The private use of public interests: incentives and institutions', *Journal of Economic Perspectives*, Vol. 12, No. 2, pp3–21

Stiglitz, J. E. (1998b) 'Towards a new paradigm for development: strategies, policies, and processes', Prebish Lecture given at UNCTAD, Geneva, 19 October

Stiglitz, J. E. (2000) *Economics of the Public Sector*. New York and London: W. W. Norton

Stiglitz, J. E. (2002) *Globalization and its Discontents*. New York/London: W. W. Norton/Penguin

Süddeutsche Zeitung (2003a) 'Wie in der Dritten Welt', 16 August

Süddeutsche Zeitung (2003b) 'Das Geschäft mit dem Blackout', 1 September

Suganami, H. (1989) *The Domestic Analogy and World Order Proposals*. Cambridge: Cambridge University Press

Sweden Ministry for Foreign Affairs (2001) *Financing and Providing Global Public Goods: Expectations and Prospects*. Report prepared by F. Sagasti and K. Bezanson on behalf of the Institute of Development Studies. Stockholm: Sweden Ministry for Foreign Affairs

Synovitz, R. (2000) 'Romania: Hungary complains about second toxic spill', *Radio Free Europe, Radio Liberty*, March, www.rferl.org/nca/features/2000/03/F.RU.000314135336.html (accessed 22 April 2003)

Tavernier, M. Y. (2001) 'Le financement et la gestion de l'eau', Assemblée Nationale, Commission des Finances, de l'Économie Générale et du plan de l'Assemblée Nationale, Rapport d'information, No. 3081, p10

Terada, K. (2001) 'Railways in Japan: public and private sectors, railway operators in Japan 1', *Japan Railway & Transport Review*, No. 27, pp48–55, www.jrtr.net/jrtr27/s48_ter.html (accessed 4 April 2003)

Terenzi, F. (2002) *The Business of Space*, Business of Space Forum, November, www.fiorella.com/bizofspace.htm

Teubner, G. (2000) 'Contracting worlds: the many autonomies of private law', *Social Legal Studies*, September, Vol. 9, pp399–417

Thompson, J. (2001) *Private Sector Participation in the Water Sector: Can it Meet Social and Environmental Needs?* London: International Institute for Environment and Development, May

Thomson, J. L. (2003) *Air New Zealand*. Huddersfield University Business School, University of Huddersfield, UK

Torres, G. (2000) *The Tortuous Road to Privatization in Venezuela*. In M. H. Birch and J. Haar (eds) (2000) *The Impact of Privatization in the Americas*. Miami: North-South Center Press

Transparency International (1999) *Transparency International Annual Report 1999*. Lusaka, Zambia: TI-Zambia

Transparency International (2002) *The Integrity Pact. The Concept, the Model, and the Present Applications: A Status Report*. Berlin: Transparency International, www.transparency.org/building_coalitions/integrity_pact/index.html

Trouiller, P., Olliaro, P., Torreele, E., Orbinski, J., Laing, R. and Ford, N. (2002) 'Drug development for neglected diseases: a deficient market and a public health policy failure', *The Lancet*, Vol. 359, Issue 9324, pp2188–2194

Tubeza, P. C. (2004) 'Gov't wants Maynilad deal junked'. Financial Times Information. *Global News Wire*, 22 July

UNCTAD (United Nations Conference on Trade and Development) (2000) *A Positive Agenda for Developing Countries: Issues for Future Trade Negotiations*. Geneva: UNCTAD

UNDP (United Nations Development Programme) (2003) *Human Development Report 2003: Millennium Development Goals – A Compact Among Nations to End Human Poverty*. New York: Oxford University Press/UNDP

UNDP, Heinrich Böll Foundation, Rockefeller Brothers Fund, The Rockefeller Foundation and Wallace Global Fund (2003) *Making Global Trade Work for People*. London: Earthscan

Unternehmensinstitut e.V. (2003) *Der Weg aus der staatlichen Schuldenfalle: Konzepte und Beispiele für eine umfassende Privatisierung*. Berlin, Germany: Arbeitsgemeinschaft Selbständiger Unternehmer, pp49–50

Urbani, G. (2003) *Il tesoro degli italiani*. Milan: Mondadori

URT (United Republic of Tanzania) (1998) *Financial Sustainability of Higher Education in Tanzania*. Report of the Task Force, Ministry of Science and Technology and Higher Education, Tanzania

US Census Bureau (2003) *Statistical Abstract of the United States*. Washington, DC: US Census Bureau

US Department of Justice (2003) 'Key facts at a glance. Number of persons under correctional supervision', www.ojp.usdoj.gov/bjs/glance/tables/corr2tab.htm (accessed 14 September 2004)

US Patent Office (1994) 'Basmati rice lines and grains', United States Patent 5,663,484, filed: 8 July

US Space Command (1998) *Long Range Plan*. Colorado Springs: Peterson AFB, Co

US–Canada Power System Outage Task Force (2003a) 'August 14, 2003 outage: sequence of events', www.energy.gov/engine/doe/files/dynamic/1282003113351_BlackoutSummary.pdf

US–Canada Power System Outage Task Force (2003b) 'Interim report: causes of the August 14th blackout in the United States and Canada', www.electricity.doe.gov/news/blackout.cfm?section=news&level2=blackout

Valenzuela, R. G. (2003) *Der Einfluss der Politik auf Wirtschaftsreformen: Die Privatisierungs- und Regulierungspolitik in Argentinien und Chile in den 1990er Jahren*. Dissertation, University of Tübingen, Germany

van de Walle, N. (1989) 'Privatization in Developing Countries', *World Development*, Vol. 17, No. 5, pp601–615

Van der Hoeven, R. and Sziraczki, G. (1997) 'Privatization and labour issues'. In: R. Van der Hoeven and G. Sziraczki (eds) *Lessons from Privatization: Labour Issues in Developing and Transitional Countries*. Geneva: ILO, pp1–19

van Dijken, K., Prince, Y., Wolters, T. J., Frey, M., Mussati, G., Kalff, P., Hansen, O., Kerndrup, S., Søndergård, B., Rodrigues, E. L. and Meredith, S. (eds) (1999) *Adoption of Environmental Innovations: The Dynamics of Innovation as Interplay between Business Competence, Environmental Orientation and Network Involvement*. Dordrecht: Kluwer

Vitousek, P. M., Mooney, H. A., Lubchenco, J. and Melillo, J. M. (1997) 'Human domination of the Earth's ecosystems', *Science*, Vol. 277, pp494–499

von Hauff, M. and Masanja, V. G. (2002) *Evaluation Report on Misereor Scholarship Programme at St Augustine University of Tanzania*. Report for Misereor, Federal Republic of German and the Tanzania Episcopal Conference

von Hayek, F. (1944) *The Road to Serfdom*. Chicago: University of Chicago Press

von Ungern-Sternberg, T. (2004) *Efficient Monopolies: The Limits of Competition in the European Property Insurance Market*. Oxford: Oxford University Press

von Weizsäcker, E. U., Lovins, A. and Lovins, H. (1997) *Factor Four: Doubling Wealth – Halving Resource Use*. London: Earthscan

Voszka, É. (1998) *Spontán privatizáció*, 'Számadás a talentumól'. Working Paper, ÁPV RT, Budapest

Walker, M. (1994) *The Cold War: And the Making of the Modern World*. London: Vintage

Wapner, P. (1996) 'Governance in global civil society'. In: O. R. Young (ed) *Global Governance: Drawing Insights from the Environmental Experience*. Cambridge: MIT Press, pp65–84

WaterAid (2003) 'The paradoxes of funding and infrastructure development in Uganda', www.wateraid.org.uk

Weinberg, B. (2003) 'Biodiversity Inc: Mexico tries a new tactic against Chiapas rebels – conservation', *In These Times*, 21 August, www.inthesetimes.com/site/main/article/613/

Weiss, E. B. and Jacobson, H. K. (eds) (1998) *Engaging Countries: Strengthening Compliance with International Environmental Accords*. Cambridge: MIT Press

Weiss, R. and Plate, M. (eds) (1996) *Privatisierung von polizeilichen Aufgaben, Beiträge zum Workshop des Bundeskriminalamtes über das Forschungsprojekt 'Möglichkeiten der Privatisierung von Aufgabenfeldern der Polizei mit Auswirkungen auf das Sicherheitsgefühl der Bevölkerung' am 26. und 27 Oktober 1995, Bundeskriminalamt*. Wiesbaden: BKA-Forschungsreihe, hrsg. v. BKA, Kriminalistisches Institut. Bd. 41

Weiss, T. G. and Gordenker, L. (eds) (1996) *NGOs, the UN and Global Governance*. Boulder, CO: Lynne Rienner Publishers

White, O. C. and Bhatia, A. (1998) *Privatization in Africa*. Washington, DC: World Bank

Whitelegg, J. (2003) 'Railway privatization: integration, environment, safety and sustainability'. Speech at conference 'Personenverkehr der Eisenbahnen: Erschließung neuer Nachfragepotenziale und Organisation der Verkehre', 27–28 November 2003, Berlin

Williams, M. (1991) *Third World Cooperation: The Group of 77 in UNCTAD*. London: Pinter

Winpenny, J. (2003) *Financing Water for All. Report of the World Panel on Financing Water Infrastructure*. World Water Council and Global Water Partnership, www.worldwatercouncil.org/download/CamdessusReport.pdf (accessed 5 January 2005)

Witt, U. (2003) *The Evolving Economy: Essays on the Evolutionary Approach to Economics*. Cheltenham and Northampton: Edward Elgar

Witte, J. M., Streck, C. and Benner, T. (eds) (2003) *Progress or Peril? Partnerships and Networks in Global Environmental Governance*. Washington, DC and Berlin: Global Public Policy Institute

Wohlfahrt, N. and Zühlke, W. (1999) *Von der Gemeinde zum Konzern Stadt. Auswirkungen von Ausgliederung und Privatisierung für die politische Steuerung auf kommunaler Ebene*. ILS-Schriften Bd. 154. Dortmund: Institut für Landes- und Stadtentwicklungsforschung und Bauwesen des Landes Nordrhein-Westfahlen

Wolmar, C. (2001) *Broken Rails: How Privatisation Wrecked Britain's Railways*. London: Aurum Press

Wolter, D. (2003) *Grundlagen 'Gemeinsamer Sicherheit' im Weltraum nach universellem Völkerrecht*. Berlin: Duncker & Humblot

Women, Law and Development International (1999) 'Women's rights under privatization'. Washington, DC: Women, Law and Development International

Woodroffe, J. and Joyner, K. (2000) 'Conditions impossible: the real reason for debt relief delays', World Development Movement

World Bank (1994) *World Bank Assistance to Privatization in Developing Countries (Operations Evaluation Study)*. Washington, DC: World Bank

World Bank (1995) *Bureaucrats in Business: The Economics and Politics of Government Ownership*. Washington, DC: World Bank

World Bank (1999) 'Project appraisal document on proposed loans in the amount of EUR 27.6 million to the Municipality of Budapest and in the amount of EUR 2.0 million to Municipality of Dunauijvaros with the guarantee of Republic of Hungary for a municipal wastewater project' (Report No. 19024-HU). World Bank, 18 August, http://www-wds.worldbank.org/servlet/WDS_IBank_Servlet?pcont=details&eid=000094946_99091002405740 (accessed 28 May 2003)

World Bank (2001a) *Private Sector Development (PSD): Findings and Lessons from Selected Countries*. Washington, DC: World Bank

World Bank (2001b) *World Bank Project Appraisal Document for a Loan to Guatemala*. Washington, DC: World Bank, April, p6

World Bank (2002a) *Global Economic Prospects 2003: Investing to Unclock Global Opportunities*. Washington, DC: World Bank

World Bank (2002b) *Private Sector Development Strategy: Directions for the World Bank Group*, 21, http://rru.worldbank.org/Documents/699.pdf (accessed June 2004)

World Bank (2002c) *World Development Report*. Washington, DC: World Bank

World Bank (2003a) *World Development Indicators on CD-Rom*. Washington, DC: World Bank

World Bank (2003b) *World Development Report 2004: Making Services Work for Poor People*. Washington, DC: World Bank

World Bank (2004) *World Development Report 2004 on CD-Rom*. Washington, DC: World Bank

World Bank Group (1998) 'Abstracts on current studies: education, public sector management. El Salvador's School-Based Management Reforms'. Washington, DC: The World Bank Group, http://econ.worldbank.org/view.php?topic=10&type=20&id=55

World Bank Group (2004a) 'About Us' / 'What is the World Bank', The World Bank Group, www.worldbank.org (accessed June 2004)

World Bank Group (2004b) 'Site Map' / 'About Development', The World Bank Group, www.worldbank.org

World Commission on the Social Dimension of Globalization (2004) *A Fair Globalization: Creating Opportunities for All*. Geneva: ILO

WSP (Water and Sanitation Programme) (2001) *Methodology for Participatory Assessments: Helping Communities Achieve More Sustainable and Equitable Services*, www.wsp.org/publications/eap_mpa_helping.pdf

WSP, Mukherjee, N. and van Wijk, C. (eds) (2003) *Sustainability Planning and Monitoring in Community Water Supply and Sanitation*, www.wsp.org/publications/mpa%202003.pdf

Wulf, H. (2003) '"Rent a soldier": die Privatisierung des Militärs', *Wissenschaft und Frieden*, March

Yonkova, A., Alexandrova, S., Stoev, G., Kopeva, D., Gancheva, Y., Bogdanov, L., Dimitrova, T., Ganev, G., Stanchev, K. and Blagoeva, Z. (1999) *In Search of Growth: Bulgaria's Lessons and Policy Options*. Sofia: Institute for Market Economics, www.ime-bg.org/pdf_docs/papers/bg_less.pdf (accessed 5 January 2005)

Young, B. and Hoppe, H. (2003) *The Doha Development Round, Gender and Social Reproduction*. Berlin: Friedrich Ebert Stiftung

Young, O. R. (1999) *Governance in World Affairs*. Ithaca: Cornell University Press

Zambia Privatization Agency, official web page, www.zpa.org.zm

ZCCM (1999) 'ZCCM privatization status report', December

ZCCM Investments Holdings plc (2002) 'Agreement on the future of Konkola Copper Mines Plc', 19 August, http://moneyextra.uk-wire.com/cgi-bin/articles/200208200700181580A.html

Zimmer, A. and Eckhard, P. (eds) with the assistance of Freise, M. (2004) *Future of Civil Society: Making Central European Nonprofit Organizations Work*. Wiesbaden: Verlag für Sozialwissenschaften

Index

Page numbers in *italics* refer to figures and boxes